IN THE HANDS OF THE LORD

✦ AVA SAVAGE ✦

ISBN 978-1-0980-8476-9 (paperback)
ISBN 978-1-0980-8477-6 (digital)

Christian Faith Publishing, Inc.
832 Park Avenue
Meadville, PA 16335
www.christianfaithpublishing.com

Printed in the United States of America

I love the morning; the early morning before everyone wakes up is my favorite time of day. I pray to thank God for everything he has given me and tell him to help me each day to become more pleasing to him. I ask him to guide me, keep my heart pure, and make each of my steps lead me closer to him. My Lord, my Savior, he gives me breath and life each day, and I am so grateful. The Lord gives me strength to live on and not dwell on my past, but some mornings, I end up back there. I end up at six years old and looking through an empty fridge. I can remember having to pull the handle real hard just to get it open and then would feel a sense of panic rush over me because of how loud it was. I would stand there for a minute or two, being very still so I could hear every sound in that house. I can remember very clearly the feeling of being there, the feeling of desperation and hopelessness—a feeling that even at the age of six years old I could recognize. I would always wake up early to wander around, play with my cat Casper, and look for something to eat. I would listen closely as I opened the refrigerator door, trying not to wake up my parents or my little brother. Looking through an empty fridge is hopeless enough, but deciding between hardened lasagna from the week before and bologna is even worse. Usually, I chose the bologna but took some dog biscuits for later. I would carefully hide them under my pillow so no one would find them. With it being so early, I would walk very quietly down the hall and sit outside the doorway of my parents' bedroom. I am not sure why I would do that, but I think it was just to listen to them sleep. I would pull off the hard side of my bologna and chew on that first because then I knew I only had the good part after that. Sometimes, I would take a couple of dog biscuits, chew them up, and spit them out for my cat,

Casper. I usually ate some of the dog biscuits too. I loved the way they tasted and the texture. I would stare at my parents' door. I could hear snoring, and it was almost comforting knowing that they were still sleeping.

At that age, I already liked being alone, and at that age, I knew my parents were not good people. Sometimes, I would sit on the floor in my baby brother's room. I'd sit over the heat vent to get nice and warm. If my brother started to move around at all, I would hurry up and get out of there. I was scared to wake him up and get blamed for his crying that early in the morning. My parents seemed so upset when he woke up and would fight if he cried too much. My mom would yell at my dad for never helping with him, and then she would rock him while crying. Sometimes, I would quietly open their door, crawl next to the bed, and then crawl in between the back of the headboard and the wall. I think I was lonely and wanted to be near someone. I think that I was depressed even back then, and they were all I had. Some days, they would wake up to me chewing loudly, but some days, they wouldn't wake up until my brother started screaming. I liked it better when my parents woke up before my brother started crying because then they wouldn't fight about who would take care of him, even though it was my mom every time. I wanted my parents to get along. I wanted them to be happy so we could all be a happy family. The worst days were when my brother wouldn't stop crying, when the normal crying turned to screaming and screaming. He would turn bright red; he would cry so loud and hard that he would choke. His eyes would get really big like he couldn't breathe, and then he would catch his breath and keep screaming. I would stand in the doorway of his little room and watch him. My cat, Casper, would jump into the crib looking for a warm place to lie but then run off because of my brother's cries. I would stand on the sides of the crib struggling to hold myself up, and he would stop crying for a few seconds and stare back at me, and sometimes, he would laugh at me. I would walk past my brother's room some days, a lot of days, and see my mom holding my brother and crying. I don't know if she was just sad or if it was because she was always fighting with my dad so much. Sometimes, when they would fight and my mom started crying, I would go into my closet and close my eyes. I would talk to myself. I would just keep saying that I hoped they would stop fighting and my mom would stop crying. I would really think that it would happen, like a wish: say it three times, and your wish will come true. I would come out of that closet thinking I just changed the world with my chanting, but it would be the same. My dad would be yelling or leaving, and my mom would still be crying. I'm not sure if that is why I started going into my closet so much or if I had enjoyed it before that. I would pretend it was my house. I would pretend it was mine, and no one else was allowed in except for my cat, Casper. I started planning my future by that age, all of it, the whole thing, my entire life after my parents and that house. In my closet, the fantasies would come alive, and my sad life would just fade away. Casper and I would be living in a luxurious downtown apartment, and then I would go to work at a dental office also located in a busy city. I would roll pieces of paper up, tape them to the end of a pen, and pretend they were my cigarettes. I would put them in an old purse that I pretended was an expensive purse from a fancy boutique. Then my closet door would open, and it was back to reality. On warm sunny days, we would play outside all day and have the best of times. The yard was ours, and we went from one adventure to the next with no one stopping us. From the jungle to the desert or under the sea, I was always anywhere but at that house. Those were the times that I had to keep with me always. Those were the times that got me through the bad days.

As far back as I can remember, things just weren't right. The things that went on were not normal, but I didn't know it then. Almost every day after school, my dad would take me to the bar on the back of his motorcycle. I didn't mind the ride. I would close my eyes and just feel the wind blowing through my hair. I didn't like to hold onto him. I didn't like to be that close, but I knew I had to, or I would fall off. I can still remember the way I felt as we would walk into the bar. It was a shameful and embarrassing feeling. I can remember that look on the men's faces, the way they looked at me, the way they looked at my dad. They were looks of disgust. My dad would go right to his usual spot at the bar, tell me to go sit down, and then light a cigarette. Then for the next few hours, it was as if I didn't even exist to him. I existed to other men at the bar. They always came up to me or sat next to me, and I would get that unsettling feeling at the bottom of my stomach. It was like the feeling you get when you are on a roller coaster going up and up and up, and then it drops down going so fast that your stomach does flips. Every time those men sat down next to me and told me how beautiful I was or how fast I was growing up, my stomach did those same flips. Sometimes, they would ask me to sit on their lap, and at that time, I thought it was normal and didn't want to make them mad, so I did it. How was I supposed to know that a six-year-old girl should not be in a bar sitting on strange men's laps. All the while, my dad would be over at the bar drinking beer after beer and talking so loudly to his friends. The louder he got was a sign that we were closer to leaving, and that made me happy. The one thing that kept me sane was the bartender's dog, a scruffy old mutt but a nice escape from the depressing surroundings. Some of the men weren't as bad as the others. Some seemed like they could be decent men with a loving wife and children at home. Some had sweet and caring eyes and didn't make you feel like prey. Those were the ones I would look for every day. Some had guilt all over their face as they would put their arm around me, telling me how beautiful I was as they slurred their speech and got spit on my face. I can remember the sour smell of cigarettes and beer on their breath. I hated it. The faint smell of cologne on their sweaty skin and the smell of leather from their boots are clear in my mind. I would have to categorize them by looking into their eyes. I could usually tell right away who was good or bad, who would treat me like a six-year-old, and who would hang all over me like I was an older woman sitting in a bar. The bartender constantly glanced at me, always with a disgusted look and sometimes shaking his head. He always looked at me like it was me who was doing something wrong—as if I, a six-year-old girl, decided to drive myself to that miserable bar and hang out there with these horrible men every day.

At the end of my kindergarten year, they called my parents in to talk, and I can still vividly remember the teacher's face during that discussion. I can't remember the exact words that she spoke, but I can remember that certain way she looked at me. It was similar to the way some of the men looked at me at the bar, a little bit of pity mixed with disgust. The teacher said that I was withdrawn during class, even more withdrawn when they tried to help me one-on-one. They said it wasn't just that my grades were bad, and they said they did not think that they could help me any further at their school. I believe it was even said that they were under the impression that I might have an undiagnosed learning disorder. Sometimes, I wonder if that's what she really thought or maybe she knew something was going on at home. I figured she didn't want to get involved; maybe she wasn't sure. Back then, it wasn't like it is today. I don't think teachers were trained in noticing signs of possible abuse or problems at home. I can't quite explain the way I felt that day. It was almost as if I felt numb. It was as if I just wanted to fade away or disappear as they talked. The worst part was they talked about me like I wasn't even there. I just stared at the ground and imagined the black-and-white tiles sucking me in. I remember my parents fighting a lot after that meeting, and I can remember the way it started to feel around them. I felt like I did something wrong, and they seemed like they were mad or upset with me. If only I had started talking to teachers at that age about my homelife or about my dad taking me to bars, then it might have saved me years of misery. I probably couldn't focus in school, because every single day after school, my dad brought me to that bar. I couldn't pay attention in school. All I could see were those men's faces. So many men held me close or grinded me on their laps pretending to just enjoy the music. Maybe that's what I thought about during school, and maybe that's why I failed. Those men took over my thoughts that year. It bothered me because I always knew that they were doing something wrong. The way that they started breathing, the more they moved me around, the harder they breathed. I felt scared, I felt sad, and my dad never sat by me or took me away from those men. One day, I went to the bathroom, and when I came out, a man was right in the doorway of the bathroom. I smiled and tried to go around him, but he stopped me and told me not to go. He said that I didn't need to be in such a hurry and that I was so beautiful to him. I told him that I had to go back and sit down, but he picked me up and told me he liked my outfit. I was terrified and tried to wiggle myself away, but he held me tight and squeezed on my butt. I panicked and screamed at him to stop and to put me down. He told me that I didn't need to be so loud and that he was just playing around. I almost slipped and fell on water from the sink as I ran out of there. I hated that bar. I hated that my dad kept bringing me there for men to mess with me. It all finally came to an end one afternoon at the bar when that bartender's dog bit me in the face. It was actually a good thing, a blessing in disguise because after that day, I was banned from ever going in there again. After that, things got worse between my parents, probably because my dad couldn't spend every afternoon in a bar anymore. It definitely seemed like after I got banned from the bar, we didn't see my dad as much, and when we did, he wasn't very pleasant.

When I was with my mom, she was sad. As far back as I can remember, she was sad. I wanted to tell her the things that always happened at the bar, but I didn't want to make her any sadder than she already was. When my dad wasn't there, my mom was a mess, constantly crying, yelling at me, and then more crying. She was full of sadness and low self-esteem and always weeping uncontrollably when my dad was gone. When he was there, she had a fake and very desperate smile in between their fights. Even as a young child, I could see that it was a serious obsession for her, some kind of obsession to please him. Before he would come home, she would desperately look at me and tell me that I better be good when he got there. She would look me in my face and plead with me like it was the end of the world if I did anything that might upset him. I felt so bad for her always. Back then, she seemed so frail and weak, weak mentally and physically. Every day, when he would come home, it was like watching a play as she tried to do or say anything that might please him or catch his attention even for a second. As far back as I can remember, that is how it was between them. My mom was desperate, and my dad always acted like he was too busy for her. Honestly, it was just horrible to watch, and it only got worse as the years went on. After my mom's sad performances, my dad would leave. He would always leave, and that always left her crying—sitting on the couch crying, pretending to watch TV and crying, or on the phone with my grandma and crying. She always cried to my grandma about how she had hoped that he would change when they had kids and how she didn't understand why he didn't want to be at home. It was just sad. Her sadness made me sad. Her sadness put a dark cloud over my childhood, and that, too, only got worse. My mom trying so hard to turn my dad into some kind of loving father or husband was a major part of our childhood, and it just never stopped. That winter was the worst; there was so much crying, so much sadness in that house. I remember standing in my doorway of my room watching her hold her belly and rock back and forth as she cried. I would try to block it out by going in my closet or by holding a pillow over my head, but I could still always hear her. Sometimes, I would feel so sad that I would cry too. I didn't even know why exactly, but I would feel overcome by sadness and weighed down by the misery that lived in that house.

As if my homelife wasn't bad enough, I also had to go to day care every day. The kids at day care would make fun of my old gym shoes, my thrift-store clothes, and my nappy hair. When my dad would drop me off from the back of his motorcycle, they made fun of me. I didn't tell him. He thought I liked it and that it made me look super cool. As soon as I got dropped off or walked in, I felt their judging eyes on me, and if it weren't for the sweet day care teachers meeting me at the door, I would have run the other way. The girls wore dresses with tights and shiny dress shoes. They wore cute little sweaters over their dresses that had little pearl buttons. They would have ponytails or braids in their hair almost every day, and it was always so neat. Sometimes, they had fancy hair clips, painted nails, and little gold earrings with matching necklaces. I didn't have dresses or dress shoes. I had mostly clothes from the thrift store, and sometimes, they weren't so cute; sometimes, they were boys' clothes. I didn't have all those extra things that made the other kids so much more popular than me. In the morning, they were happy when they got dropped off and smiling when their parents came back to pick them up in the evening. They would tell the other kids all about the new toys their parents had gotten them over the weekend or about the latest toys they were going to get soon. Unlike them, I didn't get the latest toys that came out right away unless it was Christmas or maybe my birthday, but I was okay with that. Maybe it wasn't even all those extra things that made us different. Maybe it was something else, something on the inside. One day, when I wasn't feeling good and my mom couldn't come to get me right, the teachers set me up on a cot in the corner of the room so I could lie down to rest. They put a stack of puzzles on the floor next to me just in case I wanted to play. A little boy came up to me, stuck his tongue out at me, took the puzzles, and dumped them all over the floor. So there were pieces to about six puzzles all mixed up in front of my cot. My stomach hurt, so I just lay there angry and disappointed. Even at that age, I questioned the intentions of everyone around me. I questioned whether or not they had good or bad inside of them. I would stare at the other kids at day care. I would stare at the teachers and the parents coming and going from there. I could sense things about them just by looking at their eyes and the way they moved. A lot of them had a darkness to them, a lot of them seemed like they were not good, and that bothered me. Instead of constantly being bothered by them, I became numb to the people around me. I started building an invisible wall around me so these people couldn't get close. Day care was an addition to that dark cloud that seemed to be hanging over my life, and I don't think anything could have made me feel differently about it.

Around that time, my cat, Casper, died. I can't remember how, but I can remember the pain. I can remember the pain in my chest and how the world suddenly felt so scary without him. I could connect with him even though he couldn't talk. I could stare into his eyes and feel his love. I felt more love and friendship from him than from any other person I came into contact with at that point in my life. The worst part was that for the first time in my life, I found out what death was. Not just death, I found out that we all can die and will die one day. I remember waking up after that and the darkness was overwhelming. The fact that I was going to die at some point was an unbearable truth. Life became lonely after Casper was gone, very lonely, and I think I had depression that no one noticed. If it wasn't for a big change, I might have disappeared into darkness or just faded away forever.

That summer, we moved to a new town, from a tiny house to a bigger house, from a dirt road to a neighborhood. The new house was closer to my grandma's, so things were looking up, and this move seemed like just what everyone needed. I liked my grandma's house. I liked my grandma and often thought how it would be better if I lived with her instead of my parents. She was different from my parents. She was calm and had patience, unlike them. She was a strong woman who liked her house kept clean and everything in its specific place. When I would wash my hands, she would then come wipe the sink down, straighten the soap bottle, and fold the towel I dried my hands. She would then lay it perfectly on the counter and straighten the rug I stood on. Her entire house was like that, perfectly clean and organized. When you came in, she would put your shoes in the corner and straighten them then sweep by the door before she closed it. My grandma was a very neat person, so it's funny that she was a smoker, two packs a day if I remember correctly. Anything you left at her house or that she gave you would smell like cigarettes, but it wasn't a bad smell. It was mixed with whatever good candle or scent spray she had in her kitchen. Since we were going to be five minutes away from her, I knew I would be there a lot, and because she was my babysitter. The move wasn't the only big change. Another big change was in the making. My mom was pregnant with another baby. I remember sitting on my grandma's couch watching cartoons and hearing my grandma yell at my mom about being pregnant again. She sounded very upset, and my mom sounded like me when I would get into trouble. My mom sounded like a child that had done something wrong and was getting put into a long time-out. At that age, I couldn't fully understand why being pregnant very soon after having a baby was a bad thing, but I could understand some of it. I knew that even when my mom was pregnant with my brother, she had to work a lot, and she looked very tired and was sick all the time. I also knew that my brother cried a lot and that my mom would cry just as much as he did, so I could understand something about this situation. I knew that my dad was never home, and I would hear my mom yell at him when he was about how he never held my brother or helped take care of him. These are all the things I would hear my mom and grandma talk about. Sometimes, they would fight about it. My grandma's voice sounded like she was mad at my mom, like my mom was making some big mistakes. I tried to not think about another baby coming because I didn't even like the last baby she had.

When my mom had my brother, life seemed to get more hectic. There was more crying, more fighting, and more unhappy conversations among everyone. After he came, even when I wasn't getting into trouble, I think I became a bother to my family. They had this cute little blond-hair and big- and blue-eyed little boy to hold and kiss all day. He looked just like my mom. Both of them had that shiny blond hair and sparkling blue eyes. I would climb up onto the bathroom sink and look in the mirror really close. My hair and eyes were brown, just brown. My dad would tell me almost daily that my eyes were ugly because they were brown. I tried to pay no attention to it, but it made me feel ugly all the time. When my dad was around, the way he looked at and talked to my brother was different, as if he liked my baby brother more than me. Everyone always wanted to hold him, and the compliments about his beautiful hair and eyes were never-ending. I wondered if when I was a baby, if everyone talked about how beautiful my brown hair and eyes were and always wanted to hold me.

The move was a big change but definitely a good one. Maybe my mom would cry less, maybe my dad would stay home more, and maybe we would all finally be a happy family. The new house was awesome. It was a lot bigger, and my room was so much nicer than my old room. There was a nice-size backyard, a deck, and a playhouse where you could climb all the way to the top. The playhouse had a slide that came out the side and a sandbox at the bottom; the playhouse was going to be my new apartment. No more playing in a closet. I had a clubhouse now, and things were looking up. The neighborhood seemed so big at that age. Even though it was only a few blocks, it seemed like a city to me. I started to take walks up and down the block every day with the hope of finding new friends, and sure enough, I found some rather quickly. A couple of blocks from my house, I found a friend; on the other side of the street, another one; and two houses down from there, another one. The girl I met first, Brenda, was neatly dressed, very quiet, and polite. You could tell right away that she had a very loving family that raised her right and taught her how to show respect and speak properly. Her mom was very friendly, so sweet, one of those loud and friendly women who definitely made you smile. She had a warmth to her, and she was one of the people I could tell had good inside of her. Her stepdad was quiet and didn't talk much, just a hello here and there, but he was one of the people whom I could tell had good in them too. Brenda had two older brothers whom I didn't see much of. They all talked differently. You could tell they were from somewhere else. I liked the way it sounded. There was a girl, Candace, who lived on the other side of the street who was hesitant when I first met her. She was nice and not as quiet as my new neighbor, but I liked how much she joked around. I figured she had to get to know you better before she could really open up and show you who she really was. Her mom seemed hesitant, too, but still had a big smile. She seemed as if maybe she was stressed out in a similar way as my mom was. Her dad was a strange man. At first, I felt like he didn't like me much, and I couldn't quite read him at first, so I tried to keep my distance and would figure out later how I felt about him. Candace had an older brother who was a teenager, so he wasn't home most of the time. They talked differently, too, but not like my neighbors. They sounded like how the people on the country music stations talked. Down the street from her was a very energetic girl named Amber. She was happy, fun, and just full of life from the very moment I met her. She was polite, and you could tell she was loved and raised to be respectful. Maybe her parents didn't fight a lot, maybe they didn't fight at all, and they probably all spent a lot of time together. From the first time I met her, I really liked her. I even showed up at her house first thing in the morning the very next day to see if she wanted to play. Her mom, Lisa, was really nice, and I really liked her right away also. She was kind of quiet but so sweet and looked me in the eyes when she talked to me. Her dad was equally as nice, and I could tell they were all people who had good on the inside. She had an older sister, a teenager who was quiet but seemed like she would be nice if you got to know her. She had a younger brother whom I really liked. He played Nintendo a lot. Every day, I would wake up, walk to her house, and hope that it wasn't too early for her to play. Most days, they would still be eating breakfast when I would get there, so I thought they would make me come back later, but instead her mom would let me in and offer me cereal. At first, I felt weird because I had never had a friend like that and because I felt like they were different from me, maybe better than me, but I didn't really know why I thought that. Their house was always clean, and it always smelled good even though her parents both smoked cigarettes. They had two dogs. Cubby was an older fluffy dog that was grouchy, so they said to just leave her alone, and the other one, Bones, was a young and very hyper pit bull. When they would let them out of their cages, Cubby would run up to Amber's parents shaking her little tail and licking them. She loved them and was always so excited to see everyone. She was a very old dog, sweet to people that she knew, but strangers couldn't pet her, because she could get scared and bite them. The second that the cage door opened, Bones would leap out like a lightning bolt. Then she would bounce from the couch to the floor and on top of everyone. You had to watch out because Bones would knock you down if you let her. She was just full of energy, and it was so hard to control her. Her family had this sort of order to them, like before you walked in, you knew who would be where and doing what, and it was like that every day. The consistency was almost comforting to me, and it made me wish that my family was like that. It made me wish they were my family. The more I went over there that summer, the more I liked it and the more I hoped all that would never change.

Amber liked sports, almost all of them, and she was really good at them too. Baseball, basketball to hockey, she was into all of it, and her family even liked sports too. She even had baseball and basketball jerseys, and her parents had sports blankets and jackets. Besides the sports accessories, she had the important stuff that I didn't have, the sports equipment. Her parents made sure she had all the necessary gear to play all the sports she was into, and she had extra stuff for me to use. Whatever Amber liked, I was right behind her because I knew she had good taste with everything and I thought she was so awesome. We had so much fun that summer, every day something new or exciting. We had made friends with a few boys from the next block, and most mornings, we would play baseball for hours until we got too hot. Most days, we would head to Melissa's house for cold drinks and lunch if her mom let us. In the afternoons, we played street hockey or checked every ditch or puddle of water for toads and frogs. If we couldn't find them, we looked for little mud mounds to find crawdads or by the sewers to find tadpoles and caught them in sand buckets or anything we could find. The neighborhood was ours, and there was nothing in that neighborhood that we left alone. I can still remember the way it smelled every morning and the way the sun felt on my skin. Those were the signs that it was going to be another fun and adventurous day. As the summer days passed, we became the best of friends, and that was only the beginning of our friendship.

The days were great, but during the week, I had to go back home, and every day as it got closer to 6:00 p.m., sadness crept up on me. Walking into my house, I always felt nervous and uneasy. The negative vibes hit you as you opened the door. Right when you walked in, you had to give the door a hard push to move the pile of shoes out of the way, but then you still tripped over them trying to get in all the way. I would feel embarrassed, embarrassed for myself but mostly for my mom because she let the house get so bad. Every single shoe, coat, and sweater that everyone in the house owned was all right there almost blocking our front door. That wasn't even the worst part of the house. The kitchen was definitely the worst. The counters were covered from end to end with papers piled on top of each other, stacks so high they would constantly get knocked down. You had to rush around picking them all up, and then you would feel like part of the problem just piling them back up. The sink was always full of dirty dishes, usually a week's worth, and when it got full, they were set in the dish rack. That rack was disgusting. It smelled so foul from stagnant water and rotten food. The table was just like the counters. There were so many stacks of paper and other things that you had to move a pile if you wanted to sit at it to eat. The only part of the house besides my room that was livable was the living room because the couches were only covered with a thin layer of stuff that you could move out of the way. I spent most of my time in my room to avoid the mess and the awkward predicament of knocking over piles of junk. I was just a kid, so I didn't know that what my mom was doing was called hoarding. That summer was amazing, but I was so excited for school to start. That summer flew by, and before you knew it, it was time for my new school.

That school year, my first-grade year, was enjoyable with the great teacher that I had. My teacher was so smart. She was also kind and full of patience. I looked forward to seeing her each day, and she never once made me feel like the teachers at the last school did. There was never a mention again about me possibly having some kind of learning disorder or retardation. In first grade, I would watch the kids and mentally put them in categories of good, bad, and undecided. Most of the other kids were just like the kids in day care; they had something on the inside that was very different from me. I had problems being able to see the chalkboard, so I was taken to an eye doctor and found out that I needed glasses. Normally, this kind of situation wouldn't affect you too badly, especially at a young age, but it was the glasses that did. My parents chose the only frames that the insurance would fully cover which were not very flattering. They weren't stylish or cute like the other kids at school who wore glasses. These glasses were thick plastic in an ugly brownish color. They were big like how older women wear their glasses, and to make it worse, the lenses were thick. I cried. I was angry and told my parents I couldn't wear these to school because they were so ugly and I would get made fun of. I pleaded with them to take the glasses back and let me pick out a pair that were not free through the insurance. I pleaded that they get me a cute pair even if they had to pay for them, but they told me I was being dramatic. I wanted the thin metal frames that came in pink or purple, but my dad said they were just glasses. Sure enough, I was right about all of it. The second I walked into class with those things on, every single kid stared at me with that look of judgment and criticism. The boys pointed and laughed at each other while all pounding their fists on the desks, causing all the other kids to shout mean things about me and my glasses. I looked around, and even the girls whom I normally talked to and thought I was friends with were laughing. Everyone was saying things like four eyes or saying how ugly I looked with glasses. There was a girl who barely ever spoke or talked to anyone, a girl who was so shy the teacher would say she was going to send her to the office if she wouldn't talk. Even the shy girl who didn't talk was laughing at me. At that moment, I felt like every single one of those kids hated me. I felt like I wasn't even a person. The teacher wasn't in the room yet, so I had to slowly walk through them to my desk, knowing that I would suffer through this until she got there. They stuck their arms out trying to block me from getting through, and a couple of the boys kicked me in my legs rather hard. I had to hold my emotions down and my tears, which was extremely hard. The minutes until she walked in seemed like an eternity, and I thought I would explode from embarrassment. My face must have been a bright shade of red, my ears felt like they were on fire, and I felt as if someone was sitting on my chest. My stomach started to feel sick, and I just wanted to disappear and never ever return. When the teacher came in, I wanted so badly to run up to her and tell her what happened or ask her to go to the office, but I didn't. I just sat there pushing down the pain while dying inside.

Sometimes, we had class parties where parents could attend or days where parents came in for various activities. We had a day where a parent was supposed to prepare a food dish or a baked item for us to and then together explain how it was made and share with everyone. I remember that day very clearly and the feelings that came with it. We didn't do any planning, prepping, cooking, or baking for that day; and I kept asking my mom what we were going to bring in. She said we were going to bring in graham crackers and vanilla frosting and call it a graham cracker surprise. At that moment, I felt so sorry for her, and I felt like I just loved her so much. I know she felt guilty for being so busy or too tired from work to cook or bake for that day. We went up in front of the class like everyone else did and explained how to spread frosting on a graham cracker. I didn't want my mom to feel stupid, so I told the kids how I just loved graham cracker surprise, and even though it was so simple, we ate it all the time at our house. I know she was embarrassed or ashamed, and I wished that I could take that away from her. The moms that brought in chocolate fondue, three-layer cakes, or little fancy appetizers in little containers with each child's name on it. I didn't even feel embarrassed for me at all. I only felt embarrassed for her. I didn't care what the other students thought about me or my lame desert or whatever it was supposed to be. I didn't care if I looked stupid to them or if they thought we were poor for not having an extravagant food or baked item to share with the class. I cared how my mom's face looked and how she pretended not to care how the other mothers looked at her or what they thought about her. I cared that she felt bad. I cared that she felt like she wasn't as good as those other moms. I felt so bad for her for weeks after that day and tried to be nicer to her. The kids did laugh and make fun of me after that day with constant ridicule about our graham cracker surprise. The things those kids said were cruel, but it was the humiliation and shame that I knew my mom felt that made me not care what they said or did.

Toward the end of the year, a new student came into our class. Suddenly, the negative attention and everything these kids were doing to me were shifted to this new student. On the first day, he walked in with his head down, and there was not even the trace of a smile on his face. His clothes were dirty and appeared to be old. They were almost tattered even. His jeans were so stained and inches too short. There was dirt at the bottom with some kind of dark stains on the knee and thigh area. The knees of his jeans were worn with some tears in them, and you could see that they were thinner than jeans normally were. He had on several shirts, a longer black one first, which had a shorter lighter-colored shirt with a dirty flannel over it all. I don't think I had ever seen a kid wear a flannel like that, like the ones my dad would wear to work. His shoes looked like they were at least one size too small, pretty old, and some kind of really cheap brand. The laces were untied and so dirty, but you could see that they were white at some point, maybe a really long time ago. His hair was greasy, and it almost looked like it had dirt in it; his face too, dirty and greasy. He carried a small book bag that looked like it was several years old, and it was so thin. It looked like if you put a schoolbook in it, it might just tear through the bottom. I stared at him but didn't make fun of him like everyone else did. I stared at him trying to figure out where he came from and if he was as miserable as I was. He kept his arms folded and didn't move around much. He looked like he was holding himself tightly for some reason. I was in the next row as him, and as if I didn't already feel bad for him, I realized when he bent down to get his pencil that he smelled bad. It smelled like he didn't wear deodorant and hadn't bathed in a while. That would definitely explain his greasy, dirty face and hair. I later found out that his family took care of the horses and stables at a nearby racetrack and that they lived there. That was another moment where I felt like I could take away someone else's shame and humiliation. I wished that the kids could go back to making fun of everything about me instead of him. I knew once they got close to him and smelled what I did, they would destroy his feelings. I tried to be nice to him, but either he had a wall up that he didn't let down for strangers, or he felt like I was trying to be friends with him out of pity. School wasn't very enjoyable, but at least, I had all my neighborhood friends to look forward to after school and on the weekends. All those kids were about two to four years older than me, so we didn't go to the same school at that time. I never told the kids from my neighborhood that I wasn't popular in my school or that nobody even liked me in my class. They seemed to like me just fine, and that was enough for me.

First grade was when I started looking differently at how the other kids had things that I didn't, and I decided to change that. They had pencils with characters on them or sports teams, and most of the girls had all Lisa Frank supplies. It was such cool stuff, and all the girls would show it to each other before school or on the bus. It was embarrassing because I didn't even have one thing that was cool or popular. I got the brown pencils. I got the colored matte folders that were 10¢, not the cool folders that were $1.00 or $1.97 each. Parents don't understand how the little things like that can make or break you as a young child. I just wanted to feel like a beautiful young girl. I just wanted to pull out my brightly colored folders and supplies like the other girls. I wanted to look around the room and catch eyes with other girls as we both unpacked and then proudly held our new Lisa Frank supplies. I wanted to be a part of the group of girls that compared all their stuff to see who found that new sought after item that the others couldn't find. I wanted to be the girl who could casually say I found it while out on a shopping spree with my mom. You know, play it cool and act like it wasn't that important while the other girls admired it and asked to see it. I made a big decision that year. I decided I was going to have all that stuff I wanted. I wasn't going to go through another year being the poor kid that didn't even have good supplies. At first, it was just for more practical things. At that time, I usually asked the teacher for pencils. They were regular pencils, and when my mom got me pencils, they were regular boring pencils too. When I needed markers, crayons, or colored pencils, it was the same thing. I got cheap markers instead of the newer markers that were name brand and had different shades, were double-sided, or changed colors. I started by asking to use the bathroom during class so I could go into the hallway where everyone hung their book bags and take the things that I wanted. I would take books, pencils, markers, small toys, and whatever little popular things that kids were into at that time and then slipped them into my bag. Surprisingly, no one said anything about any of the stuff that came up missing. It was almost perfect, so I kept doing it. I did it all the time, at least three to four times a week. I had to use most of the stuff at home, so I, at least, felt good because I told myself my good supplies were for home. I told myself that stuff was too good to use at school, they were my personal supplies. When my mom asked me where it came from, I told her I became friends with so many girls at school. I told her that the girls I was friends with had extra stuff or their parents had a lot of money and gave them extra supplies that they could share. I felt confident with what I was doing, so then it only made sense to step it up to bigger better things.

The book fairs that they had a few times a year were the best because right afterward you walked back to the classroom and put what you purchased in your book bag hanging conveniently in the hall. I would watch the other kids purchase all the stuff I wanted but couldn't afford to get. Any of the good stuff was around twenty dollars, but I never got that much. I didn't want to beg my parents because I knew they worked hard to pay the bills and take care of us.

They would give me a few dollars, usually enough to buy a couple of bookmarks or one of the few books they had for five dollars. I didn't want to just have bookmarks to put in the old books I had at home with brown ripped pages and someone else's name written in it. I didn't want the cheap books that were supershort and about a very boring topic. I wanted to feel like I had new stuff, nice stuff, the stuff that made you feel good about yourself. At the book fairs, I would act like I had sufficient money to buy anything I wanted, no more looking through the bookmarks and having even the teachers feel bad for me. I would browse through the more expensive books, even the really expensive triple packs that included a series of popular books. I would act like I couldn't choose at first but then end up saying that I thought all the books were old. I would say I was waiting on the new stuff I heard was coming out soon. I would also say that I had most of those books at home, telling kids that my parents buy me all the new books at the store. At the book fair at the beginning of the school year, my first book fair, it was so embarrassing. I can still remember the feeling of being all the way at the bottom. To be honest, it was disgusting. I went into that book fair full of excitement and high hopes of getting an awesome new book. I looked through the books, looking for one, maybe even two that caught my eye and looked interesting enough to carry to the cashier. After looking through a couple of racks and tables, I found two books that I knew I would really enjoy reading, so I took them to the lady at the front desk. She took the two books from me and said that these were a good choice, looked at the back, and then told me how much they were. I can't remember exactly how much they were, but I remember it was nowhere near the few dollars I had. The lady repeated herself as if I didn't hear her, so I gave her the few dollars I had and acted like I had more in my pocket. I checked my pockets and looked around on the floor as if I dropped money. I asked if anyone saw a twenty-dollar bill. I even said that it was a folded-up twenty-dollar bill and I had it in my hand with the other dollars. I acted all upset and told the lady I would have to wait until I could find my twenty-dollar bill and then would come back to purchase my two books. The lady looked right through me as if she could see my every thought, as if she knew that

I didn't have a twenty-dollar bill that I misplaced. She looked at me like I was a homeless person on the street begging, asking everyone if they could spare any change. She didn't even help me look for the twenty-dollar bill I said that I lost somewhere while looking through the books. She didn't even look or lift up one single book. She didn't even move from her little area behind the table. I think it was her reaction that made the other kids not even attempt to help me either. Not even one kid helped me or asked me where I had my money last. Everyone looked at me just like that lady did. They didn't look at me like they felt sorry for me; they looked at me like I was garbage. After a few minutes of looking around for my fake twenty-dollar bill, the lady told me I had enough to buy a bookmark. A bookmark, one single bookmark. Who goes to a book fair and buys a bookmark but not a book to put it in. So I did. I bought a bookmark and went back to class holding the single bookmark. Most of the other kids had one or two books, a bookmark, and a pencil to show the other kids and the teacher. I sat there feeling ashamed and as if my face and ears were bright red with embarrassment. I kept that bookmark under my pillow and looked at it for days until I wanted to scream and cry. At night, I would just hold it, play with the tassel, and replay that day over and over in my head. It was safe to say that I never wanted to be put in that situation again, and I would make sure I never was.

I continued to take anything I wanted out of other kids' book bags, and I had a collection of items in my closet at home. I quickly was no longer amused with the small things I was taking, so I decided that I would start taking bigger things if the opportunity arose. Once a week, kids brought in stuffed animals, toys, or things that were important to them for show and tell. For me, it was like a fashion show, but with toys, it was like I got to see what was available for me to take later. Just like with the supplies and books, I would either ask to use the bathroom or say I needed to go to the office and call my mom for something so I could go into their book bags. It was such an anxious feeling, especially when taking out bigger items because if someone walked out, it would be obvious what was going on. My heart would beat so fast I could feel it in my ears, and I would get this sick feeling in my stomach, but at the same time, I would feel so excited. It was almost too hard to decide what I wanted the most, but I took just one toy that first time, a stuffed animal of a popular character. I watched and waited the next day for the teacher to announce that there was a missing toy, but nothing was said. The next week, I decided to take two things I wanted after watching yet another awesome lineup of toys at the show and tell. I went out and took a set of figurines from one bag and put them at the bottom of my book bag; then I took a big puppy stuffed animal with a baby pup. The dog stuffed animals were bigger, and I was scared to put them in my bag right away because you would see them if it was opened. So I quickly carried them right down the hall to the restroom, lifted the garbage bag out of the can, and put the toys under it. After class, I went to the restroom and took the toys from the garbage can, shoved them in my bag, and went home. The next day, the teacher said something to the class. She said that a student misplaced their stuffed animals they brought for show and tell. No fingers were pointed, and the word *stolen* was not used, just the word *misplaced*. I guess that the child's parents felt that the toys were just misplaced, lost at school or on the bus perhaps. Nothing was even mentioned about the other kid and the figurine set that I took. The following week while looking through book bags after lunch, I couldn't believe what I found, an entire book series. They were the most popular books out, the books that everyone collected and talked about daily. They were brand-new. You could smell how new they were, the covers so shiny and pages so crisp. I felt amazing. I felt like I hit the jackpot, and I just couldn't wait to get home so I could look at them. I didn't think about the fact that I stole the books until the next day the teacher said she needed to have an important talk with us. My stomach dropped, and I felt sick as soon as I saw my teacher's face change. She was always so nice, so sweet, and always had the biggest smile on her face throughout the day. Her kindness and constant smiles were a consistent comfort to me, so when I saw that disappear, it was very scary to say the least. After she said she needed to talk to us, she sat down at her desk and put her hand on her forehead. There was a pause that seemed like it took forever, and you could hear her take a deep breath as if she was struggling to even talk to us. When she began to speak, she looked down at the floor, held her hands together, but nervously kept rubbing her one thumb up and down her hand. She said that she was very sad and very disappointed to have to tell us that someone has stolen something from another student. She said that they were going to be investigating this incident and were hoping that if anyone had any information, they would tell her. She said that she was very upset, and if someone took these books, they could set them on her desk during lunch and no questions would be asked. I told myself that I didn't take the books. I figured if I convinced myself mentally that I didn't take the books, then everything would be fine. After lunch, nothing was mentioned again, and I felt relieved. That night, I told myself I needed to be more careful and not steal such big items that would have kids or parents upset by the disappearance. I didn't like the way I felt. It was a feeling of shame and embarrassment. I felt stupid, careless, and embarrassed even to myself. I told myself that the next day would be a fresh start for me, a chance to be more careful and do things differently. By the next morning, I was feeling better and was ready to put this incident behind me and move forward. I decided to be friendly and say hello to the kids at school that day which I normally never did, and it made me feel good about everything. The teacher came in, and it appeared to be the start of a normal day; so I sat back, took a deep, breath, and let go of the stress from the day before. Soon after class started, there was a knock at the door, and it was the principal. Instantly, I felt like my heart was going to explode. What the principal said was very similar to what our teacher had said the day before, but he added that if they found out who stole the books, they would be suspended. I felt like my face was burning bright red again. I felt like my guilt was going to pour out of me onto the desk, and then everyone would see that I was the guilty one. I didn't even want to go back to school after that. The next few days were full of gossip, and all the kids were talking about what happened all day. Most of the kids acted so stuck up about the situation, repeatedly saying that their parents buy them anything they want so they couldn't be the one who stole the books. It was three days after the principal talking to us that the fingers started pointing at the possible book thief. It was right before the start of class when one of my classmates went up to the teacher's desk, right in front of the room, and loudly announced that they knew who stole the books. Fear ripped through my body so fast I thought I was going to throw up or get up and run all the way home. I could hear my heart pounding. I could feel my temperature rise and sweat start to form by my hairline. The teacher stood up with an angry but intrigued face and asked the student to show her who did it. I tried to just look at my desk and appear to be so into what I was doodling in my notebook that I had no idea they were walking toward me. I stared down at my desk trying to act relaxed, trying to act as if I wasn't concerned with anything that was going on with this stolen-book business. I wanted to appear as if I wanted nothing to do with the whole situation because I was a good kid that would never gossip or steal, so why would I take part in all of this? Even as I tried to play it cool, the thumping got louder, my face got hotter, my teeth were so clenched, and my forehead was twitching. I felt my stomach getting uneasy, and right when I thought I couldn't take it anymore, they walked past me. I didn't even know what to think. I couldn't process what had just happened fast enough. I was still trying to breathe normally and calm myself down. Then I realized where they were standing. They walked past me. One seat behind me in the next row was where they stopped. Everything was in slow motion as I turned around and looked up and saw his face. It was the new kid, the dirty one, the kid whose family lives at the horse track. I died inside seeing his innocent and confused face, the embarrassment he must have felt at that moment as everyone stared at him. He was fair skinned and had blond hair and blue eyes, so his face turned so red; there was no hiding his embarrassment. I wanted to jump out of my seat, grab his hand, and just run away from there. The teacher didn't ask if he did it. She just asked him to come with her to the office as she shook her head in anger. As he got up, he tried to mumble something, but he was choked up, on the verge of crying so I couldn't hear what he said. I don't think she did either.

When the teacher was out of the room taking him to the office, the kids all came to a similar conclusion on why he was the book thief. It was because he was poor, because he was dirty, because his family lived in some kind of tiny house or barn, so he must have stolen it. Not one kid questioned his innocence, not even one. His appearance must have been a red flag to everyone that he was too poor to afford new books, so he had to be the one that stole them. There were about ten long minutes until the teacher came back, and in those ten minutes, the other kids completely picked apart this poor kid's life. I was so angry and full of disgust toward those kids and couldn't help but think bad thoughts about them as I looked around the class. I didn't see compassion in them. I really didn't see much kindness, and in my mind, they were horrible kids. It took me some time to go back and forth in my mind about how horrible all those kids were. Then it hit me. I came to a horrible conclusion: I was the horrible one. It was my fault, all of it. I created this and let the only kid in class who might not be a bad person get blamed for what I did. I wanted to fall to my knees and cry. I was so ashamed of what I did. I wanted to go down to the principal's office and say that it was me. I was the one who stole all those books. It was just then when everything was rushing through my brain that I realized I didn't want to be the thief, I didn't want to be a thief at all. I wanted to help the poor kid sitting in the principal's office for something I did, but I couldn't. I imagined his parents coming in to get him because he got suspended. I imagined how he would look up at them with a hurt and confused look on his face. I also imagined the look they would have as they walked in to get him. I imagined them looking at him and wondering if they did something wrong when raising him or if they weren't being good-enough parents. I wondered about as they walked out of the school, what would be said in the car, or when they got home. Were they the kind of parents who would believe him when he told them that he didn't steal the books, or would they tell him they didn't want to hear his lies? Would they yell at him, would he cry, would they spank him or hit him with a belt? His face stayed in my mind all night, and it was hard to fall asleep with the guilt that was building up inside me. After that, it felt like each day was either supposed to be a punishment or some kind of test, and I became determined not to fail it. Instead of following the latest gossip or watching the same routine repeated day after day in that classroom, I sat back and observed. When you take yourself out of the circle of madness that is called elementary school, you can really know what's going on and who you want to be. After everything that had happened, I hoped that it would make me not want to be a thief, but instead it just made me not want to feel the way I did. I didn't want to feel guilt, shame, or sadness. I didn't want to have to feel bad for the mistakes that I made. Over the next week, each day got easier. The sadness and shame slowly drifted away, but inside me the guilt held on tight. The boy who was suspended for stealing the books came back, and after that, I pushed the whole incident out of my mind and was determined to move forward. I stopped stealing out of the other kids' book bags and decided I wasn't going to do anything that would cause such a big situation again. It was very surprising that no one mentioned that situation much after that, so all those feelings and emotions that I felt were so far away.

The holidays came; and before Christmas break, the school had a little shop for students to buy Christmas gifts for each other, teachers, and parents. It was similar to how the book fair ladies came in to sell the books but for Christmas gifts. Santa's gift shop was a great way for kids to be able to buy their Christmas gifts without having to get help from their parents. Your parents had to provide you with the money, of course, but other than that, you did the shopping and the wrapping of the gifts. I had told my parents about Santa's gift shop for weeks and asked them for money to buy them and my teacher a gift. They gave me ten dollars, and I was very happy to have money to shop for them. We were able to go to the gift shop several times over a three-day period, so I went on the first day our class was able to go. They had a lot of different items, mugs that said "Best Mom" or "Best Dad," all sorts of Christmas decorations and ornaments. They had watches, candles, and rustic decor that was mostly made from wood. It smelled like pine and cinnamon, and it was set up in a classroom that was only used for extracurricular activities at the end of the day or after school. They set it up very nicely. It was like being in a real shop. The tables were covered with white clothes and had glittery snowflakes on them with silver ball ornaments. There were large snowflake decorations hanging from the ceiling and Christmas music playing in the background that you almost couldn't hear with the chatter of excited children. After looking through a section of ornaments, I found the perfect gift for my teacher. It was exactly the kind of gift I wanted to get her. She was the best teacher, so when I saw a cute little "#1 Teacher" snow globe ornament, I knew that I had to buy it for her. It was clear, and inside there was snow and a tiny little apple and pencils with a little tiny chalkboard that said "#1 Teacher." It was the cutest little ornament, and I was excited about it. I purchased the ornament for five dollars and decided to come back the next day to buy other gifts because the ornament was fragile, and I wanted to focus on getting it home safely. I would wrap it in class, take it home for a couple of weeks, and then bring it back in to give to her, the last day before Christmas break.

After school, I was excited to show my parents the gift I had bought. The feeling of being an independent shopper at that age was nice. Upon showing them the gift, they immediately asked why I bought my teacher a gift, as if she wasn't good enough to get a gift from a student. They asked how much it cost and pointed out that by buying the five-dollar ornament, I only had five dollars left. They both shook their heads at me, and my mom made a sarcastic remark, saying if it really made me happy, it was okay. They made me feel stupid for not only wasting money on my teacher but also for spending half of my money doing it. This wasn't the first time they acted as if anyone besides them wasn't worthy. They acted as if they were royalty and no one else was good enough for anything. Even at a young age, I found it strange and unsettling that they had unrealistic visions of themselves. Sitting on a couch or at a table covered in junk in the middle of a house so dirty that you almost couldn't walk through, these people thought they were better than other people. I took my ornament to my room and told myself that I did a good thing by buying my teacher a gift. Even if my parents thought I was stupid, I didn't care. My teacher was so sweet and kind. I wanted her to know that she was very much appreciated. At that time, she was one of the only good things in my life. I often stared at her in class and imagined that she was my mom. I bet she would be a great mother. I imagined her being so caring and patient. I just knew she had a clean and organized home full of fancy decor and nice furniture. She probably had all of the matching dishes and cookware with a full and organized refrigerator. I imagined walking into her house and there being a welcome rug with a wooden coat rack near the door with a wooden seat that you could sit on to take off your shoes. I bet her house smelled like flowers from potpourri and scented candles in every room. I didn't think about the fact that I only had five dollars left to buy both of my parents' gifts until later that evening. I remember it hitting me and feeling panicked because it reminded me of the book fair earlier that year. I knew what I had to do, so it's safe to say, I planned out the next day and what would occur at the gift shop.

The next day, at school, I told myself not to be nervous, because there was nothing wrong and I wasn't going to be doing anything wrong. It came time for anyone in our class who had money to visit the gift shop, and I went down the hall ready to do what I needed to do. I decided to start by looking for a gift for my dad on the tables that were targeted for dads or men in general. I can't remember exactly what I picked out for him, but I went to the table where you purchased your items and paid. While I looked for a gift for my dad, I noticed that there were two classes of kids all in one small area. The lady was so busy, and she was not paying attention to everyone all the time. The teachers of the two classes were outside the room talking to each other and looking like they were having a good time, so there was only one lady in the room. After I paid for my gift, I acted like I might make an additional purchase and started looking at a rack of ornaments that caught my eye. I chose one that I thought my mom would like for our tree, and I put it under the item I already purchased for my dad and walked out. I headed back to the class, put both items in the little brown bag they gave me, and put it safely in my book bag. I felt so relieved once I got back to my class and sat down. It was as if I was safe now that I was there and the items were in my book bag. I guess I thought since I bought something, I wasn't guilty, that I just took something extra that I needed. What a relief to have my Christmas gifts for my teacher and both of my parents. With those gifts and the ones we would make in class for our parents, it felt good knowing they would get more than one gift from me. After all students made it back to our classroom and settled down, we started back with our schoolwork. Not too long after that, there was a knock at the door. It was the principal and the lady from the Christmas gift shop. Even before that gift shop lady set eyes on me, I knew what they were there for—for me. The walk to the principal's office was silent, and the hallway felt colder and longer than usual. The pause from entering the office to all three of us sitting down seemed like an eternity. The principal asked me if I knew why I was there, which seemed to me like a silly thing to ask, but I still acted as if I didn't know. I acted as if I was very confused and oblivious to why I had been brought to the office. They asked if I had taken something that I did not pay for the gift shop when our class was in there. I told them that I had purchased a gift for my dad and then went back to class. It turns out that the lady from the gift shop could do multiple things at one time. Even though she was helping quite a few other kids, she still managed to see me walk out with something that I did not pay for. She described it to me exactly how I did it. I was shocked that she had seen that while appearing to not pay any attention to me. I told them I completely forgot about the second item I had picked up and must have forgotten to stop at the front table to pay for it. They took me to the hallway right outside of the classroom where we hung our book bags, and they told me I could pay for the ornament or give it back. As I opened my bag to get it, I realized I had books that I stole from other kids and felt terrified that they would see them. I then rummaged through my book bag, searching every pocket and pretending I couldn't find the rest of my money that I had brought for the gift shop. I acted very upset that my money was gone and told them I must have dropped it in the gift shop or someone stole it from me. To my surprise, they acted as if they believed me had even brought me back to the gift shop to look for it. After not finding any money, I gave the ornament back and was told I could purchase it the next day. When the kids in my class asked me what happened, I told them I forgot to pay for one of my gifts so they came to get the money for it. I made sure to put a big smile on my face and act as if I had done nothing wrong. I convinced myself of that all afternoon, and it worked until I got home.

I don't know why I was surprised to find my parents waiting to talk to me when I walked in the door. Again, I acted like I had no idea what was going on but then acted like I think I knew what they wanted to talk about. I told them that I totally forgot about it and then repeated the same story that I told at school for the third time that day. I should have just acted like I didn't know what they were talking about and wait to see what they wanted to talk to me about. After I told my story that I had perfected at that point, they shook their heads and told me that wasn't what we needed to talk about. I really had no clue what the problem could be if it wasn't the whole situation with the gift shop. They asked me if I had anything I wanted to tell them, and for the first time that day, I was honestly confused about what was going on. To my surprise, this was about the books I had taken weeks before, which then led to the supplies that I had been taking all year. The next morning, my mom had to bring me to school with all the books and supplies that she knew she didn't buy. I tried to convince her that it was only the one set of books I took and all the supplies and other books were given to me. She told me I could not be trusted and collected all of it to bring to school. Another unpleasant surprise was when we met with the principal the next morning and the mother of the boy whose books I took were there. Walking in, being the only student there and accompanied by parents, I was obviously the accused book thief. Even before being told who she was, I suspected it because of the way she looked at me with disgust. By that age, I knew very well what a look of disgust was. It is a bit different from a look of anger. A look of disgust is much worse and makes you want to just disappear. In my defense, I told them that the books were given to me because the child didn't want them anymore. They brought the child's mom into the office with us and told her what I had said about the books being given to me. She got angry and raised her voice as she said that there is no way her son would give up books that he begged for repeatedly until she bought them. She looked at me and said there is no way her son would give me the new books. It was the way she said "new books" that really hurt. She said it as if I wasn't good enough for new books, like I was too poor to even have them. The principal said that if this was an isolated incident, she would think it was just a misunderstanding between two students, but because of what took place the previous day, it was clear what was happening. She said that I needed to learn that it was not okay to take things that didn't belong to me, and this was something that could turn into a serious problem. My parents said this was very surprising to them and this wasn't behavior that they had ever seen from me. They looked at me with what I was expecting to be looks of anger, but it wasn't anger. Yet again, I was getting looks of disgust. They had brought a whole bag in of other books and supplies that I took from book bags throughout the year, but the principal didn't want to even look in the bag. She said that she couldn't try and find the owner of each and every item if they were actually taken from other students, so she said they could take it back home. The principal didn't suspend me, no punishment was given to me at school, but I would definitely be punished. When I was sent back to class as if I hadn't been through enough that morning, I had to deal with my teacher who couldn't look me in my eyes. When she passed out a worksheet, I said thank-you, but she didn't look at me or say anything back. I had to be a horrible child, a horrible person for my teacher to not want to look me in the eyes. I tried to pretend that she wasn't treating me any differently and be as nice as I possibly could to her with added smiles and comments about how nice she looked. I raised my hand to answer every single question and offered to gather and pass out all of the worksheets, but she remained cold toward me all day. The kids in class really didn't seem like they knew what happened with anything besides the Christmas gift shop incident the previous day. I spent the entire afternoon convincing myself that everything was okay and that I didn't do anything wrong. I had to do that in order to not feel like I wanted to die from guilt and embarrassment from the person that I was becoming.

When I got home, my parents were not very nice to me. They called me a liar and a thief. My dad told me that the two worst things you can be are a liar and a thief. He said I was both, so I was already the worst kind of person I could be. After that, they almost acted as if I didn't exist, as if I was on my own in that house, no longer a child because of what I had done. When they did speak to me, it was short and rude, and they sounded aggravated by my presence. The ridicule and gossip did not come as I expected it would, not that next day and not after that either. The teacher didn't look at me the same after that. In fact, she barely would look at me. When she did look at me, she acted like she was busy so she didn't have to look me in the eyes. I left the stealing alone for a while to try and show my parents that I wasn't the worst kind of person in the world and that I was still just a kid who made a mistake. I'm not sure how long after that it was that I decided I needed to steal again, but I remember very clearly doing it. I know it was in a colder month, maybe late winter, because I had a big winter coat on. I was at a department store with my parents, and after a long period of looking through the toy aisle, I found a toy that I just had to have. It was a rather large toy, a set with a mom dog and three puppies stuffed animals that moved like real dogs. They were in a pretty good-sized box, and because they secure and seal toys very well, there was no way I could have gotten all four animals out of the box. They were secured to the inside of the box with so many plastic fasteners and then taped on top of those, so I knew it would be so obvious I was stealing if I tried to remove them. I came to the conclusion that in order to get the toys I want so badly, I had to take the whole box. I don't think my plan was logical, holding a large box under my coat—nope, not very logical. I figured if I said my stomach was hurting and held my arms around my waist like I was in pain, then my parents wouldn't see the box under my coat. It seemed to work as I walked around with my parents shopping, probably because they weren't paying much attention to me. I don't know if it was my behavior or if they could see the box under my coat, but my mom stopped and asked me to come closer to her. She pulled my arms away from my waist and patted down the bulging area, which caused the box to fall on the ground. Her eyes got big, and her face turned very angry as she yelled at me, asking if I was planning on stealing the toy. My dad just shook his head and mumbled obscenities under his breath. Yet again, I lied even though my intentions were so obvious and said that I was waiting to surprise her by showing her the toy I really wanted. She grabbed my arm, and we left the store without getting whatever they came there to purchase.

The ride home was worse than when I came home from school after the Christmas gift shop and book incident. They both told me how it seemed inevitable that I would end up a loser and a criminal when I became an adult and there would be no chance at having a good future. They told me that this type of behavior would guarantee me a life of crime and crime leads you to jail time. I heard everything they were saying, but it just didn't fit in my eyes. I was a child, and I was not going to do this forever. I wasn't going to keep stealing, and I wasn't going to be a criminal. Even though I knew what I had done and I knew that this was only the beginning of hearing my parents degrade me for my recent behavior, I wanted it to be over. It wasn't exactly the words and what they were saying that bothered me. It was the sound of their voices and the looks they gave me. Every time I had ever gotten into trouble or needed to be lectured, I wanted to disappear. The more they talked, the more I would imagine this dark cloud hovering over me slowly getting closer and closer until it suffocated me. Sometimes, I wish it would have suffocated me, helped me to completely disappear and escape the misery. Sometimes, I would go inside my head to get away from them, drift away into a happy fantasy that involved anything besides them and the words coming from their mouths. When we got home, my parents sent me to my room to think about what I had done and to think about how I had let them down with my recent actions. When I tried to think about it and go over it in my mind, it made me too anxious, so I would try to push it out and not let it bother me. It's not like I was disillusioned thinking that what I was doing wasn't wrong. I knew that all the stealing and lying wasn't okay, but I guess it just escalated quickly. At first, I just wanted to have the kind of things that the other kids at school had, the new supplies and books that made me feel good. Then I just wanted to be able to give my parents Christmas gifts, but after that, I think I lost myself and got greedy. I almost wanted to be grounded, spend some time alone in my room, and think about everything that had gone on that year. Maybe a chance to just slow down and process each incident would do me good, help me mentally move past them and not do it again. My parents were making me feel so guilty for doing these things, and I wasn't feeling good about any of it anymore. When I took the school supplies from the kids at school, I was happy. I didn't feel horrible guilt, and it was great having the supplies I wanted. All of the times that I took the books, even when I took the book set, I didn't feel bad afterward. I felt good having the latest books I wanted. At the Christmas gift shop, I started to feel guilt for what I had done—happiness to be able to get gifts for my parents but also guilt for my wrongdoing. I had pushed down the guilt just as fast as it came on, and my conscience told me that I shouldn't have stolen to get Christmas presents. I remember mentally doing a pro-and-con list before I would steal, but I would end up just letting the fact that I so selfishly wanted the things win every time. When it came to trying to steal the toy in the store, I didn't even bother with any kind of mental reasoning. I just let my selfishness take full control. I was hard on myself for what I had done in that store, but it wasn't for the fact that I was trying to steal the toy; it was for other reasons. There was zero planning involved in that situation, and that was downright reckless, disappointing really. I had thought about the school supplies and even the books before I decided to start taking them out of the book bags at school. I asked to use the restroom several times, found out what book bags belonged to which students, and watched to see what times the hallways were empty. I didn't do any of that this time. The whole situation was an embarrassment, especially since Christmas was right around the corner. Like I said, pure selfishness. I knew that I would be grounded for quite a while, but what I didn't know is that my parents being disgusted with me might never end after that. In my head, I told myself that they shouldn't be so cold toward me because I was just a small child, but I guess when you look at the whole picture, I was really messing up in life, especially for a small child. I really felt like they loved my brother and sister more than me, and if this was true, it was probably all my fault. I had hoped that my grandma's response to all of this would be different, but she said all of the same things my parents did.

When the holidays came, I received a ton of gifts like usual but opened them with cold eyes upon me and distrust lingering all around me. I expected to hear some very negative remarks for all of the bad things I had done that year, but for the most part, everyone just paid attention to my brother and sister. As the gifts were distributed and the holiday conversations started, I did end up becoming a topic of interest even on Christmas, a thief to everyone even on Christmas. I guess it was silly to think that I would wake up clean from my bad decisions and actions just because it was Christmas. My extended family treated me a little better; but behind their smiles, hugs, and kisses, there was hesitation and confusion. Little did I know that this would be the normal scenario for most of our holidays after that. House full of holiday decor, with large holiday feasts, and with so many gifts that they went halfway to the ceiling—all of these things would be present along with all of the usual family members; but for some strange reason, love would be missing. To someone looking in, it would appear to be a healthy and loving home, but right under the surface, it was rotten to the core. My grandma's warmth and kindness were always a pleasant distraction from the darkness that always hovered above me. The moment I stepped through her door, I would quickly close the door behind me and leave the darkness outside. Her house was like a sanctuary for me, a place where I could feel safe and happy even if it was only for a short while. I would always try to stay there as long as I could, always asking for a second pop or bringing up a different topic of conversation to drag out my visit a little longer. We usually did Christmas Eve at my grandma's house and then Christmas day at my cousin Theresa's house. The hardest place to leave was Theresa's house. Imagine a magazine showing a perfect home and family, just minus any kids. The only place that I didn't feel second or third best to my siblings was at Theresa's house. To be honest, it almost seemed like she liked me best. Theresa didn't have children, which makes it great for us because she bought us gifts throughout the year for no reason and a ton of presents for Christmas. We would often spend the night or the weekend with Theresa and her husband, who was also pretty great. I imagined being just like Theresa when I grew up, beautiful, smart, and sophisticated with a fancy job downtown somewhere. She always had somewhere to go and someone to see, never just lying around or letting life pass her by. She was so different from my mom, maybe even the opposite of her. Theresa got her hair and nails done all the time, had lots of hair sprays and products in her bathroom to keep her hair done nice. She had all the makeup that you see in the middle of the mall and the expensive kinds with the perfumes they sell there too. I loved just taking a bath at her house because I would come out feeling like I had just spent a day at a spa. Theresa's house was big, so for the holidays, there was room for everyone, and everyone had their place where they liked to sit and play or watch TV. I knew that Theresa wouldn't be too upset with me for my poor decisions, and I was right. She asked me to come upstairs to talk to her, as if I was an adult who had private business to discuss with her. She said similar stuff as my parents and grandma, but when she said it, she almost cried, and you could feel that she cared. The way she talked to me, I could tell that she cared about me. She cared about what I did because she believed that I had a good future ahead of me. When my parents talked to me about it, their main points were mainly that the worst things you can be in life are a liar and thief and that a thief never makes it anywhere in life. They weren't specific like Theresa was. They didn't care to elaborate from there, maybe because they didn't imagine my future like Theresa did. Theresa told me this behavior could hold me back from an amazing career as a doctor or lawyer and that this kind of behavior didn't fit my amazing personality. In our ten-minute conversation, Theresa told me that she loved me more times than my parents probably did in a year. I walked out of that room not feeling like a failure or a criminal. I walked out of there feeling like I really had someone behind me in this world. She always did that, made me feel like I could do anything, made me feel like my life was important to her even though I wasn't her daughter.

For being a thief and such a bad person that year, the holidays weren't too bad. The holidays were the hardest times for me to leave her house because that warmth that her house had just didn't exist at ours. I thought the holidays would clear the slate for me. Maybe they would see it as a new year and a new me. I think once you become a thief and a liar, you just can't get away from that, even if you're just a child. I wanted to be a good kid and make my parents happy, no more angry faces and no more being grounded. Second grade was going to be my year. I was going to take a hold of my life and be the kid everyone wanted me to be. I remember really enjoying the schoolwork that year. I loved learning, and I had a good teacher, so that always helps. My teacher was nice but not as nice as the year before. She was older than my last teacher and didn't have that young-teacher glow to her. She looked like she might have less patience with us and get angry sometimes, but she also looked like she loved being a teacher. My new teacher made me realize even more how amazing my teacher was last year; you might even say she was the perfect teacher. I would ask for a bathroom pass and take the long way to the bathroom so I could pass her class and watch her teaching her new class. She looked so happy, so full of life and ambition that it made me really miss having her as my teacher. Watching her made me happy, her smile was comforting, and I wished I could still be in her class. I told myself that I wouldn't take anything that didn't belong to me this year and that I wouldn't be that kid watching and worrying about what other kids had. I needed to be okay with who I was and what my parents could give me even if it wasn't all the latest or most popular stuff.

School was going great, and when I wasn't at school, I got to be with my friends who were the best. At school, I didn't have any real friends, but in my neighborhood, I had kids who always wanted to be around me. All my friends were older, more mature, so I think that's why I couldn't relate much with the kids in my class or grade. I was always mature, not like other kids my age, never childish. I think I was born that way, born with the spirit of an old lady in me or something. Maybe it was from all the long afternoons of sitting in the bar with my dad and observing that made me like this or watching my mom and her emotions closely. All of these things made me have to grow up fast, so I think it was only natural to relate easier with older kids. School was fun, playing with my friends was even more fun, but going home was the complete opposite. I hated going home. I wanted to love going home to my family every day, but it wasn't a happy place. It was a healthy place to be for a child. There was this toxic and never-ending cycle going on between my parents, and I so badly hoped it would end soon. I know my mom wanted to be a nice person, a fun and loving mother, but she just couldn't. If you stared at her or watched her when she wasn't looking, you could see it for a brief moment, see a tiny bit of happiness that hadn't been turned to sadness yet. I don't think she ever meant to end up like that—so unhappy I think it slowly happened and there was nothing she could do about it. I always wanted to help her, take away her sadness, but I was just a child and couldn't do anything about it.

My mom's sadness always turned into anger. The anger that she had toward my dad and him never being home or there for her, turned into anger toward me. At that time, she was at work a lot, so when she was at home, she was stressed out or tired but never relaxed because she was always waiting for dad to come home. I know it had to be exhausting to work all day and then come home and take care of kids all while wondering why your husband was never home. Even when she would yell at me for everything, I still felt bad for her because I knew the anger wasn't even meant for me; it was meant for my dad. I would feel her anger, her stress, her sadness. I would feel it all the time. My dad was always out drinking either at a bar or a friend's house. He would go straight from work to anywhere besides at home with my mother. I remember day after day of her sitting by the phone waiting for him to call. She would frantically answer it every time and almost always say the same thing. The million-dollar question was always, "When are you coming home?" I would hear those five words for my entire childhood, "When are you coming home?" The words seem so simple. It seems like such a simple and easy question, but it wasn't. I don't know what he said, but her answer was always, "Why can't you just come home and be with your family?" It was such a relief when I would hear his truck pull up before I went to bed because the later he would stay out, the more it would hurt my mom. I hated telling her good night while she was sitting on the couch crying or repeatedly trying to reach my dad. I hated it so much. Bedtime was hard because bedtime meant there was no reason that a husband and a father would still be out drinking and not be at home with his wife and kids. It was the worst when her sadness and crying made my little brother and sister cry. It was confusing to me why my dad would do this almost every single day knowing how bad it hurt my mom. I would wonder if he knew that she sat at home, crying and spending her entire evening waiting and hoping for him to come home. Did he not know, or did he know and just not care? Sometimes, my dad would come home so late he would stumble in, knock stuff down, bump into walls, and cuss a lot. Those nights it would be so late, just hours away from morning, so he would only get a few hours of sleep. I'm sure my mom would only get a few hours of sleep, too, after sitting up all night crying, wondering what he was doing and hoping that he would come home. It was hard to even want to be nice to my dad the next day when he would do that. It was hard to love him or even look at him most days. Even when he was trying to act like my mom was the love of his life after being out all night, I could sense his bad intentions and disrespect for her. In his eyes, you could tell that he no longer wanted it—my mom, us, this life that he was sitting in the middle of. In his eyes, he was unhappy, maybe even trapped by everything around him.

Things were bad at home, and I was definitely being affected. We all were. The more days he stayed out all night, the meaner he got when he was home, and it wasn't just toward my mom anymore. I think my dad knew that I knew what kind of person he was, and it made him uncomfortable and angry. When I was a dumb child, unaware of what was going on around me, that worked for him but not anymore. There were some days or moments I wanted to grab my mom and scream at her, look in her eyes, and tell her how could she be so stupid to be with my dad. I constantly went back and forth in my mind from her being a victim to it all being her fault. Could she really be surprised by this? Was his behavior really a surprise with the stacks of pornographic magazines sitting in our bathroom? Stacked high on the back of the toilet and stacked on the floor next to the toilet on both sides were the kinds of magazines that no one should have to see. Every kind of sinful and sexual behavior was in the pages of those magazines, not just nudity; nudity is nothing compared to the stuff in those magazines—girls doing sexual acts to other girls, men doing sexual acts to girls and even multiple girls; and it was just so disturbing. We, of course, were told not to look at them, told that they were my dad's and to leave them alone, but it was hard with them always sitting there. I would use the bathroom and look next to me to get toilet paper and have to see people doing very disturbing sexual acts. I know we weren't supposed to look at the magazines, but it was so hard as a young curious child and with the magazines all around you. They were right there, and with the kind of material that was on every cover, it was too hard not to. I wanted to resist the urge to look at them, but as I sat on the toilet, the nasty behavior on the covers drew me in. I would lock the door, turn on the sink, and look through them quickly but quietly so I wouldn't get caught. My heart would beat fast, and my palms would get sweaty, but it gave me a funny feeling in my stomach, and I kind of liked it. I didn't quite know what I liked about the magazines and the behavior that was going on in them, and I don't know why I looked at them. I don't know if it was because I wasn't supposed to be doing it or if it was because it was so intriguing to me, maybe both. After seeing so many sexual acts, I think I completely lost my innocence. There was no going back after seeing what was between the pages of those pornographic magazines. It changed me. It was hard to see people the same way after that. I figured that the private life of all adults consisted of the behavior in those magazines. I knew one thing for sure at that point, after seeing what my dad enjoyed looking at: my dad wasn't a very good man or husband. He would spend at least one hour a day in the bathroom looking at those magazines. I knew how many he looked at by the order they were in. I would look at the ones I knew he looked at and think of how my mom looked so different from those women doing those dirty things. I wondered what kind of woman my dad liked. I wondered if he even liked my mom or if he only liked nasty women. I was just a kid, but the things that the women did in those magazines had to make them nasty women. Not too long after that, I started to realize what my dad liked or more so what he didn't like.

It wasn't a shock when my dad started staying out later and coming home less, as if he wasn't already gone a lot. When my dad was home, he was in his shed. It wasn't a shed like the kind that you keep tools in, even though that's what I'm sure he wanted my mom to think. His shed was bigger than a normal shed. It had a TV and chairs, and it was more like a big clubhouse for adults. I think it was a regular smaller shed at one point, your average-size tool shed, and then he added onto it. There was a big door with two locks on it. When you walked in, there was just a small area in front of you, and to your left was a wall and then a few stairs. If you went up the stairs, there was a bigger area with chairs and a tool bench with a TV and VCR on it, and on both sides of that, there were tool cabinets. I went in there a bunch of times when we first moved into that house. At first, I kept my bike and a few other outside toys in the area right when you walked in. As time went on, my dad turned it into something different. It went from a normal shed where tools, bikes, and lawn mowers were kept to a sinful place where he spent all his time. After the shed became my dad's hangout, we were no longer allowed in there. My dad even put two different locks on the door. At that point, he always made sure that his shed was locked and told us to knock on the door if we needed him for anything when he was in it. After that, I only made it to right in the doorway, and my dad would come down the steps and ask me what I wanted. I could never see what was going on in there with him blocking the doorway that went up to the second level. Even if he wasn't standing there, I couldn't see up there, because he hung a large flag in the doorway so you couldn't see too much of what was going on. The more time that my dad started to spend in there, the more my mom and dad fought and the more my mom cried. My dad would tell her that he was just outside in the shed and would she rather him be out all night somewhere else. I know that my mom had to have felt very confused with why my dad would rather sit in a shed all night, day after day instead of being inside with her. I came to the conclusion that my dad either didn't like us very much or had something that he just liked better in the shed.

I wasn't exactly sure what went on in the shed, but I was pretty sure that it wasn't anything good. The funny thing was that when he was out there, she would still sit and cry waiting for him to come in as if he wasn't at the same place we were. She would even call him just like she did when she had no idea where he was at. She would call and beg him to come in. She would cry to him, asking him what was so great about the shed that he never wanted to come in and spend time with his family. She wouldn't go out there. In fact, I never saw her go out there, not even one time. Before that, my dad used to just stay out on Fridays, Saturdays, and sometimes Sundays; but it was different now. Now when my dad got home from work, he would put his lunch box in the kitchen, go to the bathroom, sometimes change his clothes and boots, and then go out to the shed for the night. When my dad would stumble in, it was worse than when he would go out somewhere else. I think because he didn't have to drive, he would drink more or do more of whatever had him looking the way he did. Sometimes I would get up when I heard him come in. I would act like I needed a drink of water just so I could see what he looked like. It was always the same. He could barely walk straight. Sometimes, he would stumble and have to grab a hold of something to avoid falling on the ground. His face would be red and sweaty, but sometimes it would be very pale. His mouth was always hanging open, and I'm sure if you got close enough to him, you might see him drooling. His eyes were the worst part of his nightly appearance, and it was hard to look at him if he was even capable of making eye contact with you. When I was younger, I used to come into the kitchen to look at him and tell him I loved him, but I stopped doing that. After looking into dark, dead eyes so many times, you learn not to do it anymore. It was confusing at first, even a little scary, but I learned pretty quickly that there was no point in talking to him when he was like that. He was there physically; his body was right in front of me. From a distance, it would appear that he was present. It would appear that he was looking back at me, but a look closer would prove otherwise. A closer look into his eyes and you could see that he wasn't there. I couldn't tell you where he was those nights as he stood in the kitchen, but I can tell you that he wasn't there, at least not mentally. When I was younger, I would look into his eyes with such confusion, because I felt like it wasn't my dad looking back at me with those eyes; it was someone or something else. Even when I tried not to look at his eyes, look down, and just talk to him so I could hear his voice, it still wasn't him. I would tell him I loved him so I could hear it back and really feel he was the same dad he was every day, but he wasn't.

Whatever my dad did in that shed took away who he was. He went in my dad and came out a hollow shell of a man. He went in smiling, saying he was going to sit in the shed for a little bit, and then came out so many hours later as if he was abducted by something that took over his body. When he would finally come in, he did the exact same thing every night. He came in the back door; walked to the kitchen table; and took his wallet, keys, lighter, and cigarettes out of his pocket; and then placed them at the edge of the table. Then he would take off his shoes, and I always knew when he was doing that because of the sound of the bottom of the kitchen chair scraping across the laminate tiles. That was the sound of him grabbing onto the chair at the end of the kitchen table to prevent himself from falling. I would imagine exactly how it was happening in my mind as I heard the noises. I imagined he would lift his foot up to remove his shoe, struggle to hold himself straight, and then lose his balance. He would then grab the back of a kitchen chair as it slid until it was stopped by the table. I would have to put my pillow over my face so he couldn't hear my giggles, even though I was on the other side of the house and he probably wouldn't be able to hear me, anyway. After so many times of hearing that sound, my giggles turned into silent disappointment. After he got his shoes off, he opened the door to the garage and sat them under the utility sink. After that, he would take off his pants, which, a lot of the times, turned into a struggle for balance as well. He would put his jeans in the garage over the side of the utility sink or hang them on a hanger over the utility sink. The garage was next to the kitchen. There was a door on the west wall that led you right there. In the garage, there was a utility sink to your left; and next to that were two washers, a dryer, and a kerosene heater. There were two washers because my dad's clothes were always so dirty from work that he needed his own washer so our clothes wouldn't be affected by all the mud and dirt. He did construction work and remodeled houses on the side, so his clothes were often wet and muddy. At that time, I wasn't sure what he did at work. I knew it was some kind of construction work, something with large construction trucks that involved getting dirty enough to need your own washing machine. He did the construction job during the day and always did the remodeling jobs at night and on the weekends. On the wall directly in front of where you walked into the garage from the kitchen were big plastic totes with cracked lids; old deteriorating boxes; and piles of old, dirty, and very dusty clothes on top of it all. In front of that, there were piles of even dirtier clothes, clothes with so much cat and dog hair on them that you could barely even see what color they were. The cats and dog would go to the bathroom on them occasionally even though they had a litter box right next to it all. There were so many piles of clothes on the ground that sometimes you could barely walk through without having to take a broom and push it all back. With the litter box right next to the huge mess, the animals probably thought it was all their litter box. Next to this but on the south wall of the garage were two tall blue lockers, similar to the lockers in a high school locker room but a little taller and wider. In those lockers was where my dad kept all his clothing, neatly stacked and separated by underwear and socks on the first shelf, flannel shirts on the second shelf, and his jeans on the third shelf. The other locker had the few coveralls that my dad wore over his clothes in the winter and extra neon-green work shirts that construction workers have to wear. Those lockers were neater and more organized than our entire house, the only piece of the house that he had any control over. Next to them was the back door that led outside to our backyard. To the left, there was a large unfinished wooden deck, and to the right, there was a short path that went right to my dad's shed.

Sometimes, I would imagine waking up the next day and everything being different: my mom in the kitchen making breakfast and my dad kissing her as she cooked. I imagined my dad being at home, maybe watching TV with us and laughing as we all joked around with each other. I imagined a neat and tidy house like my grandma's, one that smelled like apples and cinnamon with a hint of lemon cleaner. I just imagined the opposite of how our life really was, the opposite of how my parents were, and the opposite of what our house was like. As a child, you have high hopes, so when things are bad, you can't imagine things being that way forever. I could have had the highest of hopes, but that wasn't going to help anything. Things were never going to get better. When we were at my grandma's, the things my dad did were all she and my mom talked about, as if it wasn't bad enough that we had to live it. They would sit in the kitchen and try not to talk too loud, and they would tell me to go play in the living room as if I didn't know what was about to take place. As if I didn't know that, they were going to sit and talk about my dad not being home or not being in the house. Even if I couldn't hear them all the way, I knew what they were talking about because my grandma always made the same noise when she was upset or disappointed. I would sometimes wish that we could talk about me, or maybe they could talk about how I was right there with my mom dealing with what my dad was doing. I was in the same house as my mom. I was on the same list she was on, the list of people that my dad didn't want to be around. I knew they were just trying to let me be a kid. I knew they were just trying to shield me from what was going on. They probably didn't even know that I was completely aware of what was going on with my dad, or at least that's what they told themselves. Even when we went shopping, my mom was angry. No matter what we did, you could always see her sadness and anger. I couldn't blame her or get mad at her for being angry. I just got used to it and told myself that, under the anger, she still loved me.

It was hard to focus on anything else besides what was going on at home, but I found that I really liked drawing. I enjoyed drawing my favorite characters from TV shows and from popular books or movies. Drawing, coloring, and anything artistic became my new hobby; and I loved it. At first, I was able to push everything out of my mind and just focus on drawing and imagining the characters in my drawings coming to life. The level of negative distractions in my house was just too high, so it yet again became too hard to just be a child. I started looking at the pornographic magazines in the bathroom again, and with my newfound talent, I combined the two. Instead of spending my time drawing my favorite characters, I started drawing my favorite pages and people in the magazines. When I drew the naked people doing the nasty things I saw in the magazines, I got that funny feeling that I liked. I liked that I was in control of my drawings. I controlled what was in them, and it made me feel like I was a part of something. I had a few notebooks that I used to do these drawings. Two were regular-sized notebooks, and one was a small one that I got from school. The smaller one was the size of the little notebooks that people carry in their pockets to jot down notes. I got it from this booth at school that we sold pencils, erasers, and odds and ends of school supplies. It was called the School Store. They sold these little yellow notebook pads for fifty cents, and they had the logo of our school mascot on it in bright blue. I liked this little notebook, and it fit perfectly in my pocket, so I decided to draw small little naked people in it and carry it with me everywhere. No one really paid any attention to me drawing naked people in my little notebook. Even when I drew them in class, no one noticed. I can't remember if I left it in class or dropped it somewhere, but my teacher found it or ended up with it somehow. I remember not being able to find it and feeling a sense of panic, but I just told myself I would find it. I didn't find it, and when I got called to the office for it, my parents were both already in there waiting. My teacher was also in the room. She was standing next to the principal's desk with her hand on her forehead. The look on everyone's face was different, very different from when I got called in there for stealing. The principal almost didn't know how to ask me about the notebook or the drawings. She didn't even make eye contact with me. It was my teacher who started talking. She held out my notebook and asked me if it was mine. I don't know why I didn't just lie, like I usually did, but I said it was mine. This was different from when I was stealing. I knew that the stealing was a bad thing. I knew it wasn't something to be proud of. These drawings were mine, and I was proud of them. I knew that I shouldn't be drawing naked people, but they were still good drawings. I guess I felt like I was mature for drawing these pictures of naked people, and I felt like adults should recognize that maturity and the fact that they were good drawings. For a kid, I had talent, and I was proud of it. I wanted them to say that my drawings were excellent, but I shouldn't draw naked people. The compliment didn't come, but instead I was questioned several times on why I was drawing naked people doing disturbing sexual acts. My parents were part of the questioning. How ironic was that? They were questioning me about drawing things of that nature when we had stacks of pornographic magazines in our bathroom. After a few minutes, I felt the direction of the questions shift toward my parents, so now they were being asked the same questions that I had just been asked several times. At first, my parents both had the same answer. They both said that they had no idea why I would draw things of that nature. They both even looked at me and separately asked me several times why I would draw such nasty pictures. The conversation was clearly going nowhere, and the principal and teacher both gave each other a frustrated look before they both turned and looked at my parents. There was a long pause, and my teacher looked at the ground for a moment before she looked up. She told them that I would have had to have seen this kind of behavior somewhere to be able to draw it. She firmly told them that a child isn't able to draw something like that without having seen it first. Both of my parents acted confused and insisted that they were unaware of how I could be drawing pornographic pictures. The principal shook her head, took her glasses off, and looked directly at my mother as she repeated the same statement that my teacher had just made to my parents. She then told my mother that this was serious and that it was her job to make sure that everything was okay at home. Finally, for once, I wasn't the one in trouble. I wasn't the one being treated like some kind of criminal. For once, my parents had to answer to someone. For once, they had to explain what took place in our home. The tension rose in that office as the conversation took a drastic turn. The questions turned to statements pointing toward abuse by my parents. I looked at my mother as the color drained from her face, and fear filled her eyes but then turned to anger as she looked at my dad. My dad already knew what her look meant. He knew that this was his fault and he needed to bring honesty into the conversation fast. He sat forward in his chair and insisted that this was an innocent mistake on his part because he had been keeping a few magazines with nudity in the bathroom. I wanted to shout that he was a liar and tell them that he had stacks of magazines, a stack on the toilet and on both sides. I wanted to tell them that the stacks were so high and they didn't just have a little bit of nudity, they were nasty and filled with pornographic images. As my dad spoke, all I could think about were the nasty things I had seen in them and wished I could explain to my teacher exactly what I was exposed to on a daily basis. I wanted my teacher and principal to know what my parents exposed me to; they should know that they were not very good parents at all. He insisted that he had no idea I was looking at the magazines and should have taken them out of the bathroom. I wondered if this was true. I wondered if my dad was really unaware that I was looking at those magazines or if this was a lie to make him look like a responsible parent. My dad told them that he would immediately remove the magazines from the bathroom and hide them somewhere so I could no longer look at them.

I can't remember if I was suspended or not with that incident, but I do remember getting in trouble when I got home. I remember my dad angrily taking the magazines out of the bathroom as he and my mom fought about it. My mom told him that the magazines were disgusting and should never have been in the bathroom, and she said she had no idea why he would look at them. She looked angry, but she also looked very hurt. Maybe she was hurt because the school now knew what my dad liked to look at. I felt bad for her. I felt bad that she had to sit in the principal's office and had to answer for something that she wanted no part of. To have to be questioned because your husband likes to look at pornographic magazines and keeps them where your kids can look at them, that's a bad day. My dad took a stack at a time and brought them out to his shed, slamming all the doors as he went. When he walked back in, he yelled at me and told me that it was disgusting for a little girl to look at those magazines, and it angered me. Before I could even argue back with him or tell him he was the disgusting pig for having all the magazines, my mom told him this was his fault. He yelled at her and told her to clean the filthy house, and before she could say anything back, he said he was going to be out in the shed. When I looked at her, she tried to put a fake smile on her face, but she was so hurt that it looked so strange. I know that my mom probably already felt stupid that her husband had kept stacks of pornographic magazines in the bathroom, but now other people knew. My dad stayed in the shed the rest of the afternoon and late into the night. He never even came in to eat dinner or use the bathroom. I knew he was mad, but I refused to say I was sorry for drawing images that I had seen in magazines that he kept out for us to see. After that, things got bad between me and my dad. They got really bad. I don't know if my dad was angry that I drew naked people or if he was angry that I looked into his magazines. I don't know if he wasn't angry about any of that but just angry because he got dragged into the situation with the school. Or maybe my dad became so angry because I was no longer a small child who went along with whatever he said and did and now he had to be a better role model if he didn't want me doing bad stuff. Maybe it was a combination of all of those things. Either way, he was angry, and he started to take it out on me. Before that night, my dad didn't pay much attention to me when he came in from the shed, even if I was obviously going into the kitchen just to see what he looked like. He used to not say anything to me. He would just look straight in front of him as he tried not to fall all over the place. Sometimes, I would be right next to him, and he either didn't know I was there or didn't care and went right to his room.

That night, I went into the kitchen to see what he looked like, maybe to see if he still looked angry or if his night in the shed cheered him up. As I walked around the corner and looked up, his eyes instantly locked into mine, and he wasn't looking too cheerful. He looked at me with an angry face. Even his mouth had an angry cringe forming, and he started to shake his head. He said that he wasn't even mad, just very disappointed with me. He said that I made my family look bad to the school. My dad said that I gave the school the wrong idea and "now what if they think something bad is going on at home between me and him?" He told me I was on a path to becoming a nasty girl, the kind of girl nobody would want and the kind of girl nobody would want to marry. I was so angry that my anger turned into a different emotion or attitude from I had ever experienced before. I thought I was going to yell at him for talking to me like that when all of this was his fault. I felt my face get hot, I felt a wave of heat come up though my body, and I opened my mouth to yell or to say hurtful things, but that's not what came out. Instead of screaming or yelling at him, I laughed—I laughed and told him that he was the nasty one and my mom probably didn't want to be with him. It felt so good to finally say something to him, for him to know that I wasn't just a young and stupid child. I wasn't just a little girl who had no idea what was going on. I wasn't unaware of what kind of person he was, what kind of husband or father he was. I could almost see flames in his eyes as I said that. I could see the anger completely consume him as he moved so quickly to grab me. I don't know if I was shocked. I don't know if I expected him to just let me say those things or not. Maybe I didn't care what happened to me next. Maybe I just wanted to have a voice in that house. I tried to lean back as he came toward me. There was a brief struggle as I tried to avoid him getting a hold of me, but he got me. I think he was trying to put me over his lap to spank me, but because he was trying to keep his balance and I was trying to get away, I ended up on the ground. I remember feeling the cold floor on my face. I could even feel it through my pajamas. I could feel how dirty the floor was as my cheek hit it. I could smell how dirty it was and could see everything on it from that view. I had never been on the floor in the kitchen before, so it felt so strange. Everything looked different from that point of view. He spanked me and spanked me. I could feel him struggling to keep his balance as he hit me. I think because he was standing up and I was on the ground, he ended up hitting my back instead of my butt. His open hand changed to more of a closed hand, and his spanking changed to him just hitting my back. The stinging on my butt quickly changed to pain as he hit me harder, and my whimpers changed to screams. The pace at which he had been spanking me changed from swift and evenly timed spanks to fast and wild hits to my back. I felt him go from just punishing me for disrespecting him to him just taking out his anger on me. I screamed and tried to grip onto the tiles to pull myself away from him, but he quickly grabbed my legs and pulled me back. His nails dug into my skin, and I tried to turn over as he pulled me by my legs, but he grabbed me by my waist and shoved me back down. I could feel his spit hit the side of my face as he yelled at me. He was spitting everywhere and slurring his words at this point as he yelled and hit me. I screamed for my mom to come and help me. She must have heard what was going on with their room being so close to the kitchen. Where was she at?

Why wasn't she running in there to help me? I screamed louder as he continued to hit me. My back felt like it was on fire, and my legs burned from where he scratched me when I tried to crawl away. Just as I thought it was hopeless, my mom came around the corner, and my dad stopped hitting me. I felt like I could breathe again and was happy to see that my mom had an angry look on her face. I knew that she wouldn't allow my dad to hit me like that. I knew she would hate him now for what he just did to me. She asked my dad what was going on and why was he in the kitchen hitting me in the middle of the night. I went to get off of the floor, and I could barely get up. My back felt like there was a knife in it. The pain was very different from anything that I had felt before.

When we were bad, my grandma would often spank us with wooden spoons. She even brought them with us when we went to a store, so that's the worst I had experienced. Up until that point, the punishments and spankings were for the most part up to my mom, which made sense since my dad didn't usually participate as a member of the family. I couldn't even tell you how long my dad had hit me for that night, but I can tell you that it seemed like an eternity before my mom interrupted it. I felt ashamed as I struggled to get off the floor, and I tried to not make eye contact with my dad. I stumbled out of the kitchen and stood next to my mom in the living room. I stood halfway behind her as if she was my bodyguard, and with the anger she had in her eyes, I knew she would protect me from him. I, for sure, thought she was going to yell at my dad or even smack him. She had to do something for what he just did to me. Maybe she would call the police on him for child abuse. My dad told her that I had a mouth on me and wanted to act like I was all grown up now so he had to show me what happens to women who are all grown up and act like I did. I expected my mom to yell at him and tell him he was an animal or an out-of-control drunk for beating me like he did. That's not what she did, not even close. She shook her head and then turned to me. She told me I needed to stop causing such big problems. I felt a knot in my throat as I tried so hard to hold back my tears. I wanted to scream. I wanted her to feel the pain I felt. Her husband just beat me like I wasn't a child, and instead of being angry at him, she was angry at me. I was furious, hurt, and confused all at the same time. I thought, *How can this be happening to me?* So many things were rushing through my mind at the same time, so many questions like *What did I do to deserve this? How could my dad do something like that to me? How could my mom be okay with it?* I felt like the whole world was crashing down on me, and I couldn't even hold back my tears anymore, because the pain in my throat had gotten so intense.

Before I could run to my room screaming and crying, my mom told me to go to bed. She said it as if nothing happened, and the only thing she said to my dad was that she was mad because he woke her up. I threw myself into my bed crying, and I was so mad that I screamed into my pillow as loud as I could. I shook back and forth and pounded my arms and legs into the bed as I cried. I cried as loud as I could, hoping my mom could hear me, hoping she could hear the pain I was in. I was angrier than I had ever been, and I felt like I was going to go crazy because I just didn't know how to process what just happened to me. I felt so alone as I lay there hoping and waiting for my mom to come and comfort me. I didn't know how to make the anger go away or how to feel better, so I cried even louder and kicked my wall. My mom didn't come to comfort me, but my dad did come, and it wasn't to comfort me. He came stomping down the hall, and before I could take my feet off the wall, he was already in my room. He was yelling and trying to grab my legs, but I tried as hard as I could to wiggle around so he couldn't get a hold of me, but he did. He held my legs so hard that I couldn't get away and flipped me over exactly like he did in the kitchen, so I knew what was next. Before he started to hit me, he pulled my pants down and spanked my bare butt as hard as he could. I tried to scream, but it took my breath away, and I started choking as I felt my butt burning. I was crying loudly until that point, but I couldn't catch my breath, so I started gagging, but that didn't stop him. He spanked me harder and harder, and it burned so bad that I thought I was bleeding, I thought that I couldn't take any more pain. I gagged so much that I almost threw up, and my throat started burning. I was already in so much pain that I thought I was going to die as it burned my dry, chapped lips. I don't know if my dad stopped because of that or because he was so drunk that he almost fell as I threw up. Either way, he moved away from the bed, caught himself as he almost fell on my little sister's bed, and then stumbled out of my room. Just as he went through my doorway, I saw that my mom was right there—my mom was right there the whole time. She shook her head as she reached for my doorknob and told me that I better go to sleep before he comes back or I wake up my sister. The door closed, and the darkness was comforting to me. I had to calm my breathing because I felt like I was going to pass out. I took deep breaths and told myself it was okay. I even said it out loud. I held my arms around myself and said, "It's okay. It's okay." It actually made me feel better hugging myself, that and the sound of my little sister breathing. I was so worn out not just physically but mentally as well, so before I knew it, I must have just gone right to sleep.

The next morning, I must have woken up as my dad left for work, because when I jumped up, I could still smell his coffee and deodorant but he was gone. It was very early. The sun wasn't even up yet, and the house was so cold and still. I had a startled feeling. My hairs were all standing straight up on my arms, and my heart was beating fast that it was scaring me. Either I woke up still terrified from the night before, or I just woke up from a bad dream. I sat down on the couch and couldn't even believe it as I mentally walked through the events from the night before. I wanted to die as I remembered each little detail. I wanted to just go back to sleep and pretend this never happened. After I finally could stop myself from replaying every moment in my mind and step back into the real world, that's when I felt my body and the pain I was in. I had fallen off my bike a bunch of times, so I knew what a little bit of pain felt like, but this was different, a lot different. This felt like when I fell off my bike, scraped my knees up, and then had to pick gravel out of them as they bled. The difference is I felt that all over my whole body. I felt like my entire body was scraped up with gravel stuck in it. It hurt and it ached. My back hurt the worst when I tried to sit all the way up or completely straight. It really hurt and made me want to cry. I didn't know what to do. I tried to cry very quietly because I would be too embarrassed if my mom would get up and see me. Even though she had seen everything the night before, I still wasn't ready to see her face. I was just too hurt and confused. I went back into my room and slowly got into my bed because I didn't want my bed to make its usual squeaking noise and wake up my sister. I wasn't ready to see anyone, not even her. I had to try and mentally prepare myself before I could face anyone. I was so exhausted from the night before. My body ached from head to toe, and some parts hurt pretty badly. I went back and forth from sadness to anger at my dad, to anger at my mom, to confusion, and then to embarrassment as I continued to replay the night before in my mind. My pain must overruled my racing thoughts, because the next thing I knew, I woke up to the sun in my eyes and my mom yelling at me to wake up. I sat up and heard my mom going in and out of the bathroom drawers as she got ready for work and put the little bit of makeup she wore on.

In the mornings, I was always comforted by the smell of the hot curling iron and hair spray and the faint smell of her perfume. I think the little things like that comforted me because there wasn't much affection in our house—no hugging, kissing, or saying, "I love you." Even before I saw how other families do those things, I already knew that our house, our family, was missing something important. I wanted so badly for my mom to run into my bedroom and hug me tightly. I wanted her to kiss my forehead and hold her face against mine as she told me she loved me. I wanted her to say that she was so sorry for letting my dad hurt me and not do anything about it. In a perfect world, I imagined her telling me that she called the police on my dad and, because he beat me up so badly, he was going to jail and wouldn't be able to live with us anymore. That was in a perfect world, and since my life wasn't in a perfect world, she said nothing like that. I was so sad that I couldn't wait to see my mom's face. No matter what she said, I just wanted to see her and me near her. I knew I didn't live in a perfect world, but it still shocked me when she didn't say a word about the night before, just told me to get dressed or we would be late. I got dressed slowly to give her another chance to come in and acknowledge what happened the night before, but she just yelled at me from the bathroom to hurry up. I tried to move fast enough, but it was like I forgot how to move or maybe it just hurt too bad to move like I normally did. I felt like I was in a daze, and it was so hard to remember who I was the day before or what I felt like. I didn't know who I was that morning, I didn't feel like myself, and I didn't know what to do. I couldn't recognize who I was. My mind was different, and I didn't like it. My head was spinning, and my body ached as I tried to pull off my pajamas. I felt relief as my head slipped through the gown, and I felt like I could breathe until I looked down at my red scratched-up legs. I felt like I was going to be sick; my stomach was so uneasy. The scratches on my legs were from my dad dragging me from the living room back to the kitchen, and as I looked down, the details replayed in my mind. I tried to stop thinking about it, but I think mentally I needed to match the marks I was seeing on my body to details from the night before. I ran my hand over the scratches, and as I closed my eyes, I could see where this happened. It was the metal strip where the carpet ended and the linoleum floor began in between the living room and kitchen that scratched my legs like this. I could see the metal screws in the middle and the sharp edges that didn't hug the floor quite like they should. They were details that you would never pay attention to. They were small enough that they didn't bother you as you stepped on them every day. Now I would never be able to look at that little metal strip the same as I replayed being drug back and forth over it. When I had tried to crawl away toward the living room, my dad grabbed me, pushed me down, and pulled me back toward the kitchen. Under me that whole time was that metal strip with the screws poking out and the sharp edges both scratching and cutting my legs. My ankles were red, and it hurt when I got up making me replay my dad grabbing them to pull me back toward him right before he started to hit me. I couldn't take it. I wanted to forget about it. I needed to push it out of my mind and move on—I had to. I needed to get dressed, but when I opened my heavy dresser drawer, my palms and fingers burned from trying to grab the carpet. I had carpet burn on both hands and wrists. I became so overwhelmed that I fell to my knees and cried. My whole body felt heavy and sore. I just wanted to get back into my bed and hide under my blanket. Everything was different. This wasn't me. This wasn't my body. I didn't want this. This wasn't my life. I didn't even know how to do this, and I just wanted everything to be like it was the morning before. I was missing something that morning, not just something little but something very important. It was something I wasn't supposed to lose. My innocence is what I lost, but I didn't know that at the time. I didn't exactly know what was different about me after that night, but it was innocence. A child can no longer really be a child without it. Some people probably never stop to think about it, but a child is only a child because of innocence. We left the house and went out into the world as if it were a regular day, as if my whole life didn't just change the night before. You see the world so differently as an innocent child, so that day, the world was different to me, and it was overwhelming. The entire world should have stopped that day and someone, *anyone*, should have helped me, but they didn't. How could they not see it? How could they not see from my eyes that I was hurt?

As the days went on, I hoped that someone would see my pain or see that there was something very different about me. I told my grandma what happened when she was babysitting us, and I felt so relieved. I thought that she was going to help me and protect me, but she didn't. She didn't say anything. She just kept cleaning like I didn't say anything to her. I thought that I should have ran down there to her house after the first time my dad hurt me. I should have run somewhere, anywhere. When my mom came, I knew my grandma would be so mad at her for letting this happen to me. My mom would be mad that I said something to my grandma, but it didn't matter, because she was the one who did something wrong. I felt very sure that my grandma would let me stay at her house so my dad couldn't hurt me again, but she didn't. When my mom came to pick us up, my grandma told her what I had said. My mom yelled at me and told my grandma that I have been very bad lately. My mom said that I acted innocent, but my grandma didn't know how I really acted. My grandma shook her head at me and told me to make sure I behave, as if my dad beating me was my fault. I didn't understand how my mom could say this about me and was so confused by her lying to make me look like a bad kid. Up until that point, I thought it was her job to protect us from everything bad in the world, anything and anybody.

Before I could get over what my dad did, before I could even learn how to deal with it or forget about it, he did it again. It was just days later that I came home from a friend's house and my dad was actually home, sitting at the kitchen table. It was strange to me because he was inside the house, not in the shed like he normally was. I rarely ever saw my dad sit at the kitchen table. If he was in the house, he would sit in his chair in the living room. He had an ugly old recliner sitting against the wall. It was right after the opening between the kitchen and living room. It was his chair, and even when he wasn't sitting in it, we didn't sit in it either. He already looked angry the moment I looked at him. When he asked me if I thought I was a grown-up now, I had no idea what he was talking about. He told me that I must have been thinking that I was all grown up because I came home later than my curfew, ten minutes after I should have been home. He said that I was obviously doing whatever I wanted now and he wasn't going to deal with me disrespecting him. I didn't know why my dad thought this, and I tried to tell him that I didn't know that I was late coming home. He seemed angry to even hear my voice, and I tried to tell him that I was just playing outside, so I wasn't by a clock and came home when I saw the streetlights come on. I could already tell by his face that he didn't want to and wasn't going to listen to anything I had to say. I could tell by the way his eyes looked and by the way he spoke that he was drinking all evening and was probably drunk at that point. Before I could even read his body language to see what was going to happen next, he grabbed me by my shoulders and yelled in my face. My heart started pounding, and I tried to hold my breath because my dad was so close to me. I could smell the sour scent of beer and cigarettes on his breath. I hated that smell. I really didn't understand why he had to be so close or why he yelled so loud, saying that I had no respect for him. He said that I wasn't going to behave like this anymore and things were about to change. He said that I was going to learn, that I would learn even if he had to beat it into my head. I cried and told him that it wasn't true that I had no respect for him. I tried to tell him I was just playing outside and I didn't know that I was going to be late. He said that I knew better—my curfew was at 6:00 p.m., not 6:01, not 6:05, and not 6:10. He started to loosen his grip, so I thought he believed me, but he grabbed me by my mouth and screamed at me to shut up. He shook my face so hard as he yelled. He was so close to my face. I could see the spit bubbling in the corner of his mouth. As he yelled, he got louder, and I could feel his spit hitting my face and mouth. I tried to hold back my tears, but they came pouring out along with my screams when he pushed harder and slammed my head against the wall. Even with what he did days before, I was still shocked by him doing this to me again so soon.

I managed to turn my head to avoid his spit and accidently locked eyes with my mom, who was sitting right there on the couch. She was so close, just feet away, and reading one of those tabloid magazines. She was just glancing through it like there wasn't anything else in the room catching her attention. I screamed for her to help me, and she did nothing but shake her head and tell my dad to stop screaming. At that very moment, I felt all the hope that I once had quickly fade away as sadness took over. All the trust I had in my mom also began to fade away as I stared at her. My mom, she had what almost appeared to be a smile on her face, and it killed me inside. My whole world was becoming a dark and hopeless place, a scary place. I imagined it like a cliff, where I slipped off the edge but grabbed on and then I stayed there struggling to hold on. I stayed there struggling to hold on so I wouldn't plunge to a brutal death. It was hard to stay in my mind and think about these tragic thoughts as my dad kept slamming me into the wall. The dull aching turned to sharper pain as the ridge of the trim that was in the middle of the wall kept hitting my back in the same spot. I kept thinking that it was about to be over, it had been long enough; but he kept slamming me into the wall, squeezing my face and yelling at me. He was so mad, and I didn't even do anything wrong. I didn't do anything to him for him to be treating me like this. He finally stopped and just dropped me like I was a bag of garbage. I fell to the ground and stayed there as I waited to see what he was going to do. He turned around and started yelling at my mom, telling her that it was her fault that I did whatever I wanted. She told him that it wasn't her fault and to go spend more time out in the shed. This was always my mom's only response every time they fought or got into an argument. He told her that it was the very reason that he didn't like being in the house with us. The worst part about getting hit or beat is right afterward, when you have to get up and walk away. I held onto the wall as I stood up. I only glanced at my mom because I was so embarrassed and didn't want to make eye contact with my dad. Before I could say anything, she yelled at me to go to my room, and with the sadness about to burst out of me, I couldn't get there fast enough. I couldn't believe that my mom was letting this happen, and I couldn't understand why she was angry at me instead of consoling me.

At school, I wanted so badly to tell my teacher, but I couldn't. When she asked me if something was wrong because of the look on my face, I told her I was just tired. I knew that she would just call my parents if I told her what my dad did. Then they would come to the school and say that I was lying about it, so it was pointless. They would act the same way that they did when they had to meet with the principal about my sexual drawings; they would act surprised and shocked by the allegations. I wished that I could just stay at school forever, and I often thought about it, imagined it as I sat in class. At the end of the day, I could hide under a teacher's desk in an unoccupied room, and then I could come out when everyone left and have the whole place to myself. I could play on the computers and in the gym, eat dinner in the cafeteria, and sleep on the gymnastics mats in the gymnasium. It could all work out so perfectly. There would be no parents, my dad couldn't hit me, and my mom couldn't yell at me about it. I knew that my dad wasn't going to stop hitting me, but what I didn't know was how bad it would get. It was hard to concentrate in school, and even harder to participate in any classroom or gym activities, but I pushed myself to do it. I looked like a normal kid on the outside, sad but normal, but inside of me, I was already all grown up. Every day, as 3:00 p.m. approached, my stomach became uneasy, and when I was on the bus, I wanted to slide down in the seat and let the bus driver pass up my stop. After school, I went to my friend's houses and stayed there as long as I could to avoid going home, but every day, it ended the same—me going back to misery. There wasn't a day that went by that I didn't hope that my parents would change and become better parents, parents who cared about me. Sometimes, several days would pass after my dad beat me, and every time, I hoped that it wouldn't happen again, but it always did. My dad hitting me increased rather quickly, and his anger toward me grew even quicker than that, making each time worse. He started to tell me that I ruined him and my mom's marriage, and by the way he would say it, I know that he truly believed it. Even at such a young age, I often got the impression that my dad didn't want to be a dad. Maybe he never wanted my mom to have us. At night, I could hear my mom cry from my room, and even though she didn't seem to care about me, I still felt bad for her. One night, I came out of my room and asked her what was wrong. She yelled at me and told me that it was nothing. I told her that I knew she was crying because my dad was never home or always outside in his shed, but she told me I was just a child and didn't know what I was talking about.

I tried to always keep myself busy and focus on the good things in my life like school, playing with my friends, riding my bike, and drawing. That summer, I tried to go to my friend's houses every day and stay the night as often as their parents would let me. My best friend, Amber, was into all kinds of sports; so we would gather up kids from the whole neighborhood and play baseball, basketball, street hockey, and anything that involved being competitive. I wasn't very good at any of them, but she was; she was very good at each and every one. I never minded Amber being better than me at everything, because I knew I wasn't any good at them. I was just happy to have her as a best friend. When we weren't playing sports, we were riding bikes; roller-blading; or catching toads, frogs, and salamanders. That summer, we must have caught a hundred of them and discovered so many spots where we could regularly find them. I stayed the night at Amber's house as much as I could, and it didn't take her parents too long to figure out what was going on at my house. After they realized what was going on, they let me stay at their house more. Sometimes, I would stay for several days at a time. I became a part of the family, and I am pretty sure that if it wasn't for Amber and her family,

I would have never made it through my childhood. Amber's house always made me feel safe, and at night, I would lie awake just thinking about how life would be if that were my house. In the mornings, Amber's mom, Lisa, would do our hair. She would put them up into ponytails with bows to match our clothes. Sometimes, she would do our hair exactly the same, and we loved it. I often wore Amber's clothes because I didn't have the cute kinds of outfits that she had but wanted to look cute like she always did. She was a tomboy and would wear jerseys for the sports teams that she liked. Her whole family had them—jerseys, shirts, and even coats. I would feel so good wearing her clothes and getting my hair done by her mom. I would go outside to play and feel good about myself. Even on the days that I didn't spend the night there, I would still eat breakfast, lunch, and sometimes dinner there. Her family never turned me away and understood why I never wanted to be at home. I never went into details with them about my dad hitting me. I even left a lot of it out when telling Amber, but they for the most part knew what was happening to me. I never asked Amber to keep what I told her a secret, so I figured she told her parents what was happening to me. There were a few occasions where I could hear them talking about how I never wanted to go home and then would ask me to come and have a talk with them. They would ask me what was going on at home. I would tell them everything but leave out some of the details. I felt somewhat embarrassed about all of it, and when they would ask me if I needed them to do something about it, I would say no. I told them it wasn't that bad and that they didn't need to do anything about it. I think that because I liked them so much, I didn't want them to have to deal with my mom and dad. I didn't want them to have to experience the negativity and darkness that came from my parents and my house; they were too good for that. There were times when Amber and her family had to go places without me, so I would spend time with other girls from the neighborhood. Even though I didn't spend nearly as much time with them that I did with Amber, they still understood why I never wanted to be at home.

Candace lived a few houses away from Amber, and when I couldn't be with her, I was at Candace's house. Candace's parents were very different from Amber's parents. They weren't as easygoing about everything. They were more serious and strict. They didn't let her come out and play until her and her brother finished all of their daily chores, which took a long time. Her chores had to be done perfectly, or she would get into trouble and not be allowed to play or have friends over. I helped them do their chores a lot of days because I couldn't take a chance of Amber not getting to play or have me over. Candace's parents were not nearly as nice as Amber's, but even when Candace got spanked, you could still tell how much they loved her. I was at her house a few times when she got into trouble and got spanked, but it was nothing like what my dad did to me. Her parents would only allow me to stay the night on the weekends because they had to work every day and didn't want our talking or laughing to keep them up. One afternoon on a day that my dad had really beat me up good the night before, Candace asked them if I could stay the night, and they said no. When she came back into her bedroom to tell me, I couldn't hold back my tears, because I so badly didn't want to have to go home, and her parents heard me. They sat me down to talk just like Tiffany's parents did and told me I needed to tell them why I didn't want to go home. I told them everything and watched Candace's dad's face completely change. It went from curious to concerned and then to angry. They asked me when and where this occurred and what my mom was doing about it. They were shocked to hear that my mom sat and watched my dad beat me on a regular basis and didn't do a thing about it. Candace's dad shook his head, stood up, and started pacing back and forth, asking if this was the absolute truth. I told him it was and then told Candace's mom that she could come in the bathroom with me to see the marks and bruises. We went into the bathroom, and I took off my shirt to show her my back that had many bruises and scratches. I was facing the mirror, so I could see her face. She put her hand over her mouth, and I could see her almost tear up as she touched my back with her other hand. She ran her fingers over the bruises, almost looking as if she hoped they weren't real. Even with her warm and gentle touch, I could still feel it; it hurt when she went over the more recent areas that were still a little swollen. I pulled down my shorts and showed her the top of my butt where it hurt the worst. It was hurting pretty bad, so I knew it probably looked really bad. Those bruises and scratches were from my dad repeatedly grabbing me and shoving me against the end of our countertop in the kitchen. The end of the countertop was missing a piece of laminate, so the wood was exposed. It was rough and had a few pieces of jagged wood sticking out that were pretty sharp. I felt embarrassed and could feel my face get red, but I also felt relieved to show someone what was happening to me. I looked up at the mirror and could almost see tears form in her eyes as she helped me put my shirt back on and took me back into the living room. When Candace's dad saw her face and that she looked like she was going to cry, I think he already knew what she was about to tell him. She told him what she just saw, and he started yelling and cussing as he told Candace's mom that this wasn't okay. He kept repeating that I was just a little girl, just a child, and that this isn't supposed to happen. He yelled that he was going to beat my dad how he beat me. She told him to just sit down and take a breath so we could all talk about it. He said that my dad wasn't a real man, because real men do not hit women and children. He said that my mom was worthless and shouldn't even be allowed to be a mother for letting my dad do this to me. They were both so angry and confused. I know it was hard for them to hear that my mom just watched as I got beat. Candace's dad said that he firmly believes in discipline and spanking Candace when she's in trouble. He said that what my dad was doing to me was different, a lot different, and that it wasn't okay. Candace's parents seemed very angry and sad about what I told them. They told me to go back into her bedroom so they could talk. After about twenty minutes, they called me back into the living room and told me that I could stay the night for a few days. They said they didn't want me going home. They told me that I needed to tell them if my dad hit me again, and if it did happen again, they would both be going to talk to my parents. Even after we went back into Candace's room to play, I could still hear them talking about it. I could still hear so much anger in their voices. It felt good to have them care about what was happening to me, and it made me feel safe, at least for the time being.

Sometimes, Candace and I would stay up all night joking around and playing cards. It felt good to be able to laugh and feel good. We would mix a few Kool-Aid packets and sugar together, put it in a ziplock bag, and dip our fingers in it. Our Kool-Aid mixture would keep us up all night, and we had many long nights of fun with it. That summer came and went like all the summers before, but the happy times I had with my friends would stay with me forever. It was the end of that summer that I would be truly changed forever. Some weekends, I would get to go at my grandparents'—my dad's parents'—house. They were the best, not affectionate people, but they always made me feel safe and loved. Most kids hate having to visit their grandparents but not me. Mine were different. My little brother and sister never came, so it was like my own special place to go. My grandma would always cook breakfast, lunch, and dinner for me and my grandpa, which was very different from my house. At my house, we did not eat together very often. Besides the fact that my parents were miserable most of the time, the table was stacked high with junk. At their house, we sat down at the table for every meal, and afterward, we watched talk shows which were their favorite shows. When my papa would go into the basement to work on something, my grandma and I would paint our nails. In the living room, under one of the end tables, there was every shade of red nail you could imagine. That's all she ever wore, but I didn't mind. I always felt like I was away at a spa when I was there. I would do my nails and take relaxing bubble baths. My grandma always bought me big bottles of bubble bath from the Avon magazine and always had Skin So Soft bodywash, which I loved. At the top of the wall at the end of the tub, there was an open area where shampoos, conditioners, and lotions were kept; and it was full with many different brands and types. I always picked the best-smelling ones and felt so good after getting out of a long bath. Spending time with my grandparents always kind of reset my mind. It gave me a chance to unwind. Once I got done and was in my pajamas, my grandma would have me pick out a scary movie from her collection. She loved scary movies and collected them, and I loved watching them with her even though my parents kept telling her not to let me watch them. Sundays were the best and worst day there because we always went to a local restaurant for breakfast, but then I always had to go back home in the afternoon. This particular time at their house would be different, not the usual relaxing getaway. My dad's brother, wife, and two kids came to visit; so we all went there for lunch and visited with them. My cousins were not my favorite people to be around, but my grandma asked me to stay the night there with them, so I stayed. We watched movies late into the night and then sat down talking about everything we could think of. We started sharing our secrets and talking about any secrets or personal stuff that our families were dealing with. The topic of our parents spanking us and punishing us came up, and I started to talk about how my dad had been beating me. I told them how bad it had gotten over the last year and how he started constantly telling me that I ruined him and my mom's marriage. I told them that I felt like my dad hated me, like he didn't even care about me at all anymore. They did not seem to be very surprised. Their faces were nothing like Candace's parents found out that my dad was beating me. They told me that my dad probably didn't love me or care about me, because he wasn't even my real dad. I was a little confused at first until they explained to me that I was adopted. I felt blood rush to my face and ears as the walls suddenly seemed like they were closing in on me. I swear I could hear my heart pounding in my ears as I started to feel a great sense of panic build up inside of me. I felt a knot in my throat and burning in my eyes as I tried so hard to hold back tears. I had so many emotions flooding in all at once, and I could see both of my cousins' lips moving but couldn't even hear what they were saying. I took so many deep breaths that I felt dizzy but pulled myself together so I could focus on what they were saying to me.

My cousin explained that I was adopted when I was a baby, that I was taken away from my biological parents because they were drug addicts. My cousins said that they heard their parents talk about it the year before, after we all had celebrated Thanksgiving together at my grandma and grandpa's house. They said that their parents had talked about it several times since then; they heard them say that the whole situation and what my parents did to get me was wrong. They said that my parents were not going to tell me until I was an adult or whenever they thought it was the right time and that no one was supposed to tell me. I found out that I was actually a cousin to my parents and that they took me away from my mom and dad. The person I had known as my grandma, my mom's mom, was actually my aunt. Her brother was my dad, my real dad. It was so confusing and frustrating to hear something like that. It was just as shocking to find out that I had two sisters and a brother out there in the world and I never even knew. There was a whole family out there that I belonged to that I would have never known existed if my cousins had not told me. I wondered what my real family was doing. Maybe they were lying in bed thinking about me just like how I was thinking about them at that moment. I closed my eyes and tried to imagine them. I tried imagining two people who looked like me. Without knowing how they looked, it was hard, and it made me feel so much anger toward the two people who had been pretending to be my parents. I just knew deep inside me that they looked like me, beautiful brown hair and eyes, and I knew that they had to love me more than the people I lived with. I also imagined my sisters and brother with brown hair and eyes also, a whole family that looked just like me, and I couldn't help but to smile as I thought about that. My dad always would tell me that my eyes were brown because I was a liar; he always told me that. It always hurt my feelings when he said that because my brother and sister had blue eyes, so he made me feel like they were better than me because of that. He always made me feel like he didn't love me, like he only loved my brother and sister, and it never made sense until that night. It made sense why he treated me the way he did: I wasn't his daughter; I was nobody to him, just an inconvenience to him. I wondered if my real family missed me and if they wanted me back. I wondered where they lived and if it was close by. I felt so sad, scared, and confused; and I couldn't hold back my tears any longer. I must have cried off and on for two hours while trying to process the fact that I was adopted. My cousins made me promise that I would never tell my parents that I knew. They told me that something very bad would happen if I told anybody that I knew. Suddenly, the world felt so big and scary, and I felt so lost and alone that night. They told me that it was my mom's idea for them to adopt me, and their parents said it was to trap my dad into marrying her. I told my cousins that I was very tired and wanted to go to bed because I couldn't listen to anything else that they had to say. I had heard enough. I could not handle any more details. I was too overwhelmed.

So many thoughts were racing through my mind, and I must have lain there for hours after my cousins fell asleep, just trying to calm myself down. I tried to clear my mind and just let my body sink into the floor that I was lying on. I cried and I whispered to my real mom and dad with both desperation and anger pouring out of me. I cried, and I told them I was alone and needed them. I held my fists so tight, and I punched the floor, and if it wasn't for the few blankets underneath me, my hands would have been bleeding for sure. I put my face deep into my pillow, and I screamed, I screamed to my real parents. I screamed for them to come and help me. I screamed for them to come to me, to help me get far away from there. Something inside me hoped that they somehow would appear before me, but something else told me how stupid I was for even imagining something so silly and childish. I felt like the whole entire world and everything in it suddenly changed and it would never again be the same for me. I felt so hurt and betrayed by everyone. I thought about every single person in my life up to that point and couldn't believe that they kept this from me. After thinking about it for hours, it started to make perfect sense. when my dad told me that I ruined his marriage with my mom, this was what he was talking about. My dad was beating me because he never wanted me. I wasn't even his daughter, and now it was clear why he wanted to hurt me. My cousins had told me that they were surprised that I had never figured it out about being adopted. They said it was obvious due to my appearance. I felt so stupid that I never thought about why I had brown hair and brown eyes but my family all had blonde hair and blue eyes. I had never even thought about the fact that there were no baby pictures of me, just pictures of me when I was a few years old. I never even wondered why there were newborn pictures of my brother and sister but not me or why there were no pictures of my mom holding me right after birth. My entire life up to that point was all a lie. Everyone around me had been keeping this from me, and

I didn't know if I would ever be able to trust them again. Thinking about everyone in my family knowing about this and not telling me was something that I had thought I would never be able to handle or forgive. I knew that after that night, my life would never be the same. I tried to tell myself that my cousins were lying, that they were just trying to upset me, but they had no reason to lie to me. Plus, after replaying my childhood in my mind, a lot of it just made too much sense to be a lie. I had never once questioned why I didn't refer to my grandma as Grandma. I called her by her name. It now made perfect sense; why would I call her Grandma when she was really my aunt? I wondered what was real in my life and what was just a lie told to me by people who weren't who they said they were. I went to bed that night hoping that I would wake up the next morning and all this would just be a bad dream. I woke up the next day feeling so empty and alone inside. I wished that I could go back in time and change everything that happened the night before. I wanted to wake up my grandma and tell her that I knew about being adopted. I wanted her to hug me and tell me that she still loved me. I wasn't quite sure if I would be able to look her in the eyes anymore or anyone in my family now that I knew I was adopted. Even after just waking up, I had a million different thoughts and questions racing through my mind. My cousins had told me that my mom thought she couldn't have children due to a reproductive issue. A couple of years after adopting me, she found out she could and did. It all made sense; my parents only wanted me because they thought that they couldn't have children of their own. I was an unwanted child. I was a second option, and they couldn't have what they really wanted, so they took me. I didn't want to get up. I wanted to pull my blanket over my head and go back to sleep for a very long time. With everything that was said the night before, I wasn't sure if I could face anyone, and I definitely wasn't sure if I could keep it all inside of me without saying anything. I was a different person now. With what I learned the night before, there was no going back to who I was the day before. I, for sure, thought that everyone was going to be able to see a difference in me, see it written all over my face. They didn't notice no one noticed, just like how no one noticed the difference in me when my dad started beating me. My grandma made breakfast, like she always did on a Saturday morning, but I could barely eat. Even the smell made me sick. She made eggs, the kind that you could dip toast into, and bacon too. The whole time we ate, my cousins both kept making eye contact with me and putting their fingers over their mouths to silently remind me not to say anything about knowing that I was adopted. I wanted to scream and throw my plate at them for telling me that I was adopted but telling me I had to keep it a secret. It was like setting a bomb off inside me, inside my mind, and everything was a tragic mess in there. I felt so alone and so betrayed by every single person around me. I wanted to hug my grandma and hold her tight, but I was so angry and knew she was a part of the betrayal. It was hard to carry such a burden at that age, especially without having someone to confide in. My cousins told me that it would be very bad if I told anyone that I knew. They told me that they couldn't tell me what would happen, but they knew it would be bad. How they explained it was that a lot of people were involved in keeping it a secret, a lot of people helped for it all to work out. They said that there were more people than just my parents involved and that there were things done that weren't okay.

My cousins said that I wasn't exactly just given to my parents. It was more along the lines of me being taken away from them. I didn't quite understand exactly what they meant but took it as they did things that were bad and nobody was supposed to know about those. I imagined telling my family that I knew I was adopted and then getting very angry and everyone turning against me. Thinking about a huge conspiracy that I was directly in the middle of was enough to scare me out of telling someone that I knew. I tried to think of a family member whom I could really trust, someone who could help me figure all this out without it causing a huge problem. Every time I thought I had really figured it out, I remembered how I told my grandma that my dad was beating me and she did nothing. I came to the conclusion that I couldn't tell anyone. I couldn't risk my life getting any worse than it already was. What was the point of telling my family that I knew I was adopted? My dad was already beating me for no reason, and my mom and grandma both didn't care. I, at least, still had comfort in coming to my grandma and grandpa's house, and I didn't want them to hate me too. I couldn't handle everyone hating me. I couldn't handle not having any safe places like my grandma's that I could escape to. I wasn't strong enough yet. With my dad beating me and no one stopping him, I was mentally and physically too weak. For now, I would just keep moving forward and continue to have hope that everything would get better one day.

Third grade came fast, and the months went by faster, probably because I was having a lot of fun that year. My teacher was great, and I had a great group of kids around me that year who helped distract me from what was going on at home. Most days, I wished school would never end, and I wished that I never had to go home to my parents. I couldn't wait to get to school every day. I loved everything about it from my teacher's kind words and patience to the peace and quiet of the library. I had a few kids whom I regularly talked to, and it was nice to finally have friends and not just the kids who lived in my neighborhood. We had two field trips in the beginning of that year and a third one coming up that I was so excited about. The first two were to museums, a science museum and then a space museum, and both were so much fun. The field trip coming up was to a roller rink, so it wasn't a field trip where we had to learn about stuff; this was just for fun. I already had my own roller blades, and I would go roller-blading around my neighborhood all the time, so this was going to be a really good time. I had friends now, so I wouldn't be sitting in a corner staring at other kids having fun. I would finally be in the middle of the excitement like everyone else. There was a DJ who played so many popular dance songs, so we would skate and roller-blade as we swayed and danced to the beats. We would hold hands, form a line with four or five of us, then skate fast, and swing the last person off so they would go faster. Some of us would even skate backward so we could skate and talk to each other face-to-face. The DJ played a few slow R&B songs and would announce that it was time for a couple's skate, which was where a boy and girl would hold hands and skate together. I would sit on the bench staring at the couple's and imagining that it was me out there, holding hands skating slowly as a cute boy smiled at me as we skated. I imagined one of the cutest boys telling one of the prettier girls that he didn't want to skate with them anymore and then coming up to me and asking me to skate with them. There were kids at school who dated each other. They met each other outside of their classes and held hands in the hallways. At lunch, they would always sit together, and after school, they would hold hands and then hug each other as the busses pulled up and then went their separate ways. I had never experienced anything even close to that, but I did think about it a lot, daydream about it in class. I wasn't like any of the girls who had boyfriends. They were popular, and everyone at school wanted to be friends with them. They wore cute clothes, dresses with matching dress shoes and sweaters, and bows in their hair. Those girls wore lip gloss and sometimes eyeshadow and would have curls in their hair some days. Those were the girls whose moms would volunteer for all the field trips and parties in our classroom. I wasn't one of those girls, and I wasn't anything like them, not even a little bit. That's not the kind of thing you can fake. Even if I had nice dresses or shoes, I still wouldn't be able to look like them with their beautiful hair and happy smiles every day. I couldn't pretend that I had a mom who did my hair or bought me lip gloss so I could look nice for school. I could still sit and daydream about it, hoping one day I would grow into a beautiful girl who had a boyfriend. As I sat there imagining these things, a boy started to skate toward me smiling, but I thought for sure he just needed to sit down on the bench and rest. It was Jermaine, a kid who sat right by me in class. He skated right to me and stopped in front of me holding his hand out. My heart started to beat so fast, and I got so hot and almost embarrassed as he asked me to skate with him. I thought I was going to pass out or trip and fall as I took his hand, stood up, and skated to the rink. We skated to a fast dance song and didn't hold hands, but he stayed right next to me talking to me about how he loved skating. I was confused but very excited for Jermaine to want to skate with me. He chose me out of all the popular girls who were there. I felt like I was on top of the world. I felt like it had to be a dream, but I was wide-awake, and it definitely wasn't a dream. After the dance song, they announced the last couple's skate since it was getting close to the end of our time there. Jermaine just reached and took my hand so casually, and I still couldn't believe it. His hand was so warm, and I got so nervous that I could feel my hand starting to sweat. He held my hand so tight that by the time the song was over, our hands were almost dripping with sweat. We skated over to the benches as the teachers told us that it was time to get ready to leave and head back to school. At the counter where kids took back the skates that they rented if they didn't have their own, they had items that you could buy if you brought extra money to spend. My parents had only given me enough money to eat lunch there, but a lot of the kids brought extra money and went to the counter to spend it. They had glow sticks, glow-in-the-dark necklaces, bracelets, stickers, and rabbit's feet for good luck. Jermaine took off his skates and then went to the counter and came back with a rabbit's foot, and he gave it to me. He told me that he hoped it made me think of him, and then he asked me to the upcoming dance at school. I, of course, said yes and could barely even wait for him to finish talking to tell him that I would love to go to the dance with him. I could not believe what was happening. Nothing like this had ever happened to me, and I was just full of happiness and excitement. Finally, someone noticed me. Finally, someone like me and was treating me like one of the popular girls. This was something I could have never imagined would happen to me, something that I thought would only ever happen in my day-dreams and in my mind. I had never been to a dance at school even though there had been one earlier that year and one at the end of second grade also. There was never a reason for me to go before now. I didn't even have friends before this year and assumed that if I went, other kids would make fun of me. The girls always talked about the dresses and shoes that they were going to wear for the dances and would go back and forth about if they would wear their hair up or down. I always thought they were so stupid for making such a big deal about the school dances and would get so annoyed listening to them talk about it every chance they got. Now I understood what the fuss was all about, and it felt so good to finally be a part of something.

There was an hour left of school when we got back from the field trip, but I couldn't focus on anything the teacher was saying with all the excitement that just happened. Every time I looked over,

Jermaine was looking at me and smiling, and I couldn't help but to blush as I smiled back at him. At the end of class, he came up to me and held my hand as he told me that he couldn't wait to go to the dance with me and then held my hand as we walked to the busses. As we stood and waited for the busses to pull up, Jermaine told me that he wanted us to be girlfriend and boyfriend, and I was happier than I had ever been in my whole life. This was the best day of my life. On the bus, kids who had never talked to me before talked to me; kids whom I never thought existed acted as if we were good friends. They told me that I looked cute with Jermaine, and they acted as if I was in some special club now that I had a boyfriend. I couldn't wait to get in the door when I got home, I told my mom everything that happened, and I expected her to be happy and excited for me. After telling her everything, I stared at her, waiting for her response to the good news that I had just told her. She said, "Okay." All she had to say was, "Okay," and then told me to move out of the way of the TV so she could watch her shows. It hurt me, and I started to feel angry toward her, but I pushed it down and continued to feel excitement for everything that had just happened that day. I went to my room and just lay in my bed staring at the ceiling as I replayed the entire day in my mind and imagined what the dance would be like. I imagined myself in a long and very beautiful dress with matching shoes and my hair up in a fancy style. I closed my eyes as I imagined Jermaine in a handsome suit and a tie that matched as we danced all night and held hands. I played with my 90210 Barbie dolls pretending that they were Jermaine and me going on dates to the park and to the movies. When my mom told me that dinner was ready, I went out and asked her if she could buy me a dress for the dance, and she said she would think about it. I went and got the rabbit's foot that Jermaine gave to me so I could show her and tell her how we skated together and then how he asked me to the dance. I had forgotten earlier to tell her Jermaine gave me the rabbit's foot and wanted to go to the dance with me. As I told her all about it, I saw her face completely change, but I continued to tell her everything even as her face went from bad to worse. She asked me, "What was the boy's name again?" even though I had just told her what it was, and I told her his name was Jermaine. I thought maybe she was just interested and wanted to confirm what his name was, but that's not what was happening. She asked me what I thought my dad was going to say about me going to the dance with someone named Jermaine, and I told her that I didn't know. I thought that she was trying to imply that I was too young to be talking to a boy or going to a dance with one. She said that the name Jermaine didn't sound like a White name and that I knew how my dad felt about Black people. In an instant, my happiness was crushed by my parents' continued ignorance and hatred. I told my mom that I didn't care what they thought, because Jermaine was not a bad person like how they thought all Black people were. He was kind and liked me. She told me that Black boys and Black men were all the same. They all just wanted sex and to use White girls and women. It made me angry hearing her say these things about someone she didn't even know and for her to act like Jermaine was a horrible person just because he was Black. We were just kids, and we didn't have sex. Most kids in my grade barely had their first kiss yet, so how could Jermaine be trying to have sex with me? I went to my room without eating dinner. I was angry, I was upset, and my mom made me sick to my stomach. I knew how my dad felt about Black people. It was hard not to with the way he called them the n-word every single time he saw a Black person on TV. He said that Black people were taking over football and basketball because they were so much like animals, that it made them better at sports. He said that there were rules with jobs now. He said that they had to hire Black people even if they weren't good enough to do the job. He yelled at the news every time I saw him watch it, calling them other horrible and degrading names. Sometimes, I cried when he said such horrible things about people, especially people he didn't even know. His hatred toward people he didn't even know was repulsive, and it often made me so angry that I stayed in my room. How could he even for a second think he was better than them? He was a horrible man and father, and being White couldn't automatically make him better than a Black person. I thought this was so stupid.

My parents took anything good and turned it all around until they made it into something bad. How could my mom not see the good in this? How could she not see that a boy finally liked me, and nobody had ever liked me? I barely ever had friends. Girls never wanted to be friends or even talk to me, so a boy liking me was a huge deal. This was supposed to be a happy time. A girl getting asked to a dance for the first time was supposed to be a happy time in her life. I wanted this to be a happy time, and I just knew that in other families, this would be a happy time. In normal families, this wouldn't be turned into something bad. I was beyond upset. I knew I would be punished when my dad got home. He would barely be able to get in the door, and my mom would tell him about Jermaine. After I was done feeling angry at my parents, I put my pillow over my face and screamed and cried as I kicked my legs into the bed. I almost tired myself out to the point of falling asleep before my dad decided to stumble in, but my anger crept back up and kept me awake. I had hours to think about everything, and I decided I wasn't going to let my dad win. I wasn't going to let his stupidity and ignorance affect my life. I braced myself mentally as I heard him come in. I heard my mom tell him that I had something to tell him about a dance at school. The way she told him was like she was trying to set it up to be worse than it needed to be. It was like a child trying to taunt another child so they would get into an argument or fight. My dad called me out there, and I could already hear it in his voice that he was drunk and ready to take his anger out on me. He asked me what was this dance stuff that my mother was talking about, and I told him just like I told my mother. I explained it in the happy and exciting manner that I used when telling my mom about it. I was going to stand strong on the fact that this was supposed to be a happy moment in my life, getting asked to a dance by a boy was supposed to be a joyous time in a girl's life. My dad was almost too drunk to even pay attention to what I was saying, and my mom had to tell him to listen again to what the boy's name was. I told him that the boy was so nice and his name was Jermaine and I couldn't wait to go to the dance with him. I was playing stupid and acting like I had no idea what the problem could be with me going to a dance with Jermaine. He told me that I knew better, that there was no possible way after hearing what he always said about Black people, that I could be stupid enough to get involved with one. My dad said that I was doing this on purpose to make him angry and that I wasn't going to make him or my family look bad. He said I was going to go to school the next day and tell Jermaine that I wasn't going to the dance with him and that I could never speak to him again. I told him that I wasn't going to do that, I wasn't going to treat Jermaine like that just because he was Black. I told him that Jermaine didn't deserve that and it was my decision to make how I felt about Black people. He pounded his fist on the kitchen table, knocking off piles of papers, and threw his boots that he just took off against the wall. I cried and told him that Jermaine was a nice boy and he was different from the Black people that they thought were so horrible, but he grabbed me as he told me that they were all the same. I got angry as he got angrier and screamed at him that he was the bad person. I told him he was evil and that there was no possible way that Black people could be worse than him. He beat me so bad that night that I could barely get up off the floor when it was over. He pressed my head and face into the wall so many times that I thought I might pass out; I almost hoped that I did. As I walked past my mom, she smirked at me, almost smiling, and told me that I brought this all on myself. Every time that I thought that there might just be happiness in my life, my parents took it away from me. As I lay in my bed, my body hurt so bad, my head was pounding as I cried, but I was almost relieved that I stuck up for myself.

My little sister stared at me as I cried, but I told her that everything was okay and to go back to bed. Even though I was the only one getting beat all the time, I still felt bad for my brother and sister. I felt bad that they had to hear it, because I knew that it scared them. Sometimes, they would get in their beds and hide under their blankets, and they would cry for my dad to stop because it scared them. I would tell them that my dad hated me but it was okay because he loved them and that was all that mattered. I dreaded having to go to school the next day and tell Jermaine I couldn't be his girlfriend and that I couldn't go to the dance with him. He seemed so happy and calm all the time, and I didn't want to be the reason that made that change. I told him—I told him everything about how my dad felt about Black people. I told him everything except for how my dad beat me. I just didn't want this to turn into him feeling bad for me. The look on his face when I told him that this was about him being Black was horrible. It was like I took a part of his innocence away, and I hated myself for it. He told me that we could still be girlfriend and boyfriend and we would still see each other at school every day. I'm not sure why I told him that I couldn't. My dad probably would have never found out about it. I still said I couldn't do it. I think that I just didn't want to drag him into any of the misery in my life. Being with me was just too close to him being near my dad's hatred, as if my dad's racism would somehow go through me. It sounds stupid, but my life was such a sad and horrible place, and I didn't want to bring any of that into Jermaine's life. Jermaine was so sweet; he didn't deserve it. I don't know how as a child I was able to have the strength to worry about somebody else's happiness when mine was almost nonexistent. Jermaine took it well, and that was the end of that. I don't think I ever even talked to him again after that. I should have just dated Jermaine while at school because after that things only got worse at home and having him or anyone might have helped me get through it. My life wasn't getting better like I had hoped, but I kept hope inside me even if there was barely any left. My dad had almost beat every little bit of hope out of me, but I never let him take the little tiny bit that was hidden deep inside of me. The beatings got worse. They went from every two weeks to every week and then to almost every single day. Every time it happened, I would look in his eyes and try to figure out what was inside of him to make him keep doing it. All I could ever see was pure hatred. He just hated me so much, and it seemed to be getting worse every time.

I knew that I messed up the family that they wanted. I was their last hope at having kids, the last possible option for them. After they had two kids of their own, kids who were their real children and looked just like them, they hated that they adopted me. I knew that I was a mistake that they had to look at every day, and maybe that's why my dad never wanted to be around my mom. He probably blamed her for wanting to adopt me. I was an unwanted child and couldn't help but to imagine a family out there somewhere in the world that loved me. I imagined two people who looked like me, two people who actually loved me and wouldn't hurt me like these people did. It was hard to imagine it for too long, because I just couldn't see it. I kept just making up faces in my mind, but they never seemed to fit right. Some days, I started to think about killing myself. If I didn't focus on something to keep me or my mind busy, then my mind started to shift to a dark place.

Throughout fourth grade, I struggled to make it through class. Thoughts about what was happening at home heavily weighed upon me. There were small things that I would find that helped me get through each day. I had a passion for drawing, for sketching, and for anything that had to do with art; and it made me happy even if it was short-lived. I didn't just enjoy drawing; I was pretty good at it and started to think that maybe I could be an artist. The biggest distraction from my misery that year was my history teacher, who not only was a great teacher but was also a very kind and caring man. He was so nice to all his students, and the comfort that I felt around him allowed me to learn a lot in his class. Later in the year, I found out that he had been my mom's history teacher also, and he actually remembered her quite well. He would often tell me how smart I was and that I was full of potential. He said I was a good student just like my mom had been. He would go on and on about how my mom was a perfect student and how she always turned in her homework and got perfect scores on all her tests. I would listen to him, nod and smile, and act as if I was so happy to hear stories about how wonderful my mom was when she was younger. As I would stand listening to him, I would get nervous thinking about what would happen if he could hear my thoughts and how I really felt. If he could, he would find out that everything he said about my mom was surprising to me, considering my mom was no longer that good girl she used to be. If he could hear my thoughts, he would know that she was a very bad person now, so bad that she would just sit and watch as my dad beat me all the time. I wanted to tell my teacher these things that went through my mind every time that he brought up my mom, but I didn't. I just continued to keep a smile on my face, listen to his stories about my mom, and enjoy his kindness. At that point, I didn't have any friends in school, just the neighborhood kids; and they were all a few years older than me and in different grades and schools. I think that's why I didn't have any friends at school. Everyone whom I hung out with outside of school was older. I even hung out with kids that were in high school, so the kids in my grade seemed a bit childish. School was still a nice distraction from home. Between that and hanging with the kids from the neighborhood, I made it through the day.

I decided to start trying to avoid my dad, and for a while, it worked because he was in his shed almost all the time now. My dad was coming in looking a lot different from just drunk, and it became very confusing for a child. The more he came in looking strange, the more curious I became, and I wanted to know why I looked that way. His eyes would get so wide, unnaturally wide, kind of like when you try to open your eyes as wide as you can. He would look very nervous and shaky, and it was very different from when he would stumble in drunk every night. I would see cars pull up in front of the house and would see guys walk around the house to the shed. Sometimes, they would knock on the door and ask if he was home, as if they didn't see his truck parked right in the driveway. I knew most of the guys who would come over. Some were the dads of kids whom I went to school with. I found it so strange that a bunch of grown men would sit in a shed all night together. I could hear them when they would come out because when they came out of the shed I could hear the loud shed door. I would rush to the window or to the back door where I could see them walk past, and sure enough, they looked very strange also. There were several times where these men would bring women with them, and they weren't the kind of women like my mom was. These women looked like the women that were in the bar that my dad would bring me to when I was little. They wore leather skirts and tall leather boots with tops that showed a lot of their boobs. They would have on a lot of makeup, like bright-blue eyeshadow, but it wasn't the kind of makeup that made them look nice. Some just wore jeans and t-shirts, but if you got a glimpse of their faces, you could see that they were not good women. These women would have a beer in one hand and a cigarette in the other even when they came up to the door. It wasn't just the way these women looked that bothered me; it was the way they talked when they asked if my dad was home. They would sound almost ashamed and would avoid making eye contact with me as they asked for my dad. On the weekends, there would be more than a couple people out there with him. There would be several cars in front of the house when I looked. My dad used to come in most of the time around midnight, but now he was coming in no earlier than 3:00 a.m. most nights. I would try to talk to my mom about it, asking her what she thought about my dad staying out till the early morning with a group of people in a shed. She would tell me that she didn't care what my dad was doing out there and he was just hanging out with his friends and having a few beers. She would get mad at me when I would bring it up, and she would tell me that she was watching TV and to go to my room. I would get upset with her and ask her why he had women out there in his shed with him all the time. She would get really angry when I would bring that up but always told me they were girlfriends of his friends and that I was being too nosy. I would tell her that sometimes most of the men would leave and there would still be women in there with him. She just never wanted to hear what I had to say. She seemed to be in denial of the kind of person that my dad had become. I didn't want to hurt her feelings, but I would get angry when she would get mad at me for bringing these things up. I hated how my mom would act like she had no idea what was going on with my dad; it just bothered me. I didn't want her to be sad, but I also didn't want her to be naïve about what was going on with my dad. I watched this go on like this for so many months before I decided to take a look into what exactly was going on with my dad. I decided to go into his shed to try and find out what he was doing out there and why grown men and women would sit in there all night. My dad kept double padlocks on the shed door, so I would have to take his keys, or I would have to wait until it was open if I wanted to look inside. Sometimes, my dad would go in and out of the shed when he mowed the lawn or when he worked in his garden behind the shed. I would have to just watch and wait for a good time to go in there and find out what was going on during his late-night hangouts.

One day, I got the perfect chance. My dad had been going in and out of the shed all day but then had to run to the gas station. He needed gas for the lawn mower, so he had to run to the gas station, and the closest was about ten minutes away. I was watching him off and on, so when he just left without locking the shed up, I knew I had to go in there. I knew I had at least twenty minutes, but to be safe, I got the kitchen timer and timed myself for 8 minutes. I wasn't going to stay in there long enough to get caught, just long enough to figure out what was going on. I was so nervous that I almost decided not to do it, but I just needed to know what my dad was doing out there instead of being with his family. It wasn't like my dad was out there once or twice a week; he was out there every single day and never spent time with my mom or with us. I couldn't even think of one single time where my parents watched a movie together or went out to eat together. It never happened. The same went for me, my brother, and my sister. My dad never spent any time with us and probably didn't even know much about us. I swear my mom or one of us could go missing and it would take days for my dad to even notice that we were missing, and that's if he ever noticed at all. As his truck pulled out of the driveway, I felt my stomach become uneasy, and I had to take a few deep breaths to calm myself down as I went outside. I stood there right outside the back door. I set my cooking timer for eight minutes but stood there for at least a minute questioning if this was the right thing to do. I gave myself a mental pep talk and then headed toward the shed to do what I needed to do. After stepping into the door, I quickly stepped back out, went up the side of the house to check, and make sure that my dad didn't come back for something. I was worried that maybe he forgot his wallet or the gas can and would come back and catch me in there. It had also crossed my mind that this was a setup for my dad to catch me in his shed but realized that was ridiculous. I walked back and went in. With six minutes on my timer, I had to just do it. I felt my heart beating so fast, and I think I was even holding my breath as I stepped up to the main part of his shed.

I thought I was going to have to search through everything to figure out what was going on, but I didn't. It was right out in the open. He had a large piece of wood on top of one of his tool carts, so it was like a table, and there were chairs in front of it. On the table, there was a mirror with powder on it, and some of the powder was put into a few little lines. Next to the powder was a razor blade and what looked like a cut up straw next to it. I was only ten years old, but since I hung out with kids who were so much older than me, I knew what it was. The powder was drugs. It was cocaine. My dad was staying up all night out there because he was doing cocaine. Even though I had found enough, I decided to still look around because I was so curious because I had never been in his shed. On top of his big tool chest, there were three different kinds of pipes. One had burnt green stuff in it, which I knew was weed, but the other two were different. The one with weed in it was made of colorful glass. It had swirls of color and was actually kind of beautiful looking. The other two were like short glass tubes. They were clear so you could see all the burnt stuff in it and could see that it was very burnt looking, like the glass was turning a dirty-brown color. The weed pipe had a top part, almost like a little bowl to put the weed in it, so it wouldn't fall out when you were smoking it. These pipes were straight tubes without anything on top, so I wondered how they smoked out of them without stuff falling out. I looked into the end of one of them, and you could see that there had been something white in it. Next to the pipes, there were a lot of empty bags, tiny little bags all over the place, and some had a little bit of white powder in them. On the top of all the other tool chests, there were a little TV and a VCR with movies stacked up all around them. The movies had covers that looked like the pornographic magazines that used to be in our bathroom, and there were a lot of them. There were movies all over the place, on the tool chest on the shelf above it and a few stacks on the ground in front of it. I had seen enough, and it was making my stomach hurt, so I got out of there with a minute still left on my timer. I thought I was going to have to search through everything in his shed to find out what was going on, but it was all right out in the open. It was just ridiculous that my mom never stepped foot into that shed to see these things, and my dad knew she wouldn't. My dad didn't even have to hide his horrible behavior, because my mom was too dumb or too much in denial to go out and look in his shed. I can't say that I was shocked to find out that my dad was doing something like this, but I guess I was just shocked to see something like that for the first time. It's one thing to hear older kids talk about drugs and using them, but it's something a lot different to see them right in front of you. I didn't want to know that my dad was on drugs, so I don't know why I even went in there, but it was too late. I knew and then had yet another burden to carry on my shoulders, as if I didn't have enough already.

I sat for hours wondering what to do with my newfound information about my dad. I knew that I had to tell my mom what I found in his shed, but I knew she would be mad at me. I repeated what I was going to say in my head over and over until I got it right and imagined what my mom would say. I imagined her being very upset and having to hug her and tell her that it was going to be okay. I also imagined her being very angry with my dad, being so upset by the news that she would scream at him when he came home. My mom didn't drink beer. She didn't smoke cigarettes. In fact, she told us she had never done anything like that. She said that just one time when she was a teenager, her brother held her down, sat on top of her, and made her take a drink of beer. I knew that she would be heartbroken to find out that my dad was using serious drugs all the time out in his shed. I knew that I had to tell my mom right away because all the drugs were right where she would be able to see them if she walked into the shed. I imagined her storming out to the shed with a very angry face, and I imagined her knocking the cocaine onto the floor and telling my dad that she couldn't believe that he was dumb enough to use drugs. This was serious, a big deal that I knew wouldn't change everything at my house. I waited until later that night for the perfect time to tell her, and I got the chance when my dad went to do a side job. I was so nervous. I'm not sure why I was nervous, because I didn't do anything wrong, but I was. I stood in the bathroom for what seemed like forever, looking in the mirror and practicing exactly what I would say to my mom. I decided that I didn't need to make a perfect speech to tell her that my dad was using drugs in the shed every night. I took a few deep breaths, walked out, and headed down the hall to the living room where my mom was watching TV.

None of the several scenarios that I had imagined all day happened—none of them, not even close. I told my mom that I knew why my dad was staying out all night and the shed and that I knew exactly what he was doing out there. My mom used a sarcastic voice and had an aggravated look on her face when she asked me what it was that I thought my dad was doing out there. She said it as if no matter what I said after that, it was going to be some kind of silly lie. I don't know why I even proceeded to tell her anything, because by the way she looked, she wasn't going to listen or believe anything I had to say. I had come that far, so I just came out and said what I had planned on saying to her. I told her that I was tired of seeing my dad come in looking like something was wrong with him and watching people come and go from that shed every night. I told her that my dad wasn't just out there having a few beers—he was smoking weed, sniffing cocaine, and smoking it. I told her about the three pipes that I found and what was in them. I told her about the pile of cocaine on the mirror with the straw and razor blade. The evidence that I presented to her was solid, and I felt relieved after getting it all off my chest. I felt like I sounded very mature. I was able to get it all out just like I had practiced so many times in the bathroom and was so happy that I was able to do it and not sound childish.

After I stopped talking, that aggravated look that my mom had turned into an evil-looking smile that made me very nervous. I started to get the feeling just by my mom's face, that she was angry or upset with me and not my dad. She told me that my dad would never do drugs and said that he smoked weed in high school but that was a long time ago. She acted like it was a joke, as if I just made it all up for no reason. I told her that I was just in there hours before that and saw it all with my own eyes. I swore that I wasn't making it up. I explained to her in detail where everything was, how it was laid out, and exactly what it all looked like. She kept giving me that evil smirk while shaking her head at me as she told me that I was acting very childish. She made me so angry as I pleaded with her to go out to the shed and take a look for herself, but she wouldn't. She turned it all around on me, telling me that I must have been looking to do something wrong by going into my dad's shed. It made me even angrier when my mom started telling me that my dad didn't deserve this kind of behavior from me, because he was a good dad. She said that he worked hard to make sure we had everything we needed and I had never had to go without anything because of my dad. I felt like I was going to explode with anger as she said that, and I couldn't help but to start yelling at her. I told her that she must be completely blind and stupid because my dad was a bad father and a bad husband. I told her that she must have forgotten about my dad constantly beating me and never come home to her almost every night. I yelled at her to get up and stop being lazy. I told her to walk out to the shed and just look. I begged her to please just go out and look in the shed, but she refused to as she told me that she trusted my dad. I was so mad and didn't care about anything that I said after that point, so I just kept speaking my mind. I told her that I was so sick of my dad beating me and her not helping me but instead watching him do it. I told her that I was sick of my dad staying out all night as she sat in the house crying and acting so weak. I told her that I was tired of seeing my dad stumble in drunk and high out of his mind almost every single night. I told her that she was a horrible mother for letting all this happen and that they both belonged in jail for child abuse. I told her that she must be the stupidest woman ever for not realizing that my dad was a nasty man who looked at and watched porn all the time. I told her that there was a big problem if my dad chose to watch porn and looked at porn magazines over being anywhere near her. I told her that my dad was probably having sex with one of the nasty-looking women who were always going in and out of the shed, even when there weren't other people in there. I lost it. I spoke my mind and let all my anger come out, and it actually felt so relieved to just let it all out. I was relieved but felt sick to my stomach when I looked up at her face and saw what looked like shame and embarrassment. I felt so stupid for letting this go from being about my dad doing drugs to me taking out my anger on her and saying so many hurtful things. Everything that I had said was true; it was all true, but I should have never said any of it in the way that I did. I watched as she tried to hold back tears and hold onto the tiny bit of self-worth that she had left. She tried to pretend that she was interested in whatever was on the TV so that I would think she wasn't torn apart by everything that was just said. Part of me hated myself for doing that to her, but the other part didn't care, because she was allowing all this to go on. I knew that she was somewhat a victim like I was. Even though he never physically abused her, he mentally abused her with his actions. I couldn't believe how all that came from me trying to tell her that my dad was using drugs. It just killed me inside that she refused to look in my dad's shed; it was right there, and it would take her one minute to just look in there. Maybe she trusted him, or maybe she didn't want to see it, because then it would be harder for her to stay in denial. Either way, I was so sick of her and my dad, and I was just sick to death of having to be in that house.

After finding out what my dad was doing, it made sitting in the middle of it feel more chaotic. It felt like I was in the middle of a bad nightmare that seemed to never end, and I didn't have the feeling that it would end anytime soon. I felt so stupid to think that my mom would listen to me, and I knew that by telling my mom about what my dad was doing, I would later regret it. I had been in my room trying to mentally process my discussion with my mom. I stared at the wall and replayed it, trying to find out if I could have said anything differently. My mom must have called my dad to tell him what I told her, because he actually came home and even went into the house that evening. Not too long after he came home, they called me into the kitchen to talk about what I told my mom. Since my dad had come in before going out to his shed, he didn't look too angry and wasn't high or drunk yet. I was surprised by his demeanor as my mom repeated everything that I had told her just hours before and closely watched his face for reactions. My mom laughed as she spoke. It was more of a fake laugh and sounded like she wanted to imply that this was too outrageous to be true. My dad also laughed. He had the biggest grin on his face as he denied doing drugs or ever having even had drugs in his shed at any point. He said that he used to smoke pot in high school but that was a long time ago and he had no need for that kind of thing in his life. He told me that my mom and I were welcome to go take a look in his shed at any time because he had nothing to hide. I told them that we needed to go out to the shed. I asked my mom to please go out to the shed with me, but she said no. She tried to casually laugh as she said that she trusted me dad and had no reason to ever need to go into his shed. They were both grinning from ear to ear. They were both laughing at me like I was some kind of liar or fool. Then my dad told me that I needed help and that they would make an appointment for me to talk to a doctor about my lying. This was the first time in years that I had ever seen them appear to be on the same page, even if they were just pretending. My mom was always looking for any possible way to make my dad happy with her or to get him to even want to be around her. It was disgusting to see them pretending that they were some kind of team and acting as if they had a marriage involving any trust or honesty. It was so hard for me to control myself after witnessing their little performance, but I did; I held it all in.

I think that I was mentally exhausted and knew that there was absolutely no point in arguing with them, especially with them acting as if they were an unbreakable team. I was physically exhausted, too, with my dad beating me several times a week. I was just so exhausted, and I just didn't have it in me to fight about this. My dad told us that we were welcome to go in his shed at any time because he would never hide anything from his family and that we were everything to him. He looked at me and told me that he loved me, that he didn't want us to fight with me, and that he wanted his sweet little girl back. I was so disgusted by him and the lies that were coming out of his mouth. How dare he say that he wanted his sweet little girl back. I wanted to grab his face and stare into his eyes and tell him that she was gone. He must have beat that sweet little girl right out of me. He was a joke. He and my mom and the little shows that they randomly put on like this, this was all a sick joke. My dad knew how to mentally manipulate people, especially my mom, and the sad thing is, I don't even think she ever knew that he was doing it. My dad knew that if he acted like a team with my mom, she would never even question him, because she was so desperate for his attention, so desperate for his love. That's why she never even did anything when he beat me.

She hoped that by letting him do it, he would be pleased with her. I often wondered if it was always like this with them. I wondered if, when they were younger, my dad loved her and actually respected her. I tried to imagine them as a young couple still dating and being crazy in love with each other, but it was hard to see that having ever happened. I tried to think about my dad wanting to be around my mom or sitting down with her to have dinner or them going out together, but I couldn't. I couldn't imagine them having ever been in a normal relationship that involved loving, trusting, or fully respecting each other. I just could never figure out why or how my mom ended up like this, so desperate for my dad's love or even a little bit of attention. When I would stay the night at my friend's houses, I would look at their parents and try to imagine my parents being like them. My friend's parents spent evenings cuddled up watching movies together or going on walks around the neighborhood while holding hands and smiling as they enjoyed each other's company. They went out on dates to nice restaurants and looked forward to going to concerts together or baseball games. Things couldn't be more different at my house between my parents, and it was confusing to witness as a child. It was hard living in a house that had desperation instead of love, lies instead of trust, and chaos instead of peace. I wondered if my parents knew that their relationship and behavior were affecting us. I wonder if they even cared.

My dad actually stayed in the house that night. He moved a few piles of junk off the couch and sat watching TV with my mom. It was obvious that he wanted my mom to believe him or not question him about the drugs, so he showed her the little bit of attention that she so desperately needed. He knew that she wouldn't dare ruin it by bringing up anything involving the earlier conversation, and he was right: she never said a word about it. I went to the bathroom a few times so I could peek around the corner at them. I could see both of their faces from where I was standing. My dad's face looked unhappy, like he couldn't wait for the night to be over, and he looked like he was being punished. My mom's face looked so happy but so desperate at the same time, and she looked like she never wanted that moment with my dad to end. Even with everything that she did to me or allowed to be done to me, I still felt bad for her and didn't think that she deserved to live like this. As I stood there in the hallway tucked around the corner where they couldn't see me, I thought about my mom and what he put her through over the years. This desperation that my mom had, it wasn't something that happened overnight. This was years and years of her hoping and wishing that my dad would change and be the husband and father that she wanted him to be. At first, in their early years, my mom probably waited and begged for him to take her out and spend more time with her. After so many years, I think she just waited and begged for him to just come home. Even if he went straight to bed or stayed in the shed all night, she just wanted him home. It hurt to see my mom being treated like this. This wasn't how women were supposed to be treated, even the bad ones. What my dad did to my mom changed her. It changed her as a woman but also as a mother, and that's not something that can be reversed. What my dad was doing to my mom affected us. She might not have realized it, but it affected everything about her. She couldn't fully love us, because of how broken her heart was, so we became just like her, waiting and hoping for love and affection that would never come. I had become like her. I would imagine her hugging me, kissing me on my forehead, or telling me that she loved me, even though that would never happen. I could see in her eyes that a long time ago, she was probably a good person and her life and future was full of hope and possibility like any younger person. It doesn't take very many bad decisions to end up damaged like that. For her, it probably took just one mistake. I wondered if she knew the kind of man my dad was when she met him. I wondered if he was different or if he always was a bad person. I wondered if my mom knew but thought that she could change him or if she really had no idea that he wasn't going to be a good man and husband. I always felt bad for her, but at the same time, I despised her for the weakness and desperation that had consumed her. I imagined that everything would change and my parents would be in love again, sitting cuddled up how they were in that moment, and them both staying happy. I could imagine and hope all I wanted, but it would never be like that. There was no hope for our family.

After that night, and after my mom didn't believe anything that I had to say about my dad, it was hard for me. I felt alone and betrayed by everyone around me, and it wasn't the first time, and I'm sure it wouldn't be the last. My hope that things would get better yet again didn't happen, and my dad beating me only got worse. Every time that my dad hit me after that, it was like he was punishing me for going into his shed and exposing him for the drug addict that he was. I think that even though my mom was blind to what he was doing, he felt angry and ashamed that I knew, and he hated me for it. He would tell me that I was a liar, a thief, and I would never amount to anything in life as he shoved me all over the kitchen and beat me. There were times where he beat me so bad that I couldn't even get up, and I would beg him to stop and tell him that I was just a child and to please stop hitting me, but he wouldn't. If I said anything to him while he was doing it, he would hit me harder and scream at me to stop talking back. If my mom was in the room when it was happening, he would tell her that I was trash and that she let me ruin their marriage. She would tell him to shut up but never tell him to stop beating me. Sometimes, when he was done and I was trying to get up, she would look at me so angrily and tell me that I brought this on myself. I would scream and cry, asking her to tell me how all this could possibly be my fault, and I would beg her to tell me why they hated me so much. I would ask her why she let my dad beat me, but she would laugh and tell me that I was just being dramatic. She would tell me that I didn't even know what it meant to get beat and then tell me to go to my room and stay there.

I am pretty sure that it was around that time that depression came into my life, and it would be a long time until it left me. I felt like I was trapped, not only in my life but inside of myself, inside the darkness of my mind. I needed someone, anyone, to love me, to look after me, and to take care of me; but I didn't have that. The closest that I got to love and feeling cared for was by my grandma, but it stopped being enough for me to hang onto. I would walk to her house almost every single day to my grandma's house and sit with her for about twenty minutes just to feel her kindness. I would find anything and everything to talk about, so I could stay as long as possible, but I couldn't stay there forever. Our visits were almost always the same. I would come in, and she would greet me, and I would instantly light up just by being in her presence, and I needed that. She would offer me something to drink and ask me if I wanted the rest of what she cooked herself for dinner, and I would decline but ask her for a snack bar or something that she had sitting on the counter next to the refrigerator. Our conversations always started with how my day was and then would shift to whatever was going on in both of our lives, and that was always the extent of what we talked about. Here and there, we would discuss any minor issues that we were going through, but they were always just the superficial problems, nothing too deep or serious. It angered me that she wouldn't talk to me about my dad beating me or about her daughter sitting and watching my dad beat me like it was a movie in a theater. I had tried several times to talk to her about it, to get her to care about it or say anything to my mom about it, but she seemed to not want to get involved. She wouldn't get any further into it than telling me to be good so my dad wouldn't have a reason to do it or say that I must have been doing something to provoke him. I hated that she was right there in the same boat as my mom when it came to doing absolutely nothing for me when it came to my dad and the abuse. As bad as I wanted to scream at her and tell her that she was a monster for letting this happen to me, I didn't, because I needed that little bit of hope and happiness that I got from her. I kept telling myself that I would get stronger and that once I did, I wouldn't need her or anything that she did for me. It sounded good, but I never got stronger, and I still needed our little visits to keep me hanging on to the light and not fall completely into the darkness. Sometimes, I would need to bring her something from our house, but I would go there without it and tell her that I forgot, so I would have a reason to come back. Some days, I would purposely leave something in between the cushions of her loveseat and then go home for a while and then come back to get it so I could talk to her a little more. Until I got stronger or until anything got better, I still needed her. Even though she wasn't helping me with what my dad was doing to me, I still needed her. I would feel so safe and would feel good about myself when I was there, and my self-esteem was almost nonexistent, so I needed that so badly. This kept me going for a while, but as soon as we started saying our goodbyes, sadness would rush through me so fast. Most days, I would cry as I walked home from her house. I would cry and scream at her as if she was right there with me. I would beg her to let me stay with her forever. In my mind, it felt like I was really saying these things to her, so I would feel a little better as if I had actually just expressed myself to her and told her how I feel. I would stop halfway between my house and hers and stand there in the middle of the road just staring back, wishing she would come out and signal at me to come back. I would stand there and just hope I would hear her calling my name so I could run back, hug her tightly, and get to be with her a little bit longer. My grandma made me feel good, she made me feel safe, but it was just temporary, and I couldn't be around her all the time.

As things got worse for me at home, I started to feel like it was pointless to go and visit her every day, to be so desperate for the small amount of love and affection that I got from her. I started visiting her less and less as my depression grew stronger, and that only made me feel more alone in the world. I would close my eyes and try so hard to see myself with my real family—my real mother, father, sisters, and brothers; but I couldn't. It seemed like no matter how hard I tried, I couldn't imagine anything about them, and it was hard for me. I had no images, no faces to hold onto and keep me going, no family even in my mind to call my own. I wanted to at least have faces so I could close my eyes and see them, see my real family, a family that was mine and would keep me safe. My thoughts were the only thing that my dad couldn't take away from me, the only thing that he couldn't destroy. I spent so many days playing out every possible scenario in my mind as I tried to figure out why I was adopted by these people and why my real parents would give me away. I often wondered why I had to go through all of this. I wondered if I was born only to be tortured and to suffer by the hands of these evil people. I had to hold on tight to what I did have that was good in my life. It may not have been a lot, but it was enough to keep me hanging on. If it weren't for my friends from my neighborhood and their parents treating me like family, I wouldn't have made it through everything that was going on with my dad.

That summer, I tried to stay away from my house and my dad as much as possible, and it did work for a while. My friends were everything to me, and our summers together were nothing less than awesome. Even though they were just kids, they understood me and what I was going through more than any adult whom I had tried to confide in. They seemed to know more about life than a lot of adults, and they helped me through my troubled childhood and let me get out alive. Just like I had started pushing my grandma away, I think that I unconsciously started pushing Tiffany away, too, so I started hanging out with Candace more. Tiffany was so good at everything, and I mean everything, so that often left me feeling inadequate. I spent years in her shadows, and I was always okay with that because I loved and adored everything about her. I had always been so proud to be her friend because of how amazing she was, and I didn't even care that everyone knew me as Tiffany's friend and probably didn't even know my name. Just being with her and around her family was all I had ever wanted up to that point, but something changed inside me, and I rebelled from being in her shadows. I think I just needed a break from it. Maybe it was because I was depressed, or maybe it was because I wanted to stand in my own light and not in Tiffany's anymore. Candace was almost the opposite of Tiffany in so many ways, and at least for that summer, that was exactly what I needed. She wasn't obsessed with sports, and she wasn't so good at every sport that it made me look horrible. She liked to just hang out and have fun. She loved to laugh and always kept me laughing too. We would laugh so hard at the stupidest stuff. Stuff that Tiffany would say was stupid, Candace thought it was hilarious. I just needed a break from the pressure of trying to be so athletic like Tiffany, and I just needed a chance to try and be me, the real me.

That summer, Candace's parents had a trip planned, a vacation without kids and just for the two of them. During the time they were away, she couldn't have anyone over at their house. She or her brother couldn't let anyone in, since their parents were gone. Candace knew that I needed her more than ever that summer, so she asked her parents if I could stay there while they were away on vacation. They asked me to come over and talk to them the day before they planned to leave, and they told me that I could stay there with Candace even though they wouldn't be there. They both told me that they normally would never do this, but they knew what my dad was doing to me and wanted to help me anyway they could. Unlike my mom and dad, Candace's parents trusted me and said that I was a good kid whom they wouldn't have to worry about causing any trouble while they were away. Sitting there with them as they said that, it made me feel so good and safe, and it made me feel like someone actually cared, which I normally didn't feel very often. I may not have had good parents, not even a little bit, but my friends did; and that was enough for me, even if it was only temporary. It was like a vacation being at Candace's house when her parents were gone. It was just us and her old brother, Brandon. We stayed up late watching TV and playing cards. We only knew a few games, but we had so much fun playing them. We talked for hours about everything you could think of, and after hours of talking about everything we loved, somehow the conversation always changed to what we hated. I don't think that Candace really knew how bad things had gotten at home for me until that summer until I went into detail about my dad beating me. It started off as me telling her about the most recent incident with my dad, and then I just kept going back further and further, explaining to her each and every time he beat me. I cried to her, and I knew that she cared about me, because she cried, too, and told me that she was so sorry that I had to go through all of this. We would always talk for hours about me being adopted and would try to guess what my real parents were like and where they lived. We could never really come to a conclusion on why we thought that I ended up getting adopted or why I ended up with the parents that I had. What we both could never figure out was why my parents adopted me if they were going to abuse me and not treat me right. What we both did always agree on was that we thought they adopted me because they couldn't have kids and then they did and started to hate me. That was the only scenario that we could ever put together without having any other facts or any information on my real family. Candace would listen to me, really listen to me, when I talked about how I felt knowing that I was adopted and had a family out there somewhere. It felt good having someone to talk to about my life, and I always felt better after we stayed up all night talking. I wished that I could stay in those moments forever, the moments that I felt like I had someone that cared and felt like it was okay to be me and not be judged for it.

Candace's brother Brandon made us promise him that we would not tell their parents that he was having a few friends over to hang out and drink beer with him. He stayed out of our way and never said anything about what we were doing, and we knew that if we were doing something that we weren't supposed to, he wouldn't tell on us. He never really talked to me much, and it was probably because he was a lot older than us. He was halfway through high school already. I had always thought Brandon was cute with his long messy hair; and I loved his style of ripped jeans, a chain wallet, and old concert T-shirts. He played the guitar and had that laid-back musician vibe to him, but it was hard to tell what he was really like, because he never talked much and always had a serious face. We could always hear him listening to loud rock music in his room because it was next to Candace's, and he always seemed so mysterious and rebellious just sitting in there alone with his music and guitar. He was in high school, but he was so mature, and even had a truck and a part-time job to save up for an apartment. I wasn't sure if he didn't pay much attention to me because I was younger than him or if it was because he thought I wasn't cool enough, or maybe it was both. When he had friends over, I could see through the crack in the door when I was going to the kitchen, and I could see what they all looked like. The boys looked like him with long messy hair, ripped jeans, and old tattered concert T-shirts that were almost falling apart but still looked good. The girls wore similar clothes, but theirs were tighter, and sometimes the shirts were ripped so their belly would show, and they some wore tall leather boots. The girls had long messy hair, too, but it was a little neater and had a few streaks of green or pink in it with a few loose braids. I loved the way they looked. All of them looked so effortlessly cool and laid-back all the time. When they would come out or walk past me when they were leaving, I always tried to play it cool, but I know that I looked and sounded so lame and childish to them. I knew that I wasn't cool like them, and even if I dressed like them, I probably still wouldn't be anything like them, not even a little bit.

Candace's brother and his friends would stand outside and smoke cigarettes, and even though I hated the way they smelled, they looked really cool and mature doing it. The girls especially looked like the sophisticated women you would see in commercials, the way they would casually laugh and hold their cigarettes up near their face. Sometimes, I thought about what would happen if I went out there and asked them for a cigarette. I wondered if they would laugh at me or think I was cool. That was me, always sitting back and imagining myself in someone else's shoes or in someone else's life and always trying to get out of my own. Candace's brother asked us both if we were okay with him having a small party which he referred to as more of a get-together and less of a party. He said that they would be drinking and just wanted to make sure that we wouldn't tell on him, so he said that we could drink a little bit too. I was ecstatic but played it supercool and said it didn't matter to me what we did and I was down for a little drinking if Candace was. At the time, I really didn't understand why her brother was asking us to drink with him and his friend. I later realized it was because if we drank, too, then we couldn't tell her parents. I didn't care about that. I was just so excited that he actually talked to me like a real person. Before that, he had never even looked at me. My eyes and mind were clouded by things that I only thought were important at that time but would later find out that I was being so childish and naïve. All day as I helped Candace clean up for Brandon's little get-together, I acted as if it were a regular day, even though I was screaming with excitement on the inside. This was definitely my chance to show Candace's brother that I wasn't just a boring little kid, I was mature and I was fun, and I just needed a chance to show it. I just wanted to be able to hang out like they did, everyone just laughing and having a good time was exactly what I wanted to be a part of. I was a little bit nervous to drink beer or alcohol with them, only because it was my first time and I didn't want them to make fun of me for that. I wished that

I had better-looking clothes and shoes that day. I never had cared about my clothes that much but regretted it that day. Everyone else had name-brand clothes and shoes, but I never had any of that, just the cheaper stuff, and sometimes it came from the thrift store. When I wanted to look cool, I would wear Tiffany's clothes, but I couldn't go and ask her to borrow any, since I had barely talked to her in a while. Candace didn't have clothes as cool as Tiffany's, but they were still better than mine, and she had some of her brother Brandon's old band and concert T-shirts. I picked an old Def Leppard shirt to wear with my shorts and sandals, which weren't the most awesome outfit to wear, but it would work. I had so badly wished that I had a pair of black leather boots to wear, maybe with some ripped-up jeans or shorts, but at least I had the old band T-shirt to help me look cool.

Later in the evening, Brandon's friends started to show up, but Candace and I played it cool by acting like we weren't interested in what they were doing and continued to watch movies. Only four guys came over that night, and it was surprising to me that none of the girls I had seen Brandon hang out with came. Two of the guys brought cases of beer and both brought bottles of brown-colored liquor, which they later told me was whiskey, and a pop to mix the whiskey with. They just hung out listening to loud rock music in Brandon's room, and we could hear them laughing and joking around as we watched movies in the living room. They didn't start drinking for a few hours until it was nighttime, and when Brandon came out to ask us if we wanted a drink, we casually accepted the offer. He told us to get ourselves some pop and ice so he could mix some whiskey into it for us, so we did as we continued to act like it was no big deal. We acted as if this was something that we had done before, and when Brandon asked if I had drank before that, I told him I had tried it a couple of times already. He laughed when I said that, so I am pretty sure that he knew that I hadn't drank before but didn't say anything. The pop and whiskey had a horrible taste to it, so I drank it very slowly and was still on my first cup when Candace started her second. Candace was a couple of years older than me, so this wasn't her first time. She had drank with Brandon a few times before that. It was actually funny how big of an age difference there was from the youngest to the oldest person there. I was ten, Candace was a few years older than me, and Brandon and his friends were eighteen and older. I finished my first cup and just sat there for a while until Brandon came out to use the bathroom and told me to have his friend pour me another drink. His friend poured some whiskey into my cup, and I went into the kitchen to mix it with pop and ice. I was nervous because I had never drank before, and it was starting to make my stomach hurt, so I poured half of it into the sink. I was already feeling very silly because of the first cup I drank, and everything Candace said to me made me laugh. We sat on the couch telling jokes and laughing at everything. I had never laughed so hard and was having a really fun time. Brandon said that we couldn't have any more to drink after we both had two cups, because, he said, we were too young. I felt stupid being told that, but as everyone started to drink more, they came out and sat in the living room with us, and we all actually hung out together. This was the first time that Brandon and his friend's didn't ignore us or treat us like we were little kids, and it felt good. They looked right at us, laughed, and joked around as if we were all the same age. Even though I was so young, I was mature and not just for my age; I was mature in general. I never felt like I could connect with anyone my age. A lot of the times, even Candace seemed too childish to me.

With Brandon being so much older than me, before that night, he had barely ever spoken to me. It was great sitting back and listening to Brandon's friends talk about what they did that day or the plans they had coming up. Brandon talked about how hard they worked him at his job, which was a local garage where they did oil changes and small car repairs. His friend Martin, who worked at a as truck driver, said that his back was hurting from a long day at work; so he asked if one of us would give him a back massage and said he wished he knew someone who gave massages. He said that he also had a bad headache and maybe needed to sit in a dark room for a while to try and get it to go away. Candace told me that I should give him a massage, and then she told Martin that he could go and lie on her bed because her room was the darkest in the house. She had dark blinds over her windows, so even during the day, her room was so dark and peaceful and stayed nice and cool. Candace gave me a bottle of lotion so I could give Martin a real massage, and I went into her room where he was lying facedown on the bed. He told me to squirt the lotion right on his back and to massage hard but not to worry about hurting him. I knew how to give a good massage because I often gave my grandma massages when her back would hurt from a window falling on her back and breaking when she was a teenager. I would use a lot of lotion and massage her back until it was bright red, and then I would look very closely to see if there were any glass shards coming up. Even though it was so many years later, pieces of glass would still come close to the surface in her back, and I would use tweezers to pull them out. I was never really sure why, but she actually liked it, and it was something we did on a regular basis. I felt like I was important when she would ask me to do it. I felt like I was a doctor and I was performing a much-needed procedure for a patient. I guess that giving someone a much-needed massage made me feel the same way. It made me feel like I was wanted and needed. Having always given my grandma massages as a small child, it didn't even cross my mind that it might be inappropriate for a ten-year-old girl to massage a grown man's back. I massaged Martin's back firmly, really trying to get the tension out of his shoulders, which is what I did when I gave my grandma massages. Martin seemed to be enjoying it, and I knew I was doing a good job because my hands were feeling so tired, but I kept kneading and massaging his upper back. I kept going until he told me that he knew my hands must be tired and that I could stop and go find some lotion to use. I got up to look for some lotion, but Martin told me to lie down and he would give me a massage now since I gave him such a good one. He told me that I looked too stressed out for such a young girl, and he asked if I had it bad at home and if my parents hit me. It was like he knew what I was going through just by looking at me or by being near me, and it made me feel comforted. He told me that it was going to be okay and that whatever didn't kill me would only make me stronger. Martin told me that I was a beautiful young girl and that he knew I would be something really special as I grew into a young woman. He said that my dad was probably just a loser who didn't go far in life so he was jealous of me because I was going to do something with my life. He told me that he could tell that I was one of those smart girls who didn't care about silly stuff and didn't let anyone tell me what to do. He said that my beauty wasn't just on the outside, that he could see it shining through from deep inside of me. He asked me how old I was, and I told him that I was ten years old, and he told me that he couldn't believe it, because I acted like I was sixteen years old. I knew that I was very mature for my age because of everything I had been through but didn't think I could look much older than ten. Martin told me that he was eighteen, but he said that he didn't feel that a number or an age should defy who you are. That made perfect sense to me because I could never connect with anyone my age, because they were so childish and I was so mature. I hated that people saw me as a little child when I was more mature than people in my neighborhood who were sixteen years old. I told Martin that, and he told me that it was because I was a diamond that nobody ever noticed, because I just needed someone to polish me so that I could shine again. Nobody had ever said anything like that to me before, and I felt like I was on top of the world. I felt safe, comforted, beautiful, and like I was actually worth something instead of just being good enough to be beat all the time. Nobody ever even paid attention to me or paid attention to what I was going through, and of course, nobody ever said anything to me that made me feel like I mattered to them. I would have never guessed in a million years that I would be sitting in a room with a handsome man and being compared to a beautiful diamond. Sitting there with Martin as he smiled at me, I felt something that I had never felt before and almost wanted to cry because it felt so right. I felt everything that I had never gotten but needed from my dad while sitting there with him. At the same time, I also got everything that I often thought about or daydreamed about when it came to having a boyfriend. For the first time in my life, someone could see me, someone could see that I was important and my feelings were just as important too. He touched my cheek softly and then held it with his hand. I closed my eyes and just enjoyed the warmth of his skin against mine. After that, everything happened so fast.

Martin turned into a predator and molested me. I wanted to say no. I wanted to tell him to stop, but for some reason, I didn't. I didn't even know him but had some deep desire to make him happy with me. No one had ever been so sweet to me, so I just lay there and waited for it to be over. Martin's face had been warm and kind, but when he was done with me, he was different. He told me that I could never say anything about what we had just done and he stopped because he knew that it was wrong. I was confused by what he was saying, because he didn't act like what he just did was wrong. I waited for him to smile at me, maybe touch my face and tell me that it's okay and that I was still very beautiful to him. I stood there hoping, needing him to reassure me that I was the smart and beautiful girl that I was before he wanted to have sex, before he told me to lie down. Martin didn't do that. In fact, he didn't even make eye contact with me again. He crawled onto the bed and lay down, and he told me to walk out of the room as if none of that happened. He told me to tell everyone that I massaged his back for so long that he fell asleep and that I didn't even realize he fell asleep until I heard him snore. I took a deep breath and walked out of that room trying to look as normal as I possibly could—as normal as I could for a ten-year-old girl who was just molested by a grown man. I thought I would have the whole room staring at me as I walked through the living room where everyone was still sitting, but I didn't. I went straight through the living room into the kitchen and held my breath the whole time, as if they wouldn't be able to see me if I wasn't breathing. As I entered the kitchen, I almost gasped for air as I stopped holding my breath and went straight to the sink. I guess it was just instinct to walk toward the sink because it was facing away from everything. I could pull myself together and just think for a minute. I felt like the room was blurry and spinning around me. Everyone's voices and the music was all just one loud ringing sound. I needed to pull myself together, and I needed to do it fast before I passed out. I needed a moment to think, and I needed my heart to stop beating so fast, and I needed to slow my breathing down because I was getting dizzy. I started washing my hands and got lost while staring at the water and suds going down the drain. I let the water run until it turned warm and kept my hands under the water as I closed my eyes and imagined that I was taking a bath. The warm water running over my hands was the bathwater, and I imagined myself lying back in the water and letting it cover me, just washing over my whole body. I stood there with the water running over my hands until it soothed me enough to calm me down and let me breathe again. I felt like I was able to breathe again, like the warm water brought me back to reality and calmed me down. I was okay; no one was even paying attention to me or what I was doing, so I could just calm down and relax.

I walked over to the doorway and peeked into the living room. Everyone was talking, laughing, and having a good time. They were doing the same thing that they were doing before I went into that bedroom, and they were doing the same thing still. I felt relieved knowing that they did not notice me panicking as I walked past them but felt sad at the same time. I guess something inside of me hoped that someone would see me and realize that something just happened to me, but no one noticed anything. I felt the same way that I did after my dad beat me for the first time, and I went into the world the next day thinking everyone would know. This was the exact same thing; I just thought someone would notice. I thought they would see something different about me. So many thoughts went through my mind as I stood in that doorway. I had so many questions that I would never have answers to. Did Candace or her brother have any idea what just happened in that bedroom? Did they know or even think there was a possibility that Martin would try to have sex with me? Did they know what was going to happen and think that it was okay? Did they think it was okay for me to go into that bedroom with Martin because they thought he just needed a massage? The questions were endless, and the answers were nonexistent, so there was no point in trying to figure anything out, at least not that night. The world wasn't stopping because of what just happened. It was a normal part of life. At least I thought it was at that time. I went and sat on the couch next to Candace. I smacked her leg as I plopped down, and we both laughed as if someone said something hilarious. As we sat there, she smiled at me, and it felt good to be back with her. It felt as if I had been gone for so long. We listened to her brother and his friends tell jokes and act so stupid as the night went on. Martin eventually came out of the bedroom. He looked like he had actually fallen asleep for a couple of hours. He just said goodbye to Brandon, never looked at me, and left. I was actually relieved when he left because I knew that with him gone, that wouldn't happen again. We didn't drink any more liquor that night, but enjoyed watching Brandon and his friends get drunk and act like fools. I didn't need to drink any more. I didn't want to. I just wanted to feel like a little kid again. I was happy with staying up all night, eating sugar mixed with Kool-Aid, and laughing till I couldn't laugh no more at Candace and her stupid jokes.

That night came and went like any other. When the morning came, I was relieved to be even further from what happened the night before. The sun shining through the side of the blinds was a small comfort as I woke up and realized that the thoughts in my mind weren't from a dream; they really happened. I looked over and watched Candace as she slept, and I wished I could have the innocence that she still had. Candace was years older than me, but she was still a child, and I wondered why I couldn't still be a child too. I leaned toward her to feel the warmth of her body and slid my foot under her blanket just to be closer to her. She was only inches away from me, but I was so alone. I wanted to just hug her so tight and tell her that I needed her. I replayed the night before in my mind several times as I tried to figure out how and why it all happened the way it did. I tried to figure out if there was a certain moment where I could have changed the direction of where Martin was leading me. I guess I would have had to know his intentions to know that I needed to change anything. I felt so stupid thinking about how I went into that room with a grown man and thought he would only want a massage. I used to think that I could trust older people. I thought that they were here to protect us, but I knew that that wasn't true—my dad and what he was doing to me, my family who let him, and now Martin along with a house full of people who let me go into a room alone with him. I wondered if there were any grown-ups who were good on the inside or if they were all bad and had no intentions of keeping us safe or doing right by us. My emotions were all over the place, and it was hard to say exactly how I felt that morning. I think my biggest emotion was disappointment. I was so disappointed with myself, but sadness closely followed. There were too many times when I could have said something or asked him to stop. He wasn't holding me down, he wasn't forcing himself on top of me, and he wasn't hurting me. I had sat there and listened to his every word as he flattered me, and I let him trick me into thinking that he cared about me. I was just a child, but I knew what was going on, and I could have stopped it at any time, but I didn't. The more I replayed it in my mind, the more I blamed myself for all of it, and I felt so ashamed. I couldn't even be mad at Martin, because I allowed it to happen, and I probably even unconsciously gave Martin signals that I wanted him to do it. He must have known that I was so alone inside, that I was broken and vulnerable. I lay there wondering if anything that Martin said to me was true or not. Did he think that I was beautiful and smart, and did he really think that I was special? I wanted to believe that he really felt that way about me, and I wanted to believe that what we shared was beautiful, but he didn't, and it wasn't.

I was smart enough to know that he probably only said all of those things to make me comfortable with him and so that I would trust him enough to not get scared. I wondered if he did this to other young girls or if he thought I was mature and only did this kind of thing with me. I couldn't stop replaying it all in my mind and wondered how it would have been different if I wouldn't have been so flattered by everything he had said to me. I also wondered if he had seen the loneliness and desperation in my eyes before we went into that bedroom and decided then that he was going to have sex with me. Or did he feel a connection with me as I massaged his back, or was he a predator, a man who preyed on young girls? After all of that, my emotions went from confused and naïve to angry and ashamed for what I allowed to happen to me. I had never even had a real boyfriend, so how could this have happened? It was because I was desperate for love, any kind of love, the love I didn't get and would never get from my parents. I was so messed up inside that it was affecting my life outside of my messed up house and everything that went on in it. I was so happy that Candace was still sleeping, because if she was awake, she would see my face and know that I was a mess. That morning, I came to a horrible realization about what kind of person I was already becoming, but I was too young to have any idea how to change it. I tried to stay still as long as I could. I must have lain there for an hour just thinking about everything over and over. I had to go to the bathroom so bad that I had to get up. I stood up quietly and stood very still, took a step, and stood still again. I almost made it to the door of the bedroom, but then the floor squeaked, and Candace moved around. I went around the corner as fast as I could and sat on the toilet without closing the door, hoping that if I was quiet enough, Candace would still be sleeping. I didn't even flush the toilet, because I needed Candace to stay sleeping, because I really needed more time by myself, with my thoughts. I needed to figure out how to process it all. I needed to know which emotion I was supposed to be feeling so I could start my day and move forward.

I walked back into the room, and Candace was sitting up and smiling at me. She looked so happy and refreshed as she stretched her arms into the air. I didn't think that I would be able to keep a straight face or leave all of the mess that was going on in my mind, but I did, and it made me feel so much better. Standing there in front of Candace, I felt like I stepped out of the chaos of my mind and right back into reality with her. I felt like I had been lost and Candace found me, and I was so happy to be with her that morning. I took a deep breath as I watched the sun shine through the corner of the sheet that was over her window just above her bed. I wasn't near it but felt like I could feel it's warmth on my face. I went over to the window and moved the sheet out of the way so I could feel the sun on my skin and smell the fresh air. It was warm outside, but since it was so early, it wasn't hot out yet, and that's when you could smell everything. In just a moment, you could smell the mulch and bushes that were next to the window on the side of Candace's house and the fresh-cut grass in the front yard that Brandon had mowed the day before. I could smell the chlorine from the pool they had in the backyard, the creek in between their yard, and the neighbors and the few tulips that hadn't been stepped on in the front of their house. I could hear bees, the frog that sat on a rock in the creek, and birds, all kinds of different birds. I don't know how I did it, but I managed to make it until that night without even thinking about telling Candace what had happened the night before. She was in the kitchen cleaning up and washing the dishes while I sat and watched TV in the living room. She was almost done and told me that we could go in her room and hang out, so I went in there and waited for her. I heard cabinets closing and the sink draining as I heard the back screen door slam shut and then heard her brother's voice. I lay back on the bed and was staring at the ceiling when Candace gave in and asked me if I wanted to drink with her brother again. I told her that I wasn't sure if I felt like it but told her that I might want to in a few hours. I didn't know if I even wanted to drink liquor again after everything that had happened the night before. I wasn't sure if us drinking liquor had anything to do with what happened to me, but I wasn't sure I wanted to take a chance. I felt like I was in the clear, because Candace didn't even ask me why I didn't want to drink; she was okay with my decision. I always liked that about her. She wasn't bossy, not at all, not ever. She was easy to be around, because you could be yourself around her and not have to try and make her happy. She was okay with you having different opinions on stuff, and she was okay with you liking rock music when she only liked country. She respected my decisions, and that made me feel comfortable, and it made me feel like she was okay with who I really was. Tiffany was my best friend, but she didn't share those same qualities that Candace had. She was pretty amazing, and I loved everything about her but couldn't quite be my true self with her. If I said I didn't want to do something, she would try to change my mind and sometimes keep talking about it until I changed my mind. She was always laughing and smiling when she did it, but sometimes, she did it so many times that it was too much. Most of the time, I just did what she wanted to do and told her I liked all the same stuff that she did even when I didn't. It's not that she was mean to me or aggressive about it; it just got tiring when she always tried to change my mind about everything. I think that was why I started hanging out with Candace more. Maybe because the more broken I became, I felt like Candace would be able to accept it better than Tiffany would.

We decided to play a game of cards, and the game War was our favorite most of the time because it took so long to play considering one person had to end up with the entire deck of cards. It was during that time that she told me that Brandon's friends were coming over again. My heart started to be faster, and I could feel blood rush to my face, and I tried to breathe normally as I asked Candace which friends would be coming over. I tried so hard to keep a normal facial expression but had no idea if I was or not because I was uncomfortable. She said it would probably be the same group as the night before, and I felt like I was punched in the throat as she said it. I got that knot in my throat that you get when you need to cry, but I wasn't even sure if I needed to cry. I held onto my emotions as strongly as I could. I tried to casually ask if Martin would be one of the friends whom Brandon had coming over. She told me that she wasn't sure, but she figured that he was, because Brandon said he had the same people coming over again. I was caught off guard. I guess I didn't think that I would have to see him the very next day. It had taken me so long to step out of the chaos and confusion of my mind that I hadn't even once thought about having to see Martin again. All the thoughts that I had all night and morning came flooding back all at once, and in that moment, I felt like I was going to explode. I tried to take a deep breath and tell myself that everything was okay, that I could figure this out. I felt like the room was getting smaller and hotter as I tried to quickly calm myself down, but it wasn't working. Candace knew something was wrong, because I'm sure that the look on my face said it all, not to mention that I couldn't look directly at her. She asked me why I cared if Martin came over or not, and this was the part I had never even thought about, because I promised I wouldn't tell anyone. I hadn't planned on telling anyone, not just because Martin made me promise but because I was too ashamed. I planned on just forgetting all about it. I guess I thought that I could just move forward and not look back. I didn't plan on having to face this, especially not that soon, so I hadn't thought about exactly how I would say it. I wanted to run away, get as far away from Candace as I could, away from that bedroom and from the memories of the night before. I tried to casually tell Candace that I didn't care about who came over and that I was just asking if he was coming over. She sat there staring at me, and I couldn't quite read her facial expression but hoped that she would be satisfied with my response. Her facial expression changed from a neutral expression to more of a concerned or even upset expression, and I knew that I was going to have to tell her. The hardest part was finding the right words and talking even though I had a horrible knot in my throat and wanted to cry. I tried one more time to get myself out of having to tell her the full truth on why I was asking if Martin was coming over, but it didn't work. It was too late for that. She knew that there was something going on, and I wasn't going to be able to keep it a secret like I had planned.

I told her every single detail of what occurred right after I had given Martin a massage, and the more I talked, the better I started to feel. I didn't make direct eye contact with her as I spoke. I just stared down at the cards that I was holding in my hand. I looked at them so I would stay calm. I just slowly shuffled through them one by one as I tried to focus on the color or type of card it was. I was only able to do that for so long, because after telling Candace about all the sweet things that Martin said to me, I then had to tell her some very uncomfortable details. It was hard to find the right way to explain everything to her without fully knowing how I felt about it. Should I explain it in a way that I sounded like I wanted it to happen and that I thought Martin really liked me and made me feel wanted? Or should I explain it in a way where Martin was more like a pedophile that molested a ten-year-old girl. I tried as hard as I could to just tell her what happened, just the plain facts without adding my confused emotions into it. She didn't say one word the entire time as I explained everything to her. She just sat there in silence. I hadn't looked up at her at all, so I wasn't sure what her face looked like or what emotion she appeared to have. Telling Candace what had happened felt good. It was exactly what I needed, and I didn't care that Martin made me promise not to tell anyone. I said what I needed to say. I took a deep breath, and I looked up at Candace to find comfort or reassurance that everything would be okay. She had always been good at that, good at making me still have hope inside of me even after my dad tried so hard to beat it all out. I thought that Candace was hurt by what I had just told her. Because of the look that she had on her face, I thought that she was hurt that this happened to me. That's not what was happening. She told me that I was probably dreaming and there's no way that Martin would have done that to me. She said that she was pretty sure that he had a girlfriend and that there was no way he would do that kind of stuff with a little girl when he had a girlfriend. Was she implying that I wasn't good enough for him, or maybe she was saying that I was too young for him? I told her how I gave him a massage after we went into her bedroom. I told her every detail of what happened after we walked into that bedroom. I don't know how the very specific details that I just told her didn't grab her attention. How could I just make something like that up? She asked me why I didn't tell her last night and why I waited so long to bring this up, but it was hard to explain why I didn't. I didn't even know how to explain something like that. How could I explain to her that I thought Martin liked me and that at first I thought that what Martin was doing was normal? Would she understand that because I thought he cared about me, that I let it happen and don't know why? I didn't fully understand why I allowed it to happen, so I couldn't fully explain it to her even if I really tried. Maybe I was the bad guy in this situation. Maybe I somehow unconsciously seduced him and made him want to do those kinds of things to me.

Candace's face was enough to make me just drop the subject even though I needed to talk about it. After trying to tell her what happened to me and her not believing me, I lost all trust in her. In an instant, she betrayed me like everyone else—like my dad, my mom, and my grandma. My mom was able to sit and watch my dad beat me, my grandma was able to hear about it and not care, and now Candace was able to not care about her brother's friend molesting me. I would have never in a million years have guessed that Candace was one of those people who could just ignore something so serious, one of those horrible people. For someone else, they might not be able to handle one of their best friends not believing them about something so serious, but I was used to disappointment in the people around me. I was used to everyone around me, whether it be family or friends who failed me and let me down. They all allowed me to be hurt, so why not Candace? It hurt and broke my heart, but I couldn't be too surprised by it.

After that, Candace didn't mention any of it again, but her attitude toward me was different. She was distant and seemed like she was annoyed by what I told her, and that didn't go away. I could only deal with a couple of hours of that, so that night, I went home even though I was supposed to stay there for one more night. I could feel that Candace no longer wanted me there and was mad at me for what I told her. Maybe she didn't want to believe that something so horrible could occur in her house without her knowing about it. Maybe she wanted to believe that Martin wouldn't do something like that, because he was a good person or because he was such a good friend of Brandon's. So many questions filled my mind as I lay in my bed that night, and I couldn't help but to feel like I had done something wrong. How could one of my best friends not believe me when it came to something so serious? The day before, Candace was one of my best friend's, someone I thought I could trust and someone I thought would always be on my side. That day, everything was different. She was now on the list of people who let me down and acted as if I didn't matter to them. She was now just like my mom and my grandma. Like them, she wanted to just pretend that something horrible didn't just happen. I couldn't stop thinking about her face and how her eyes looked after I told her what happened. They both became so cold. I couldn't understand how she could listen to the details of what happened and not have any other response than that I must have been dreaming or that Martin wouldn't do something like that. It was like she didn't want to believe it, because if she believed it, then she would have to have that in her mind as something that happens in the world. I wondered if she just didn't want to believe that something like that could happen so close to her. Maybe it would shatter her view on the world or at least the world directly around her. Maybe it was too much for her to accept. Maybe it was just way too close for her, this happening to one of her friends, in her house and being done by one of her brother's friends.

As if I wasn't miserable enough, the next day, Candace called to tell me that her parents were home and they wanted to talk to me. By the sound of her voice and being let down enough, I knew that her parents weren't inviting me over to be sympathetic about what happened to me that weekend. At that point in my life, I wasn't stupid enough to think that her parents would offer support or a shoulder to cry on. I wasn't that stupid anymore. I could hear my heart beating so loud as I walked down the street to Candace's house, and if she wasn't already standing outside the door waiting, I might not have gone in. Her face said enough as soon as I saw her, and she didn't even say hello, so I already knew what I was about to walk into. Her parents were both sitting in the living room together waiting, and her dad never sat anywhere besides at his spot at the kitchen table. Candace not believing me about what had happened that weekend was enough to prepare me for whatever they had to say. I figured it would be a combination of what had happened with Martin and us drinking that her parents wanted to talk about. Her mom looked so angry, and even though I knew that I was somehow being blamed for this, it still hurt to see her look so angry. Her mom wasn't the most cheerful person. She actually was kind of grouchy most of the time, but she was a good person. She may have been grouchy, but she was a good mom, and I knew that if I ever needed something, I could talk to her. Candace's mom and dad were both like that. They worked a lot, so maybe that's why they weren't usually in the best of moods, but they were still good on the inside. They both had shown me a lot of support with what I was going through with my parents, and I had always been able to tell that they genuinely cared about me. Her mom shook her head as she looked at the ground, and it made me nervous the way she was avoiding eye contact with me. The way she shook her head and looked at the ground was something I had seen so many times before. Her mom said that they said that they were both very disappointed with me for my behavior when they were gone on their trip. Her dad said that I was the only person they ever trusted to be in their house while they were away and that they did that to help me. They reminded me of what I told them my dad was doing to me and said that they were trying to help me escape that even if it was only for a couple of weeks. As if I needed a reminder of what was happening at home or what my dad was doing to me, I was the one who was going through it. Candace's mom said that Candace told her everything about how we had been drinking. She said that drinking at our age was not acceptable and that she really hoped that I would never do something like this again. The saddest and most upsetting part was that neither one of her parents asked me about what happened to me; Candace didn't even tell them.

As we were sitting there, Candace's brother, Brandon, walked in and shook his head at us. The seconds that it took for him to walk past me felt so long as he stared at me and gave me the meanest look he possibly could. Right before he got to his bedroom door, he turned around and told his parents that we were annoying kids who drank by ourselves. He mumbled something under his breath, grabbed his doorknob so hard that you could hear it rattle, and then went in and slammed his door. I couldn't help but to wonder about what exactly Candace told her parents and brother for them all to be acting like that. I had to hold back my tears. I wanted so badly to cry. It was confusing to have everyone treat me like I had done something wrong when something so horrible had happened to me. I would be able to understand them being upset if they knew what went on between Martin and me, but I couldn't understand them being upset about us drinking. Candace's mom said that she knew how hard things were for me at home but drinking at my age wasn't okay, wasn't right. I wanted to scream and just run away when those words came out of her mouth, and it was so hard for me to sit there and keep listening to her. Candace's dad mumbled something under his breath a few times, and all I could hear were a couple of cuss-words, but his face summed it all up. They both told me that I wasn't allowed there for a long time and that they would let me know when they thought it would be okay for me to come over again. Candace's dad said that they would talk later and decide if they were going to call and talk to my parents about it. I left that house having not just one person against me but a whole family against me at ten years old. I held my breath for days every time the phone rang and imagined what I would do if it was them calling, but they never did. The decent people that were somewhere inside of them didn't want to be the reason that my dad was beating me, so I am almost positive that's why they never called. I told myself for weeks that it didn't bother me. I tried convincing myself that Candace and her whole family were garbage, but I still felt horrible about what happened. That wouldn't be the last time that I would be let down by the people around me or by people whom I thought I could trust. After that, when my dad would hit me, I would think about what I did with Martin and tell myself that I was being punished for being so dirty.

That summer started off so bad but would later get better for me in a strange way. For a few weeks after that, my dad started acting very nice to me. He smiled more, and he actually started spending more time in the house instead of in his shed. It was really nice. I would sit on the couch and watch TV with him, mostly the History Channel. It was exactly what I needed after what happened with Martin just weeks before. I even started going places with my dad, just normal stores mostly, and out to eat a couple of times. We went and visited his parents a couple of times a week, and it was nice, just me and him, father and daughter. Just as fast as his loving behavior came, it left. Around that time was when I finally released the long-held secret about knowing that I was adopted. One afternoon, my dad came home looking very angry. He looked like he was back to his old self. He and my mom started arguing, and my mom brought me into it like she always did. Most of the times when my dad beat me, well, at least half of the times, it was because of my mom. She hated when he was angry with her, so she would change the subject to me not listening to her or to me misbehaving when my dad was at work. Then the whole conversation would jump to me, just like that. I knew that it happened like that, because even when I wasn't in the room with them, I could usually hear them from my room. My dad would scream my name, or my mom would yell at me to come out of my room, and then that's how it would start.

My dad would say that I was being disrespectful no matter what I said to him. Then he would start grabbing me, pushing me, and hitting me. Just like that, just like that my mom would shift the misery and anger from her to me. That day, my dad started beating me pretty good. He kept pushing me into the edge of the counter, and it was so painful. Our kitchen counter was like an L shape, so the long portion was against the back wall of the kitchen with the sink in the middle of it. It had all the normal kitchen appliances on it and a small TV at the end right before it curved out into a sort of table-like area. That area that came out in the L-like shape had lost some of the laminate; well, most of the laminate on the front edge of it was gone. With the laminate being gone from that area, it was rough, unsanded, and unfinished wood under it. That seemed to be my dad's favorite area to slam and push me against, and I am not sure if it was because it was rough or just because it was there. On that particular day, he slammed me into that rough edge of the counter for maybe the third time, and that's when my anger started to rise more than normal. I think it might have been because I had really hoped that my dad wouldn't start hitting me again, and I had really wanted to have a good relationship with him. I had been trying so hard to not give my dad even the slightest reason to hate me or want to hit me. I talked to him like a loving and sweet girl every time I was around him. I would even act intrigued by whatever he was talking about and ask questions like I thought it was so interesting. I had this idea in my head of being daddy's little girl, and I had almost convinced myself that it was all going to work, but I was wrong. I was wrong, and it angered me. That third time he slammed me into the cabinet, my shirt must have risen up, because it was wood-to-skin contact that I felt. I quickly got around my dad and was then standing in the middle of the kitchen and the living room with both my mom and dad staring at me from each side.

My mom had been sitting on the couch just watching the whole time. Sometime during my dad hitting, she might have mumbled something, but I wasn't sure. The anger was rising, and I felt like I was burning up. I told them that I hated them with a smile on my face. I laughed, and I put my hand on my forehead as I tried to gather my thoughts about the situation. I bent over and put my hands on my knees in an attempt to brace myself, and then I just laughed. My dad came across the room and grabbed me by my arm and pushed me to the ground and then started hitting my butt and back. That was always how my dad attempted to spank me, or at least I told myself that he meant to spank me, but then he closed his hands.

Where he was hitting me on my back was where the counter scraped me, so it burned and felt like it was shocking me. He kept smacking and hitting me there, so I quickly rolled over and used my legs to push myself away from him. I got away and was able to get off the floor. Then I went toward the wall in between the kitchen and living room and held onto it. That's when I said it—that's when I told them that they were not even my parents and that I hated them. I told them that I didn't care if they hated me, and I told my dad that he could beat me every day, and it didn't matter, because he wasn't my dad. I felt the room stand still as I said those words. It was like the air even stood perfectly still, and then they just looked at me. My mom had been looking through a tabloid magazine the whole time, but she looked up and sat the magazine down when she heard me words. My dad just stood there as if he was frozen, just frozen right where he stood. His mouth was slightly open and one foot in front of the other like he had been about to take a step but then just froze. They, of course, first asked me how I knew, and I told them that my cousins told me when I was younger, in first grade maybe. They started rambling in an attempt to apologize for not telling me and told me that they wanted to wait until I was older to talk to me about it. I told them that they were stupid for even caring about that and that it made no sense, because my dad constantly beat me. I told them that it was okay; I told them that I knew they hated me and had only adopted me because they thought they couldn't have kids. I told them that I knew they hated having to look at me every day after having their own kids and that they hated being stuck with a kid with brown hair and brown eyes. I told them that if I ever found my real parents, I would leave and never ever come back. That's when some of the biggest lies my parents would ever tell me spewed from their evil mouths. They said my parents were heroin addicts who abandoned me, that they left me and never came back to get me. They both went on and on about how my real parents wanted nothing to do with me and didn't care about me. I felt like they reached into my body, grabbed my heart, and then ripped it out. I felt a feeling that I had never felt before, a sick but sad and so lonely and hurt feeling deep inside of me. My heart ached at that moment. It hurt so bad that I felt like I couldn't breathe, but I couldn't let them see that.

My mom told me that my biological mom couldn't take care of me and left me alone in an apartment with my older sister and someone found us there. She said that my mom had a choice to get me back but never even tried to, because she didn't want to. She told me that my dad was in prison at that time and that no one was even sure if my dad was really my dad, because my mom was a drug addict. My mom told me that my real mom could have gotten me back but did not, that she didn't even try at all. My parents told me that was how they got me and that my grandma wasn't my grandma, she was my real dad's sister, so she was really my aunt. So my parents were really my cousins, and that was how they got me. They told me that I had an older sister, a younger sister, and a younger brother and that they all lived with my real mom and dad. My dad looked at me with a smirk and said that my biological parents got my other siblings back but did not care about getting me back. It was about an hour of that, that hateful and derogatory talk about my real parents. They made it very clear that my parents would never want to meet me. It was confusing to hear everything they were saying, but I didn't lose hope. My hope was still there. I would find my parents one day, and they would want me. They would love me and want me. I couldn't hear them say any more hurtful things about my real parents, so I changed the subject. I asked if I had any other family members who lived near us, and they told me that I had an aunt. A real aunt, my aunt Sarah, and that she was my mom's sister and lived just a couple of hours away with her family. When I heard that, I felt this warmth in my heart, this tiny bit of warmth that I hoped could grow. My mom said that most of my real family lived down south, about five hours from where we lived. My mom said that my aunt Sarah had been wanting to meet me and went to a drawer in the kitchen and gave me a little piece of paper with her number on it. That little piece of paper was a beige color but looked like it had once been a white piece of notebook paper that had been in that drawer so long that it changed colors. That little piece of paper brought me great excitement. The numbers were in my grandma's handwriting, so I figured she must have been the one who last talked to her. I didn't know my aunt Sarah yet, but I knew that she would bring me some kind of hope to my sad life. That turned out to be true.

Within a week or two of talking to my aunt, they came and picked me up. My aunt was married, and her husband, my uncle Will, was just as wonderful as she was, and it felt so good to be with them. When I first saw both of them, I knew in my heart that they were good people, just good on the inside and the outside. It only took a glance to see that they were not bad people like my parents. Their hearts were good and kind. When I first saw them, it was like they were appearing to me as angels, like in the movies, angels with light beaming on them. I probably had never been happier in my life than when I met my aunt and uncle, and the best part was that they were mine. They were my family, not my adoptive family; they were my real family, so I knew they would love me. They took me to their house. It was about two hours away in this cute little town, and their house was just as cute as the town was. My aunt and uncle had two children. My cousin Will was my age, and my cousin Eric was a few years younger. They were great to me. They were the ideal family, the family in my dreams that I always wished that I could have had or at least been a part of. The best part of it was that I could feel that my aunt was my real family. I could feel and even see my real mom through her. She treated me like I mattered, like I was important mentally and emotionally. She cared how I felt, asked me questions, and actually cared that I ate every meal and liked it. My aunt was different from anyone else I had ever been around. She acted so differently, and her house was different too. She talked about God and being a Christian, and I felt something inside of me when she spoke about it. My aunt looked in my eyes when she told me that God loved me and that I was special to him. She even told me that he had a plan already made for me. My uncle and my cousins were Christians too. At the time, I just saw it as that they were nice, that they were good people. That is what I made of it all, that being a Christian meant believing in God and being a good person and being kind to everyone. I had never met people like that—people who were kind to you for no reason, people who didn't have selfish or deceptive motives. I had never been in a house that felt like theirs. Most people's houses lack trust, lack happiness. Most people's houses feel like they are missing something important. I had never been in a home that didn't involve kids being spanked or hit when they did something wrong or been in a house where they prayed before eating or going to bed. At first, it kind of made me feel strange, almost upset because I didn't understand it or feel like I was really a part of it. At first, I felt like an outsider looking in or an intruder disrupting their happy Christian lives. I kept expecting my aunt and uncle to want something from me. I kept thinking that their kindness came at a price, because I had never experienced anything like it before.

When my aunt prayed with me, I wanted to cry and tell her what my life was like and what my dad was doing to me at home. I wanted so badly to tell her the details of my misery and abuse at the hands of my dad. I wanted her to know that the smiles my mom gave her when she picked me up were fake and that my mom allowed me to be abused constantly. I wanted so badly to ask my aunt Sarah to help me, but I didn't want to ruin my visit with her or ruin getting to see her again. If I told her and she said something to my mom or dad, then I was sure they would never let me see her or my uncle or my cousins again. It wasn't just that. Their family was so perfect. They were so happy and lacking any chaos or any of the things that I hated about my life. I did not want to be the person to put that in their lives. I didn't want to give them chaos. I didn't want to add conflict into their lives. They were happy, they were kind, and they had amazing Christian lives; and I didn't want to mess that up. I told myself to push all of that down and to enjoy my time with my real family. I told myself that my first visit with them was not the time to tell them anything about what my dad was doing to me. My visit with them was one of the happiest times of my life, and each day was just as good as the last. My aunt Sarah, uncle Will, and cousins William and Eric were all so good to me; and I fell in love with each of them so quickly. From the very first day, they didn't feel like strangers. They felt like my family. During my stay with them, my aunt kept telling me that she had so much that she needed to tell me but it just wasn't the right time yet. I tried to talk to my aunt about what my parents told me about my real parents, but that was how she answered: she said it wasn't the right time. She later told me that when I was old enough and the time was right, she would tell me so much about my real mom and dad. She told me that my parents loved me and that one day she could tell me so much more. I normally wouldn't believe something like that, but she had tears in her eyes when she said it, and something told me that I could trust her. My aunt had baby pictures of me. When I looked at them, it felt so weird because I then realized I had never seen baby pictures of myself. Then I felt stupid. I never paid enough attention to the fact that my parents didn't even have newborn or baby pictures of me. On the wall in the hallway of our house, there were so many pictures of us, hospital newborn pictures of my brother and sister, but not of me. I was so dumb and unaware of something that noticeable, something right in front of my face. Even after my cousins had told me that I was adopted, I still hadn't noticed that or looked through any albums to see that what they were saying was true. I didn't continue to push my aunt for answers around my birth or adoption. I felt like she was telling me that she had all of those answers, but that I wasn't old enough. The fun I had while I was there distracted me but in a good way. My cousins were like the best friends I always wanted. I had best friends in my neighborhood but not like my cousins. We laughed and laughed about anything and everything. We put spoons on our noses and jumped their trampoline until we were completely out of energy. The weeks I spent with them went so fast, and each night before I fell asleep, I dreaded that I was one day closer to having to go back home. My aunt asked me every day if I wanted to call my mom. She said it was okay if I missed my family or if I was home sick. I had to just look at the floor and tell her that I was okay when she said that. If I looked her in the eyes, she would be able to see the pain, so I just looked at the floor. I went to my aunt and uncle's house alone in the world, and I left there knowing that I had a family that loved me. On my last night there, I cried harder than I had ever cried before. Going back home was going to be so hard, but at least I met my real family.

When I got back home, it was like my mom and dad were mad that I had gone to my aunt and uncle's house. They didn't say it, but it was like they hated them. My dad later said that my aunt Sarah was a drug addict like my real mom but thought she's better than everyone now because she's some kind of Christian. My dad called her a Bible thumper. He said that people like her think that everything they do is forgiven if they go around shoving stuff about God down your throat. He said that my uncle was just as goofy as she was, thinking that they were going to be able to run away from who they really were. I wanted to jump across the room and punch him in his face and scream at him to just shut his dirty mouth for once. My dad was a monster. How dare he talk about someone like my aunt or my uncle? At least they try to be good people. My dad probably never in his life cared about being a good person or a good father, or even a good husband. I refused to listen to anything he had to say about my real family. I just acted like I listened and cared. I just said, "Okay," and walked away after his hateful conversations. Almost every time my dad opened his mouth, something hateful came out, something racist, something negative, something hurtful or just unnecessary. I already knew he was going to hit me worse after going there. I could feel it; he was going to try and beat whatever happiness they gave me right out of me, and he did. It didn't matter, though. I was never going to forget that I had a real family out there and that they were not evil like the people I had to grow up thinking were my real family.

Before school started back, I decided that I was going to become someone different. I didn't want to look like everybody else around me anymore. I was different on the inside, so I was going to be different on the outside, too, because it made sense. I needed to feel better about myself, and I was tired of living in other people's shadows and following trends that everyone else did. I was never good at or even able to follow all the latest trends because my parents didn't have the money, and even if they did, they wouldn't be spending it on me. I was never able to have name-brand shoes or clothes, so I always looked stupid trying to follow trends or look like them. I wanted to be myself and feel good about it, so I was going to create my own style, and other people could follow me for a change. I decided I was going to do the opposite of what everyone else was doing, the opposite of crisp new clothes and shoes and the opposite of what was sold in every local department store. I talked my mom into taking me to the thrift store with her every week by telling her that she didn't have to buy me any new clothes for school. She didn't mind. She went to the thrift store once or twice a week already, so that made it easy at being able to get everything I needed for the new look.

That summer, I had heard some of the music that my friend Tiffany's sister Theresa was always listening to, and I really liked it. Rock, grunge, and alternative music became my new thing; and it helped distract me from everything else around me. I decided to dress the part, dress like the people in my favorite bands did, and I loved it. At that time, Nirvana was so popular. Their music and style inspired me to just be me and create a style that made me feel good about myself. Nirvana started an entire trend, a whole new style that I knew right away I wanted because I loved Nirvana. I got old ripped jeans and corduroy pants, faded oversized T-shirts and sweaters, and weathered black leather boots. Instead of putting my hair up in a ponytail, I left it down, parted it down the middle. and left it messy. No more looking like the other kids or trying to look like them. I found my new style, and I was so happy with it. I was absolutely in love with the singer and guitar player from Nirvana, a popular grunge rock band from the '90s that created a whole new style of music. The singer, Kurt Cobain, became my idol. When I heard him sing, I could get lost in his music. I could not only hear but feel his voice, and I could close my eyes and feel his pain through his songs. I felt like our pain flowed together even though he was a celebrity whom I didn't even know, but I felt connected to him somehow. His music soothed me. Even when he screamed in the louder songs, it comforted me and sort of let me embrace my pain. Nirvana not only started a new trend in music but in style as well, and I loved it. I felt like Kurt Cobain was on the same level as me, like his voice and lyrics reached out and grabbed a hold of me. The whole band all wore old jeans that were all ripped up, old and kind of retro sweaters, and old comfy sneakers or leather boots. I felt like their style was exactly what I needed. It helped me express myself, and I felt good doing it. It was a style that you could do without having parents who had a lot of money, and you could actually get most of it at the thrift store. With my mom going to the thrift store on a regular basis, she didn't mind me going, and I was able to get so much stuff for this new grunge style. Plus, I think that my mom appreciated me wanting clothes that only cost her a few dollars and allowed her to save hundreds of dollars on school shopping. Nirvana allowed me to not need everyone around me anymore. It allowed me to be free and to finally start feeling good about myself. I couldn't wait for the kids at school to see me. They would get to see me being myself and not the ugly and miserable follower that I had always been before that summer. They would finally see that I didn't need them or their style, and they would see that my pain didn't need to be embarrassing, because it was beautiful. I didn't want to be ashamed anymore, ashamed of how bad my homelife was and how bad everything had gotten in my mind in the last few years. The new music that I had discovered allowed me to do that. It made being a broken person not feel so bad anymore. It made you feel like being an outcast; everyone else didn't matter. The rest of the world, the perfect and mainstream followers, should be the outcasts.

I was so sick and tired of being in the hands of people who didn't care about me. I was tired of being hurt and let down by people who were supposed to help me or support me in life. It was that summer that I decided that I was going to love and take care of myself. I was going to love and comfort myself as I embraced my loneliness and pain. I started fifth grade with more confidence and self-esteem than I had ever had, and I was no longer that girl who was desperate for friends or anyone's approval. I walked through the hallways without even looking around me that year, and I walked without a doubt in my mind that I didn't need any in that school to like me. It's funny how the world works, and it's just too hard to figure it all out without going completely crazy. When you're nice and want friends, you don't get any, but the second you act like you want nothing to do with anyone, then suddenly the possibility of friends is everywhere. Kids who never even noticed me, and probably never knew I existed, were saying hi to me every day in the hallways. In class, they asked me how my summer was and then told me all about what they did or where they went on vacation. Everyone looked at my clothes as I walked through the hall, and I could hear them whisper to each other, and for the first time, it wasn't bad or hurtful stuff. I could hear them tell one another to look at my boots or to look at the new style that I had started. I liked it, but in the back of my mind, I didn't forget how all of those kids had looked at me like I was garbage every year before that one. It felt good to look around at the other kids and know that I no longer was trying to follow them; I was no longer a follower. I even stopped trying to hang out with the kids in my neighborhood so much. They were good friends, but I felt like they thought I was always trying to be like them. I still hung out with Tiffany on the weekends, but I no longer was so desperate for her approval with everything that I did.

With the chaos that constantly filled the walls of our house, my mom was possibly looking for help, because she took us to a church that year. Either my mom did think our family needed help, or it was yet another move to try and make herself look good. It was different, it felt strange, but something about that place intrigued me. There was something about the shape of the ceiling, tall and pointed so the music just filled it. The windows had stained glass. They were absolutely beautiful when the sun was shining through them. The front of the area where we sat was just as beautiful. It had so much to look at. I just couldn't stop looking at it. All the way to the far back wall directly in front of us, there were steps that went up, and then you could see them going back down but through a glass tank. It was a small pool. It was where they baptized people who wanted to be a permanent Christian or permanently go to that church. In front of that and to the side, there was a piano, a big and very expensive-looking piano that they used for the songs. In front of that, there was a long table that was full of white flowers, several different kinds; and in between, there were white and purple candles. In front of that table, there was a tall skinny desk that the pastor stood when he spoke to us, and it was a rich brown color that matched the benches that we sat on. The walls were halfway paneled with that wood. The trim and the whole ceiling had the same rich-brown shade of wood. Next to where the pastor stood, there were tall wooden crosses with white wood or stone in the center of them. Above all of it, there were these huge clothes flowing down from the ceiling and falling around that whole front area. Next to that, on each side, there were these huge white vertical banners that had purple crosses on them. They matched the purple candles on the table. Like I said, it was intriguing, and it was a magical feeling when you were right in the middle of it. When all the people were singing, I looked around. I looked for anything that might mean that God was there. If God was really there or answered prayers, I needed him to help me fast. I wanted that church to help me. I wanted to know God or Jesus like they talked about.

A few times, I went to Sunday school, while my mom went to the main service, because I thought I would make friends. I thought that a church would accept me, but they didn't; well, at least the children didn't. The kids in Sunday school were all so clean looking with nice haircuts, wore neat and fancy clothes with matching shoes, and had fancy attitudes to match. Every time the Sunday school teacher asked a question about a Bible verse, every one of them raised their hands. The teacher would read us chapters of the Bible and then discuss it with us and relate it to our lives. When he read from the Bible, it made no sense to me. I tried to focus real hard, but it sounded like he was speaking a different language. I would look around at each of the kids and just admire the way they looked and talked. The stuff they knew was pretty awesome. The way they just knew what the teacher was always talking about, no matter where he was in the Bible, was amazing. The Bible is so big, but somehow, no matter what part the teacher read from, they knew all about it. The first time I went to that class, I daydreamed that all the kids would help me learn the Bible, tell me that God could help me, and teach me stuff. That would have been nice, but it never happened. At first, the kids seemed curious of me, but they were so confused by how I didn't know any of the stuff they knew about the Bible. I hoped I would fit in eventually, and maybe even one of the kids would pull me aside and help me learn the Bible. That also never happened.

After a few times of going to the Sunday school class without a Bible and without being able to answer any Bible-related questions, the teacher asked me to stay after class. It wasn't just that I didn't know any of the chapters of the Bible. I wouldn't have even been able to tell you what the Bible was, who wrote it, or even who was in it. It was sad but true. My mom brought me to a place that she never even prepared us for. Never, not even one time, did she ever talk about God or talk to us about God. I didn't even know what all this church stuff was. I didn't even have a clue who God was. He smiled and told me that he was happy that I joined his class and asked me if I could bring my Bible next time. I told him that I did not have a Bible, and he said that it was very important that I get one so I could get caught up with what he had been teaching. He asked me what they had been teaching at my last church, and I just looked at him. He laughed and told me he, of course, knew what they were teaching. He meant what chapter of the Bible or lesson we had been working on. He wanted to know what chapter I had read when I had never even seen a Bible before that class. How great. I had to tell him that this was all new to me and that my family had never gone to church. Instead of telling me it was okay, he said I would have to get a Bible fast and spend quite a bit of time catching myself up. He seemed a bit aggravated that I had never been to a church, but it was okay; I could get all caught up. He told me the types of Bibles I could get and told me they sold them there at the church gift shop. Just as fast as my hopes went up, they were shattered when my mom told me that we didn't have money for stuff like that. She also told me that I couldn't have one, because if my dad found out we were going to church, there would be serious problems. I tried to explain to her how I knew nothing about anything that they talked about. She paid attention to nothing that I said. She acted as if I was mumbling about childish issues. Our churchgoing ended just as quickly as it started when my dad found out that we had been going behind his back. Just like that, it was over. The God whom everyone always talked about was out of my reach.

With my parents having even more to fight about, I often took walks around the block or went down to my grandma's house. At her house, my uncle James was often there. I had seen him quite a few times in the past few months, and he always asked me to come over. I usually just said, "Okay," because I thought he was just asking me to come over to be polite. I was hurting so bad inside, so one day when he asked, I said yes. He wasn't just being polite, because he told me to pack a bag and he would pick me up that Friday afternoon. When I was younger, I spent a few weekends at my uncle's house because he was dating a lady who had two daughters. Even the younger daughter was several years older than me, but my uncle kept asking me to come over and spend time with them. I think he wasn't sure how to do the whole family thing at that time in his life, but it was nice seeing him with a woman and kids in his house. He normally stayed in his big farmhouse all alone, just him and his black cats. His house was out in the middle of nowhere, very few houses anywhere around, just cornfields as far as you could see. I was a lot younger the last time I spent more than an hour around my uncle, so I kind of forgot what he was really like. Sure enough, that Friday, he came to pick me up, just like he said. He was excited for me to come and stay with him and his girlfriend, Mary. They had been together when they were younger and decided to get back together, and he seemed happy and relaxed with her. Very quickly, I realized how awesome my uncle was. When he picked me up, he was listening to Nirvana. Out of all the music he could be listening to, he was listening to my favorite band, the band that was my life. I told him I was completely in love with Nirvana. I told him my favorite songs, albums, and lyrics. He knew everything I was talking about and knew of all the alternative bands that I liked, and he liked them all too. He had me listen to a bunch of bands and songs that I had never even heard of, and a lot of them were pretty good. Finally, someone who not only listened to but felt the music like I did. At his house, he had tons of CDs. He sat on the floor in front of the CD case as he looked through it for the ones he thought I might like. Most of his favorites were ones that I hadn't heard of or just hadn't listened to. One of his favorites was the Depeche Mode. He loved them in the same way that I loved Nirvana. He had his favorite songs, guitar riffs and lyrics that he was passionate about, and I was absolutely amazed. His house was warm and inviting, not like it used to be, not even when his other girlfriend lived there for a while. It was a lot different now, not a single-man's house but more like a family lived there.

Mary and James treated me well. Right away, they both treated me like I was a human being. They looked me in the eyes when they spoke to me and actually waited for me to respond. My parents acted as if everything about me was bothering them. They barely looked me in my face when they talked, definitely not my eyes, and never cared to hear what I said back. Most of the time, when I talked, they said it was talking back. Me talking to them normally was too much for them, so they would say I was talking back to them. It was great talking to them. We had so many conversations about all kinds of stuff. I sat on the couch talking to my uncle James while Mary made dinner. He asked and talked to me about everything that my dad should have. He told me I was turning into a beautiful young lady and asked me about what was going on in my life. I didn't want to sound desperate, so I tried not to sound desperate and go on and on after every single question. We laughed and ate, smiled as we passed food around to each other, and acted like a family. It was so nice, just so nice to have that, especially because I really needed it. After dinner, I would stay in the kitchen and help Mary clear the table. We talked just like I did with my uncle as we cleaned up. She treated me just as nice as he did. She asked me all kinds of questions and was genuinely interested to hear my response. There was a little pantry area in the kitchen. Mary smoked cigarettes, and she would sit in there to do it. She said she was trying to quit, and she didn't want to smoke around her daughter or my uncle James. Most people whom I had been around looked old and gross when they smoked, but she didn't; she looked sophisticated. My uncle didn't like cigarettes, and Mary was a good girlfriend and mom to smoke in the pantry. It really made me see how disrespectful my grandma and dad were, always smoking in the car with us and waiting to roll the windows down. They didn't even care about us breathing in the smoke. They didn't care whether or not we wanted them to smoke by us. Mary was different, a different kind of person who had respect for her family and others. It was wonderful to get away from my house and visit them. They were so happy and alive.

My uncle James would bring up my dad sometimes. He would always start off the conversation by telling me that they used to be good friends and that he knew him before my mom did. He would say that he wasn't sure what my mom saw in that guy, because all he did was party when my mom started dating him. That's what my uncle used to be into in his younger days, heavy drinking and drug use. He grew up and became an adult, a real adult who spent time with his family and didn't spend all his time doing drugs in a shed. He said that a few times my grandma briefly mentioned that things were a little intense between me and my dad. I tried to hold most of it back because I didn't want to sound like a victim. I didn't want him to think that I was expecting him to save me from my dad. I kept it simple and just said that my dad got mad at a lot of stuff that I did and spanked me a lot. I told him that I didn't like him but then changed the subject. He told me if my dad got too out of line that I could call him. After that, I asked them if I could take a bath. They told me that the bathtub was very stained from the well water, but I was welcomed to take a bath if I liked. I went into the bathroom full of both relief and sadness—relief because I, at least, got to tell my uncle and Mary part of what was happening and sadness that I didn't tell them all of what was happening. The relief disappeared the more I thought about not telling them everything and the sadness remained but then quickly turned into anger. The hurt that I tried to keep deep down inside came pouring out. I grabbed a towel from the towel rack. It had three shelves with the same-colored towels and looked like Mary kept it neat. She had decorated the bathroom in a beachy sort of theme which made you feel like you were somewhere modern, and not in an old farmhouse. I grabbed one of those matching towels and screamed into it. To my surprise, it actually almost completely muffled the sound. How could I be so stupid? I could have told my uncle to help me, that I couldn't handle my dad hurting me anymore. The hot water felt good. I slowly leaned back and felt the water flow up to my neck then to my chin. I took a few deep breaths and imagined not ever having to go back home, never having to see my parents again. I imagined a new life with my uncle and Mary, being a family with them, and just forgetting all about my parents. I could do that and never look back, forget they ever existed and move forward, leaving them behind. Without them in my life and if I never had to see them again, I could leave the pain behind too. They were both evil people, and I would be saving my brother and sister from a horrible life. If my dad's anger and abuse ever turned to them, they would never make it. Even though they were just kids, they were weak, the kind of weakness that would probably never go away.

I wished my uncle James would just tell me that I could stay there. I wished he would tell me that it wasn't safe there and he couldn't allow me to go back. I don't know why I didn't just tell him how bad it was there. I think that part of it was fear, and part of it was that I didn't want to burden him with it. He had a good life with Mary, a family life, and he deserved it because he was one of those people with good on the inside. He was rough around the edges, but I liked that about him. The fact that he was nowhere near perfect was comforting. I felt like a mess on the inside and outside, so being anywhere near people who appeared to be perfect was not for me. My uncle was caring but joked a lot, so you couldn't see how caring he was sometimes. Maybe he did that on purpose. With the way he lived away from everyone in a big farmhouse, even as a little kid, I knew he was just like me. I couldn't burden him or Mary with my messed-up life. It wasn't their responsibility to help me or get me out what I was going through. I was thankful that they at least had me over here and there. Their kindness soothed me inside and out. We would all sit in the living room, turn the lights off, and watch a movie. My uncle had big speakers and a stereo system that made the movies so much better by making every loud noise seem so intense. I would get so relaxed watching movies with them, between the soft blanket and comfortable couch. I never made it through one without falling asleep. When I woke up on Sunday mornings, the first thing I would think about right as my eyes opened was that I would have to go home soon. The thought of going home would hit me so hard that I had to try so hard not to panic. I had to remind myself that I had a few more hours there. I had to tell myself to calm down and enjoy my morning. I loved how Mary always made breakfast, and if she didn't make breakfast, she would give me cereal or oatmeal. No one at my house made breakfast, and no one cared if I ate cereal or not. No one paid any attention to things like that. Mary was like Tiffany's mom, so kind and exactly how a mom should be. I tried pretending it wasn't coming, but it was around that time that my uncle always asked if my mom was coming to get me or if they had to drop me off. My mom was lazy. Whenever I called her to see if she could pick me up, she got mad. Her response was always the same, as if it was some kind of recording, like on someone's answering machine. She made a noise indicating that she was irritated by my question and always responded by asking me why my uncle couldn't bring me home. I was always embarrassed for my uncle to hear me respond to her, so I would try to talk as quiet as I could. I knew he would know what she asked me if he heard my answer. She made me feel stupid, even when she wasn't there. I wanted to tell her that she was lazy all the time, and when she said she was busy, it meant sitting on the couch or shopping for more unnecessary items that we didn't have room for. I wanted to tell her that maybe my uncle and Mary couldn't drive me home because they were busy being good parents—busy playing with their child, cleaning their house, and doing all the things that parents should do. How dare she try to push one of her responsibilities on my uncle. Picking me up was the least she could do. I would end our conversation by telling her that I would see her later and call before she got there, and then I would just hang up. She never called back after I did that. Sure enough, a few hours later, she would pull up outside and honk the horn obnoxiously until I came outside. It was hard going back and forth from such opposite worlds. I almost felt like I would rather stay in my miserable life than get out of it only temporarily. I hated leaving the misery because that meant coming back, and coming back was worse than continuously being there. I would have to just drown out the pain, dull it maybe; my dad seemed to be able to do that. At least he looked like it, when he came into the house in the middle of the night looking like he was somewhere else.

That year, I started taking marijuana from him. I would sneak as quietly as I possibly could and take his keys when he went to bed. Every night, after taking off his work boots and clothes, right before he went to bed, he would set his keys, wallet, and cigarettes on the edge of the kitchen table. I had never smoked it before but decided that I was doing it after thinking about it for a long time. It was nerve-racking taking those keys off the table, because he had so many different keys on it that it was almost impossible to do it quietly. I was always able to get them off the table without making my mom or dad wake up. After taking the keys, I would stand there for a while to make sure they didn't wake up and catch me going out the shed. Every time I went into his shed, I was terrified and felt like I couldn't breathe. I would check behind me several times before I went in just to make sure they didn't come out before I went in. I was always scared my mom would hear the keys or the back door open, because she didn't sleep as sound as my dad did. My mom also didn't snore or fall into a deep sleep like my dad did. Instead, she slept so lightly, barely even sleeping. He usually had one or two ziplock bags full of weed, maybe two different kinds. I was never sure, because it all looked the same to me. He had three weed pipes, but I was too scared to use them, because I would have to use one right then and there and I definitely did not want to get caught. He also had papers that were for rolling-up weed cigarettes—joints, I heard people call them. I figured that out because there was a tray with weed, the papers, and this little thing that looked like it helped you to roll the weed into the papers. Next to all that on the tray were joints that were already rolled up, so I knew that was how I was going to smoke it. I took enough weed that looked like I could roll two joints. I took to six papers just in case I messed some up, and I took a lighter and hoped he wouldn't know, since he had four different ones sitting around the shed. I could never figure out which was scarier, getting into the shed to steal the weed or waiting and wondering if he knew some was missing. I wished the weed took me someplace else and made me feel good, but it just made me feel fuzzy. I mostly did it just to be distracted. I wanted to just be distracted by anything I possibly could.

That year, I think my dad started to hate me more, maybe because I was getting older or maybe because he just hated me. The more he hit me, the more I started talking back to him, telling me that he must like beating children because he wasn't a man. As he hit me harder and slammed me into the door or cabinet, I would laugh at him and tell him that only a loser would beat an eleven-year-old so much and that he must like it. The more I talked, the angrier he got, but I refused to just lie there or stand there and let him enjoy beating me. I was going to make sure that he knew that real men didn't beat little girls and that only losers took their anger and frustration out on children. When he would beat me and I was facing him, I would look deep into his eyes, and I could see that inside of him was pure darkness and evil. I couldn't help but to stare at and think that he hated me because I wasn't his child, that I belonged to a mom and dad somewhere out there in the world. I often sat daydreaming, imagining my real parents and what they were like, what they looked like and if I looked like them. When I closed my eyes, I could see their brown hair and brown eyes, just like mine, beautiful and brown. My dad constantly told me that you couldn't trust anyone who had brown eyes. He said they were usually liars. I always looked at people's eyes because of how hateful my parents were against brown eyes. I couldn't help but turn it around and judge people with blue eyes. It seemed more and more like my parents didn't like anything about me, and it only got worse as I got older. I tried as hard as I could to love them even when it didn't feel like they loved me back. I needed something to hold onto, and I tried to appreciate what they did for me even when it was more bad than good. They had this way about keeping you hanging on by a thread. They were so mean most of the time, but here and there, they gave you a tiny bit of love and kindness that you so desperately needed. Even with all the horrible things that they did to you, that little bit of kindness would have you feeling like you were the bad person for feeling the way that you did about them.

Some days, I would sit and stare out the window hoping that my real parents would come and rescue me from them. Like a fairy tale, I constantly imagined them coming to save me, but they never came. I would close my eyes and try to focus really hard on my mom. I would try to communicate with her. I would tell her that I needed help. I guess I thought because she was my real mother that she would be able to feel me trying to connect with her. So many times I cried and screamed for her, I needed her to hear me, to feel me and know that I needed help. I felt like if I could just get her to hear me, then maybe her and my dad would come to save me from the people who hated me. If my real parents knew how bad things were for me, then I just knew they would come and take me away. I would imagine my real dad beating up the monster that I currently called my dad, beating him how he beat me. After thinking about it for so long, I would get angry and confused. How could my real parents let these people take me and treat me so badly? Even though I hated my dad, I went with him to visit my uncle in Tennessee. He didn't just live in Tennessee. He lived deep in the woods where there was nothing but huge trees and mountains for miles and miles. My uncle was my cousin Theresa's dad. I'm not sure why, but I called him my uncle Woody. I had only visited him a few times before that, and even though we had barely spent any time together, I always felt close to him. I think it might have been because I actually felt like he cared about me. Even though we barely ever saw each other, he actually cared. Most kids would probably be scared of an uncle whom they barely ever saw just from the fact that it was a strange man that they did not know very well. Then when you add into the equation that he was tattooed from head to toe, gave tattoos out of his house that was in the middle of the woods, and cussed and drank worse than any adult that I had met so far. None of that mattered to me. Because of everything that I had already gone through, I could tell that he was good on the inside. It was the way he hugged me. It wasn't fake like the feel times that my parents hugged me out of pity or some reason that benefitted them. He would quickly put his arm around my shoulder, pulling me in. Then he squeezed me real tight for a few seconds while patting my back. That wasn't the kind of hug that you give to somebody you don't care about. Those hugs were genuine. It wasn't just the hugs. It was the way he showed me how he got the house ready for me to come. He told me that he had to get it ready for a young lady, something so little, but it showed me that he really cared about me. I heard him tell me dad that he had to get rid of all the dirty magazines and the calendar that had a naked woman on it, clean up the house, and make his extra bedroom into a room for me to sleep in. Just that right there meant so much to me. I almost cried just hearing him say those things to my dad. My dad never cared about leaving all his disgusting magazines out, and I am sure he really didn't care about how it would affect us if we started looking at them. He looked at me right in my eyes when he talked to me. He saw me.

Nobody in my family besides my cousin Theresa ever saw me. Maybe it was because Theresa was his daughter, or maybe it was a coincidence and they were both just good people. I asked him to give me a tattoo, and he told me that I probably wouldn't want a tattoo when I got old enough to get one. I told him I didn't just want one, I wanted them all over my body. I told him that I wanted to look just like him with all his tattoos, and I think that made him feel good. I think that was just how he made me feel good, and I made him feel good in that same way. He had me look through all the samples of his drawings so I could pick out which tattoo I wanted to get when I was older. I picked one, and he told me I could get one when I was a little bit older. He said that I had to be at least sixteen. Later, we somehow came to the agreement that he would give me one when I was twelve, and I never forgot that. The funny thing is, my uncle Frank didn't even have a TV, but I still liked being there. I was a different kind of kid, the kind who could appreciate nature and being around anyone who had my well-being in mind. I didn't mind just sitting in that little cabin; I didn't mind it at all. I would wake up to the sound of pots or pans and would lie there and smile as I listened to him cuss many times while trying to make breakfast. When the cussing slowly stopped as he was almost done, I would go out there as if I hadn't heard a thing. The best days were when my dad wasn't there, when he went out to go visit some of the people he knew out there. He knew some of my uncle's friends and neighbors, so while being out there, he would go fishing or hunting really early. My dad would always say that we could all get up early and go together, but my uncle said that a little lady didn't need to be out doing that stuff so early in the morning. I loved that, how he cared about me being just a child, or how he cared how a young girl was treated or what she did. My uncle would make things for breakfast that I had never eaten for breakfast, stuff that you ate for lunch or dinner. He made me fish that one of his neighbors had caught, with baked beans and a big bowl of some kind of spicy peppers. I didn't care what he made for me. It was how he tried so hard to make me happy. Normally, it was unbearable to be anywhere near my dad, but when we were at my uncle's house, in the North Woods, he wasn't as angry and abusive as he was at home. Being there took him out of the circle of chaos. It took him out of the evil pattern that he had developed in the last few years. I think that my dad also saw me as someone different when we were there. There were so many different things that made everything so bad at home, and when all of them were put together, that's what made it the way it was. My dad being stuck in a marriage with my mom that he clearly didn't want to be in, and then having adopted a child when they were so young was the core of the madness. Then add in two kids coming into the picture when they thought they wouldn't be able to have any, and add in that my dad probably never wanted even one to begin with. The days with my uncle would go so fast, and before you knew it, it was time to go back to my miserable house. I would hug him and casually and say goodbye as if I wasn't screaming and crying inside for him to let me stay with him. I didn't care that he didn't even have a TV. I would be happy just sitting there with him, just the two of us. I could deal with no TV if it meant getting away from the abuse, the abuse and the misery that came along with being anywhere near my parents. When I was walking to my dad's truck, I would look back at him and try so hard to communicate to him through my mind and my eyes. I tried to make him feel my pain so he would help me. It was so hard holding back my tears on the ride home with my dad, so I would stare out the window as if I was distracted by the scenery.

The eight-hour ride from Tennessee back to Illinois seemed like it lasted forever, and the pointless conversations that my dad started only made it more uncomfortable. I remember getting home from that particular trip. I remember my mom standing outside in the driveway when we pulled up. I got out of my dad's truck, and right away, my mom walked up to me. She told me that she had to tell me something important. I was confused by her face. I had never seen that face. All I could make out of it was that it looked serious. She told me that there were three girls whom I might know were hit by a semitruck and killed that weekend. It turned out I did know them. I wasn't very good friends with any of them, but I knew them. Two of the girls, Marla and Margaret, went to my school and were a year or two older than me. They were popular, so, of course, we weren't friends. We weren't friends; but most of the kids in my school, along with me, lived in that town their whole life. That meant that we all went to school together since kindergarten, some since day care until we were old enough for school. So even though we weren't friends, it still hurt finding out that kids whom you went to school with for so many years have been killed. The third girl, Lena, went to a different school, but I knew her because her mom lived a block away from us, and she spent most weekends there. I had played with her several times the last two summers. She played baseball with me and the other neighborhood kids. Tiffany knew her a lot better than me because they had both played on the same softball team for the last year or two. I sat there for a moment. I remembered knocking on her door and asking her mom if she was there or at her dad's house. Tiffany would always send me to get her so we could all go to the park and play baseball. When she would play with us, I would get jealous of her because she was good at sports like Tiffany was. They were both obsessed with sports and knew a lot about them, so they always had a lot in common. Even though we didn't see Lena very often, when we did, Tiffany would act like they were the best of friends. Thinking about my jealousy toward her made me feel horrible as I stood there thinking about her. I wasn't even sure how to process what my mom had just told me. It was hard to think about three girls whom I knew being dead. I had never thought about the fact that kids can die. The thought hit me so hard that I felt like I couldn't breathe. Nothing seemed the same anymore. Life felt so temporary, so short, so pointless. It was hard to even know how I was supposed to feel or how to act. Honestly, I felt numb and confused.

At school, I had that same feeling. All the other kids seemed to know exactly how they felt, and they all grieved together. I felt like an outsider looking in, looking into a window at the emotions that I was supposed to be feeling. I looked around at everyone rushing up to each other and grabbing each other. They then pulled each other in so tight and looked as if they never wanted to let go. Everyone had red eyes and started to cry every time they looked at each other. All you heard in the halls were weeping and kids blowing their nose because they had been crying too much. The teachers barely taught their classes. Instead, they gave everyone the option to talk about how they felt. Everyone cried and talked about how close they were to the two girls who went to our school and how much they would miss them. I think one of the hardest things for everyone to grasp was that someone hit three young girls walking down a road and didn't even stop or get help. It was hard thinking about and not knowing who was evil enough to do something like that to innocent girls, three children. They made announcements over the intercom and held an assembly in remembrance of both Marla and Margaret. All of this lasted the whole week, and it was as if I was alone in a dark tunnel, unable to get out or connect with anyone around me. I felt like I was the only one not a part of the grieving. I was grieving, just not with everyone else. It was like I was completely invisible. I was on the outside of everything, on the outside of the crowd. Everyone seemed to be acknowledging each other's sadness, jocks with geeks, conservative kids with the gothic kids; but no one acknowledged me or my sadness. Even my sadness and grief wasn't good enough for everyone. Like always, I was the outsider. I had become the darkness that nobody wanted to get close to. Even during a tragedy, nobody had open arms or hearts for me or my feelings. It seemed like forever before they had their services. They had all three girls together for the wake: Marla, Margaret, and Lena. I think because they were together for their last moments and together when they were killed, it was only right to keep them together for people to say their goodbyes.

I thought long and hard about going to the wake. I felt like if I went, I would be so close to death and something even darker than what I was already trapped in. I felt like I was already in such a bad place, and I just knew that going to see those girls, three girls who were so tragically killed. It was only going to get worse. I decided that I had to go. I knew that was something that you had to do when someone you know dies. It was more than what I was supposed to do. I felt like I had to go because they were kids just like me, and everyone should at least say goodbye to them. My mom took me, and it was shocking as we got toward the funeral home, and there was a line of vehicles before we even got close. At first, it looked like there was a car accident ahead of us, but as we got closer, we saw cops directing traffic toward the funeral home and the library across the street. The whole parking lot was full; people even parked in the grass all around the building and even along the curbs. There was a large grassy area in between the funeral home and a car lot next to it, and it was also full with cars so close to each other that it looked like it was going to be difficult for everyone to get out. There were signs that additional parking was available across the street at the local library, but that, too, was completely full. My mom had to pass the funeral home, turn around in town, and go back down a little ways past it to a gas station where she dropped me off. She would drive around and wait for someone to leave so she could get a parking spot while I walked over to the funeral home. The closer I got after stepping out of the grassy area, reality hit me hard as I walked up to the long line of people waiting to get into the funeral home. Even in the line, there were kids from my school crying uncontrollably and questioning why something like this would happen to these girls. I was so scared and felt like I was out of place as I stood in the parking lot thinking about what they were going to look like in their caskets.

Before I even made it close to the steps of the building, my mom came up after finally finding a parking spot. I knew that there was no turning back as we made it to the door, and I tried to look normal even though I felt like I couldn't breathe. When we walked in, it was like I entered into a whole other world. Everything felt different, so scary. It felt like there was no flow of air in there, as if the air around me was completely still, and even the way it smelled in that room scared me. There were so many people and just so much crying. That's all you could hear—people crying and weeping so loudly.

The emotions and sadness in that place was unlike anything that I had ever experienced, and it was so hard to keep walking forward. We almost couldn't even get through the crowd of people to fully get into the line to go up to the caskets. My mom asked me a few times if I was okay, and I found it strange that she was acting as if she cared about my feelings, but then figured it was because there were other moms around doing the same thing. The face she made when she was asking me was the same face she made when talking to my principal or picking up our layaway of school clothes. It was the face and voice that other people got but not us. We didn't get that face; only the people she was trying to impress did. I would hate listening to her on the phone. When she was making appointments or paying bills, she used a voice as if she was a nice and normal individual. I had enough in front of me and to worry about. The last thing I needed to be angry about was the monster I had to call my mother. To make it all worse, she kept whispering to me, asking if I was friends with any of the kids around us or who were walking past us. She whispered to me, asking whose parents were who and which kids she thought were siblings of the three girls. She would be the kind of person worrying about stuff like that at the wake of three girls who were tragically killed. I was embarrassed and did not want someone to hear her whispering these things, so in anger and frustration, I told her to stop it.

I would never have thought that so many people would go to their wake. It must have taken an hour just to make it up to the caskets, which was nerve-racking, and I swear I almost passed out a few times in that hour. I am not even sure if my mom was still by my side. The whole room and everything in it just stopped. Everything around me just faded away somehow. All that was left was me and three girls who were no longer on this earth but at the same time right in front of me. I felt different from what I had ever felt before in that moment. I felt nervous and almost embarrassed because my legs might have been shaking and my face must have looked like I was going to throw up. I had watched closely what everyone else had done when it was their turn to go up to the caskets to say their good-byes, so I had already decided that I would do just what they did. I looked in front of me, and I felt sheer terror before I could even feel sadness, and I felt so guilty that I was terrified. These girls didn't do anything wrong for me to be so scared just to look at them, so I felt horrible to be that scared to just look at them. I took a deep breath and told Margaret that I didn't know her and had never really been friends with her, but I told her that I was so sorry this happened to her. I had never even talked to her at school. I honestly barely ever noticed her much. From what I had seen, she was a nice and quiet girl, not involved in a lot of the typical middle school drama. I didn't know how long I was supposed to stand there. I wasn't even sure how to do any of it. I took another deep breath and walked to the next casket. It was Lena—right there in front of me was Lena. The girl that lived on the next block with her mom but only on the weekends, because she lived with her dad during the week. Lena, the girl whom I had played softball or baseball with so many times for the past two summers, was no longer filled with life, with energy, with happiness. How could someone be so full of life one day and then be in a casket the next day, gone, no longer here? Why would three young girls be killed? Why like this? Why now? How could three girls who were only twelve be taken from this world? Why didn't they live until they were older, have families, and do all the things that everyone else would get to do? I closed my eyes and told Lena how sorry I was. I told her that I was sorry that I didn't try to play with her every single weekend that she was at her mom's. I told her that I hoped she was in heaven playing softball on a warm and sunny day just like we had done for two summers in a row. She was such a good softball player. She played on a team just like Tiffany did, and she was good at every sport that I had seen her play. Seeing her so puffy and so different was so scary, and it made me get a sharp pain in my stomach, and then I felt dizzy and sick. They had her in regular clothes, the same kind of clothes that she would wear when we played together. I recognized the shirt she had on, just a regular T-shirt with colored strips. It must have been one of her favorites. I felt like I wanted to get away from there as soon as possible, but at the same time, I knew these were our last moments together, and then it was over. Again, I took a deep breath and walked to the next one, but the casket was closed.

Marla's casket wasn't open like Margaret's and Lena's caskets. It was closed with flowers on top of it. With it closed, you could see how big they were, so tall and wide for a child. The whole idea of a casket was terrifying to me, a huge fancy box that you put a body in and then buried it. It was scary thinking about all three of them being buried, no longer being here with us, but instead in a casket and in the ground. Then it hit me, and I realized that there was a reason that the casket was closed. What did she look like in there? Why did only her casket have to be closed? 1I was so scared. I couldn't stop myself from imagining what she looked like in there. So1 many thoughts were rushing through my mind all at once. Was she all bruised and cut up? Had something 1horrible happened to her whole face? Was it so much worse than anything I could imagine? I f1elt so sick, so sorry, so horribly sad. I told her I was so sorry that she had to die like this, that her life had to end at twelve years old, that this wasn't fair. I didn't really know her. We weren't friends, but all throughout school, I had heard her name and seen her in the halls. She had a small group of friends including her sister whom she regularly hung around with. It seemed like they were good friends, always happy, always smiling.

I walked away without feeling like I had gotten the chance to say goodbye properly. It was awkward and sad walking away from those girls and then seeing so many people crying; some were hysterical. You could kind of sort them out from friends, people who just knew them from school but weren't friends and family members. You could almost instantly see who their mothers were by how upset they were, not just upset and crying but almost screaming with tears pouring from their eyes. People would try to hold them and comfort them, but in a time like this, there was nothing that would work. Only getting their children back was the only thing that would ever comfort them at that point. I already knew who Lena's mom was, but even if the other moms weren't crying and screaming, you could find them in that room by looking for eyes that no longer had life in them. How could they ever be happy again? I couldn't imagine them being able to live a normal life with a child who was taken away from them like this. I couldn't bring myself to say anything to anyone as I walked out. I would never feel the same way about life. I almost forgot that my mom was there with me. She was waiting toward the back of the room in the doorway that led to the front doors. When I walked up to her, she looked at me with a face like I would have something wonderful to tell her. She looked at me like there was big news to tell her. Honestly, her face disgusted me, and I couldn't even look at her. I told her that we needed to leave. She didn't understand how I felt, because she didn't even go up there. She was on a whole other level. Hers was a level of curiosity and possible gossip, but mine was a level of sadness and darkness, so there was no point in talking to her. I stared out the window after we finally made it through all the people and traffic coming in, out, and around that funeral home. I hoped she would refrain from any kind of conversation during the ride home, and to my amazement, she did. There was now a dark cloud over me, but at first, I thought that everyone had it, but they didn't. I think that my cloud had been growing for quite some time, and getting worse, but I decided to embrace the darkness.

That summer, I drifted into it, and it consumed me. Tiffany's sister was into heavy metal music, wore black clothes with dog collars, and drew pictures of dark images. I decided I would do the same. I would turn the darkness inside of me into an appearance that matched. At first, I just did it to express how I was feeling, and I drew the dark pictures because Tiffany's sister did. I drew grim reapers with sharp curved blades, skulls with snakes coming out of the eyes, and several other dark images. I started going to the railroad tracks at the end of our block. You just went through one of the backyards, and you were right there, a place to be alone. Growing up, we went back there a lot. We built so many forts and would walk up and down the tracks for hours. We never told our parents that we went back there, because they would tell us that it was too dangerous because of trains. A few times, some of the people who had houses in front of the tracks would run into our parents. They would tell them that they saw us messing around by the tracks. We would, of course, tell them that it wasn't us, that it was all the other kids who were bad who played by the tracks. I started going there with Tiffany's sister because she went back there to smoke cigarettes and listen to music. When she offered me a cigarette, I accepted and told her that I had been smoking for a few months. That wasn't true. I had never smoked and found it disgusting when my grandma and dad did it. When I was in the car with my grandma and she lit a cigarette, I would hold my breath and wait for her to crack the windows. Most of the time, it felt like forever until she rolled the windows down, and sometimes, she forgot to roll them down. So when I took that first cigarette, I just knew it wasn't going to be good. In fact, it was horrible. So many people smoked cigarettes, almost every adult I knew, except for my mom, so I figured it would get easier. At first, I felt guilty when I smoked, but after a while, I started to like it, and it was nice to sit by the tracks and have a cigarette. I stopped going there with Tiffany's sister. I went out there by myself and would just sit and think about everything that was going on in my life. It was a place to get away, away from my parents, away from there fighting, and away from my dad constantly hitting me. Some days, I would sit out there for hours and watch the sun go down, and I hated it when it got dark because that meant that I had to go home. The sun going down meant I had to go back to misery, confusion, and the mess that I was forced to be a part of. My body was always hurting, always bruised, and every time I moved, I was reminded of my dad. Even when I was away from him, I still couldn't be at ease. He was destroying my whole life. I hated having to be around the rest of my family too. I shared a room with my little sister, so I put a sheet in the middle of the room so I could have privacy. I had to pretend that she wasn't there so I could have a place to be miserable alone. She and my brother had issues. My dad didn't hit them, but they still had to live in the middle of the chaos. For some strange reason, I felt bad for them, as if watching my abuse was worse than going through it. I avoided them because I was embarrassed that they constantly witnessed my abuse and because deep down I couldn't love them for not having to go through what I was. My side of our room was mine. It was just for me, and I told my parents to stay out of there, and for the most part, they did. When I was in there, I would draw and listen to music. I started borrowing CDs from Tiffany's sister. The music was dark. A lot of it was scary, but it matched the darkness inside of me. Tiffany's sister gave me her old band and concert shirts, and even gave me a block dog collar to wear. Under the shirts, I would wear long-sleeved shirts with stripes. That was the style that gothic people were all wearing, and that was the new me. I was gothic. I would get lost in my head, the heavy metal music took me away from there, and the drawings expressed what I was going through. My drawings got darker, they got scarier, and I started hanging them all over my walls. I was trapped in misery, so my room became my dungeon where I became one with the darkness. When school started, I stopped even trying to have any communication with other kids, not like I had much before. The three girls who were killed the year before, it was like nobody even cared about them or what happened anymore. I didn't know them very well, but it still bothered me that three girls could be killed and forgotten about. I used to watch the other kids with a bit of hope that they might one day talk to me or want to be my friend, at least at school. I used to observe everyone—kids and teachers—in class, at lunch, waiting for the bus to come. I stopped even looking at them, all of them. I either looked at the ground or straight ahead while somehow blocking everything around me out. I don't know if anyone noticed my transformation or if anyone even cared if they did notice.

At home, my parents barely spoke to me. The person who did was my dad when he beat me. His usual anger toward me got worse, and so did the things he said to me. He liked to get himself all worked up before he hit me, maybe to feel like he had to do it. Maybe he did it to make me say something back that would give him the feeling that he was justified for constantly hurting me. I finally did start to talk back to him, and it felt good even though it made it worse for me. He told me I ruined his marriage and that it was hard for them to love me. I told him that he was a grown man who liked beating and abusing little girls. The more he beat me, the more I said it, and the madder he got. I started telling him to beat me harder. I told him that he wasn't even a man, not a real man, because real men didn't hit children. Even after I was under him on the ground and could barely get up, he continued to beat me. I decided to start laughing at him. This was the only relationship we had, him beating me and me taking it. Laughing at him made him so angry because he couldn't control it. He couldn't make me stop no matter how hard he hit me. He told me he wished that I was never born and that I ruined their family. He hated me, and he didn't even hide it. I knew my mom hated me also because she would always just watch what he was doing to me. She never got up to help me, never tried to get my dad off me or away from me. I started saying things to her too. I screamed at her that she was a fat pig that could eat junk all day but not even get up to help her daughter. My parents were failing me. They were supposed to keep me safe, supposed to love me. They were bad people and lacked the love and compassion that I saw other parents have. This became a daily occurrence, me getting beat into the ground and degraded by those people. When I got up off that floor and made it to my room, I would scream into my pillow. I begged my real parents to come and help me, to come and help their child. I had real parents out there, a mother, a father; and I just knew they wouldn't hurt me like those people did. I called out to my real mother for her to come and help me, to hold me and tell me that everything would be okay. The darkness inside of me grew; the happiness, the small bit of it that I had left died. The problem with darkness is that it's not on your side. You think that it is by trying to grow with it. In the end, it wins. It grows apart from you and consumes you completely. I don't know how it happened exactly, but I got lost. I lost any ties to myself that were left, and everything became a dark blur. My dad beating me had gotten so bad that I didn't even want to be alive anymore and started to think about suicide. I wanted to get away, be free of the torture and the pain. I imagined disappearing, just fading away into nothingness. I would close my eyes and imagine a better place where I could be a beautiful young girl, full of happiness and life again. In that place in my head, I felt the warm sun touching my skin as the wind blew through my hair and made me feel relaxed. I would be in a cute summer dress and sandals so I could feel the grass tickling my toes. There would be a huge field around me of grass and wildflowers. I would run through it while dancing around and picking flowers to put in my hair. I was beautiful there in that place. I was full of light instead of darkness and happy instead of sad. In that place, my skin was glowing in the sunshine, not like in reality, where my skin was pale and full of new and old bruises. I started to lose that place, too, and ended up in a place full of misery and death.

Death became my answer to the pain, to the shame and sadness that I felt throughout every fiber of my being. Death wasn't something my dad could take away from me, so I started planning it in my mind. At first, the thoughts of suicide scared me, but after a while, they became my only comfort because they were a way to stop my pain. I visualized every aspect of my death from how I would do it to how everyone would act at my funeral. I became obsessed with it. It became all I had to look forward to, planning my death. Some days, I imagined cutting my wrists and falling back onto a beautiful all-white bed with white silk sheets all around me. There would be a canopy above me, four poles around the bed that go across the ceiling, attached was beautiful silk that came down all around the bed. Tables in the four corners of the room with several candles burning on each one. The flames from the candles would slightly sway and flicker, and a gentle breeze came in through an open door that led out to a large balcony. I would lie there like a brokenhearted princess quickly bleeding all over the soft silk sheets. It would be a beautiful tragedy. I would be lying there in a long and lacy white gown, arms gracefully and so perfectly laid next to me. My head would be slightly to one side with loose curls covering part of my face and neck, natural pink cheeks, and my mouth slightly open. I would look almost posed like a doll but natural and so innocent. Sometimes, I imagined my parents coming in and finding me lying there dead, it being too late to even try to save me. They would gasp at first, shocked and trying to catch their breath as they tried to fully understand what had even happened. After taking it all in, they would fall to their knees, my dad saying he couldn't believe I would do this and my mom screaming and loudly crying. They would cry and argue right there on the floor in front of the bed, blaming each other for my suicide and death. They would get up and stand at the sides of the bed, gazing at what was in front of them, but too scared to touch me—completely horrified, not wanting to keep looking but not wanting to look away either. Sometimes, I wouldn't imagine my parents as the ones who find me but someone else. A prince or handsome man who would walk in with a smile and a tray in his hand, bringing me tea and fancy pastries. He would look so happy until he looked up and saw me. The terror of what was in front of him would make him drop the tray. The metal tray with a mirror top would hit the floor, making such a loud noise. Between the mirror from the tray, the teapot, and little glass cups, there was glass everywhere. He would scream at the top of his lungs as he rushed to the bed and cried as he pulled me into his arms. My head falling back and hanging as he held me and cried into my chest, begging me to come back to him. He would hold me so tight and not want to let me go and hold my head up to him as he kissed me and said goodbye. In my mind, it was all so beautiful, a beautiful way to end my miserable life.

As if I wasn't sad enough already, the harsh realization that my death would not be beautiful in any way was hard to accept. I'm not sure if my parents would even care if I died, but it would still be a way to punish them for every single thing that they had done to me. I wanted them to pay. I wanted them to be held accountable for neglecting to be the kind parents that every kid needs. I don't know how long exactly that I was in that darkness, that sadness and that state of mind where you are so far in that no one can reach you. I lost track of day and night, weekdays and weekends. The lines for everything faded. I was gone. I was lost in some sort of nightmare. Just darkness and abuse were there. My body and mind must have, for the most part, shut down, because the next thing I remember was taking two full bottles of Tylenol and two bottles of some kind of prescription pills. I wanted to die. I wanted to drift off to sleep and never wake up. My mom must have found the empty pill bottles on my floor and rushed me to the emergency room. The hospital staff pumped my stomach and made me drink charcoal to dissolve any pills left in my stomach. My mom was angry at me, but my dad didn't even come to the hospital. I honestly don't even think my dad came home from wherever he was partying at. I am not sure why the hospital didn't admit me right away, because I really needed to be hospitalized. I needed help. I needed something to fix the sadness inside of me. When I got out of the hospital, I wanted to kill myself. I wanted to try it all over again but do it right. I would have, but a few days later, my mom took me to what I thought was just a doctor's appointment. She told me she was taking me to see a doctor who could help me, so I just looked out the window and stared at everything we passed. At that point, I wasn't even sure how long it had been since I even realized what was going on. I knew I had been lost, but I wasn't sure if it had been weeks or months. I did start to get the feeling that I hadn't been in reality for quite a while. What I did know is that I was so tired. I was more than tired; I was exhausted. I didn't care where we were going. I had no reason to ask and no need to talk to my mom. It was late afternoon, but the sun was still out, and it felt good on my face. I couldn't remember the last time I had felt the warmth of the sun. I closed my eyes and waited until the van stopped to open them.

We were at some sort of doctor's office or a hospital with offices in it. I just followed my mom without questioning her about where we were or where we were going. It felt so long since I had gone anywhere, or at least that I could remember. We weren't in an office building. We were in more of a hospital, a pretty big one. My mom didn't lead me into an office. She led me to more of a check in area and gave my name, and we sat down. Rather quickly, they called my name, and a nurse led us back into a room. She looked at my mom and asked if I knew what was happening. My mom looked at me with a fake smile on her face as she told me that we were there to talk to a doctor about me possibly being admitted into the hospital. The nurse did what nurses usually do when you go to the doctor: took my temperature, blood pressure, height, and weight. Doctor to come in and talk to us. During the few minutes that I had to sit waiting while my mom awkwardly stared at me, it felt like an hour had passed. Finally, a woman entered. She stood before me smiling and extended her hand. I put my hand out, and she grabbed it while telling me that she was Dr. Walland and she was so happy to meet me. Her voice and the way she talked sounded like she was from a different country. I had watched a movie the year before, and the movie had a few people in it who were from London. So she was probably from London or maybe somewhere near there. In my head, I tried to say her name like she did. I tried to say Dr. Walland with her accent and almost made myself giggle. She was bubbly, and her hands were warm. She had a comforting feel to her. She had short reddish hair, and it was short like how a boy's hair is short but styled differently. So far I liked this lady, this Dr. Walland, even though I had just met her. She was slim, not too slim, but she was in shape and looked like she probably exercised regularly. I often caught myself categorizing people: people who exercised or had a healthy look to them and people who didn't or looked overweight. I don't exactly know why I started doing that, but I am guessing it had something to do with my mom being so overweight. Dr. Walland was pretty. She looked dressed up but casual at the same time, very stylish. She looked very beautiful and had a very fit body for an older person. It was hard not to stare at her. She sat down at her desk, folded her hands, and looked up at me with a huge smile on her face. I could see that she had green eyes from where I was sitting, and it almost looked like they were sparkling. I could see that her teeth were not straight, but they were so white, and I liked the way they looked. There was a folder in front of her that she opened, which made me realize how neat and clean her office was, including her desk. There wasn't much more on her desk besides that folder, a horizontal desk lamp, a metal name tag with her name on it, and a pen. The neatness of her desk made me look around the room, and it was just like the desk—so organized, so exact. On the wall behind her, there was a large painting. It was almost the length of the wall, such a perfect fit. The painting had a dark wooden frame. It was so thin that you could barely see it and wouldn't notice it if you hadn't been staring at it. The painting was beautiful, almost breathtaking. It was abstract with mostly shades of blue and green. For a painting that was abstract, it was stunning. You could feel the artist's passion from just looking at it. On the wall to the left, there were four paintings staggered unevenly, one just slightly lower than the last. They were tall and rectangular. They were paintings of flowers, slender blue flowers. All four paintings matched each other but not just because they were flowers. They looked kind of like a puzzle. If you put them together, the flowers would match up perfectly but still looked good separated. It looked as if they took one big painting and cut it into four smaller paintings. On the right wall, there were three bookshelves. They were staggered similar to how the paintings on the other wall were. There were two books on the first two shelves but not standing up like books normally were. These books were all lying flat. The third shelf had three books on it, and they were standing up, held up by two stones, one on each side. The stones were tall. They were marbleized with white, blue, and a bit of gray in them. The door we came in was closer to that wall, and the chairs we were sitting in were closer to the other wall.

Dr. Walland said to give her a couple of minutes while she reviewed a few things, and for some reason, I began to get nervous, so I stared at the ground in front of me. The floor was dark wood. I started following the outline of the planks as I stared at them, attempting to calm myself down before I got too anxious. She then asked me if I knew why I was there, and I told her that I really wasn't sure. Her face changed as if I hadn't been truthful to her with my answer, and she made eye contact with my mom before she looked in the folder again. She said that according to my mom and dad, I hadn't been happy for a while and it was scaring everybody. I couldn't help but to laugh in my head. Of course, I wasn't happy. I was beat nearly every day. This was completely unbelievable. I sat there speechless. She said that my parents had become very concerned by the drawings in my room. They were dark and almost frightening. Dr. Walland asked me why I had drastically changed my appearance in the few months prior, so I explained it to her as best as I could. I told her that I used to fight off the darkness inside of me, the sadness, but I got tired and stopped fighting. I told her that it was all I had left; all my happiness and any other feelings or emotions were gone. I told her that I had to make the outside of me look like the inside, complete darkness. Dr. Walland said that she understood that. I was shocked to hear her say that, but it made me feel so relieved. She said that my parents told her there were drawings in my room, and they seemed to point to me being obsessed with death. Out of the corner of my eye, I could see my mom shaking her head with her usual stupid-looking smirk on her face. My mom then told the doctor that I had been hanging out with some bad influences, and that's when I changed. She said that this new look and attitude wasn't me—the gothic clothes, the dark drawings, and the heavy metal music. She told Dr. Walland that she had no idea where all of this came from and was worried that this could be a serious mental illness. The tone of her voice and the way she smirked while speaking, it seemed like she was annoyed by what I had just told the doctor. The doctor then asked me if I agreed with my mom about not being happy for quite some time now. I told her that I did agree, but it wasn't my fault; it wasn't my fault or anyone that I had been hanging out with either. I told her that my mom let this happen to me and that she is only pretending to care about me. I looked at the ground and shook my head. I told Dr. Walland not to let my mom fool her. My mom laughed when I said that. I felt the anger start to rise up inside of me, but I took a deep breath and pushed it back down. Dr. Walland's face changed when I said that. Her forehead and eyebrows became tight as she asked what I meant by that. I looked up, and she looked right into my eyes. She again asked if I could please explain to her what I meant. It was hard for me to keep looking at her, so I went back and forth from looking at the ground to looking at my hands, which were clenched in my lap. I told her that my mom let my dad hurt me and that she never stopped him. Dr. Walland asked me what I meant when I used the word *hurt* when I said my dad was hurting me. I told her that he hit me almost every single day, and she asked me how he hit me. I explained it to her but could barely get out more than a sentence at a time because of my mom interrupting. My mom kept saying that I was being ridiculous as she laughed and shook her head. She told Dr. Walland that this was what they had to deal with, me lying about everything. She told her that one minute, I was happy, and the next minute, I was sad or I was angry. Dr. Walland asked me what I thought about my mom saying that I was lying and asked my mom to let me talk and not to interrupt.

I told her that my mom was a monster who sat and watched when my dad beat me. I told her that my mom wished I was a liar. Me being a liar was what she told herself to feel better, and I didn't care what she said about me, because she and my dad were the liars. She then asked me what I thought about my mom saying that my moods go up and down a lot, and I told her that I felt that could be true. Sometimes, I felt like that, like my emotions were up and down. Sometimes, it got pretty exhausting, like I was on a roller coaster inside my head, happy and then sad. Dr. Walland asked my mom why I would say that my dad was beating me, and she told her that he spanked me and I exaggerated it for attention. She told her that I was always talking back and being respectful, so they had to spank me because they didn't know what else to do. I told my mom that she was sick in the head and that what my dad was doing to me wasn't just regular spankings. I told her that spankings were getting hit on the butt a few times. Then I told her that that's not what was happening to me. Dr. Walland asked me what I meant when I used the words *beat* and *beating*. I told her that my dad would beat me, meaning he continuously hit me until I was on the ground and couldn't get up. I told her that he would then hit me more and more as I screamed and tried to get away. I told her that he would grab me, scratching my lower back and legs when I tried to crawl or grab onto the wall to get away. I told her that it wasn't just on my butt; it would start there and end up on my back, shoulders, arms, and legs. I told her he would slam me into the door, the wall, and the kitchen counter. I told Dr. Walland how bad it would hurt my back and how it would hurt for weeks. I told her not only did it hurt my back but all the scratches and bruises would hurt so bad too. I told her that he would grab me and shake me and then slam me into the door or the ground as he screamed and spit all in my face. Again, my mom did her evil little laugh, the laugh she always did when she knew someone was right and she was wrong. She often did that same laugh when she was mad at my dad. He would stay out in the shed all night, men and women coming and going, with the driveway and front of the house full of cars. The next day, when my dad would make his way out to the kitchen in an attempt to gather up his things and leave, that's where he would have to face my mom. She would tell him that it would be nice if maybe he could spend a night inside with his family and not out in the shed with his loser friends. He would tell her that there's nothing wrong with having a few beers with friends and at least he was at home. That's when she would do that same laugh, and I always wondered if my dad hated it as much as I did. That laugh made me sick to my stomach and enraged at the same time. I wished I never had to hear it again.

Dr. Walland said that it was clear that there was a lot of tension and anger going on and that fighting about it was not going to help anybody. She turned to me and said, "I think you and I can all agree on one thing. You are depressed and want to feel better." I agreed; I did want to feel better. She then turned to my mom and said, "I think that we can both agree that Ava is depressed and needs help." She said that she agreed, but who knew what was going on inside her head? Dr. Walland closed the folder that was on the desk in front of her, smiled at me, and said that she felt that everything we told her confirmed her initial thought that I had bipolar disorder. Dr. Walland said that I had an imbalance of chemicals in my brain that caused my emotions to get seriously out of balance. She said that it can have very negative effects on someone's life, and it can cause what's called manic or depressive episodes. Dr. Walland said that my emotions could get extremely high, causing me to not sleep and have erratic behavior. That is the manic side of the illness. She said that the opposite of that was what I was experiencing, and that's the depressive side of the illness. Some of what she was saying made a lot of sense to me, but at the same time, it sounded like a way to cover up what my dad was doing to me. I wanted to believe her. My instincts were telling me that I could, but she wasn't addressing my dad beating me. She said they were going to do everything they could to balance me out and help me feel better. She then asked if I could have a seat in the chairs outside of her office so she could talk to my mom and get a plan together.

When I stood up to step out of the office, I felt so relieved. Walking out, I didn't want to look at my mom, but her eyes caught mine, and it was like I could read her mind. Her eyes told me that she was outraged that I would tell the doctor that my dad beat me and that she wished she could convince me that my dad only spanked me. Her eyes said that she wanted to be the good guy in this situation, that she wanted to be able to blame the cause of my depression on kids whom I was hanging out with. Her eyes told me that she wanted me to shut up and that she wanted this discussion to have not involved my dad beating me or anything of that nature. I tried to tell her with my eyes that she was a monster, she and my dad both. I broke away from her stare as I reached for the doorknob and quickly left the room. Once I sat down in the little waiting area outside the office, I felt so relaxed from getting to talk about what was happening to me. The waiting area was not decorated as nice as Dr. Walland's office, not even a little bit. The wallpaper and pictures didn't even match each other at all; the chairs and floor didn't either. I didn't care what they were talking about in that office. I really didn't care about anything anymore. I watched the clock on the wall for a while, and after about ten minutes, I started looking through the magazines for something to look at. There were mostly magazines about being healthy, getting into shape, and cooking. In the cooking magazines, there were a lot of pages torn out. It looked like it was the recipes that people were ripping out. There were also a lot of family magazines. They had articles about finding time to talk to your kids about using drugs, spending time together in a busy world, and fun activities for the whole family. I read some of the articles and flipped through them, but it annoyed me and made me aggravated. The families in the magazines were all smiling. Every single person had a huge smile on their face. The mom and dad in all the pictures looked like loving and kind parents, like good people in general. The kids looked so happy and full of life. They looked loved and well taken care of, not a care in the world. They definitely didn't look like they ever had to worry about getting beat or having two horrible people as parents to deal with. The cooking magazines were the same. They showed pictures of happy people making delicious meals. There would be lists of recipes that said delicious home-cooked meals for the busy mom. The mom in the picture would be holding a white dish with light-green oven mitts and standing next to a perfectly clean white oven. On the front of the oven, there was a towel hanging that matched the women's oven mitts and her cooking apron. They were all a light and pastel-looking green color, and in the corners, they had little white flowers on them. The picture showed a small portion of a nice and tidy kitchen, organized and all having a similar-color scheme. On the wall, you could see a small wooden sign that said, "Bless this

Kitchen," an off-white background with black cursive letters. The lady had her hair pulled back into a ponytail. She had on a white shirt with a long floral print skirt and brown sandals with a small heel. I tried to close my eyes and imagine my mom like that, like the lady in the picture—with the nice outfit, a neat ponytail, a big smile on her face, and the appearance that she was happy to be cooking for her family. I looked closely at the picture and compared it with our kitchen. The difference was just too much, so I closed the magazine. They were all the same, all the magazines, no matter what they were about. Looking at them made me feel embarrassed for the way my family was, the way my mom was, and the way our house looked. I wanted to throw the magazines onto the floor, take them all out of the rack, and throw them all into a big pile.

Twenty minutes later, Dr. Walland's door opened, and she asked me to come back in and have a seat. She said that after speaking to my mother, they had come to the decision that I needed to be hospitalized. If being hospitalized meant getting away from my parents, especially my dad, then I was all for it. At that moment, I felt like I was about to go on a vacation and almost felt excited. I asked Dr. Walland when I would be going into the hospital, and I was surprised to find out that it was happening right then and there. She said that there was a children's psychiatric ward at the hospital that we were in, and that was where I would be staying. She offered me a few minutes to say goodbye to my mom, but I told her I was ready. I looked at my mom, and then I walked out of the room. As we walked through the halls, Dr. Walland told me how happy I would be here, and I believed her. The hospital was big, with so many different areas and levels that it took quite a few minutes to get to the children's psychiatric ward. When we got down there, it felt strange at first. I went from a doctor's appointment in an office to being admitted into a hospital. Dr. Walland took me into a room where a nurse was waiting. She told me that I was in good hands with the nurses down there. She introduced the nurse as Laura and told me that she was one of the best nurses she'd ever had. Before she left the room, she said that we would be talking every few days but if I needed anything to ask one of the nurses to speak to her. That made me feel good.

She made me feel important, and she made me feel like she cared about me. After she left, Laura told me the next steps to being admitted into that unit. I would undress and put on a gown so that she and another nurse could examine my body. They would chart down everything they saw, down to any freckles she said.

After undressing but keeping my underwear on, I put on the gown, and Laura came back in with another nurse. The other nurse had a clipboard, a folder, and some different markers in her hand. Laura told me that they would do one area at a time. She started by checking my face, head, and neck. She called out to the other nurse that I had my ears pierced and a scar through my right eyebrow that was approximately one inch long. She said that I had a birthmark under my right ear, some scratches on the back of my neck, and a small bruise under my left ear. Laura checked under my chin and then asked me to drop the top of the gown down into my lap. I closed my eyes and told myself that these people were going to help me. She told the other nurse to mark down that I had a scrape on my left collar bone and a bruise below it on my chest. She called out a bruise at the top of my left shoulder. She held my shoulders as she looked for anything else. Laura called out that there were scrapes on both elbows and small bruises on both of my forearms. There was a large freckle—or possible birthmark, she called it—at the top of my right forearm. She then walked around me, and I felt her clench her hand because it was still on one of my shoulders. She called out that I had several very long scratches going down my back at a slight angle and a large bruise across my lower back. Laura then told me that I needed to stand up and drop the gown while she checked the rest of my body. I felt my cheeks get red as the gown hit the floor and as Laura squatted down to examine my lower half. She called out several bruises on my stomach, some smaller, some larger. Laura told the other nurse to chart down bruises above both knees and scrapes on both knees, with bruises below the knees also. She called out a birthmark on my left leg and a bruise on the top of that foot also. She then asked the other nurse to come over and take a second look at my body to make sure that nothing else was missed. The other nurse pushed her glasses up her nose and scrunched her face as she looked closely checking over each area of my body. It made me feel good in a strange sort of way. This lady was carefully checking my body. They cared enough about me to check me over twice. The doctor and now these two nurses, they were all making me feel like I was important. They made me feel like I mattered. They told me that they would be back with clothes. They said that they were giving me something to wear. Laura brought me back tan sweatpants and a sweatshirt and explained that everyone wore those in the afternoon and evening. She also gave me a pair of light-blue socks. They were the loose ones with grips all over the bottom that you get at hospitals. She asked me to put all of my things into a bag and leave it in the room and then meet her outside.

Laura led me down a hall and through a few doors that needed passcodes and then brought me to the unit where I would stay. She introduced me to a nurse named Kelly and then told me, "Good luck." Kelly took me to my room first. It was all the way at the end on the left side of the hall. She explained that for the first week or two I would not have a roommate. They had to closely examine me first. She then took me back down the hall, and the area that we started at, she explained, was the dayroom. In the dayroom, there were a few tables. Then to the right, there were three love seats and a TV. Directly next to that, there was a short hallway and then big double doors at the end. To the left, there were three doors. One was the door I came in, the middle one said, "Nurse Station," and I wasn't sure about the third one. She told me that there was a schedule that the unit followed daily and told me that it shouldn't take too long for me to remember it. We were woken up at 6:00 a.m. and had until 7:00 a.m. to get ourselves showered and ready for the day. Breakfast was brought to us between 7:00 a.m. and 7:30 a.m. in the dayroom, and we had thirty minutes to eat, and then it was time for school. I would not have guessed that there would be school in a hospital, but I guess this was a different kind of hospital. Kelly explained that we had a main class that we did for a few hours in the morning then lunch back in the dayroom, and then a different class after that. At 3:00 p.m. every day, we had group therapy and then personal therapy. Dinner was at 6:00 p.m., and then we could go in our room or sit in the dayroom until 8:00 p.m., and then it was bedtime. I wasn't really sure what I thought about that place at first. I just knew that it was better than the misery I was in at home. She asked me if I had any questions before I went to bed. I realized we were the only people around because it was almost 9:00 p.m. That whole afternoon felt like some kind of dream. I was tired so I was more than happy that it was time for me to go to bed. There were two beds in my room, but they told me that mine was the second bed, the one by the wall and the window. The window was huge. It took up almost the whole wall. It was a beautiful view. Even though all you could see was the tops of other areas of the hospital, there was something about it that was beautiful. I tried to take in everything around me in that room, but I was so tired that I couldn't do much but fall asleep.

The next morning, everything felt as if I was still in a dream. Looking around seeing other kids was the strangest part. A nurse named Lolita came and woke me up. She said it's 6:00 a.m., and that meant to get up and get yourself ready. Her voice was stern, and it startled me. She pushed the door all the way open and put a wedge under it. She told me that ready meant showered, teeth brushed, hair done, and completely dressed. Before we left our rooms to wait for breakfast to arrive, we had to clean any mess we made in the bathroom and put our dirty clothes in a bin for housekeeping to take. She had a clipboard in her hand and was writing something as she talked to me. I sat on the edge of my bed staring at her as she wrote and wondered if she was writing something about me already. Her skin was smooth. She was a Black lady and had such a dark and beautiful skin color. She wasn't wearing any makeup, but she had a subtle and natural beauty to her. Her hair was pulled back. It looked very tight and was twisted up into a bun. The all white scrubs and shoes that she wore made her look so neat, and it made her skin look even more beautiful. She was chubby, especially her stomach, but she was small at the same time. She asked me if I knew where I was. I thought it was a strange question, but I told her that I did. She asked me how I was feeling, and I told her that I was feeling okay. She asked me if I had any questions, and I said that I did not. She looked at me and smiled and then told me that she would bring me my clothes that they washed after I got in the shower. She said that on Fridays, we got to wear our own clothes, not our sweat suits. She said that it was something that the patients and staff decided on after many feuds about continuously wearing tan sweatpants and sweatshirts. Nurse Lolita said that the only reason anyone ever approved something like that was that a patient said that it helped them express who they were. She told me that once we were ready, we were able to come out of our rooms and watch TV or talk to the other kids until it was time to eat. I told her, "Thank you," but wasn't sure what I was supposed to call her. Did I call her Nurse, Nurse Lolita, or just Lolita? I wasn't sure, so I asked her. She said it didn't matter, so I told her that I would call her Nurse Lolita. She laughed and told me that worked just fine. She told me that my first day would mostly be meetings with different doctors. She said that I had a team of doctors so they could get a better idea on how to help me. She said that after that, they would work on helping me get on track with the routine of that unit. Nurse Lolita told me that they had a whole bunch of people there that were going to help me: doctors, nurses, therapists, and counselors. She said that I had to meet with some of them for the first day or two. Then they would help me get used to the normal routine there. She made me feel good. She made me feel like they were all going to help me, and I needed help.

It took me a few minutes to figure out how to make the water hot, or even warm, and after five minutes in ice cold water, I got it. The shower woke me up. Being refreshed and awake helped me to prepare myself for the day ahead of me. It had barely sunk in that I was in a psychiatric hospital, but again, it was better than being home. The towels were so small. I had to peek around the door to make sure that no one was in my room. My clothes were sitting on my bed, neatly folded with a roll-on deodorant that I only guessed was for me. It was so strange to smell a different laundry soap on my clothes. They almost didn't even feel like they were mine. I had just woken up, but I was tired. I was tired of my life and was hoping that place would help me with that. I tried to push all of that out of my mind and focus on what was right in front of me, getting dressed and eating breakfast. After staring at the wall for a few minutes, I startled myself remembering that at any time Nurse Lolita could walk through my door. Sure enough, about one minute later, she did. She must have worked there long enough to know exactly what kids are doing. She knocked and popped her head around the door to tell me that she didn't want me to miss breakfast. She shook her head and said that she could never figure out all the different styles kids were always getting into. She told me that I was too pretty to be dressed in clothes like that—"all ripped up," she said. I was wearing an over-sized beige sweater with a dark-brown horizontal stripe around it. My jeans were old and ripped on both knees and on the thighs too. They were tattered around the ripped areas and all around the bottoms of both legs. My outfit was the exact definition of the grunge style, grunge at its finest. I didn't get mad when people said anything about it. They didn't understand it, and I was okay with that. It wasn't just a fad or a style of clothes. It was more like a state of mind. I walked toward the door, and she told me that I needed to put on shoes and that she had put mine under my bed. I bent down to get them and realized that someone had taken my laces out. My shoes were not shoes. They were leather combat boots that now had no laces in them. I looked at Nurse Lolita, and she laughed. She told me that laces were not allowed in there, and she wasn't going to tell me why. I wasn't stupid or naïve. I knew where I was at. I knew the kind of stuff people did in there or at least tried to if they had the chance.

She led me down the hall into the dayroom, and in the middle, there were three tables, so I picked one and sat down. I tried to act cool as if maybe I had done the whole psychiatric hospital thing before, but it was hard. It was hard to play it cool with kids staring at you. There were probably about six other kids in that unit, and only a few of them were out of their rooms already. My initial thought was to say hi to everyone, but with awkward stares in every direction, it was hard to. I decided to just focus on what I needed to do, worry about eating my breakfast. There were boys and girls in that unit. I had thought there would only be girls around me while I was in there. One of the boys was standing in the corner singing or rapping loudly, throwing his hands up like he was throwing up gang signs. He was tall and looked even taller because his basketball shorts were sagging so low that you could see half of his boxers. Boys who acted like they were ghetto always annoyed me. It looked so stupid to me, so fake. When he saw me looking at him, he got louder and then laughed and started talking to himself. There was another boy near him but sitting on one of the three love seats next to where I was at. He was staring at the ground and pulling on his hair. He was kind of rocking back and forth. It was darker over in the area where the love seats were at, so I couldn't really get a good look at him. With the way he was sitting, I couldn't see his face. I had to take a deep breath because the thought of being stuck with a bunch of ghetto kids was so aggravating. There were a few kids at my school like that, and they drove me crazy. A girl walked in and stared at me all the way until she sat at the table in front of mine. She looked angry. She looked like a teenager but at the same time like an angry little girl. She had pigtails in her hair and a long-sleeved purple shirt, with silver dots on the bottom of it and a long tan skirt. I later found out that her name was Samantha. She had a lot of problems from being abused. That's why she dressed and acted like she was a lot younger than she was. The abuse really messed her up.

The first doctor came and got me right after I ate breakfast. She told me that she hoped I ate a good breakfast, because I had a lot of doctors to see. She introduced herself as Dr. Patel but told me that everyone called her Dr. P in that unit. She told me that she was one of the doctors whom I would be working very close with while I was there. She had a nice smile and beautiful white teeth, and her skin was so smooth and shimmery. She was Indian and had black shoulder-length hair. It was shiny and perfectly straight. I liked her already. Everything about her was warm and inviting. She was so petite, so short and small, but appeared to be so full of life. Dr. P was wearing a plain white fitted T-shirt, very relaxed looking. She wore it with black dress pants and red leather flat dress shoes. She was dressy but casual. She wore tiny gold ball earrings and a small vertical gold bar necklace that fell in the middle of her chest. She was so simply dressed, so casual, but so elegant at the same time. She smiled again and told me that we needed to get a treatment plan started and we could do it together. She explained that meant a goal that we both agreed on for my hospitalization period. She said it didn't have to be decided right away, but she wanted me to start thinking about it. Her first thought of an option to be my goal was for me to get back to being happy. She asked me if that sounded like a good idea, and I didn't know what to say, so I just said yes. The problem with that was that I couldn't remember the last time I was happy, and as long as I remained anywhere near my parents, I would probably never be happy. Dr. P said that we had to make basic categories of what made me happy and what didn't make me happy, and then we could expand from there. She asked me to name a few things that made me happy; so I said that I liked music, I liked drawing, and I liked being outside. She then asked me what didn't make me happy. I felt my ears get hot and just knew my cheeks were probably red as I felt a strong feeling of complete and utter embarrassment wash over me. I don't know why I got embarrassed, but I did, and then it made it hard to talk about what didn't make me happy. Dr. Patel asked me if I was okay, and I told her that it was hard for me to talk about it, and then I told her that I have barely ever talked about it. So then she, of course, asked what "it" was. The embarrassed feeling didn't go away, and then I felt like I was going to start sweating. She looked at me and again asked if I was okay, and then she told me that she was there to help me. It was hard to talk to someone like her about my problems, because she looked like she had a perfect life. She looked like she lived in a fancy condo, with modern architecture and tall ceilings. I imagined her living room with all white walls, mostly black and white decor, with red accent pieces. I imagined wood floors, always shiny, and large woven rugs with intricate patterns. Dr. Patel probably had parents whom she was very close with, loving and kind people whom she had dinner with once a week. I could sit and imagine myself in her place, in her life, and it would be a dream come true.

I snapped back to reality when she asked me if I was okay again, but I had to take a moment to try and brace myself. I wanted to start talking like a normal person, slowly, calmly; but it didn't happen like that. Somehow, I lost my breath before I even started talking, and it just poured out as I almost screamed that my dad had been beating me. She asked me to tell her what I meant by that, and I couldn't help but to give her a stupid look. In my head, I told myself that a stupid question deserved a stupid look, and maybe even a stupid answer. She told me that she had to make sure that we both were on the same page. She said she needed me to confirm what she thought that I meant. Again, she said that she just needed to be sure. I had to just breathe and close my eyes for a moment because I didn't want to get frustrated with Dr. Patel. I looked at her, and I told her that he hit me. Then I paused and told her that he hit me a lot. She asked me to tell her about a recent occasion where my dad hit me and told me to take my time. I told her about a typical day in my life and gave her the details of what my dad did to me on a normal basis. She told me that she was sorry to hear these things and that she was going to help me. Dr. Patel then asked me to look at her. I was looking down at my lap as I tried to calm down from pouring my feelings out so fast. She put her hand over mine, and the warmth of it almost startled me, but I looked up at her and held my tears back. Dr. P told me that she was going to be by my side and we were going to get through this together. She said that she was so happy that I opened up to her and that it was time to meet with my second doctor, whose name was Dr. Taylor. I wasn't quite sure why I had so many doctors, but I didn't care; I felt so relieved. I felt like I was as light as a feather after opening up to Dr. Patel. I no longer felt so weighed down. I was okay with talking to doctors. It was better than being at home, so it worked for me. Dr. Taylor wasn't as nice as Dr. Patel was. She wasn't mean, I guess just serious. She told me that she had looked over my chart and spoke with Dr. Walland, the doctor whom I had spoken with before getting admitted the previous day. She asked if I agreed with her that I was not happy, that I was feeling sadness that has lasted longer than a few weeks, and I said yes. She said that she wanted to start me on an antidepressant right away. She explained that it was a medication to help with sadness. Dr. Taylor said that even though we had not gotten to know each other very well, what she did know was that my brain needed help with producing chemicals that controlled my emotions. She said that they might not keep me on that medicine, but it's what we could start with. She explained that it sometimes can take months to find the right medications and sometimes medications do not work for some people. Dr. Taylor was a serious lady, but I liked her because she didn't talk to me like a child. She led me through a few doors and down some hallways until we ended up at some kind of window. It looked like it was for medication, like a pharmacy. She asked me to sit and wait for her. She said she had to put a few things into the computer. I sat and watched people come in and out of doors. Everyone used a swipe card or punched in a code on a little keypad by the doorknobs. I noticed that there were a lot of security guards coming and going. It made me feel confused on whether I was in a hospital or a jail. It felt like I was waiting for Dr. Taylor for so long. I started imagining all kinds of things. I imagined that the medication that they gave me brought me to a place that was beautiful, happy, and safe: shining sun above me, conversation and laughter all around me, maybe a park on a summer afternoon, kids flying kites, or kids playing baseball with parents behind them cheering them on. I closed my eyes and could see a young couple, a mom and dad, kissing with a little girl reaching up for them to pick her up. They picked her up and laugh, and then the dad tickled her as the mom kissed her on the forehead. I could smell the fresh air as if I was really there, a hint of flowers, sunscreen, the refreshing smell of crisp fresh-cut grass.

I almost fell out of my chair when I heard a door slam near me, and after what felt like two hours, a nurse came out and gave me a pill. I looked down at this little tiny pale yellow pill and frowned. I was almost positive that a pill couldn't give me all of those warm thoughts in my mind. The nurse told me that she would bring me back to my unit to eat lunch and then I could join the other kids for a movie. She told me that Friday afternoons were what all the kids looked forward to. The unit would decide on a few movies, and they got to sit and watch them. She said that sometimes the night nurse would bring everyone snacks to eat during the movies. When I got back to my unit, all the lights were dim, and the other kids were already on the love seats and watching a movie. I felt stupid interrupting them and more stupid when they all stared at me. The nurse told me to sit down at a table, and she would check with the nurses' station to see if they saved me any lunch. A different nurse came out a few minutes later with a plate for me, some kind of sandwich with fruit on the side. I barely ate, my stomach started hurting, and everyone staring at me had me nervous. I tried not to make so much noise when unwrapping the sandwich, but the harder I tried, the louder it got. When I walked in, the movie was so loud, but when I started unwrapping my sandwich, it, of course, got much quieter. My stomach hurt, and I started to feel sick and dizzy, probably from the medication. The nurse who brought me my food came back and whispered to me that she was the night nurse, and her name was Janet. She told me that I could join the other kids, but I asked if I could go back to my room. She said we were normally not allowed to spend time in our room until after 6:00 p.m., but she knew that I was still adjusting. I couldn't get to my room fast enough. I felt so hot and so sick, and I just wanted to lie down. After calming myself down, I just lay there and tried to take it all in. My room was just a room with four walls, two doors, two beds, and a window. Everything was white. The walls, the floor, and the doors were white. Even the bedding was all white. There was something about the lack of color, design, the lack of everything that put you at ease. It kind of made you clear your mind and just let everything go; it felt good. The rooms must have been white for a reason, because the next thing I knew, it was the next day. A different nurse came in and woke me up. She said that after breakfast, I had to stop at the nurses' station to take my new medicine. Her name was Amy. She was younger than most of the other nurses whom I had seen so far. She explained that on the weekends, there wasn't much of a schedule and we were able to come and go from our rooms. She said that we could watch TV in the dayroom, read books, or play board games, and they had a good selection of puzzles. She said that during the week, we were not allowed to go in our rooms until after dinner but on the weekends, we could. Nurse Amy said that during the week we were encouraged to be social, so not allowing us in our rooms made sense.

During breakfast, the other kids were all so loud. They were practically yelling as if they weren't right next to each other. They reached over each other's plates and bumped into each other shaking the tables. A few of the kids asked what the other kids were going to eat off their plates and insisted that they gave up what they didn't want. No one asked me my name, but the girl across from me did ask me why I was there, and I said because my parents or doctor thought I needed to be. She laughed and kept eating her breakfast and then asked me if I wanted my toast. It was hard to focus on eating breakfast in a strange place with kids you didn't even know. I asked the girl what her name was, and she said, "Maricella Mendoza, but my girls call me Mimi." I figured since she asked me why I was there, I would ask her the same thing. She said it was because her mom was always tripping and trying to control everything she did because she didn't have a life. She went on telling me that she was staying out at night, drinking alcohol and smoking weed with her boyfriend. She said that her boyfriend was older than her and her mom wanted to keep them apart. She said that's why she was there. A girl from the next table came and sat down by me and introduced herself as Jessica. She told me that I would hate it there and said I better enjoy the weekend. She and Mimi told me that during the week in the morning, there was a nurse named Brenda, whom they hated. They said she purposely tried to make everything harder for them. They said that the weekend nighttime nurse was a guy named Matt and that he was awesome. He let them get away with all kinds of stuff that the other nurses didn't. They said that Amy was okay too. They said that they always thought she and Matt would make a cute couple and acted shy around each other. There were two other kids at the table on the other side of me. Both were just sitting there and not talking. That weekend, I went back and forth from my room to the dayroom. I took a couple of naps and watched a couple TV shows. We couldn't control the TV. The nurses' station had the remote, but we could ask them to change the channel. After two days of doing nothing, I wasn't sure if I felt better or worse. That week, I got thrown into the routine. Mornings consisted of waking up, getting ready, eating breakfast, and then getting my medicine from the nurses' station.

During the week, we had a hospital version of school for a few hours. If we did all of our work, we got to pick five stickers out of the sticker box. At first I thought it was so stupid, but then I decided to collect all the stickers I liked, and I would do something with them.

There were so many different kinds—teddy bears, shooting stars, rainbows, butterflies on flowers, and almost every kind of cartoon and superhero you could think of. I started collecting all of the Ninja Turtles stickers; and the teacher, Ms. Stephanie, gave me a baggie to keep them in, and I hid them under my mattress. After school was therapy. I had long therapy sessions with two, sometimes three, different therapists every day. They all asked me the same questions like, Why are you here, why do you think you're here, how are you feeling, and what do you want to get out of your stay here? My answers were always the same. I was there because my parents obviously wanted me there, and I was feeling okay but sad before I got there and I guess I want to be happy again before I leave. I told the therapists everything. At first, it felt so good to get it all off my chest. I got to tell them every little thing that my dad said and did to me, and not just that, but I also explained how I felt. With everything that was happening to me, I always felt so many different versions of sadness, anger, and depression. I got to really explain my emotions, and I never had gotten to do that before. Sometimes, I would forget what the therapists even asked me, and I would talk and talk, telling them so much more than they probably even asked me about. The sessions were so long, and they wrote everything down. They said it was so they could look back on it later and show it to my doctors and other therapists.

The first couple of weeks went by pretty fast, and I was feeling better than I had felt in so long. After you had been there for two full weeks and had no issues with breaking the rules, your family got to come and visit you. Family visitations were on Sunday afternoons. They lasted about an hour and a half and were in a different part of the hospital. The first thirty minutes were for just visiting, and the rest of the time was family therapy with Dr. Taylor. I wasn't even sure if my family was coming to visit me. They didn't tell me, but I actually hoped they didn't. As soon as it was time for family visitation, they called me to the nurses' station and told me that a security guard was coming to escort me to the family room. My mom and dad were looking as awkward as they possibly could as soon as I walked through the door. I guess it was awkward for everyone. I was happy to see my mom. It felt like it had been longer than two weeks, so I was excited to tell her about it there. My mom asked how I was doing and how everything was going, and I told her how great I was feeling and how I enjoyed it there. It was a pretty basic visit, what you would expect out of a visit with anyone who was hospitalized. My dad didn't talk at all. I was okay with that, and I actually thought it was nice of him not to say anything rude to me. There wasn't much to say to them, and it was such a relief when Dr. Taylor came in and asked if we were ready for our session. Our first therapy session started like all my other therapy sessions did, the same questions. She asked me why I was there. I told her because my mom brought me there because I had gotten very sad. She told me that she had heard me say that for two weeks, and she was ready for me to tell her why I was really there. I told her because I was depressed, very depressed, so my mom brought me there. She said that was a good start, but I needed to do better than that and tell her why I was really there. I repeated myself several times, but she kept repeating herself until I was about to lose my mind. I got so angry. I felt it rise up from my feet to the top of my head, and my words just poured out after that. I told her that she was not listening to me. I was there because I was depressed. I was so depressed that I wanted to die. I was yelling, and I told her that my mom was a fat pig that sat and watched my dad beat me every day. I asked her if she was happy. I asked her if this was good enough. I yelled louder and told her that I had no idea why my dad was there, because he was an evil person who liked to beat little girls. I stood up. I looked at my mom and dad as the anger completely took over. I lost control. I could barely get the words out properly as I yelled. I told them that they were stupid for coming to see me. I laughed and told them that it made no sense at all for them to visit someone that they didn't even care about. It felt so good to yell at them. They looked so stupid sitting there, like kids who just got into trouble. I had no clue what this doctor wanted from me. It was like she wanted me to explode or to get upset. They were all just sitting there looking at me, all them of them just staring at me like they were watching a movie or something. They were silent, no responses, and I couldn't take it. I told Dr. Taylor that I needed to go back to my unit. I told her I couldn't take it and to please take me back. She took me back, all the way to my room, and I was so surprised that she didn't talk to me about what just happened. After the anger left, the relief that washed over me was so intense that I fell asleep.

I woke up to a nurse telling me that I needed to wake up so she could give me medicine. I told her that I already took my medicine in the morning, that they gave it to me at the nurses' station. She told me that it was a new medicine and handed me a pill and water. I was half asleep still and said, "Okay." I woke up the next day, so either I was extremely tired, or the pill that I was given made me go to sleep. I was so groggy and crabby when Nurse Lolita came into my room at 6:00 a.m. to wake me up, and I kept falling back asleep. I don't even remember that day, but I do remember a day or two later meeting with Dr. Taylor. When I walked into the therapy room, she was writing in a folder, and she didn't even look up. She told me to give her a couple of minutes. She said she had to finish up some notes before we began. Sitting there, I couldn't help but to realize how small that room was. It was almost like being in a large walk in closet. It was a dark-orange color. I think that might have made the room seem smaller. She looked stressed out, or maybe she didn't like her job. She probably saw tons of kids. Dr. Taylor always wore suits that had skirts instead of pants. She had on one that was a light-gray color with flowers on it. The last time I saw her, she had on one that looked just like it but without flowers, and it was a darker gray. Her hair was always the same too. It was long and blonde. It looked like she just pulled it up and clipped it back. She wore the big clips that looked kind of like two combs put together. You squeezed the middle to open them, and then when you let go, it grabbed the hair and kept it in place. The big hair clips never matched what she was wearing. Today's was dark blue with light-blue stripes, and I remember the one she wore last time was bright red. The only thing that matched were her shoes and her glasses. They were both dark brown. After looking at her for a while, I realized that she probably wasn't as old as she looked. Maybe she just didn't care about how she looked or wasn't confident. I always wondered how people got to the point of not caring whether they matched or not. Maybe they thought it looked good together, or they didn't care.

Dr. Taylor looked at me for a moment, and I thought it was because I had been staring at her, but she just said my name and then took her glasses off. She let her glasses fall on her chest. They were hooked onto a beaded necklace thing that went around her neck. When I saw that, it really made me wonder why she tried to make herself look so old. She must have been an unhappy person. I figured she was not married, maybe never married and never had kids, maybe just had a dog or two. She shook her head and then told me that there were consequences for my behavior during our family therapy session the past week. I looked at her like she was crazy, and I told her that I didn't do anything wrong. I told her that I was sorry that I yelled, but I had been holding it all in and it just came out. I looked at her. I waited for her to say that she understood or that it was okay to express the way I felt, just not while yelling. I expected her to tell me that she was sorry to hear about what my dad was doing to me and what my mom was watching my dad do to me, but that didn't happen. She told me that she had been in close contact with my parents and had a better idea now on what was going on with me. She told me that my mom was so upset by everything that happened at our family therapy session and my dad was hurt by what I said. I asked her why my mom or dad would be upset. I told her I was the one that was upset. She told me that I was not going to make progress if I wasn't ready to be truthful. She said that I was the only one who could help myself get better. I shook my head. I asked her what I was supposed to be truthful about, because I had no idea what she was talking about. She closed the folder that was on her lap and told me to think about it, to think about the fact that my progress there was up to me. I was confused and mad at what she just said, but I just held my tongue and didn't say a word. She said that they were going to add another medication into my regimen to help me control my emotions and that they would come to my room that evening to administer it. My parents must have told Dr. Taylor something for her to act like that. I just hoped that Dr. Patel didn't treat me the same way. She didn't take me back to the unit, and she didn't have a nurse do it either. She opened the door, and there was a security guard waiting for me, and the second I saw him, I knew that she thought I was some kind of criminal or dangerous person. I had so many thoughts rushing through my mind. *How did I go from a patient to a prisoner? How did this happen? Was I being escorted by a security guard because of yelling at the family therapy last week? Did they think I was violent now?* I had no idea. I wondered if they thought I was so unpredictable that they couldn't trust me, or maybe they thought I would try to escape.

I hadn't been in my room too long when two nurses came into my room. One was a very petite woman who looked young. The second nurse was a tall and rather muscular man. He looked middle-aged and in great shape. I knew he was middle-aged, because his head was shaved, but it was just starting to grow back, and you could see a pattern of baldness. They both had on light-blue scrubs that matched, not like the white scrubs that all the nurses in our unit wore. They both had big smiles on their faces and the woman braces on her teeth, and I thought it was strange, because I had never seen an adult who had braces. The woman asked me my name, and I told her. She said that she just had to verify that they were giving the medication to the right patient. She told me that her name was Nadine and she was very happy to meet me and give me my medication and that she would not take up too much of my time. I thought that it was funny of her to say that, because it wasn't like I was in the middle of doing something important; I was in a hospital and just sitting in a bed with nothing to do. She pulled a small plastic package out of her front pocket and told me that this medication was different from the ones that I was already taking. She said that it was not taken in a pill form, but instead it was absorbed by my skin. It was a patch that would go on my back. I was relieved, almost happy, because when I heard my medicine wasn't a pill, I, for sure, thought that meant it was a shot. A patch sounded great compared to a shot, and a patch sounded even better than a pill. She asked me to stay sitting on the edge of the bed, lean forward, and lift up my shirt. She asked me to reach over my shoulder as far as I could and to stay like that for a moment. She asked the male nurse to put his finger where my hand ended and then told me I could bring my arm down into my lap. I just put my head down. I could see her open the little package and take out a little white patch. I felt the other nurse's finger lift off my back just as Nadine wiped the spot off with alcohol, waved it dry with her hand, and then stuck the patch on my back. I don't remember eating that day, and I thought it was around dinnertime, so I went to sit in the dayroom. It was after 6:00 p.m., and there were empty trays on the tables, so I asked the nurse where my dinner tray was. The nurse told me that she was under the impression that I wouldn't be eating dinner that evening, but she would send someone down to the cafeteria. I felt so stupid that I got so mad inside. All I could do was tell the nurse that I wasn't hungry anyway and was just checking.

I sat in my room staring out the window and imagining my real mom and dad coming to take me out of that hospital. I imagined my real parents telling me how sorry they were that I was put in there. They would tell me that they were sorry that they ever let me end up with those people who weren't even my real parents. I closed my eyes and could see them. Even though I didn't know what they looked like, I could see their love. Wherever they were out there in the world, I knew—I could feel—that they loved me. I could feel that my real parents would love me for who I was; they would really love me. I tried to clear my mind and use the energy inside of me to connect to my mom. I tried to talk to her, trying so hard to get her to feel me. I would tell her that I needed her so bad. I needed her to help me and to find me. I would tell her that I was her daughter and I needed her. I would try so hard to connect to her. Wherever she was, wherever in the world, I needed her to feel me trying to talk to her. I would try so hard that I would give myself a headache and make myself dizzy, but it was worth it. I hoped she felt. Deep down inside of me, deep in my heart, I knew that they must have had a good reason to let me get adopted by my parents. I knew if they met me, they would want to get me back and away from my adopted parents. I was so tired, and with my eyes closed, I couldn't stay awake anymore, so I drifted off as I talked to my real mom with my mind. The days after that, all started to blur together, I was so tired and barely remembered anything or knew what was going on around me.

Somewhere in that fog, a new girl came into the unit, and they put her in my room. I was lying down staring at the wall when she came in. They introduced her as Amber, but she just looked at the ground and didn't say anything. She just sat on the bed, moved to the middle, and hugged her knees to her chest. She put her head down on her knees and kind of rocked back and forth. She was skinny, more like scrawny. From what I could see, she had no curves to her body. I had forgotten that after two weeks, I would get a roommate if anyone new came in. There were other rooms available, but for some reason, they didn't use them. They just paired us up. Maybe it was easier for them to monitor us with two kids in every room. There was one kid, one of the boys who had his own room, Shawn, the ghetto one who was always rapping. They said that he needed his own room because he had serious anger issues and they didn't want it to affect someone else's progress there. I had seen him get angry several times, most of the time in our school class, when he didn't know how to do the schoolwork. He would get very angry if he didn't understand how to do something or if the teacher told him he wasn't doing it properly. He would stand up and yell at her, telling her that she was stupid and he wasn't doing it anymore. He would shove his chair, and most of the time, he would cuss at her. I'm not sure if she was a teacher or if she was just some sort of counselor. One time, I saw Shawn get so angry in the dayroom that he kicked the wall, and then he clenched his fists and started hitting himself in the head. He paced back and forth while hitting himself and screaming until Matt, the counselor, tried to stop him. He couldn't get him under control. Shawn kept pulling Matt's hands off of him and screaming. He kept running and then jumping all over the love seats, so Matt couldn't grab him, so he had to call security to help him. When security had to come to the unit, they made us stay in our rooms, but we would stand by the doors so we could see what was going on. They would put a jacket on him that wouldn't let him move his arms, and then you wouldn't see him for a couple of days. When you did see him again, he wasn't angry. He wasn't really anything; he was just there. He would look very sedated and just sit in a chair and stare at a wall, like a zombie, like an empty person.

My therapy sessions started to all sound the same. Each doctor and each therapist told me my progress was up to me. They said that how long I spent there was up to me, so I needed to start cooperating. They started saying things like my parents were so worried about the friends I was getting mixed up with. They were worried that I became depressed from using heavy drugs. I didn't even know what they were talking about, but it made me angry because heavy drugs sounded exactly like what my dad was doing. Then one day, Dr. Taylor said that my parents told her something that was very disturbing. She said that they told her that I was hurting myself. I felt like I completely lost control mentally. So many thoughts were going so fast in and out of my mind. I became frantic. I looked down at the ground trying to focus, trying to figure out how this happened. I told Dr. Taylor that I wouldn't hurt myself and the only reason I became depressed was that my dad was beating me. I told her I was so depressed because he had been beating me for so long that I didn't know what else to do but to start thinking about suicide. I cried. The tears poured out, and I felt my nose running, but I didn't care. I needed her to listen to me. I told her that my mom was always sitting right there when my dad beat me. I told Dr. Taylor that he beat me so bad some days that I could barely walk. I could barely get off the floor. I cried and cried and told her that my dad hated me, my mom, too, and I couldn't take it anymore. I cried, and I begged her to take me away from them. I told her I didn't care where I went. I just couldn't be anywhere near my parents anymore. She was writing in the folder and asked me to take a breath while she got caught up writing down what I told her. She took a minute or two, then took off her glasses and folded them, and then placed them in her lap. She looked like she was trying to figure out what to say to me. I heard her take a deep breath as she looked at me. She asked me why my parents brought me to the hospital. She asked why they would care to hospitalize me if they didn't love me. I told her that they wanted to find a way to not have to deal with me anymore. I told her that they didn't beat my brother and sister, just me. I told her that they probably put me into a mental hospital so that no matter what I told people about what they were doing to me, no one would believe me. I told her that with my dad beating me worse than he used to, now that I always had bruises, they had to cover it up. Now everyone would think I was a crazy person, and they would then believe what my parents said. She asked me to listen to myself, to listen to what I was saying. She said that it sounded like I was blaming everyone one else for what was going one with me, everyone except for myself. She told me that I had to take ownership for what was going on with me, and until I could do that, I would never get better. I couldn't believe that my parents could do this, this was my fault, and I should have told everyone what was happening to me. I should have told my school. I should have called the police every time my dad hit me. I should have showed the school all the bruises. When he beat me and I couldn't get off the ground, I should have crawled to a phone and called 911. This was my fault. I let my dad beat me like I was garbage, and I never did anything about it. I told Dr. Taylor that it was all my fault that I let him do this to me and never did a thing about it. I told her I never hurt myself or hit myself or whatever stupid stuff my parents were saying. I told her that I no longer cared what she thought and that I would never say anything, nothing but the truth. She told me that was my choice and that I was the only one that would suffer from that. She had a nurse take me back to my room, and then before I knew it, they came to put another patch on my back.

The next day, I woke up feeling so strange, so dizzy, with my head feeling so heavy that I could barely hold it up. I woke up before a nurse came to wake me and Amber up, because my stomach was hurting and I felt like I had to throw up. As soon as I stood up, I almost fell over with my head feeling so heavy. I stumbled and was able to catch myself on the bathroom door. As soon as I got in there, I fell to my knees but couldn't make it to the toilet and threw up all over myself. I remember my head jerking back and forth. I struggled to keep it up as I choked on pieces of food in my vomit. I felt better after that; at least my stomach did. I was still dizzy, so I just leaned back and lay on the ground. I almost fell asleep until Amber came in. I thought she was going to help me, but instead, she yelled at me and told me that I was letting them do that to me. She said that they put the medication patches on my back where I can't reach them, because they knew I would be sick. She said that this wasn't her first time in that kind of place. She had been in four of them. She said her parents kept sending her back for depression and because she made herself throw up and refused to stop. She told me that I had only two options in this situation. The first option was to tell them whatever they wanted to hear so that they wouldn't keep me so sedated. Option number two would be to start throwing up the pills and having someone take the patches off. I just wanted to lie down and go back to sleep. I was so dizzy, and the smell of my vomit was making it worse. Amber kept going on and on about the doctors and nurses and what she thought was going on. I felt too sick to deal with it while I was lying on the ground in my own vomit. I couldn't help it, but I had to yell at her and tell her just to go and get a nurse for me. Amber picked the absolute worst time to decide that she wanted to talk to me, so it was hard to not get mad at her. One of the daytime nurses who was only there a couple of days of week came in. Her name was Carol, and she was not the nurse for that situation. Carol looked like she hated herself and her life every single time I saw her. It was disgusting to see a nurse act like that. I hated people like that. That's exactly how my mom acted all the time, so miserable. Carol looked at me and shook her head, and instead of helping me up, she complained first and scolded me. She said that there was no reason I couldn't have made it to the toilet or the garbage can. She said I was too old for that kind of behavior. I lay there with my head spinning, listening to her complain, and telling me that there were no excuses. She said that she shouldn't have to clean up vomit from someone my age, especially with her having back problems. I was annoyed and wanted to smack her and tell her that her back was hurting because she was so overweight. How dare her. She was a nurse, and her job was to help me, not make me feel stupid for throwing up because a medication they gave me made me sick. Her scrubs were so tight, and her belly bulged out in several places. She was one of those people who breathed heavily when she did anything. She lifted her arms a few times, and you could hear her. She had red curly hair. She looked like she got perms and dyed it auburn frequently. She wore two sets of small gold hoops and had on a small gold necklace with a heart that had a blue and a red stone on it. She only ever wore blue eyeliner, no other makeup, just blue eyeliner. At first, I thought she just didn't have time to finish her makeup but later realized she did it on purpose. She was such a mean person all the time, and her white scrubs were always so tight that I'm sure that didn't help her out. Nurse Lolita was chubby, but because she had such a sweet personality, it was cute. Nurse Carol's attitude was just like my mom's attitude. Their outside looked just as ugly as their inside. Every time I saw her, I thought that she must have a bad relationship with her husband, just like my mom did. They were both so hateful. They both had the same miserable vibe when you were near them. Nurse Carol reached over me and turned on the shower. She told me to get myself off the dirty floor and into the shower. She told me that I needed to get myself cleaned up so she could send someone in to clean up my mess.

For the rest of that day, I couldn't help but to hear Amber's words repeatedly in my head. I knew she was probably right. I knew that the patches were making me sick and they were making me so dizzy. I couldn't help but to go over everything in my head. It started to all make sense. I got upset at the first family therapy session, and then that night, they gave me a second medication that made me feel so tired. Dr. Taylor was acting as if she didn't think that I was telling the truth about my dad hitting me, and then it happened again. That same day, they put a medicine patch on my back that made me so dizzy that I got sick. I felt my heart start to beat faster after I realized there definitely was a connection with what was happening to me. It scared me, I didn't understand why everything was happening the way it was, and I was confused. A few days later, it was time for a family therapy session, and this time, they wanted to do separate sessions. One session where it was just my mom in the room, and one session with just my dad. My mom barely even said anything. She waited for Dr. Taylor to ask questions, and I could see her trying to figure out what to say. Dr. Taylor asked her, in her opinion, how this all started and what here biggest concerns were. My mom told her that I started dressing differently, wearing all black, and listening to dark music. She told her that she thought I started using drugs and might be having sex. She said that with me, anything was possible. My eyes were so heavy that I kept struggling to keep them from closing or rolling back in my head. I was also trying so hard to keep up with the conversation. I was dizzy, and my stomach was still hurting. What did that even mean, that "anything was possible with me"? Why would she say that about me? I couldn't believe she was saying that. My mom made it sound like I was some kind of out-of-control kid. That wasn't even me. She said it was a possibility that drugs were what started all of this, the attitude change and the disrespectful behavior.

Dr. Taylor told her that, during their phone conversation, she had mentioned that I was harming myself and wanted to know more about that. My mom looked confused for a moment. It looked like she had forgotten that she lied and said that. She didn't even do a good job at acting like that was true. Her face looked like she just got caught doing something wrong. All she said after that was that she and my dad were very worried about that. Dr. Taylor asked her how she knew I was hurting myself and asked her if she had seen me do it. My mom said that she didn't but she knew that I was doing it. She then asked my mom how I was doing it, and my mom told her that I punch myself in my face and on my body. Even with feeling so sedated, I yelled at her to stop all of the lying. I told her that I couldn't take it anymore. I told Dr. Taylor that my mom didn't even make sense. She said that she never saw me hit myself but said I punched myself in the face. I asked Dr. Taylor if she had realized how much of a liar my mom was, because she definitely was a liar. I told her that she had to notice that my mom froze up when she brought up her saying that I hit myself. I told her that she clearly froze up because it wasn't true and that she had forgotten that she ever said it. I told her that my mom was just trying to cover up the fact that my dad was constantly beating me while she just watched him do it. My mom told me that I was completely delusional and that my lies were hurting my dad. She said he loved me so much. I got up and told them both that I couldn't deal with any more lies. I told my mom she would be punished one day for doing this to me. I couldn't deal with any more of my mom covering up for my dad. I looked at Dr.

Taylor, and I told her that if she believed the lies that were coming out of my mom's mouth, then she was just as stupid. I yelled for her to take me back to my room, but she told me that I still had to do a therapy session with my dad. I asked her if she really needed to hear my dad's lies, too, because I didn't feel like it. She told me that I needed to sit down before she called security. I did sit down, but it was only because yelling at her got me so dizzy that the room started to look like it was spinning.

The session with my mom was bad enough, but then the nurse brought my dad in, and I knew that the worst session was yet to come. My dad sat down, and without even looking at him all the way, I could see his face. He wanted to look and act like he was a victim, so then I couldn't be the victim. My dad looked at me and told me that he didn't know why I was doing this, why I was hurting him and my family. He tried really hard to make it look like he was being sincere and distraught. He looked at the ground so that he would appear upset. Really it was because he had no idea how to actually care, so he didn't know how it looked. The only person that my dad probably ever really cared about was himself. He was the most selfish person I had ever met in my life. I had to dig deep inside of me and gather up the strength to control myself, because I was having a hard time. Dr. Taylor asked my dad why he thought that I was showing signs of having anger-management issues, and my dad acted like he had no idea. I laughed at him and asked him if he was really going to just lie to her face. I asked him how he could feel good about himself knowing that he had been beating me and then lied about it. I asked him if he would do me a favor and disappear from my life. I told him that he hated me and clearly didn't like the rest of his family much either. I told him that everybody would benefit from his leaving and never coming back. I told Dr. Taylor that when he wasn't beating me, he was either gone or in his shed doing drugs all night. I told her that she would be scared and probably horrified to see what he looked like stumbling into the house in the middle of the night. The madder I got, the dizzier I felt, and it was making my head and my stomach feel so much worse than they already did. My dad looked at Dr. Taylor and told her that this is what he and my mom had to deal with all the time and that it was affecting the whole family. He told her that he did sit outside in his shed but only because he was scared of me and what I might do. I couldn't deal with him anymore. I was drowning in their lies, and there was nothing I could do. I stood up, and I cussed. I said bad things to him, and I cussed more, and I knew that I made myself look horrible.

I was so tired that I started slurring my words and could feel spit coming out the sides of my mouth. I had a little plastic cup of water in my hand that I had got before I walked to the therapy room. I threw that cup of water at the wall, and I told Dr. Taylor that I did not want to look at my dad anymore. I told them both that they had serious issues and that I couldn't be in a room with them anymore. My head was spinning, and my anger was at an intense level as I called Dr. Taylor a few inappropriate and derogatory names. I didn't get escorted back to my room by a nurse. I was grabbed by two security guards and pulled out of the room. They put me into one of the white jackets that they put Shawn in when he had his anger episodes and was hitting himself. It was a type of jacket. It looked like a big white coat with a bunch of straps and buckles hanging off. They put it on you from the front, like a hospital gown, and you could feel that closing it with straps. Then they held your arms across your chest and strapped them down with a bunch of straps, and they did it very tightly. It wasn't that it hurt to have it on, but because you couldn't move, it was aggravating and put you into a state of panic. I think the worst part about it was that they put you in it when you were angry, so then you felt like you were going to lose your mind. You're angry and then furious, and you're no longer in control of even moving your own body. Then to make it even worse, they didn't let you walk. Two security guard nurses dragged you wherever they wanted you to go. You would try to calm down and just catch your breath, but you would panic even when they drag you to your bed. Somehow, even when I was nowhere near my parents, they were controlling me. I gave them so much time to figure out a way to cover up what he was doing to me. I gave my parents so much time to drown out the truth with their lies and performances in front of Dr. Taylor. I could see myself drifting off, losing my voice and losing any of the power

I might have had to help myself out of this. Sinking into nothing-ness, I was losing; I was losing at everything. I wanted to matter. I wanted my life to matter, but it wasn't, and it never did. It was hard to even lie down with the straightjacket on. They set me on my bed, and then I had to fall back and push myself with my legs. I felt like they had a camera hidden somewhere and were probably watching me and laughing. They must have thought I was dangerous even in the jacket, because they sent a nurse in to give me a shot. The nurse must have been from a different unit. She didn't even talk to me, not a hello or anything. She just came in and pulled my pants down without even asking me to lift my butt up, just roughly pulled them down. Then she wiped my upper thigh with alcohol and gave me a shot. It stung it first, but then it started to burn, and then it felt like fire or poison was ripping through my veins. I couldn't help but scream and kick my legs up and down in an attempt to stop the pain. My leg felt like it was itching and burning at the same time, and it didn't stop for a minute or two. The nurse was already gone before it stopped burning, and I could focus on what was happening. I didn't even care that Amber was sitting on her bed right next to me. I still cried loudly and kicked my legs on my bed. I didn't know her. She was just some girl whom I had to share a room with, so why would I care about what she thought? All I remember after that was that the burning in my leg turned into a feeling of intense happiness and relaxation, and then it spread through my body.

The next day, I was so tired again, and it was hard to wake up even when they came and took the straightjacket off of me. Usually, I only had to see Dr. Taylor a few times a week, but she had a nurse come and get me right away. She didn't waste any time as I walked in. She told me that my behavior was not acceptable. She asked me if I was planning on changing my behavior or if I would still waste my parents' time every week. I told her that I didn't understand what she meant by that, so she told me that they would give me time to think about it. I was so happy when I realized it was going to be a supershort meeting, but then when two nurse guards came to the door, I knew my happiness was premature. They, at least, didn't grab me and yank me around. They just held my arms and walked me out. They were male nurses, but they were also the security guards for the unit. There were always two male nurses there who stood by the doors or in the hall near the rooms. They were pretty much security guards most of the time, but they were nurses when they needed to be. If you needed to be forced to take your meds or held down to get a shot, they were your nurses. One was a skinnier Caucasian guy with red hair, light skin, and freckles. He seemed nice, held me gently, and gave me reassuring smiles when I definitely needed them. The other guy was almost the opposite of him, if you look at it like that, meaning his features were much different. He was big and a lot taller, and he had very big arm muscles. He obviously lifted weights. He had dark-brown hair and a mustache and beard. He looked like he was Mexican but might be Italian. He gave me the feeling that he wasn't a good person, he was bad on the inside; I had seen it before. They brought me up to the front of the unit, toward the right side, and told me to wait for a moment. One of them squatted down, and then I noticed a square in the wall in front of us. The walls in there were gray. They were like a thin gray carpet. When you go to someone's house and they have an inside porch, sometimes there's a thin scratchy carpet. The walls are like that. I then saw the nurse grab a little knob on the wall. It was a white knob, and I had never even noticed it. The outline in the wall was only about three feet high and maybe three feet wide, so that's probably why I never noticed it before. He pulled the knob, and then a wooden door came forward, but it didn't have any hinges. The door thing came all the way off, and he sat it down on the floor next to him. He then grabbed some keys from his front pocket. Under the wooden carpeted door, there was what looked like a cage, and then the nurse unlocked it with one of his keys. It was a small cage or some kind of room, and it was right there in the wall where you wouldn't even see it. I was so distracted by the door being right there in the dayroom that I wasn't even thinking about what it was. The nurse looked at me with a serious, almost mean face and told me not to make it harder than it needed to be and pointed down at the door. I almost thought it was a joke at first, but both of the nurses didn't look like it was a joke. I took a step back as I tried to process what was going on. I was scared, but they grabbed me and told me to kneel down. I fell to my knees, and they told me to crawl into the door, and I did. I found myself in a small space in the wall. It wasn't big enough to even call a room. It was too small to stand up. You could only stay on your hands and knees. I heard the nurse's keys, and then I heard them jiggle and lock the door. Panic set in, but before I could even try to breathe, I heard them pick up the wooden door. As soon as they put it over the cage door, the light was gone. There was only darkness and then silence. I could hear my heart beating, and I could hear my breathing get faster and harder. There was just enough room to lean back onto your legs and then push yourself back into a sitting position but with your head down. I reached my heads out, and the walls were right there. All four of the walls were right there. It wasn't a room; it was a box, not even a small room but a small box. I was locked in a box in the wall. It was too small in there to scream. It was too small to cry. You couldn't hit the walls or kick the floor, because there wasn't enough room. I wanted to die. I wanted to scream and to yell, but I couldn't do anything. I started shaking, and I was already not feeling good from all the meds. In that box in the wall, I wished that I was dead. All I could do was close my eyes and try to focus on something. I had to find something to think about. I picked my parents, my real parents, and I tried so hard to reach them with my mind. I needed them. I needed them to come and help me. It was hard to not feel like an animal trapped in a cage, because I was being treated like one. They were doing more than controlling me; they were taking every little piece of me away. They sedated me when they got mad at me for refusing to stop saying stuff that they didn't like. They put me in a straightjacket when they didn't like how I refused to go along with all of the lies. Then they put me in a cage after refusing to let them drown out my voice completely. They put me in the darkness and the silence that they wanted to keep me in, the same kind of darkness and silence that I was already in at home. I sat there hunched over, feeling my legs cramp up from sitting in such an awkward position. I had to slow down my racing thoughts and try to put a hold on the questions that were flooding into every crevice of my mind. I wanted to figure all of it out, make sense of it, and find a solution or a plan. That wasn't the time and definitely not the place, so I literally had to just breathe. I couldn't, I couldn't just breathe; I cried and I cried, and I got myself so worked up. My emotions went back and forth from one to another, and I no longer had control over them, none of them. I was trapped, I was alone, I was scared, and I was panicking. Somewhere in between the crying and breathing heavily, I either passed out, or I fell asleep. I woke up to the sound of Nurse Amy's voice asking me to back out or get onto my knees and crawl out backward, and I gladly did. My body was sore, and I just wanted to lie down. Being in that place in the wall had me feeling horrible. I wanted to rest. I wanted a shower and get a good night's sleep to get rid of my headache and the cramps in my legs. As we walked to my room, Nurse Amy gave me a vile smirk and told me to get ready for breakfast and school. When I realized it wasn't still Sunday afternoon, I got a sick feeling deep in my stomach. I wasn't in their cage for a couple of hours; I was in it all afternoon and all night. I was tired, but I liked going to our school class, because it took my mind off what I was going through. Focusing on something simple that was so easily solved was a small comfort to me. I looked forward to getting my five stickers at the end of our class, and I always got them. I carefully chose them, and then I hid them under my bed until I figured out what I wanted them for. Most of the other kids didn't even want the stickers, because we weren't little tiny children. I was so tired that I felt myself drool sometimes, and if I wasn't doing something, I would drift off to sleep.

I realized that I hadn't met with Dr. Patel in what seemed like weeks, so when a nurse came to get me for her, I felt hope. I knew I had to explain to her what was happening to me. Her warm smile comforted me as I walked into the room. I felt the good vibes radiating from her. Right away, I could smell her perfume. It was an intense floral aroma, and under that, you could smell a hint of woodsy scent. It was intoxicating. It took me away from that hospital for a moment. It actually lifted my spirits as I smiled at Dr. Patel. I quickly sat down, and I held my composure because I didn't want to look like I was unstable in front of her. I just didn't want her to think I was lost in my emotions or unbalanced. I wanted her to really understand what I was about to tell her. I needed our conversation to be simple and clear, no confusion. She asked me how I was doing, and I told her that I was not doing very well at all. She looked up at me with a concerned face and put down the folder she was holding. She looked genuine. Her face showed true emotion and concern for what I had just said to her. I told her that I had become so confused by what was happening to me there, and I didn't know what to do. I explained to her that I have been honest with every single doctor and therapist and everything started to go downhill after my first family therapy session. I told her that my mom and dad were both lying about everything and my dad was pretending he didn't beat me. I told her that at both sessions, they acted like they were worried about me and Dr. Taylor believed their lies. I told her about all the medication that made me sick, the straightjacket, and the small space in the wall that they put me in. Dr. Patel's face went from concerned to almost frightened by what she was hearing. She told me that she was going to talk to Dr. Taylor right away and find out what was going on. I told her that I told Dr. Taylor so many times about my dad beating me but she told me that I needed to start being honest. I told her that my mom told her that I was hurting myself and I was pretty sure Dr. Taylor believed her. I told her that Dr. Taylor told me that there would be consequences if I didn't start telling the truth, and I told her I was being 100 percent honest. When I told her that I wasn't going to be quiet about my dad hurting me, she had the security guard nurses put me into the little space inside the wall until the next day. I could tell that Dr. Patel didn't want me to know how upset she was getting by what I was saying. She tried to force a normal smile as she told me to be patient while she got to the bottom of everything and met with Dr. Taylor. I don't know why I didn't ask to speak with Dr. Patel before it got so bad there. I guess it just all happened so fast. I knew Dr. Patel was going to expose Dr. Taylor for what she was doing to me, and it was such a relief. I no longer felt helpless. If I had any other problems, I would have Dr. P. help me. I watched her write down notes from our session, and the way her hand moved, I could tell she was upset. Her hand wasn't loose. The pen wasn't moving lightly across the page. I could see how tense her hand and arm were from where I was sitting, and she was pressing the pen rather hard as she wrote. I closed my eyes for a moment. In my head, I imagined her asking Dr. Taylor what she was doing. I imagined her angry and telling her that she couldn't treat me like that and that it was completely unethical. Dr. Patel would tell her that my parents were clearly abusing me and that she was going to do something about it. There was no way that Dr. P. was going to let this go on. She was going to help me; I trusted her. Before the nurse took me back to my room, she told me to hang in there and not to worry anymore. I felt good about everything. I felt like things were going to be moving in a whole new direction. I had a newfound hope. and I kept my spirits high that week even as I felt so sick from the new patch they put on my back. Between the patches and the pills, I could barely tell what day it was or if it was day or night. I went from awake, thoughts racing, and my head pounding to so tired that I drooled on myself when I tried talking.

A new girl came in. Her name was Marquisha, and her room was across from mine. At night, I could hear her cry, sometimes scream, and I didn't see her a lot. She didn't come out to eat most of the time, and she didn't attend our school class. One day, I was eating lunch and in a medicated stupor. When she sat next to me, she just sat and stared at me. She had dark-brown skin and dark-brown hair pulled into a tiny ponytail. She wore an old purple hoodie that looked so worn that it was starting to get thin in some spots. It looked like she had worn both her hoodie and jeans for a very long time, like those were some of her only things to wear. Even her shoes looked like they had been scrubbed and put through the washer many times. Her skin was dry, and it looked like she hadn't taken good care of herself for a while. I didn't care about all of that. When she looked at me, she looked deep into my eyes. She told me things but with her eyes, and I told her things back with mine. She was broken. She was in the same darkness and couldn't get out. I felt it. I felt like we were on even ground with each other as she looked at me, and I felt like we were old friends even though we just met. She didn't smile. She just told me her name was Marquisha, and I told her mine was Ava. She just sat next to me and ate and then sat next to me while I watched TV, and after that, she was always next to me. We didn't talk much, but it was because we didn't need to. It was the darkness that was in us that talked, that connected. All we knew was that we were the same. My medications made me so tired that I wanted to give up, but I kept going and waiting for Dr. Patel to figure it all out. Family therapy sessions continued to be full of lies, their lies mixed with my sadness and anger. Dr. Taylor continued to tell me that with my actions came consequences and I would then end up in the wall—the dark, very small, and hidden area inside of the wall that no one could see; the tiny cage right beneath the wall that you wouldn't know existed if someone didn't show you. After several times in there, I figured it all out, the point of it all. That little cage was to change you, to quiet you, to erase you so they could then turn you into something else. It made sense. It was a tool, and it worked in combination with all the pills and patches to shut you up. The space inside the wall was my enemy until I learned how to relax my entire body and remain calm. I learned to take myself to a place of peace, and I would stay there in my mind while leaving my body behind. I would close my eyes and clear my mind completely, and then the darkness would turn into fluorescent colors. Bright colors shooting toward me and then past me, I would pick one color and focus on it. That color would intensify and then turn into a bright white light that filled my entire mind. Every section and corner of my mind would be illuminated, and then it would roll downward like smoke, filling up my entire body. My head would get warm and fuzzy, and then that, too, would drift down and take my body over. This meditative state that I learned how to achieve was the only thing that got me through being put in the wall. I went from coming out of there shaking and fragile to calm and clearheaded. While in there, I decided that I wasn't going to just roll over and die, and I wasn't going to let them kill my spirit. I was going to live. Sometimes, on the weekends, Matt, one of the weekend nurses, brought us to the roof. He wasn't supposed to, but he told us that everyone deserved fresh air and that it was good for the nerves. I would close my eyes and feel the wind and the sun on my face. I would try to identify any smells in the air, no matter how faint they were, and then focus on each one. Bringing a bunch of unstable kids outside probably wasn't the smartest idea, especially on a rooftop, but I enjoyed it. In the hall right before we got to our unit's side door, there was a big lost-and-found box. Shawn, the kid who was always rapping, would joke around and tell Nurse Matt that he needed to go shopping in the box. He would say that he needed to find new gear and tell Matt he should step his game up and do the same. Nurse Matt never really understood that Shawn was joking, making fun of the items in the lost-and-found box. He also didn't understand that he was at the same time making fun of how he dressed. He was the only nurse who often wore his normal clothes to work, and not scrubs. I don't think anyone cared since he only worked on the weekends, and weekends were very relaxed there. One day. we were walking back to our unit, and I saw a lunch box, the old-school kind of lunch box, the ones that were square and hard plastic, often with cartoon characters from movies or TV shows on the front. It was hot pink, and whatever was on the front had been scratched or peeled off, but I didn't care. Nurse Matt told me that I could keep it, and I did. I set it in the corner of my room and kept my stickers in it. I don't know why I liked it or even wanted it in the first place, but I had it. I started talking to Marquisha at meals and in the dayroom and would sneak into her room to talk privately. We weren't allowed in each other's rooms, but some of us did it when the nurses were not paying attention.

In some of the rooms, you could barely see the bed from the door. There was a small corner by the doors. In my room, the beds were directly in front of the door, and the room was a perfect square. Marquisha's life was like mine, full of darkness, but in a different setting. Her mom was a drug addict and could never take care of her the right way. She always chose crack over her. Her mom wasn't what you call a functioning drug addict, meaning she couldn't get high and take care of her responsibilities. My dad was a functioning drug addict or at least a functioning drug user. Her mom couldn't keep a job and an apartment and pay the bills while using or being addicted to drugs. She told me that her mom made a lot of money prostituting but couldn't keep any money set aside for anything but drugs. After the money was gone and her mom needed more, she started letting men have sex with Marquisha. She said that it started when she was eight years old, and her mom would do it whenever she wasn't in DCFS custody. Marquisha's mom would lose her off and on for not properly taking care of her, but she never told DCFS about her mom selling her for money. She told me that she never said anything because that was better than living in a group home. She told me that group homes were like jail and that she'd rather live with her mom even with having to have sex with grown men. Her grandma took her off and on, but she was too old to take care of her, and DCFS knew that. I told her how I have these memories, bits and pieces of someone molesting me, but can never see their face. I told her about my dad bringing me to bars and strange men making me sit on their laps. I told her everything that my dad was doing to me, and she consoled me as if she didn't have her own problems. I thought she would think what I was going through wasn't as bad as what she was, but she didn't. She had to have sex with grown men but still told me how sorry she was for what I had been through. She was there; she was right there with me in the darkness. Marquisha had been in a group home and was supposed to be going back to live with her mom. She said her mom was doing well. She had gotten a job and a new apartment. Then she stopped coming to see her and stopped answering the door for the DCFS caseworkers. Marquisha said she had gotten her hopes so high up that they came crashing down and she tried to kill herself. She asked the group home staff for pain relievers every day and saved them. Then during a weekend visit to her grandma's, she took a bottle of her painkillers from a hip surgery. Marquisha took all of those pills she had saved. She took them all at once and waited to die. Someone must have found her before she did, because she ended up in that hospital with me.

On a day that I was so drugged up that I kept falling asleep while trying to talk to Marquisha and watch TV in the dayroom, she told me something bad. We were sitting near Samantha, the girl who dressed and acted like she was younger than she was. Samantha was quiet. She never talked much, and she carried around a stuffed animal, a tattered old monkey. Samantha and Marquisha were roommates, so sometimes they would watch TV together in the dayroom. She told me that I better start pulling the patches off my back. She told me I couldn't be like that in there, it wasn't safe. She kept trying to talk to me very quietly, but I was so tired that I couldn't hear her. After several failed attempts of her quietly talking and whispering in my ear, we went into the hall near her room. She told me that she couldn't say it in front of Samantha, but when you are drugged up, you have to be careful. I was confused, but she explained that she had seen male security guards near Samantha's bed. I was so out of it that I couldn't even comprehend what she was implying. Marquisha told me that the last time she was hospitalized, there were a few girls who said the male security nurses were coming into their rooms at night. I could hear what Marquisha was saying, but I didn't know what to think about it or how to even process it. I asked her what exactly they were doing when they were coming into the girls' rooms at night. She told me that they were touching them, and one said that they had sex with her when she was drugged up on medications. I told her that there was no way that she could know that this was even happening or had happened before. Marquisha put her head down and told me that she did know for sure because she was one of those girls. I felt panic shoot through my body, and I could feel the hairs stand up on the back of my neck. I had almost understood and accepted that place. I told myself that it could be worse and to just deal with it. I almost lost my breath asking her the details of what happened to her. She told me that the last time she was there, she was there for five months, so it happened several times. I wanted to hear what she was going to say, but I wanted to run away all at the same time. She said that the first time it happened, she woke up to one of them touching her, and she was so scared. I asked her why she didn't tell someone, like one of the nurses or doctors. She said she did. She said that no one believed her, that no one believes kids who go in and out of group homes. She said that the doctors knew her mom sold her for drugs, they knew that grown men had sex with her for money. She said that after something like that got put in your file, no one would believe that would happen to you again. She said the male nurses knew who to target because of something like that, those were the girls who they probably thought were used to it. Marquisha said that the male nurse who kept messing with her threatened her and told her not to talk about it. He told her that he would make sure she was put in the space in the wall every day if she talked about it. I told her that I would rather be put in the wall, but she told me she was terrified of the dark. She said that after that, it was the same male nurse who would come in and have sex with her, and he would choke her when he did it. I was horrified, I was scared, and I didn't know what I was supposed to do now. I would go back and forth from a feeling of panic to a feeling that I was going to pass out the more I thought about it. I had almost made my peace with what I thought was the worst part of that place, which I thought was being put into the wall. Come to find out, there were much bigger things to worry about. I told myself she was lying just to help me get through the night, even when she became very agitated as she told me that it was all happening again. I was having a hard time processing it. I had already been having a hard time with the fact that I was in a children's mental hospital.

I got caught in Marquisha's room sometime after that, and then the nurses started monitoring how much time we spent near each other. My therapy sessions got worse, but I continued to stay patient and wait for Dr. Patel to figure everything out. Whenever I spoke to Dr. Patel, I had to tell her about what was happening and had happened to Marquisha. I couldn't even imagine how Dr. P. would handle finding out that male security guard nurses were molesting patients. After another horrible family therapy session, Dr. Taylor started to look like she was getting angry or maybe losing her patience. She no longer looked calm and casual as she sat on the other side of the room. She normally leaned back slightly in her chair with her legs crossed and gently shook her foot as she spoke. The way she spoke was always in a calm manner, and she always sounded like she had no concern with any of my responses, whether they were to her liking or not. She met with me immediately after that particular therapy session, and she did not hold back when telling me what she thought. She wasn't sitting back comfortably in the chair with her legs crossed this time. She was sitting forward toward the edge of the chair, fingers crossed, and her chair right in front of mine. Dr. Taylor told me that I was wasting her time and she did not deserve it and nor did my family. I had to tell her that I did not care about whether or not she thought I was wasting my parents' time. I told her that I thought I had made it very clear about what I thought about them. I wanted something good to come out of it all, but how could it with everything based on lies? She asked me what she could do to help me move forward with my treatment and with mending my relationship with my family. I tried to just stay calm and not get upset with her. I told her I did want to move forward. I told her that the only way my relationship with my parents could be mended was for my dad to stop beating me. I told her that I knew she believed my parents with all their lies but the only way we could move forward was for her to open her eyes. I told her that she was supposed to be helping me and I didn't want to hear anything else from her. I told Dr. Taylor that I was done talking to her if she wasn't ready to help a child who needed her so desperately. I told her that I just didn't understand why she couldn't help me, why she couldn't get my dad to stop hurting me and my mom to stop watching it. That's not what Dr. Taylor wanted to hear. She had already chosen to believe my dad's side of the story. I guess it made sense: that hospital probably was expensive, and it was my mom or dad who would pay for it. So why would she accuse the person paying the bill of beating their child? I had always heard that money ruled the world, so, yes, it made perfect sense what was happening to me. She told me that I had left her with no choice but to start taking a more drastic approach to my treatment. Every time Dr. Taylor didn't get what she wanted out of our sessions, they either added more medications to my list or increased the dosage. It got to the point where I could barely walk, and when I spoke, my words were slurred and distorted. I just wanted to stare at the wall and laugh. I was completely drugged up, and I knew it. I asked a couple of the nurses to tell Dr. Patel that I needed to talk to her immediately. After a few days, she met with me, and I told her what Marquisha told me was happening to her and to Samantha. I told her that the male nurses were molesting patients and it had been happening for years. I told her that every time I met with Dr. Taylor and said something she didn't like, then they drugged me. I stood up and walked around the room, I was wobbling, stumbling to keep my balance and told her to look at me. I told her to listen to my words. I told her that I knew she had noticed that I was slurring my words and probably drooling on myself. I leaned against the wall and then slid down it, ending up on the floor, sitting on my butt. I was tired, and I felt strange. I put my head in my hands, and I cried for her to help me. She quickly got up and walked over to me. She knelt down and put her hand on my shoulder. She told me that she was going to help me and that I needed to stay strong for a little bit longer while she figured some things out.

Dr. Taylor must have found out about my visit with Dr. Patel and must not have been happy. After that, they gave me some kind of medicine that made everything start to look and feel like a dream. Then the next thing I knew, I was waking up, and it was several days later. I went from being drugged up to being in the wall. There were days where I didn't eat and days where I went to the bathroom on myself. There were days where I don't think I even woke up, or at least I didn't remember it. My back burned from the patches and from being in such a horrible position when in the wall. Being put in the wall over and over had my neck cramped up, and I think my hip and pelvic areas were bruised. They had me locked away in the wall like an animal in a cage. I could smell myself, and I could feel how dirty my body was from so many days of not showering. From so much medication and not eating, I felt weak, and I felt so sick. I found out that I was no longer allowed out of my room except or to eat and attend my school class. They moved Samantha to a different room. I guess I was being punished good this time. I ate my meals, and then they put me back into my room. I didn't see Marquisha at any of the meals. I asked nurses, and they told me that I needed to worry about my own treatment and stay focused. When they told me that, I knew that Dr. Patel had told them what I said about Marquisha and the male nurses. I told the nurse that I needed to talk to Dr. Patel, and she told me that she would let someone know. I found out later when meeting with Dr. Taylor that Dr. Patel was no longer a doctor there. When those words came out of her mouth, I could see a slight smirk and happiness wash over her. I don't think she even cared about how she looked when she said it, as long as she looked like the boss. I asked her why Dr. P. wasn't there anymore, and I could tell that it bothered her that I called her Dr. P., and not Dr. Patel. She told me that it wasn't working out for Dr. Patel there, that she was having a hard time handling her patients. I was calm at first when I told her that it seemed like such a coincidence, the timing and all of Dr. Patel getting fired. Dr. Taylor said that she was aware of my conversations with Dr. Patel and all of my allegations. She said that my allegations toward her and the male nurses were very serious and that kind of stuff is nothing to joke around about. I could see what was happening: she was in control of this place; she let all the bad stuff happen. I felt sick to my stomach as my heart started to beat harder and harder until I could feel it in my forehead. *How could this happen to me? How could I have a doctor who was a bad person, an evil doctor?*

As I looked at Dr. Taylor, I knew that she didn't have kids and that she probably hated them. There was no possible way that she could have children with the way that she treated the kids at the hospital, the kids who needed her. She had the perfect chance to be a great person, a kind and loving person to tons of kids whose lives she could change. The other idea that kept popping in and out of my head was that Dr. Taylor was doing what she was paid to do. I started to think that she was being paid by my parents to drug me, punish me, and brainwash me into being a different person. It made sense; it was too much of a coincidence that I was put into a hospital with a doctor who acted as evil as my dad. This hospital visit was to brainwash me into forgetting about how bad my dad was, how bad my family was. I told her that they weren't going to be able to cover up the male nurses molesting patients. I told her that I would expose them when I got out. I would tell the police, and I would call every news channel. I told her she would get in trouble for drugging me and keeping in the wall, not feeding me, and allowing me to urinate on myself. She leaned in toward me and told me that could only happen if I ever made it out of there. Her words did frighten me. I felt the hairs on my arms stand up straight. There was absolutely no point in talking to her anymore. She was an evil woman and an even more evil doctor. I heard crying one day as a nurse walked me to my room, and I knew it was Marquisha, so I ran into her room. It was Marquisha, lying on her bed, crying her eyes out. I slammed the door shut and told her to get up, and then I pushed her bed into the door to help it stay closed. I told her that they had been keeping me drugged because I told Dr. Patel what the male nurses were doing to her and to Samantha. She yelled at me and told me that she couldn't believe that I did that. I was confused. My heart dropped to the floor when I saw the anger in her eyes. She pushed me, and I didn't know what was happening, but from the way she looked, I knew she was mad at me. I asked her what was going on, why she was angry; and I told her how confused I was. She told me that I made everything worse, worse for her and worse for Samantha. She told me that I was a silly little girl who thought I was going to change something, but no one would ever be able to change that place. She told me that Samantha tried to kill herself, the male nurses started going into her room more. She told me that it was the same for her, too, and that they hurt her bad. She cried and cried, and her hot tears splashed onto my arms as I tried to hold her.

The nurse had gone and got security guards. We could hear their keys jingling, so we knew they were coming. Marquisha told me to hurry up and help her to hold the beds against the door so they couldn't get in yet. She told me that I had to stop. She said that I had to do whatever it took to get out of that hospital. She was looking directly at me, and her voice was so serious that it grabbed my full attention. She said that I actually had parents, most kids in there didn't, so I needed to do what I had to do to get out of there. She told me to start by having good family therapy sessions and to tell my parents what they wanted to hear. Then when I was on good terms with them, I could tell them what was happening to her, and they could stop the abuse in the hospital. The security guard nurses were yelling at us to get away from the door, to stand against the wall so they could get in. I didn't know what to say. My mind had so many thoughts, and I was so irritated with what Marquisha had told me. I was even more agitated by what she asked me to do. My dad was beating me, and now she wanted me to pretend that everything was fine, and I didn't know if I could do that. How could I go from standing up for myself to kneeling before my parents and Dr. Taylor and saying, "You guys won"? I told Marquisha that I would do it, I would help her, but I wasn't sure if that was true. I had to think about it. I had to really think about everything because I had no idea what I was going to do. We stood up and let the security guards push through the door and the beds. It felt like we were being ambushed, as they acted like we were criminals. They pushed us both onto the bed and put us in straightjackets. The nurses were not happy as they mumbled and cussed under their breath. They put me back in my room and then laid me on the bed and told me not to move. Lying there, I could feel my heart beating through the straightjacket and the sweat that just started to bead on my forehead just right under my hairline. My mouth was dry; it felt so dry that it was making my teeth hurt and I was getting a headache. I was uncomfortable and couldn't process what had just happened. It was too much for me to handle. I barely knew what day or time it ever was. I always felt sick, always dizzy and drugged up, always struggling to walk or talk properly. I was a mess, and now Marquisha expected me to put on a show and try to talk my parents into helping her. My thoughts kept going back and forth so fast, one idea to the next; but clarity on the problem or the solution was nowhere to be found. My racing thoughts and confusion quickly turned to anger, and I couldn't help but to think that Marquisha was not my problem. I tried to help her by telling Dr. Patel everything she told me, and it made everything worse. I had enough to deal with, and now all of this was thrown at me.

I was so upset that the tears just started pouring out. I cried and sobbed uncontrollably. I shook my head back and forth as I yelled and cried. I kicked my feet into the bed, and I cried harder. I cried angrier, and I cried until I fell asleep. I woke up knowing that there would be unpleasant consequences for my actions the previous day, and there definitely was. They gave me medicine that made the room spin, and if that wasn't bad enough, they put me into the wall. I could normally deal with the wall but not while everything was spinning. I couldn't be all hunched over like that. Being in there like that was unbearable. Even after I threw up, I was still so sick and needed to get out. I had to sit with my face right above my vomit, I was hot, I was sweaty, and the smell made me even sicker. I started to continuously feel like I had to throw up, but nothing would come out anymore. Hunched over and dry heaving, I needed to get out of there, I was panicking, I was sick, and I needed help. I couldn't relax my whole body and drift away from there like I had trained myself to do. Not like that, I couldn't. The dry heaving got so bad that my head started pounding. I could feel my pulse through my eyes and could hear my heartbeat. I couldn't control anything when I was dry heaving, including any muscles near the pelvic region, so I went to the bathroom on myself several times. I needed to get out of there. I was too sick to be stuck in a tiny area inside the wall. I felt like the space was getting smaller, like the walls were caving in, and I couldn't breathe. My head and nose felt like they were burning, and everything started feeling very different, very fuzzy. That wasn't the first time I passed out and woke up the following day still inside the space in the wall. I was so tired, not the kind of tired that I usually was when I came out of there. I was a different kind of tired that day. My chest was painful to the touch and felt so heavy. My nose and mouth were dry and slightly burned, and I had a headache that I felt through my eyes. I was weak, not just tired; but my body felt so heavy, so sore, and it was hard to move. It was morning, because I could hear the nurses telling everyone that breakfast was on its way. I could hear the news. In the mornings, the nurses always turned the news on before all the kids came out of their rooms. It was the weather portion, cloudy with a 60 percent chance of rain and scattered thunderstorms in the afternoon. It sounded like a beautiful day for someone who wasn't in a mental hospital or crammed into a tiny space in the wall. I felt like an animal in a cage, like a dog, and I felt like I should be sniffing around in an alley looking for scraps to eat. If I were a dog, I would be the angry unpredictable kind of dog that you didn't want to approach. I tried calling the nurses or security guard nurses. I yelled at them to please take me out of the wall. My bladder was full, and I didn't want to go to the bathroom on myself again. My underwear were, for the most part, dry. They must have dried some during the night, and I didn't want to sit in wet underwear. My stomach was hurting from being bent over for so many hours, and I imagined my organs being pushed up against each other. I heard a buzz and the main door open, and then I could hear the squeak and rattle of the wheels on the food carts. It was almost time for breakfast, and that meant that all the kids would be at the tables maybe twenty feet away from me. If I yelled long enough, maybe the nurse would think that I was too much of a distraction and let me out. Sure enough, it worked. I was out and told myself that I couldn't go back there again.

I was escorted to my room by a male nurse and told to take a shower before eating breakfast. That shower felt euphoric after what I had just gone through. It was such a relief to feel the water on my face and skin. I closed my eyes and cleared my mind as I listened to the different sounds that the water made. I was so torn between what to do, keep fighting for the truth to be exposed, or just shut up and play nice. My life and my problems, Marquisha's life and her problems, it was overwhelming. It was all a lot to handle, even for someone a lot older than me. That situation was a lot to go through at any age. Getting nice and clean, eating breakfast, and feeling better were my first priorities. Then I could think about the bigger stuff. The shower had been so relaxing that it allowed me to just release. I cried and cried. I yelled into my pillow. I got so lost in my sobbing that I didn't even hear one of the male nurses come in and almost jumped when I saw him. By the time I looked up, he was right there kneeling in front of me and telling me that it was okay to cry. He told me to just get it all out and not hold onto anything that wasn't good for me mentally or emotionally. It was comforting to hear him say that, to hear him say that it was okay. It was comforting until he touched my face and told me that I was too beautiful to have so much sadness inside of me. He rubbed the side of his hand across my face, then down my neck, and then held both of my shoulders. He told me that it was okay as he moved his hands from my shoulders to the tops of my knees and gave me a big smile. He told me that he always helped out girls who were so sad, and I jumped up before his hands touched anywhere else. I didn't even think. I just told him I had to use the bathroom and quickly walked across the room. I waited in front of the bathroom. He walked toward the door slowly as he stared directly into my eyes. He walked right by me and stopped. The look in his eyes frightened me, but I tried so hard not to let him see that. I just smiled and told him, "Thank you," as he walked out. Suddenly, all the images from my dad's pornographic magazines flooded my mind, and I almost screamed. So many images rushed through my mind all at once. It made me gasp for air as I imagined me in those images. I imagined that nurse doing some of those things to me, and I couldn't help but to fall to my knees and cry. Then Marquisha's words pierced through my brain like a knife; the details of what she told me had me panicking. The thought of that nurse holding me down and molesting me, raping me, it was terrifying.

I was no longer confused about what to do. I would get out of that hospital—that was what I would be doing. With what just happened, there was no doubt in my mind—I would do whatever it took to get out of that place. I remember those few times my mom snuck us to church and the pastor's words about praying in times of need. I didn't know a lot about praying. That's why I never did it, and I really didn't know anything about whom I was supposed to pray to. I knew that it all had to do with God. That's whom, I was pretty sure, you prayed to or talked to when you needed help. When we had been to that church, the people were different. They all looked better than us, so I always figured God was for other people, not me. I decided to pray. I told God that I needed to get out of that hospital so I did not become like one of these other girls, molested by male nurses. I gave up after a minute or two. I didn't even know God, and I didn't see a point in asking him anything. I did what I needed to do after that day. I smiled, and I told them what they wanted to hear in therapy. When family therapy day came around, I told them how much better I had started feeling and how much I missed my family. Those words burned like fire as they rolled off my tongue, but I smiled as I said them and kept moving forward with my plan to get out of that place. I told Dr. Taylor that I was depressed and confused, that's why I said the things I did about my mom and dad, but was finally feeling better. They were all so stupid. They didn't care about me or my feelings. They just wanted everything to go their way. I felt like a robot, moving, speaking, and operating to their program that they selected for me. In our school class, I did great every day and kept collecting my stickers and placing them in my lunch box, still not knowing what I was going to do with it. I didn't forget what Marquisha asked me to do. I told my mom that I thought Marquisha needed help and that we should try to help her. I couldn't tell her that the male nurses were molesting her. If I said that, then I would be back in the same situation that I just crawled out of. Marquisha even came and visited with my family a few times at family visitation, and surprisingly, my mom liked her. My dad hated Black people with every fiber of his being, but my mom pretended not to. I think that pretending that she wasn't racist made her feel like she was a decent person, instead of a horrible person. Marquisha was happy to have any kind of attention. Anything that even slightly resembled having a family meant so much to her. All of that distracted her from the fact that there wasn't a single thing that my mom would be able to do to help her. Without telling my mom what was really happening to her, there was no way anything was going to change for her. If I did tell my mom, then between her, my dad, and Dr. Taylor, they would have my thrown back into the space in the wall until I said that I made it up. I felt bad for her, but I knew there was nothing I could do for her, and I knew that life was different for everybody.

I started thinking about what life was going to be like when I went home, back to school, back to reality. I realized that the kids at school might know where I had been, locked away in a mental hospital. In fact, I almost knew for sure that everyone already knew. Tiffany and Candace had become so concerned about where I went that they ended up having their parents walk down the street to talk to my parents. They probably tried so hard not to tell anyone, and when they did, they made whoever they told promise not to say anything. I imagined that going on and on and on until everyone knew exactly where I was at, away at a mental hospital. I couldn't help but to imagine what the kids at school were thinking about me. Maybe they were all going to be scared of me, or maybe they would all think it was cool that I was in a mental hospital. It would be up to me to make sure they thought it was cool, that they thought I was cool. I took the lunch box that I had been looking at every day, and I covered it with dark-blue glittery nail polish. There was a lady, Sally, who came around to the different units and gave girls things like headbands, nail polish, and lip gloss. I think it was to help girls or women feel good about themselves while in the hospital, help them to feel pretty. When I had only been there for a week, she came to my room and offered me some items, but I turned them down. She took a two packs of nail polish out of her bag, sat them on the end of my bed, and left. After the nail polish dried, I took all the stickers that I collected, and then I stuck them all over the inside and outside of the lunch box. At first, I had no clue what I was going to use it for, but then it hit me—it was going to be my purse, my crazy-looking lunch box purse. A crazy-looking lunch box purse for the crazy girl who just came home from a mental hospital. I decided that I was going to own it, I was going to give the kids at school something to look at and talk about. They were already going to be looking and staring and whispering in the halls, so now they would have an additional topic to obsess about. When they stared at me, I would wave with my hand held high, and when they would whisper, I would say hello with my head held high, making them feel awkward. This was going to be a fresh start for me, a new beginning, a revamped Ava.

After thinking about the new me so much, I started to think that maybe the new me would make my dad treat me differently. All of it sounded so good in my mind, and the whole thing had me excited; it gave me something to look forward to. It had been so long since I had something to look forward to. Honestly, that was the first time in so long that I even imagined the future. Before I knew it, I was back at home, and my parents were actually acting like we were a happy family. My brother and sister were happy that I was home. They were actually happy to see me, and I was happy to see both of their smiling faces. It felt good; it felt relieving. After what I went through in that hospital, I needed "good" and "relieving." What I needed was normal when I came to my family—a normal mom, a normal dad, and all normal siblings. I wanted my brother and sister to have a good childhood. They were so innocent. I hated thinking about them having to go through what I did, I felt like it was my job to protect them from it. My brother was such a nice little boy. He was always so quiet but so yet playful. I wanted to spend more time with him, but it was hard not to feel resentful toward him, because my parents favored him. My sister was just as sweet, but she was so little that with everything that was always happening to me, I barely ever played with her. Even with sharing a room with her, I barely had spent any time with her. I barely ever looked at her. I was going to make being in that hospital a good thing. I was going to make it into a second chance at everything. I was going to be a better big sister to both my younger sister and brother, not let anything that was happening to me get in the way. My dad hurting me had made me completely block them out and had me treating them like the enemy. I think that because my parents favored them, I tried to pretend that they didn't exist, but they did, and they needed me to protect them. To make life look brighter, my dad turned half of the garage into a new bedroom for me. They removed the garage door and had a wall put there and then put up a few walls and a door, and my room was born. It really was going to be a new chapter of my life. I was going to make the best out of everything. Sharing a room with my sister was always hard, and it did upset me a lot because she wet the bed every night. My mom didn't change her sheets or take out her clothes that she wore when she wet the bed, so our room always smelled so bad. Some days, it was unbearable, and a lot of nights, the smell kept me from falling asleep. So my own room was really nice—my own room, my own style. I was really going to use all of this as a chance at a new me, and I was so happy about it.

Going back to school was the beginning of a new me, and from the moment I stepped off the bus, all eyes were on me. Most kids needed a new year for a fresh start, not me. I was breaking all the rules to start fresh. My new lunch box purse wasn't the only thing that I revamped. I spray-painted my leather boots with different colors and put my hair in pigtails. I even used those old-school plastic hair barrettes that had poodles on them and those plastic ball ties that you put around ponytails. Don't get me wrong. I loved my grunge style, but I had to add onto it a bit. I had to make some changes, funk it up just a little bit with bright-blue eyeshadow and mascara. The finishing touch was the Elmo doll that I carried with me. I looked so crazy that no one dared to ask me if I had been in a mental hospital. I went from having no friends at school to have groups of people around me everywhere I went. All the popular girls, girls who were cheerleaders, were interested in me. They wanted to be around me. Some of the girls started to copy my new style and would run up to me when they saw me and were so excited to show me. It felt good. The attention distracted me from the fact that I just got out of a mental hospital, and I actually pushed it completely out of my mind. That whole year, before I went to the hospital, I was obsessed with this boy Ricky. He was into grunge and Nirvana just like I was. Before the hospital, he had never talked to me, and I don't even think he had ever even looked in my general direction. That definitely changed just a few days back, and he was all smiles as he glanced in my direction. Before I even knew it, Ricky was my boyfriend. The boy whom so many girls drooled over was now drooling over me, and it was all eyes on us. For a few months, I was on top of the world, riding the high of my newfound popularity. I did a Miss America wave to all of the kids on the waiting list to be in my direct circle of friends. I can't lie and tell you that it didn't get to my head, because it did. I loved it, every minute of it.

There was one girl whom I really felt connected with. I thought everyone was so different from me, but they really weren't. Her name was Latrisha, but no one ever called her that. She only went by Trix. She definitely did not look like a Latrisha. In fact, most people wouldn't have believed you if you told them that was her name. Trix was awesome. All her characteristics were so subtle, but if you put them all together, they were equal to amazing. She had a messy dark-brown-but-almost-black kind of hair that she tied into a ponytail. It wasn't the kind that was up toward the top of your head. It was the kind of ponytail that was down toward your neck or back. Her hair was messy, but the beach wave kind of messy, the kind of messy that people try to mimic now. She wore striped polo shirts that were worn, probably from the thrift store, and very worn, ripped jeans. She wore a thin single piece of hemp around her neck with a teeny tiny silver wishbone charm on it. Trix wore very worn Puma sneakers that matched her outfits so perfectly that you would think that she bought them in a set. The funny thing about Trix was that her family was what you might call rich. She lived in the rich area of our town, a place that I had only heard about. I would have never believed it if anybody ever told me that—parents who were lawyers, a huge house, a giant bedroom, and a walk-in closet. Nope, I would never have believed it, and you would never have been able to figure it out by the way Trix dressed or acted. I think that that's what I liked most about her; she didn't care about fancy clothes or any of that. She didn't care about looking like she was rich, and she never talked about it. She never had even mentioned that her parents were lawyers. Trix was so quiet and calm all the time, but out of nowhere, she would have bursts of energy and would spread around her happiness. When she was in a good mood or had something to be happy about, you knew it. She would run down the hall and say my name so loud and cheerful sounding. She would jump and prance all around me as she laughed. Trix had a friend named Becca. They had been friends since they were little. They lived in that same wealthier neighborhood. Trix and Becca had almost the exact same demeanor, the way they were quiet but then were full of energy. They were so similar in that manner, but Becca was a little more quiet than Trix, and her voice was softer. She dressed like Trix, but her style was a bit neater looking. She wore newer shirts, usually preppy brands, but wore them with worn, sometimes ripped, jeans and old sneakers. I became pretty good friends with her also. I became pretty good friends with a lot of the girls at school. I spent the night with Trix a couple of times; and her house, her neighborhood, it was very nice. Her house was the kind of house that you see in movies, and her room was bigger than our whole living room, and that didn't count her walk-in closet. Trix's room was an exact match to her style and her personality. There were two cheerleaders whom I talked to every day, Beth and Katrina. They were nothing like me, both constantly so bubbly and cheerful. Those two probably didn't even know how to be mean. They were so happy to see me every day and gave me at least two hugs every single day. It must have been a mix of coming out of the mental hospital and starting my new and crazy style that had all those girls flocking to me. It wasn't just girls. I had so many boys who followed me around too. It was like I had my own fan club at school. Several teachers treated me in the same manner. They waved at me in the halls as they yelled my name and gave me thumbs-ups. The teachers, janitors, and lunch ladies all told me how much they liked my new style and that there was nothing wrong with being different. My life was finally good. I finally had friends, and things were going smoothly at home. My dad was treating me well. My mom was being her normal self, which wasn't too bad, and I was bonding with my brother and sister.

It seemed like everything was changing so fast, because around that same time, I found out that Tiffany, my best friend from my neighborhood, was moving away. I couldn't believe it when I found out. It was like a knife stabbing through my heart. Tiffany had called me and told me that her parents wanted me to come and talk to them, so I hurried down there to see what was going on. Tiffany's mom started by saying that she was so happy that I was out of the hospital. She said that she was so upset when she found out that my parents put me in there. Tiffany's parents both implied that my parents could have done anything else besides put me away into a hospital. Tiffany's mom started crying, and at first, I was confused why, but then she told me that the hospital that I was in made the news. A few girls had come forward with allegations that they were molested by male nurses or security guards while they were patients there. She asked me if anything like that happened when I was there, but I had to take a moment to think before I answered her. There was no point in upsetting her further by telling her that it was happening in that hospital. Telling her that other girls were being raped on a regular basis and that it would have happened to me if I didn't get out was pointless. If I told her that, then I would get all entangled in it, and I would then probably get sent back there. If they weren't able to find the truth out of it, then I would definitely be sent back. If I said something and it couldn't be proven, then the male security guard nurses would probably hurt Marquisha and Samantha worse. Tiffany's mom said she called and told my parents that they were wrong for putting me in that hospital when it was on the news for horrible reasons. When she said that I instantly felt sick to my stomach, my mom or dad never asked me if I was okay, if I was being molested in there. They expressed no concern with the hospital being all over the news while I was in there, and the male nurses in my unit were probably whom the allegations were against. I felt sick, but at the same time, I felt a strong sense of relief because someone was at least looking into what was happening to girls at that stupid hospital. I thought that Tiffany's parents only called me down there to talk about the hospital, but it wasn't. Tiffany's dad said that they were moving, selling their house, and moving to a different state. I couldn't believe it. I didn't know what to say or do when he said those words. Tiffany's mom said that there were better opportunities in the area where they were going, better jobs, better schools, and a really good neighborhood. Tiffany's dad had a good job. He worked with computers. He had a computer programming company. Tiffany's mom worked at a grocery store. She went back and forth between that and a pharmacy cashier. I couldn't blame them for wanting a better life. Our neighborhood wasn't bad, but it sure wasn't the greatest. After seeing Trix's neighborhood, I knew that we lived in the not-so-elegant part of town, not the slums but not the best place to live. The town that they were moving to was the next state over, and it was only a few hours away, but to a child, that sounded like she was moving to a different planet. Tiffany had a great family, and if anybody deserved a better life, it was them. I tried to block out the fact that Tiffany was going to be gone from my life, and I tried to put my new friends and popularity in its place. I think it was right then that I started going full steam ahead. I stopped sitting still and made sure I was always moving forward. I let Tiffany move away while not looking back, just pass right by me. A huge part of my childhood just passed right by.

The rest of the school year went by so fast. I guess time goes by fast when you're happy. During the last few weeks of school, I think everything started to change. My popularity faded as fast as it came. I liked my boyfriend Ricky so much, and just when I thought we were going to kiss each other, he broke up with me instead. My other friendships all faded over the summer, completely faded. It was a bit confusing. I guess when all of the friends you made were because of being in a mental hospital, it makes sense that it would dissolve or fade away. I, at least, made a new friend that summer, because a new girl moved to our neighborhood. Her family moved into the house to the right of where Tiffany lived. Her name was Alicia; and it was just her, her mom, and her little brother, Sammy. To most people, they were an odd bunch. Even I thought so at first, but who was I to judge anyone? Alicia's mom worked in a factory, and being in a single-parent home, they didn't have much. They may have been poor, they may not have had a lot of food or may have been barely able to pay the rent, but I really liked all three of them. If I didn't already know my parents were hateful people, I found out when they told me horrible things about Alicia's mom. My mom told me that she used to work with her at a factory and she not only slept with a lot of the guys there but she used heroin. It hurt to hear them say such negative things about her even if it was true. She was a kind woman and, from what I had seen, a good mother. As a child, there was no way to keep something like that to myself. I had to ask Alicia about it even though I knew she wasn't going to be happy. The look on her face was even worse than I thought it would be. It wasn't anger in her eyes, not at all. It was pain and embarrassment. She couldn't even find the words she wanted to say before she put her head down and cried. Alicia told me that before she moved into my neighborhood, she lived with her grandma Joe while her mom was getting back on her feet. She said that her mom has had a few problems with using heroin, so she and Sammy were living with their dad's mother. Alicia told me that her mom went to a rehab program. She had never done that before, so she knew she was serious this time. She and Sammy lived with their grandma for a large portion of their lives, but her mom really wanted to be there for them as a mother again. She did what she needed to do and saved up a bunch of money and then found them a house to rent. Hearing her say that made me really have a lot of respect for her mom. It sounded like she really loved them. It sounded like it took a long time, but Alicia's mom did what she needed to do to be a good mom. Alicia told me that, for the record, her mom said that my mom didn't like her, because she had a Black boyfriend. I didn't know that Alicia's mom had a Black boyfriend, but I knew that if she did, my mom would definitely not like her. My parents acted like dating anyone who wasn't White meant that it was the end of the world. After that, I really understood Alicia's family a lot better. I really appreciated them for everything they did and for how far they came. Alicia made me forget about Tiffany moving away. Without her, I have no idea how I would have made it.

Summer flew by, and seventh grade was suddenly the new reality. Another strange school year started. Over the summer, I let go of a lot of the silly things I had been doing the year before to get kids to look at me or pay attention to me. No more pigtails or Elmo dolls. I even retired the lunch box purse. I went back to the regular grunge style—old shirts, ripped jeans, and boots with a small dog chain as a necklace. All the kids who crowded around me and screamed my name in the halls barely even said hi to me, even when I said it to them. The kids who did say hi or wave to me, they did it in a kind of way like their mom was making them do it. It was so strange. It was like I was only a fad, not one of the permanently popular kids. The cheerleaders' faces when I waved to them were as if they were ashamed to have ever been friends with me. It was all so bizarre, like in a strange dream. I went from being a nobody to being the most popular girl in school and then back to being a nobody all in a few months. I was happy with my new friendship with Alicia, but it was hard not to feel sad about it. Alicia's mood and personality was on the darker side of the spectrum. She was always on the verge of serious depression, and it was obvious. She said that she had something called manic depression and that her mom had it too. That seemed very plausible because her mom was the same way. Alicia had a lot of mature and very childish sides to her. I often was surprised by her moods. I liked her because she saw the world from the very middle, not from my side, not hers, just from the middle. She had an unbiased view and opinion of everything, so I always knew I was getting the truth from her, even if I didn't want to hear it. Sometimes, I couldn't stand her because of it. We always say we want the truth, but when someone gives it to us, we get mad. My dad's evil ways slowly creeped back into our lives. I should have known that his anger would slowly build back up toward me. I guess I had hoped for the best for all of us. I had hoped to be a loving and functional family. My dad must have truly hated me, because before I knew it, I was back in the middle of his hatred and chaos. I tried not to complain to Alicia about my dad hitting me. I figured she had been through enough with her own situation to tell her about my problems. After the really bad fights with him where I ended up pretty beat up, I would climb out of my window and run down the street to her. Alicia never had anything off-the-wall to say, like other people always did. She just hugged me and told me it was okay. My other friends had always talked about running away and never having to see my dad again or them hiding me at their houses forever. Alicia's mom was the same way as she was. She was down-to-earth and minded her own business. I could have been seriously hurt when she asked if I was okay, but as long as I said I was okay, she just went back into her room.

At least I had Alicia that year, because it got really bad at my house. It wasn't just with me. My dad seemed to hate all of us. He really hated my mom, but he never hit her. I think my dad took his hatred toward her out on me. Maybe that's why he hit me so much, because he was hitting me for her and for me. My dad also seemed like he hated that he had kids at all. He rarely ever had anything to do with us. I always tried to figure out the deal with my dad, and my thoughts were that he didn't want to be married to my mom and he didn't want to have kids. I imagined my mom and dad as young people. They probably had some happy years and thought that it would be a good idea to get married. Maybe after that the fun ended and my dad didn't want to be a husband or father, he just wanted to stay in that young-minded mentality and have fun. It always felt like we made my dad miserable, and I could see how miserable he was with my mom. No matter how many times my mom watched my dad hit me, I still felt bad every time I saw her face as she begged my dad to spend time with her. She would ask him to watch a movie with her or to go shopping with her, but whatever she asked him to do, the answer ended up being no. He never actually said no; he would say he was busy, he had a lot to do in his shed, or he would say he was tired and then go to bed early. I hated seeing the pain in her eyes. Even at that age, I knew she loved him, but he did not love her anymore. Seeing that made me feel guilty like I had something to do with ruining their marriage. I started to realize my dad wasn't just trying to hurt me when he would hit me and tell me that I ruined their marriage; it was true. I think it was a combination of things that ruined their marriage, an adopted child maybe and then two unexpected children. Maybe my dad didn't want children at all. I wondered if maybe my dad only wanted one kid but then my mom wanted more. I wondered if my mom wanted to have a happy little family, but my dad wanted to enjoy being young and just have fun. Maybe my dad wanted them to be a young married couple who went to bars, watched concerts, had big parties, and got high on drugs together. Whatever it was, they just didn't work; the whole dynamic of our family just didn't work at all. Sometimes, after asking my dad to do something with her and getting denied, she would take her anger out on us. She would do it by yelling at us to stop bothering her and go to our rooms. She would yell that we never let her relax and have alone time. Her voice would sound strange, very deep because she needed to cry. Sometimes, she would cry, and we would ask her if she was okay, but she would yell at us for asking. I hated it because we could hear her cry, and then we would always hear her open bags of chips or cookies. My mom ate junk food when she was sad or unhappy with my dad, or when my dad was nowhere to be found, she ate. Sometimes, she would take several pieces of bread, smash them together, and just eat them. Sometimes, she would eat a box of individual brownies or cupcakes or ice cream cone sundaes. No matter what it was that she ate, it was sad, and I could feel her pain, and I could feel her needing love. In my mind, I always made excuses for her on why she let my dad hurt me. I told myself she only did it because she was trying to please him. I told myself that she just needed my dad's love and affection, and hoped he would give it to her if she supported him hurting me. I often saw us on the same level. We both were hated and abused by my dad, just in different ways. He abused me physically, but he abused her mentally. Most people would think that I got the worst of it with the physical abuse, but they didn't have to see what my mom went through. My mom did for the most part what she was supposed to do as a wife and mom, but that just didn't matter to my dad. My dad was a monster, but at the same time, my mom was dumb for letting it go on like that. At the end of the day, my mom should have stood up for herself and for me, but she never did.

That year, I started off my normal skinny self, but somewhere along the way, I gained quite a bit of weight and became very self-conscious about it. That year was the start to a never-ending battle between me, my weight, and food. I couldn't control my family and all of our problems, my mom's constant sadness, or my dad hitting me. Somehow that year, I realized that I could control my weight even if it was in an unnatural way. My appetite started growing, and I wanted to eat more and more, I think it was a hormonal girl thing or something. Whatever it was, it wasn't good, and I couldn't let myself get even fatter than I already was. I would make a grilled cheese sandwich and tomato soup, but after I ate it, I would still be hungry and make another sandwich. Some days, I would keep making sandwiches and then be so unhappy after eating three or four sandwiches. I would think that if I could just go back and stop at only one sandwich, then I would be okay, or if I could just take the food out of my stomach, then I would be okay. Somewhere in the middle of the unhappiness, guilt, and disgust, I realized I could take it out of my stomach by throwing up. I still do not know how I actually started doing this, but I did. I learned how to make myself throw up my food. I could eat as much as I wanted, but at the same time, I didn't have to feel guilty and so disgusting. I got to feel happy and satisfied when eating and then relieved and refreshed when I threw it up. I got a whole system down rather quickly. It was fast, easy, and effective. I kept a big bag in my closet that was full of plastic shopping bags, bags from when my mom went grocery shopping or to department stores. I would take a bag and put it in my little garbage can, putting the bag around it, so I could throw up right into it. I would put the garbage can in the opening of my closet, and that's where I would do it. At first, it took me sometimes fifteen to twenty minutes to get myself to throw up, and it wasn't easy. When you first start to do it, it isn't pretty, and you feel like you are a bit crazy. I would use my fingers. I would wiggle two or three fingers down my throat in an attempt to make my food come up. At first, it hurts. At first, your eyes feel like they are going to pop out of your head. At first, you scratch your throat, and it burns. At first, you cry. After so many times, you have to stop and gasp for air as you squeeze your stomach and tell yourself you are a fat pig. Sometimes, I would push my stomach as I cried. I would tell myself that I better toughen up and get the food out. After some practice, I started to develop a better routine and was able to just put my fingers down my throat and easily throw up. I would go into my closet and throw up my meals, then tie the bag up, put it into two more back, and tie them up. I would put each bag of vomit into the back of my closet under clothes, and I would line them all up, only throwing them away every seven to fourteen days. Normal-minded people wouldn't understand the aspect of keeping those bags of vomit for that long. It was like keeping trophies. I knew that right in the back of my closet, I had seven to fourteen days of self-discipline, control, and commitment. Being able to quickly execute the process of throwing up meals gives you an intense feeling of accomplishment and control over your body. It makes you feel good about yourself and makes you feel like you have somehow tricked your body. I lost that weight I had gained, plus a lot more, and I was starting to feel great about myself.

With my parents not ever paying much attention to me, they never even noticed or realized what I was doing. Alicia actually did not think I was crazy for what I was doing either and didn't put that much of an opinion in at first. I felt like I had a way around gaining weight, and the more I lost, the more amazing I felt. I was finally in control of something. The problem with making yourself throw up is that your gag reflex starts to get used to your fingers going halfway down your throat, so then you have to go all the way down. The problem with sticking your fingers all the way down, your throat is that you gag very hard, so hard that you feel serious pains in your chest. At that point, you have to use something to go even further, so I started using the end of a spatula or a hairbrush and pushing on my stomach at the same time. It feels like a lot for your body to handle, but that extra work then makes it feel like even more of an accomplishment. After losing twenty pounds at such a young age, I felt so tired, so I found a way less stressful way to maintain my new slim physique. I started eating every other day, and that worked perfectly without the stress on my body. It just simply worked. When my dad hit me, it was different. I at least controlled the body that he was hitting, and that meant something. That year, my seventh-grade year, had a lot of ups and downs and a few temporary friends, but I made it through to another school year. The summer between seventh and eighth grade was fun. I had a few different friends, and a couple of them were boys. Both of them liked me, and it definitely felt good, so I took the qualities that they both liked about me, and I intensified them. They both told me that I had a beautiful face and that I shouldn't let my hair get in the way of it. I decided to cut my hair off. I just picked up scissors and did it myself. I cut my hair boy-short. It gave me a sassy tomboy sort of look, and it definitely defined my face. I loved it even though it gave my dad a new reason to hate me more; he started calling me a lesbian. A few times, he screamed in my face and told me that I looked like a stupid little boy, an ugly little boy. He told me that I would never be able to find a husband if I kept my hair short and dressed the way I did. He told me that I needed to grow my hair out and wear some nice dresses—"look and dress like a lady should," he said. Both of the boys said that I had a beautiful smile, and even though I had a lot to frown about, I decided to smile more. It took a lot of looking in the mirror to find a smile that I was comfortable with and that I didn't find repulsive. When looking in the mirror, I couldn't help but to smirk and give myself some flirty and sassy smiles, because that's how I felt about myself, flirty and sassy. That summer, I pushed away all my self-conscious issues that I had with myself, and I put myself on a pedestal. It may have been selfish, but I let both of my friends that happened to be boys do the same, put me on a pedestal. I needed to explore my feelings, so I let both of them think that I was interested even though I was too damaged to have a boyfriend. I needed attention and a slight bit of affection to help fill in the holes that were left from my dad's constant abuse. I think that leading them on was like my new bad habit of only eating every other day. It was something I had control over, and I did feel like I had some kind of control over them. The downside was that Alicia had a crush on one of them, but he liked me, and I don't know why, but I still let him think that I might want him to be my boyfriend.

The trust between Alicia and I was strained to say the least, but when I would run down there after getting into a fight with my dad, she was still there for me. Our friendship came to an end in the last weeks of that summer when a similar situation happened. There was a boy whom Alicia liked, and they had been hanging out and talking on the phone. He lived near us. His name was Carter, and he was older than us, maybe sixteen or seventeen at that time. He hung out with kids that were even older than him, so he somehow got a hold of a bottle of liquor, so we planned on getting drunk when Alicia's mom was at work. We did just that, we listened to loud music, and we joked and laughed as we passed the bottle back and forth. It was fun, and we were drunk and lying around in Alicia's room. Alicia and I were on the floor. Carter called Alicia over to where he was lying on the bed, and he boldly kissed her. It wasn't just a regular kiss. It was the other kind of kiss, so I got up to leave the room. When I was about to walk out the door, Carter told me to come over to them and then pulled me onto the bed with them. Alicia was on one side, and I was on the other, and we were both kissing Carter off and on. It took just a few minutes before things were no longer divided equally between Alicia and me. Before I knew it, Carter was only kissing me. He was telling me how beautiful I was and told me that he wanted to have sex with me. Alicia got mad and pushed us as she got off the bed and slammed the door as she stormed out. I don't know why I kept kissing Carter, and I should have left the room with her, but I didn't. I stayed, and I kept kissing him and acting like I was going to have sex with him, but then something scary happened. He started kissing me faster and harder. When I put my hand in his hand, he grabbed it and slammed it onto the bed so hard that I got an adrenaline rush. My heart started beating so fast as images started to flood my mind. I shoved him hard and pushed him to the floor. I stumbled over him and quickly left the room.

Alicia was right there with an angry look on her face and didn't care to hear that I didn't have sex with Carter. She told me that I knew she liked him and should have never got onto the bed. I was drunk and had let Carter and the other two boys who liked me get to my head. I started liking the attention too much. When I was in her room with Carter, something serious happened in my head. I needed so badly to talk to her about it, but she was so mad. When Carter was on top of me, kissing me and touching me, I started having these intense flashbacks. They were so frightening, so real and scary, and I knew what they were. They were flashbacks of someone molesting me when I was little, but I couldn't see their face. He told me that I was a pretty little thing and not to go telling anyone about the game we just played. He bent over and gave me a few dollars and told me I was a good kid and to make sure my dad bought me some candy later. I was angry that Alicia refused to talk to me. I needed to tell her what happened. Instead of even trying to apologize to her, I told her that it wasn't my fault that Carter liked me, and I left it at that. Alicia told me to go home even though I had already told my parents that I was staying the night at her house, so I left. I had brought my own pillows and blankets because they didn't have any extra stuff like that; they barely had their own bedding. I took my stuff and slept on the side of her house that night. I cried and I cried. I smacked myself repeatedly while replaying the flashback in my mind. I felt so dirty. I felt so disgusted and so angry that I didn't know what to do. I just wanted to feel better. I didn't just smack myself. I punched myself in my jaw and my thighs while gritting my teeth. I felt like an animal that was out of control, like a vicious and wild animal that needed to be caged. There was nothing I could do that next morning but push that flashback down and move on with my life, and I did just that. After that night, our friendship faded away as quickly as it started, and I had too much pride to try and change that. I started cutting myself with razor blades after Alicia and I stopped being friends. I found them in my dad's shed, and cutting myself helped give me a release. Nothing that I did ever helped release any of my pain or anxiety, but cutting myself helped. It hurts at first, and you panic, but then you feel this rush of relaxation hit you. At first, I only did it on my thighs, but after a couple of months, I started doing it on my wrists and just wore long-sleeved shirts all the time.

A few months after Alicia and I stopped being friends, I met a new friend. I started hanging out with a girl from school named Erica. She had been in all the same schools as me, but we haven't talked much. After talking a few times and going to her house after school, we became best friends. Her house was great because her parents were always gone, either at work or out all night at the bar. Erica was sad. She had a darkness that hung over her, but since I was sad and had that same darkness, it worked. We just existed together in this close but lonely and distant relationship. Erica had an older sister and brother; so we could stay out late, get in all kinds of trouble, and still have a ride home. We used to meet up with boys, and one night, I met and started talking to a boy named Joey. I had been in school with Joey probably since elementary school but had never really talked to him. I always thought he was too different, in a different group of kids at school. All schools have different groups: there are the gothic kids, skater kids, and preppy kids who are very smart or whose parents have a lot of money. There are ghetto kids and the kids into sports who are football players, baseball players, and cheerleaders. There is usually a group of kids, sometimes a big group that just do not fit perfectly into one of those groups. Erica and I were in that group of misfits; any friend I had ever had was in that group, except for Joey. Joey was not a misfit. He was a football player, a jock. He not only was on the football team but also on the baseball team, so definitely a jock. He was the sweetest boy at first, but then he started to get weird, and I guess you could say he got into my head. I was so broken on the inside, and I didn't know how bad I was longing for genuine male affection. At that age, you do not understand why you feel the way you do, especially about the opposite sex. I was just crazy about hearing Joey say nice things about me; his notes in school gave me goosebumps and had me smiling the whole day. His kisses in front of everyone in the halls were the best thing I had ever felt. He made me feel so special. Joey made me feel like I was the only girl in the whole world, and all I could think about was him. It went on like that for a while, but then he wanted to have sex, and I was worried about doing that at such a young age. Joey acted distant after I expressed how I felt about it, and after a week or two, he acted like he didn't know me at all. Our relationship just stopped, and I was heartbroken and so sad.

I cried so much to Erica. She told me that it wasn't a big deal. She said there would be other boys, but she didn't understand. She didn't understand how sweet he was to me, and more importantly, she had no idea how he made me feel. I wasn't just sad. I needed Joey and his affection back. I was dying inside for it. When he stopped talking to me, I felt like my whole world ended, and I couldn't go back to a world without him and his kind words. I couldn't go back to being lonely and not having someone hug or kiss me. I thought I couldn't get any sadder, but then one day, I got to school, and Joey was kissing another girl. I just died when I saw it. I must have looked crazy as I ran to the bathroom. I put my face into my book bag, and I cried so hard. After that, I went into a deep depression. At Erica's house, I just sat there talking about Joey and how broken I was. I told Erica that it was all my fault; it was my fault I didn't have sex with him. I drank liquor in an attempt to feel better but usually just ended up drunk and worse off. Erica's sister or brother always bought us liquor and cigarettes, so we got drunk a lot. At school, Joey's locker was in the same area as mine was, so I saw him all day. Seeing him kiss his new girlfriend Tamryn in between every single class was killing me inside, and my heart broke every single time. One day, Joey smiled at me, and even though I didn't see Tamryn at his locker, I thought it was an accident. I thought he must have been smiling at someone next to me or something. Later that morning, Erica ran up to me to tell me that Joey was single, he had broken up with his girlfriend. I did get filled with a sense of hope but still kept in my mind that Joey probably would still never want to be with me again. I was so wrong. Before the day was even over, he wrote me a note asking me to meet him outside afterschool. He told me he was sorry, and just like that, we were back together, and I could feel my sadness wash away so quickly. Just as quick as my sadness washed away, I found out that Joey broke up with Tamryn because she wouldn't have sex with him. It hurt—it hurt to find out that he didn't break up with her because he didn't like her anymore. He told me that he didn't stop like me. That's why he said they broke up. Joey made me think that Tamryn wasn't as beautiful and special as me. He said she was too boring. I honestly believed that Joey chose to be with me and not Tamryn, even though that's not what everything was adding up to. It didn't take long for Joey to tell me that if I loved him, I would have sex with him. I should have known that Joey was a liar, and I should have known that he knew just how to get what he wanted. I let Joey see how I needed him and so badly wanted to be with him, and he took advantage of it. Joey told me that if I wasn't ready for a more mature relationship, then he thought we should break up. He said he was tired of girls that acted so young and that he thought I was ready to be the mature girl that he needed.

It went back and forth between us, meaning he ignored me. He also didn't talk to me at school and would wave to the girls around me when he saw me in the halls. I would lose my mind. I would cry and cry and then call his house, hoping so bad that he answered. It only took a few times of him denying me his love and affection before I gave him what he wanted. I gave Joey my virginity because I believed that he cared about me. I thought I needed to have sex to be in a mature relationship, but mostly I just really wanted someone to be there for me. I believed so many of Joey's lies. I just needed someone to love me, but I was looking in the wrong places. I don't know why, but after we had sex, things were different, and Joey's personality completely changed. Most days, he ignored me at school but then would call me after school and say that he was just busy. He would act rude and say mean things to me and then call me and say he was sorry and would make it up to me. There were constant ups and downs, some kind of issue every other day or two, and it really started to mess me up. I started feeling like I had to be with Joey. He made me feel like I was nothing without him. He made me feel like I needed him and I would be a nobody if it wasn't for him. It took me a while, but I realized what Joey was doing to me. He was playing mind games. It took me seeing a Lifetime movie to really understand what Joey was doing to me. The movie was about a woman who was being mentally and physically abused by her husband. It was mental abuse that Joey was using to get what he wanted, mind games, mental manipulation. I didn't want to believe it, but it was right in front of me. All the way from the beginning, from when we started dating, he was messing with my mind; and I couldn't keep letting him do it. Looking back, I should have known that he had bad intentions all the way from day one, but being so needy, I never noticed.

As if that wasn't enough to deal with, Erica and I got into a fight, an actual fight at school. I had been friends with this boy Toby for about two years. We were pretty good friends, and we talked a lot. We talked every day at school and talked on the phone at least every other night at home. We had a relationship that felt like we were brother and sister, no interest in dating each other. I considered him a good friend, and he was so sweet. Toby had such a big heart. One day, Erica told me that she thought Toby was kind of cute, but I didn't think too much of it. After that, Erica insisted that I tell Toby that she liked him, but I was hesitant because she hung out with an old boyfriend on a regular basis. With talking to Toby at school so much and talking to Erica, it was hard to keep her away from him. She started flirting in the halls and suggested that Toby hang out with us at her house on the weekends. Toby, being overweight and never having had a girlfriend, was shocked but so eager to hang out with us; but one thing led to another, and they were dating. Erica was good friends with this boy John. She dated him off and on for about two years, and he lived right by her. When I stayed at Erica's house, we would sneak out and go to John's house to hang out and get drunk. Every time she was all over him, sitting on his lap, tickling him as she flirted. They definitely had a good vibe between them and made a cute couple, but Erica said they weren't together or messing around. At first, I wasn't happy that Erica and Toby were dating, because I wondered if she was still going to John's house during the week when I wasn't with her. Everything was great for a few months. Erica was happier than she had ever been because Toby was treating her like a princess. I knew that if Toby ever got a girlfriend that he would be the best boyfriend. He was just full of love and kindness. One day, my mom said that I could go to Erica's house during the week, because we had a 1:00 p.m. dismissal. I normally rode the bus home with her but somehow missed it because I forgot something in my locker. My grandma came and picked me up from the school and dropped me off at Erica's, but she wasn't there. Her sister said she was somewhere in the neighborhood. There were only three people she could be with. There were two girls who lived within a block from her, and then there was John. I checked the closest places, the two girls' houses, but she wasn't there, so I walked to John's. Sure enough, Erica was at John's and looked rather surprised to see me. I'm guessing she thought I wasn't coming over. She probably thought I just went home or got an after school detention. I acted like I was happy to see her and John and made sure I didn't act weird about her being at John's. That night, I didn't even tell Toby about it when I talked to him, and he even asked me what Erica and I did that afternoon. Erica was my friend, and she was a good person, so I just didn't say anything to him. It was a few weeks later when Toby asked me if Erica had said anything to me about their relationship, and I asked him why he would ask me that. He said it was because Erica barely ever answered his calls or her family said she wasn't home and she didn't call him back anymore. I told him that she hadn't said anything, but without even thinking, I said that she was at John's house. Toby didn't even know that John lived right by Erica. He didn't even know that they hung out at all. He didn't say much to me about it when I said it, but that afternoon, I found out that he broke up with Erica. I found out when she ran up to me screaming and crying that Toby broke up with her because of me. Instead of talking, she pushed me into a locker, and just like that, we fought, and our friendship was over. I tried to talk to her a few times after that. I tried telling her that I didn't mean for everything to happen like it did. Nothing I said to her mattered, so we were done. The rest of the year was definitely lonely without Erica, and I wasn't as happy as when we were close. We had always been together on the weekends, so sitting at home was so depressing at first.

That summer, I reconnected with some neighborhood kids, one of them being my neighbor, so things got better. In eighth grade, I continued the same behavior. I used boys for their kind words and affection. I would lead them on, make them think that we would be a couple, and we would date. I needed compassion, someone who at least acted like they cared about my life, my sadness, and my problems. I mostly needed someone to talk to, a shoulder to cry on, and someone to just be there for me. I loved the late-night talks, the love letters, hugs in the hallways, and the constant support from the boys at school. I did a lot of leading them on even when I liked them. It was hard to know that dating meant sex at some point, it all leading to some kind of sexual behavior. At that age, I had to lead them on because I knew what it meant to have sex with so many boys, and dating meant sex. Even though I had always been so fascinated by my dad's porno magazines, I was scared to have sex again, because of my flashbacks. That year, I got really into music, old rock music like Led Zeppelin, Pink Floyd, and Black Sabbath. I also listened to anything alternative. There were so many songs and lyrics that I could relate to. When you're that age, thirteen or fourteen years old, music can be so inspiring and influential. All I know is that if it wasn't for music, I might have never been able to keep my sanity at that age or point in my life. I decorated my room with band posters and black light posters and had two big black lights, a disco ball, and a lava lamp. I also had a big mushroom poster right in the middle of the biggest wall. Under that, I had my TV and TV stand, and next to my TV, I had two tall incense bottles that my uncle James gave me for Christmas. On the wall next to that, there was a window, and on my windowsill, I had several candles with wax dripping down the sill and onto the wall. One was a skull candle, and I had a long dragon candle with four wicks on it, and between those, I had tall colored sticks. The first couple of times, the candles dripping were accidental, and my mom got so mad, and then I kept letting it happen. I told my mom that I would scrape it all off the wall when I got tired of it, and I guess she was okay with that, because she stopped complaining about it. Next to my window, there was a No Doubt poster, and on the wall next to that, there were two big Nirvana posters, and under that was my bed. I had a futon bed, so sometimes it was down, but most of the time, I kept it up as a couch. I had a black bed set with two mini neon-green pillows and some of my old stuffed animals from when I was a small child. Next to my bed was my closet without a door. It was just open, and I had black peace-sign beads hanging. There was a corner next to my closet, and then back a few feet was my bedroom door, and on my door, I had another big mushroom with fairies black light poster. When the lights were off, my candles and incense lit, and my black lights were on; my room looked like a magical cave or a mystical getaway. My room was a hippie-and-kind-of-a-rocker combination, and I liked it. It was my place to be alone, to be me.

I'm not really sure why, but I hated having anyone over because I hated having anyone in my room. My room was mine, it was just for me, and I wanted to keep it that way, untouched and not judged by anyone. The only downside to having my own room out in the garage was that it was directly in front of the back door. My dad used the back door as he came in and out of the shed, so I was at risk of seeing him when he was extremely drunk and high. Also a downside was when my dad had sex with random women in his shed. I could hear wood creaking and moaning from both of them. Besides those kinds of things, I loved having my room out there. It was more secluded. I would spend a lot of time lying in my room and daydreaming. I had always daydreamed, even when I was very small. My daydreams had been the same for so many years, many different scenarios of me getting rescued by a handsome boy. He would treat me like a princess and help me to get away from my dad hitting me, and then we would run away together. The boys would just change as I got older, and the places would, too, but it was always the same story, getting rescued from my dad's abuse. I started using boys whom I knew from school and thinking of all kinds of situations and scenarios where they could come and rescue me. It made me start seriously wanting a boyfriend, and I started thinking about it all the time. When I was younger, I did the exact same thing with my Barbies. I had Ken, or the boy Barbie, rescue my Barbie from being beat up or hurt by the bad guy. I had a bad guy in my life, and he had been there so long; my dad was the bad guy.

That year, I started hanging out with this girl Carla. I met her at school and told her I liked the patches on her jacket. Her jacket was army green and had band patches on it. She had a Ramones patch, and I told her that I really liked them. After that, we were inseparable for the next couple of years. Right after we met, a boy whose dad was my dad's best friend told me that my dad slept with prostitutes. The next year, he told me that my dad caught two STDs from a prostitute, and his parents were talking about it a lot. His mom said that my mom must be pretty naïve, because my dad couldn't have sex with her for quite some time while waiting to get rid of the diseases. Carla's mom confirmed that my dad had been sleeping with several women for years. She said it started right after they started dating. That proved one of my theories, the theory that my dad was never happy with my mom, but it still had me confused on why they got married then. Carla was exactly what I needed. It was like she was always there for me right when I needed her. She was broken like me, not because of physical abuse but because of emotional trauma. Carla's dad had never been in the picture; so it had always just been her, her mom, and her little brother, Mark. The only other people besides them were her two grandmas. Carla was lucky to have not only her grandma but also her great-grandma still in her life. Her little brother, Mark, lived at her grandma's house off and on. Both her grandma and great-grandma lived together a few towns away.

At first, I couldn't quite figure out why Carla was the way she was or why she didn't get along with her mom. I found the answer to that rather quickly in the first few months of our friendship and fully understood it after a year or two. When I first started going to her house, her mom was so cheerful and bubbly; she appeared to be the perfect mom. She made big dinners, took us to the flea market, and even bought us both CDs. Right away, I wished she was my mom because she made me feel safe. Laura found out that I smoked marijuana and not only allowed me to do it in her house but also bought me a nice colorful glass pipe for it. That was the popular thing at that age, these colorful blown glass bowls. They were just fancy pipes for smoking weed. Carla wasn't interested in smoking weed too much, but later, she started doing it with me. Her house became my sanctuary, a safe place, a place where I could be myself. After a few months, one day, I walked into Laura's room, and her face looked a lot different. I had never seen her look like that before. She started yelling and cussing at me to get out of her room, and she said that Carla and I weren't going to just sit around her house anymore. Later when she came out of her room, she was very upset and crying. She told me that Carla hated her and that we didn't respect her. Laura said that the whole world was against her, that she couldn't take everyone judging and trying to control her all the time. It wasn't the words and what she was saying that was frightening; it was the frantic way she talked. She was shaking, and I could see that she was clenching her teeth as she talked. She was very agitated. It made me so sad to see her like that because I cared about her a lot. It was confusing to see her like that, and Carla later explained that her mom had bipolar disorder. It was even more confusing to hear that because I had bipolar disorder and felt like I had never had issues like Laura was having. My ups and downs were more gradual; hers was very extreme and scary. She was supposed to take her medicine every day, just like I did, but she didn't. Carla's mom acted as if she was her own psychiatrist, taking herself off meds when she saw fit. That wouldn't be my last time seeing Carla's mom struggle with bipolar disorder and overall mental illness.

At school, I only talked to Carla and a few other people. I had stopped talking to a lot of people when Carla and I became friends; other kids just weren't like us. I think it's because Carla and I weren't just friends—we became each other's family. My mom and dad were monsters. Carla's mom had scared her too many times with her ups and downs. The other kids at school didn't get it. They didn't know what it was like to have to go through what we did. Other kids got to worry about what new shoes they wanted; we had to worry about getting beat or Carla's mom losing her mind. Every weekend, I was at Carla's, and there were times I ran all the way to her house to escape my dad's fist. It was a long walk down a busy road to get to her house, but I did it several times a week. One night, my dad was high and angry. He started following me around the house and hitting me, so I had to get out of there. I called Carla and told her that I needed her mom to help me fast. I told her to meet me in this little park in between our neighborhoods; you could get there by walking down the tracks near my house. So I ran down the street and to the railroad tracks and then ran down until I made it to that park where I saw them waiting. Carla's mom drove to her house and locked the doors. Even with the doors locked, I was scared of my dad. I hid upstairs with Carla's little brother, Mark, who was spending the week there, and I put my hands over my ears so I couldn't hear him banging and yelling at the door. Mark put his arm around me, and even though he was younger than me, he tried to comfort and protect me from the fear that I was experiencing. Laura went outside, somehow calmed my dad down, and convinced him to let me spend a couple of days there. She said I would be better off there while everyone calmed down, and surprisingly, my dad listened to her.

Later in the summer, Carla moved to her grandma's house, so it was a little harder to escape my dad's wrath. Laura wasn't doing good, and they were fighting all the time. Carla got the worst of it all when her mom wasn't doing so well. She took most of her anger out on her. The problem with that was when Laura was doing better, Carla would still be angry at her for things she did during an episode. Then everything started to just stay bad between them, and their house became a place of anger and confusion. I hated it when Carla moved because she wasn't in walking distance anymore, and it was harder to find a ride to where her grandma lived. She only lived a few towns over, but it was a bit of a drive down one of those long country roads that everyone hated. It was around that time that I dyed my hair blonde and started dressing a lot differently. I went for a more punk rocker look, with spiked hair, plaid pants, and a studded dog collar. At first, I just liked the way it looked, but then I started to like the music that went along with it. My favorite bands became punk bands like Pennywise and Hatebreed. I listened to them all day and even listened to them as I fell asleep. I soon found my next obsession, which was '80s punk. It wasn't just the music that I liked. It was the punk rock party lifestyle. I had been experimenting with pills, taking a few different kinds to stay up and then smoking weed to come down. Pills, weed, cigarettes, and liquor were what we focused daily on getting. We could get our hands on all sorts of pills, legal and illegal, and we constantly did. Most kids our age did not have money to buy pills and drugs, but we did, only because of Great-grandma. She gave Carla a lot of money to help her do chores and other things that needed to be done. We not only had money for drugs, but we had money to buy pizzas and Chinese food almost every day. We would get so high, wander up and down the streets around Carla's grandma's house, and then order all the food we wanted. I started becoming increasingly obsessed with not just the Sex Pistols the band but with the people, Sid and Nancy. They were members of the '70s punk rock band called the Sex Pistols, and they were drug addicts, serious drug addicts. I liked everything about them, their music, their lifestyle, and their insane love for each other. It was so sick and disturbing that I liked it, and the higher I got, the more I felt like I could relate to them. Even though we weren't gay, I felt like Carla and I were Sid and Nancy. I felt like we were two outcasts, two people whom nobody wanted, just two lost souls always high. It got to the point that I was high so much that when I finally slept, I felt like I would never wake up. Carla never got as high as I did. The more pills I took, the less she did so she could watch me and take care of me. There were a couple of times where I think I was borderline overdosed and puked for days, and Carla took care of me. I threw up so many times in her bed, and instead of losing her mind, she put a towel down and lay next to me.

Our reckless behavior persisted, and before we knew it, we were in high school, our freshman year. That year, Carla and I were closer than ever, the very best of friends and still inseparable. Somehow, I was appealing enough to meet and date a boy right away, a junior. I felt like I was on top of the world when just weeks into the school year, a junior called me over to his table at lunch. He was cute. Caleb was a rocker kind of guy. He was into older rock music, so that was cool. He was a junior, so he even had a car, and that made me feel like I was finally mature. It made me feel like I finally found someone to be in a real relationship with, someone to actually go on dates with. What I didn't know was that Caleb had a crazy ex-girlfriend and that they were on and off again all the time. So my guess is that she had thought that they would get back together, but then he met me. At first, I didn't know who she was when she called me over to her table at lunch and asked me if I liked Caleb. I, of course, said yes as I smiled and acted like a little school girl. She laughed and told the other girls at the table if they heard what the silly little girl in front of her was saying. My smile, as well as my heart, must have just fallen onto the floor. I was shocked and confused. I was so confused, so I just walked away, because I felt a really bad vibe coming from those girls. They laughed and said negative stuff about my hair and clothes as I walked away. After that, as I walked toward the cafeteria door, a girl from another table called me over to her. I was hesitant but quickly saw a genuine warm smile on her face, so I walked over to her. She told me not to worry about Stacey. She said that the girl whom I had just encountered was Stacey. She said that was Caleb's ex-girlfriend and that she was angry and had issues but was harmless. She said that Stacey was clearly jealous and intimidated by me because Caleb had never liked anyone how he liked me. That didn't make me feel much better. I felt like Caleb knew he was bringing me into the middle drama with him and his ex. Being a freshman, it was almost scary having an older girl and her friends against me so early into the school year. Normally, I would have just sat with Carla and ignored anything like that, but we weren't in the same lunch period. There wasn't much I could do but to break up with Caleb, and I did. We stayed good friends, but I just couldn't deal with us officially dating and the problems that would come with that. Caleb drove me home from school, and we talked on the phone almost every day, so we were good.

The beginning of that year got even more dramatic when Joey came back into the picture. I think that I was still hurt by what happened with Caleb. I still felt embarrassed, and I felt alone. Joey was the same. He was the same manipulative person, but I felt like he knew me. The biggest thing probably was that we were both freshmen, so we were on the same level and had known each other for so long. The whole school knew about Caleb's ex-girlfriend having a problem with me and me breaking up with Caleb. I think Joey used that to creep his way back into my life so he could mess with my mind yet again. Joey convinced me that nobody else would ever care about me how he did and told me that he truly loved me. I started to believe all of Joey's lies and fell for his mental manipulation yet again. Joey had a friend Corey. They had been best friends since probably kindergarten. They lived right by each other, and I think even their parents were friends too. One day, I was at Joey's house lying in bed, and he came in the room with Corey and told me that they were both going to have sex with me. Joey tried using the same tactics and mind games that he had used before to get me to have sex with him, but I couldn't. My fear helped me to not let Joey talk me into doing something I didn't want to. Joey had me so messed up mentally. Instead of having sex because I wanted to, I had sex because I felt like I had to make Joey happy. Making Joey happy with me became almost like an obsession, and I didn't realize that was something he purposely created until that day. That wasn't the first time Joey was disrespectful to me. If I said something Joey didn't like, he did the same things he had done before to mess with my head. If I didn't walk to his house before school for sex, then he would wave and smile at other girls and whisper to me that any other girl would love to have sex with him. He would tell me that I was lucky that he wanted me, that nobody else would really care about me. He constantly brought up how Caleb let his ex-girlfriend embarrass me at lunch. He said that was what every boy would do to me. If I didn't make Joey happy, then he would wave to his ex-girlfriend Tamryn and then give me a nasty and angry look. He made me dress how he wanted and only allowed me to talk to a few people, and he chose them. If I said hi to other boys or even girls who were known to mess around with a lot of boys, he would get so mad. He would point at me and then say, "Now." When I would go over to him, he would grab my wrist and squeeze it so hard. I would have bruises on both of my wrists, and he then started to do it to my shoulders when I made him mad. I knew that I had to end it with Joey before he really hurt me or forced me to do something really bad.

I talked to Caleb here and there, but, of course, I never let Joey know, because he would lose it. I started to confide in Caleb about what Joey was doing to me, and he almost couldn't even believe it. After talking to him enough, he gave me the courage and support that I needed to end my relationship with Joey for good. Caleb was disgusted to hear that Joey tried to get me to have sex with him and his friend and told me that Joey was out of control. He gave me enough courage to end my relationship with Joey, and it was the best thing for me. I was scared of Joey, but Caleb helped me out a lot with that problem. Caleb came to my locker after most classes to keep Joey away from me, and he even drove me home a lot. Here and there, Joey would come up to my locker and slam his fist into it to scare me and tell me that I was nothing without him. He would call my house so many times, but every time, I would answer and tell him to stop calling me. He threatened to tell everyone that I was sleeping around if I didn't get back together with him, but I refused. I had already made it clear that I didn't want to be with him and that I wasn't stupid and knew he didn't love me. I had already made it very clear that I knew he had been messing with my head, manipulating me to get what he wanted. He would get so angry and scream at me, telling me that I would be sorry if I didn't get back together with him. Somewhere in the middle of the threats and degrading comments, I stopped being scared of him. Nothing he could do or say to me could ever be worse than what my dad had done to me my whole life. I finally realized that I stayed with him and allowed him to treat me the way he did because of my dad. They say that you unconsciously choose boys or men who are like your father to date or marry. I definitely did that by choosing someone who was exactly like my dad. I thought that Joey would never stop harassing me, but he did. One day, I saw him in the hall holding Tamryn's hand, and I was so relieved to see that they were dating again.

After that, I met this girl named Melissa. She was in one of my classes. I had seen her in the halls a few times but didn't talk to each other until we had a class together. From the outside, Melissa looked almost preppy. She wore NSYNC and Britney Spears shirts and dated a nerdy-looking guy. If she didn't talk to me, I probably would never have talked to her or even paid any attention to her. Honestly, I would have never talked to anyone wearing an NSYNC shirt. NSYNC was the direct opposite of everything I liked or was into, so I would not have thought we had anything in common. After getting to know Melissa, I couldn't have been more wrong; we were so much alike. Melissa was like me, broken, a lost and broken soul just wandering. She didn't just like the trendy bands; I found out that she liked all kinds of music and a lot of the same music as me. Melissa had a wild spirit and such an upbeat energy to her all the time, so there was never a dull moment with us. Our hearts were both broken from pain. Her mom was a drug addict, crack cocaine. Melissa's grandma raised her but not because she really had a choice. She and her brother lived with her grandma off and on when her mom was really bad on drugs. I know that a lot had to have happened in her childhood for her to be the way she was. She was just like me in that sense, broken. Melissa had just broken up with someone she had been with for a couple of years, so she was just as sad as I was. We were sad and compatible. I could tell that Melissa wasn't scared of much, so I decided to bring her home to meet my parents. I decided to tell them that Melissa was my girlfriend. I guess I was trying to make them mad. I am not sure what I was trying to do. My parents just thought I was messing around. They acted like they didn't even care. I thought that bringing home a Black girl and saying she was my lesbian girlfriend would get a rise out of them. Doing that just gave them an opening to call me more names, so many derogatory names. I really liked Melissa, but she was too much like me. It almost made everything too intense. Two people full of darkness, full of internal conflict, and both from chaotic lives equaled intense situations. We were just too much, we were too wild, and we both just had no limits, so things got crazy. There was nothing we wouldn't do and nothing that we were scared of, so we got ourselves into some bad situations. People always think that it would be perfect to find someone like themselves, but it's not what you think it is. I couldn't even tell you how far we would have gotten into some things.

There was an incident that caused us to have to take a break from each other, and I started hanging out with Alicia again. I said hi to her at school, and I guess she forgave me finally, because after that, we were back being friends. I'm not sure exactly how it happened, but my next obsession became witchcraft. Alicia said she had been learning about it and just started practicing it. She said that her mom used to do it, too, but made her promise she would stay on the good side of it all. With witchcraft, there are two sides to everything, good and bad, dark and white, that kind of thing. That's how the books we had explained it, and Alicia's mom told her the same thing. Alicia called herself a white witch. She said that she would always stay on the good side of magic. We had different-colored candles that we used for different spells and chanting. All colors are linked to different things. Alicia usually only used white candles. White means purity, protection, balance, peace, and healing. She sometimes used pink candles which fell in a similar category, meaning acceptance, friendship, kindness, love, and femininity. Alicia always stayed right inside the lines of basic white witch practice. Her spells and what she studied were pure and clean magic, nothing dark. I thought she was annoying for worrying about that. I didn't care about good or bad, black or white. I just cared about seeing something. I cared about being distracted from my life. I wanted to be distracted from my dad, my mom, and their constant anger and fighting. I always felt so empty, so alone even when I was with someone, and so sad even when I had a reason to be happy. My life was already dark, so I decided that the darker magic was for me. I wasn't interested in white magic. Alicia told me that she felt her magic in everything around her, in the trees, the sun, and even in flowers. She told me that she knew that Mother Nature heard her chants, and she could tell by the little things, leaves drifting her way or rays of sun through her window. I always told her that I was happy for her, and I would tell her how great that sounded. I really didn't feel that way. I thought that she sounded stupid when she said stuff like that. If I was going to practice magic, I didn't want a leaf blowing toward me to be my sign, I wanted the earth to shake. I didn't want to sound like Alicia, pretending that nature was telling her that she was a good witch and did good spells. I was willing to sell my soul to the devil if he was willing to help me. I started using black candles, spells, and chants to bring a change to my life and everything I was going through. I put a spell on Joey to make him pay for what he did to me, and I wanted to hurt him just like he hurt me. I would chant and focus so hard on what I wanted to achieve with my spells. I wanted to be in control. I would chant so long that my candles would burn out, and I would be sitting in the dark and feeling like there was something there with me. That's exactly what I wanted. I wanted to see something. I wanted to feel something that made me know there was something there, something that would shake up the broken pieces of my heart. I didn't feel like I was achieving much of anything with my spells, and the results of my chanting were mediocre. That's when I decided to start praying. I decided to pray to the devil himself. I wasn't going to waste any more time with chanting and summoning, no more trying to use the forces from the moon and fire to get what I wanted. Alicia cried when I told her what I was going to do. She told me that she was going to pray for me. I laughed at her, and then I asked her whom she was going to pray to. I didn't wait for her to answer. I knew she was going to say God. I didn't know much about him, but I figured he was probably the last person who could help me.

I did just what I said I was going to do. I prayed to the devil, and I asked him for help. I had plenty of time to pray and do whatever I wanted to do, because my mom was at work most of the time. My mom had decided to go back to school for a year or two before that. She was in school to become an X-ray technician. While she was in school, she worked as a receptionist at a local chiropractor. She went to school during the day and then at the nursing home in the evening and night. My dad went to bed by eight o'clock every night, and my brother and sister never bothered me, so I had no distractions. I had the perfect opportunity to practice my chants and spells. It was so perfect. I took a black sheet. I had an extra one from my bed set, and I nailed it over my window. That blocked out the light on the front of our house, and it made my room completely black. I drew upside-down crosses and a big pentagram on a sheet and then lit black candles in a circle all around me. I dressed in all black and used black eyeliner to draw an upside-down cross on my forehead. I even took a razor blade and cut my fingertips and then put some of my blood into a little glass dish to show the devil I was for real. I sat in the middle of the pentagram, prayed for hours, and made up chants to help me summon the devil. When my dad hit me and said horrible and negative things to me, I would pray so hard for bad things to happen to him. I prayed for someone or something to help me. I prayed that my dad would die or disappear forever. When I saw dirty-looking women coming in and out of my dad's shed when my mom was at work, I prayed harder. When I went into my dad's shed to take weed from him and found women's earrings and thong panties, I prayed really hard for something bad to happen to him. I got lost in the darkness that I created when I prayed to the devil. I felt like he listened to me, and I felt comforted. I felt like he told me that I was going to be okay. I felt like he was going to help me. One day, after praying for a long time, I felt something in my room, and then the candles blew out. A feeling of terror came over me as I saw something in the corner of my room. It was big, I could feel it there with me. I could feel something so dark and evil. I saw the shadowy figure move and feared for my life, so I quickly got up. I jumped toward the door as I felt it coming toward me, and I ran out of my room. I didn't just run out of my room—I ran out of my house and down the street. I had no idea what I was doing, but I still felt it near me or coming for me. I decided to run to Alicia's house. I ran through her yard even though I had no shoes on and banged on her door. I was scared to death as she opened the door. I pushed her out of the way and slammed her door closed. I could barely catch my breath to tell her what just happened. I could barely explain as she looked down at my muddy bare feet. I had to bend over and put my hands on my knees. I had to close my eyes and take a moment to catch my breath and breathe normally. Alicia was going on and on about what was going on, repeatedly asking me what had happened to me. She kept asking me why I was running, why I ran to her house, and why I had no shoes on. She asked why I was scared and out of breath. She was talking so fast that I had to yell at her to stop. I told her to please stop talking, stop asking me questions, and just wait a minute. I put my hands over my ears and yelled so loud and told her to please just shut up. Finally, I could think, and that's when I told her everything about what I had been doing to try and get the devil to help me. I told her what had just happened in my room and why I ran out of my house without even putting on shoes. Alicia was so upset that she started crying. She cried and told me that she was scared and couldn't understand why I would do that. She said she was scared that the thing that was in my room would come to her house. She was scared it could be attached to me. I hadn't even thought about that. I had to worry about the fact that I might have something evil attached to me. It was my fault. I definitely achieved what I was trying to do. I attracted something evil into my life. That night, I felt it, it was with me, and it stayed with me for a while.

I stopped the chanting and praying to the devil. I had gotten in over my head and didn't want to do it anymore. Every night, I had nightmares that someone or something was following me. It continued for weeks, and I could barely sleep. At school, I could barely concentrate, I swear I could feel something next to me and could almost hear it whispering. When I had to use the restroom, I used it fast. I could feel it in there with me and had to hurry, or I felt like it would catch me. In the middle of the school year, a new boy came, a boy who would distract me from the darkness in my life. Walking away from my locker one day, I saw him. He was just standing there by his locker looking at the ground. He looked like he didn't want to be there either, and the way he dressed and the way he looked caught my eye. He looked like a boy version of me, dark clothes, messy hair, and a sad face with a slight smirk. When I saw him lift his hand up to push his hair behind his ears, I could see that he had black nail polish on his fingers, just like me. He had longer hair. It was dark brown, maybe black, and fell right below his chin. His hair was wavy, a messy kind of wavy, and there were loose curls at the ends. His skin was pale like mine. He had what looked like dark-brown eyes, just like mine also. He had on an old concert shirt. It was a faded black Metallica shirt. I loved it. He wore jeans that were just as faded, maybe black or dark gray, and skater shoes. My first impression was that he wasn't a skater. He probably just liked the clothes like I had. His darkness felt like mine even from across the room, and I was drawn to it like a magnet. Our eyes met, and we stood there staring at each other from across the hall, and I couldn't help but to smile at him. I walked over and said hi. I asked him if he just moved here, and he said yes. I told him that my name was Ava, and he said his was Mark. He said he moved her from a few hours away and lived with his aunt and uncle. The neighborhood he lived in was in the nicer part of town. I told him we had to hang out soon, gave him my number, and smiled as I walked away. It drove me crazy waiting, but Mark called me the next night just as I predicted. After talking that night, we found out that we were a lot alike, and suddenly, I had a new best friend. I didn't pay too much attention in school already, but after that, Mark had my full attention every day. From notes back and forth, hallway chats, and ditching class together, we became more than just friends very quickly. We started dating, and he helped me glue back the pieces of my broken heart. It was hard to spend time with him. I wasn't allowed to date, so I had to lie about where I was all the time. I would say I was with Carla or with Alicia or say I was going to someone's house from school. I tried to have an actual conversation with my parents. I tried to tell them that I was mature enough to have a boyfriend. I asked them if he could come over and hang out with me, but they would say that I wasn't allowed to. I didn't want to sneak around. I wanted to be able to date him like girls I knew at school did. I wanted it to be a normal relationship, but my parents didn't allow that to happen, not at all. Even though it wasn't easy, we did it. We did everything that we needed to do to be together.

Mark was nothing like the other boys at school. He was quiet but sweet and so mature all at the same time. It was great. We did everything together, and I finally felt like I had something to be happy about. The only downside was that it was hard to be in a mature relationship with someone when your dad still hits you like a small child. It was also hard because of having to sneak around. I had to lie so much to be able to spend time with him. I couldn't keep it a secret for too long. My emotional state told a clear story. I thought that Mark would want to run when I explained to him what my life was like and everything my dad had done to me. I always hated seeing people's faces when I told them the story of my life. It was a bad story that no one wanted to hear. It was different with Mark. It wasn't like when I told other kids; his face was different. Other kids had a look on their face usually expressing that they were sorry—sorry, but there was nothing they could do for me. It's not that I ever expected anyone to help me or any of them to know what to do, but I always wished they wouldn't look so helpless. I just wanted them to listen, just be there for me, but other kids always looked like I was asking them for something. Mark didn't do that. He looked like I had told him something horrible, and he wanted to be there for me in any way he could. Mark was respectful. He never brought up sex, or even anything sexual, and told me he wanted to wait until I was ready. I didn't have to tell Mark about the flashbacks I had of sexual things happening to me when I was very little. I think he just knew there was something that happened to me in that department. It wasn't until months later when Carla's mom was gone for a few days. We stayed there, and that's when we had sex. Mark was older than me, a few years older, and he knew people out of high school who sold drugs. I would tell my parents that I was staying the night at friend's houses, and we would go to parties and get so drunk. We just drank a lot at first and smoked a lot of weed every day, but then we moved onto ecstasy. We would have ecstasy parties, like five to ten kids would all buy it, and then we would do it together at someone's house whose parents were gone. With Mark's aunt living in a rich neighborhood, he became friends with all the rich kids who smoked weed and did drugs. So almost every weekend, one of their parents would be out of town at their lake house, on a boat somewhere, or on a fancy European vacation. So we always had big houses to party in and several places to have fun and get very high or drunk.

The rest of my freshman year was a blur, a blur of heavy drug use and parties. The drug use made me obsess even more about my weight. I loved how it allowed me to go a day or two without eating, and it made me want to be skinnier. I got this image in my mind of a superskinny model, the kind of model where you could slightly see her ribs. Skinny to the point of looking frail and starved somehow was beautiful in my mind. Superskinny and drugged out was apparently the look I was trying very hard to achieve and maintain. In the tabloid magazines, they sometimes showed celebrities who had eating disorders, and I loved the way they looked. I obsessed over it. The more days I went without eating, the more beautiful I felt. I felt like I had accomplished something so big. Before I knew it, I went from being bulimic to being anorexic. It was confusing to be fifteen years old and to be going through the kinds of things I was, and I am sure that didn't help it. It was confusing to be in what I considered a mature relationship but still get hit by my dad when I was at home. My mom was always gone, and my dad was always high, and when he was high, he hated me the most. I was torn between telling Mark and not telling him every time my dad hit me or beat me into the ground. It got really bad that year. My mom and dad were constantly fighting when they were both home. It was bad. My mom was working so hard, school during the day and work at night; so she was tired. When she was home, she had to try and figure out where my dad was, and sometimes, that wasn't easy. My dad was always out partying and sleeping with other women while my mom was working so hard to give us a better future. Even though she never helped me when my dad hit me, I still felt bad that she had to go through that. My mom once told me that my dad was the only boyfriend she had ever had, so that means she never slept with anyone else, just him. I always figured that was why she dealt with everything that he put her through, because she didn't know any better. I often imagined my mom with someone else, a man who treated her like a princess, a man nothing like my dad. I wished my mom would marry someone else, and I told her that. I told her that a real man would love her. I told her that he would make them dinner and watch movies with her while kissing her or rubbing her feet. I told her a real man would take her on dates, take walks with her, and truly respect her. My mom laughed at me when I told her that, so I asked her if she thought my dad really loved and respected her. I told her that the way my dad acted and the things he was always doing, that wasn't love or respect. My mom's only reply was that I didn't understand it, because I was too young. I couldn't fight with her. I felt too bad for her to go further than that. She probably started to believe her own lies. She probably thought that was how a husband was supposed to treat his wife. I wanted to try and save my mom, but I couldn't. I had to save myself.

My dad's drug use was starting to get hard to ignore, even by my mom, who always pretended it wasn't happening. My dad had turned into a crack addict, and everyone knew it. I was visiting my grandma and crying to her when my uncle James stopped by to visit her, too, and he knew something was wrong. He asked me to come and stay at his house that weekend, and normally, I would have declined, but I said yes. I was a teenager who loved to party, so normally, I wouldn't have agreed to spend a weekend with my uncle, but I felt like I needed him. I didn't want to be away from Mark, but he understood and wanted me to tell somebody what was going on. I needed to tell my uncle the full truth this time. I wasn't a stupid little kid anymore. I needed help this time. It was time to tell someone who could help. I needed to get the truth out there. I wasn't there more than twenty minutes when my uncle James sat next to me on the couch and told me to start talking about why I was crying a few days prior at my grandma's house. I started with how my dad used to just stay out late getting high but then he looked high during the day and it was getting scary. I told him how the boys at school whose dad was friends with mine, said that he was smoking crack a lot. I told him about the drug bags in the shed with little white rocks in them and the glass tubes next to them. I told my uncle about the arguments I heard my parents having about where all the money was going from my dad's side jobs. My dad would tell her that he had a lot of expenses, that he had tools or machines that broke. Month after month of hearing him say that same thing, it just got embarrassing. I had to tell him about my mom crying to my dad and telling him that she didn't have money to pay the bills and that she was scared of what was going to happen. I hated listening to them when they were having those arguments. I could hear my mom's pain, but my dad just sounded like I couldn't wait to get high. I had to tell my uncle how my dad had been cheating on my mom as long as I could remember, and from what I heard, it was since they met. I told him how he slept with my friend's moms, and even caught STDs from prostitutes. I hated having to say that kind of stuff out loud, but he had to know. I explained to him how I went to school with his best friend's three kids and how they told me every time my dad slept with a nasty woman or prostitute. The look on my uncle's face when I told him that my dad had women with him out in his shed was indescribable. I know it had to disgust and anger him to hear that his brother-in-law slept with other women. Hearing that it happened right outside while his sister sat in the house, that was something really disturbing to hear. I could only go on and on about my dad being a drug addict and a cheater before I had to move on to the next part.

I put everything aside, and I let it pour out of me like a pipe exploding and water pouring out everywhere. Instead of using the word *hit* like I had when I was younger, I used the word *beat*. I said it over and over. I told him how he did it, where he did it, and how hard he did it. I don't know why, but I wanted him to feel what I was saying. I wanted him to know what I had been going through for years. My uncle put his head down. He looked at the floor and then just sat there. He shook his head with a stunned look on his face and told me that I could have come to him for help. I know he was hurt. I know he was probably angry that I didn't tell him how bad it was when I was younger. I could see that he felt guilty just as he tried to bring up our talk years ago, but I had to stop him. I told him that it was my fault. I told him that I was the one who told him that I would be okay. I told him that I didn't want to disrupt his life back then but thought it was time now to get help. It felt good to have him listen and to see him shocked, and I wanted to just hug him. I wanted to cry on his shoulder, but I was embarrassed. I told him I was sorry. I just wanted to let it all go when I was little, but then it got worse and never stopped. My uncle looked up at me and said he was sorry and that he loved me. He said he would do anything for me. He asked me what Mark thought about my dad hitting me, and I told him I was worried he would try to kill him. I wasn't joking when I said that. I really was worried that Mark would be pushed over the edge by my dad's abuse. I just knew that it had to be horrible seeing it all from his side, the side of a guy whose girlfriend is being abused. He got on the phone after that and called my grandma. I had never heard him talk to her the way he did, mad and almost yelling. He asked her if she knew that my dad was smoking crack and spending up all their money on drugs. He yelled and told her that this was out of control. He told her that she better put some sense inside her stupid daughter's head. He asked her if she knew what my dad was doing to me, and it sounded like she said yes. He then asked her why she would let this go on and not do anything about it, not get me out of that house. He asked her why my mom was letting this go on and said that she was part of the problem. He slammed the phone down without even saying goodbye to my grandma and put his hand on his forehead as he looked at Mary. He asked me if I had bruises on my body. He had a serious look on his face and asked her to take me into the bathroom to look at my body. My body was so skinny, so frail, and so bruised; but it told a story. The bruises that she looked at told her a clear story about the night my dad came in high and I was in the kitchen making a sandwich. It showed her without words how he told me that I wasn't going to be doing whatever I wanted all the time. It showed her that I only told him that I didn't know what he was talking about when he grabbed me and then started hitting me until I fell. The bruises then showed her how he grabbed me up after smacking me to the ground and slammed me into the table and then grabbed me and slammed me into the cabinet. That's what the bruises told her, but the scratches showed her that he liked slamming me into the cabinet and kept doing it. He liked doing it because he knew it hurt me and that the laminate was missing and it would cut my back. He liked doing it until I just fell to the ground and didn't make a single noise. Only then would he walk away telling me that I wasn't as tough as I thought I was.

All Mary had to do was lift up my shirt in the back, and she had seen enough to know that it was all true. We walked out of the bathroom, and Mary shook her head at my uncle. He knew that it meant I had told them the truth. He asked me to start from the beginning and tell him everything, from the first time it happened. I asked him if he was serious, because the first time would have at least been ten years before that, and I couldn't remember it. It took a while, but I told him most of it, but I had to hold back from telling him some of the really disturbing parts. There were some things that hurt to say out loud. Some stuff was just wrong, and I didn't like to talk about it. I just couldn't tell him about the faint memories or flashbacks that I had of molested as a small child. I couldn't tell him that when I was real little, someone had stuck things in my butt. I couldn't look him in the face if I ever told him that. Mary had gone into the kitchen to smoke a cigarette and maybe to take a moment to gather her thoughts after the bathroom. After we came out of the bathroom, she looked as if she was crying a little bit or as if she needed to cry and said she needed a cigarette. He called Mary into the room to catch her up on what I just told him. Her reaction showed me that she and my uncle really cared about me. Mary actually cried when hearing about the abuse that I had been dealing with for so many years. My own mother just watched it happen, but Mary couldn't even stand to hear it, and that proved my mom was a monster. A monster is just a word; she was something else. She and my dad were more than just monsters.

My uncle James asked me if I had been talking to my cousin Theresa lately, because he suggested that we call her about what was happening to me. It sounded like a good idea to me. With all three of them caring, I knew something good could come from it. I hadn't talked to my cousin in a while, but I knew that she would help me. I knew I could trust her. The next morning, I was barely awake when I heard a car door. I looked out of the window, and my cousin Theresa was already there. It didn't take long for my uncle James, Mary, and my cousin Theresa to come to the conclusion that something had to be done immediately. I can't remember exactly how it happened, but after that, I started staying with Theresa a lot. I was left out of most of the details, but at some point, it was planned to be a permanent arrangement. I wasn't around when the initial conversation took place, but I figured my parents had to have been threatened to let it happen. I actually only heard one conversation, and it was between Theresa and my mom on a day where I was supposed to go back. I had told Theresa the day before that I hated going back with my parents and that I wanted to stay with her permanently right away. The next day, Theresa told my mom over the phone that she's not going to be playing any games, she would go straight to DCFS if my mom wouldn't allow me to stay with her. So I am pretty sure that my uncle James and my cousin Theresa told my parents that they would call the police or DCFS on them if they didn't allow me to leave. In my head, I imagined them saying that to my parents, and it made me feel good. Thinking about their embarrassed faces made me smile just a little bit. Even though I was being left out of the verbal arrangements, I felt like I had some kind of leverage over them. I still did not feel as good as I would have thought being in a situation like that, with them losing their power. Theresa asked me if I wanted to live with her. When I said yes, she told me that she would make it happen. She said that she talked to a lawyer and that she would take my parents to court if she had to. She said that there were a couple of different ways we could do it, but either way, she would make sure I stayed safe. She did just that. She not only kept me safe, but she made me feel safe too.

One of the first things that became so apparent to me after leaving my parents' house was that it was so dirty. It wasn't just dirty—it was out of control, and someone needed to do something about it. During my whole childhood, I had to fear that one of my friends would unexpectedly come over and someone would let them in. My mom and dad should never have let our house get so dirty and so full of stuff. Back then, no one really used the word hoarder, but that is exactly what my mom was—she was a hoarder. Every room of our house was absolutely filthy, and there was no excuse for it. I think that if I had to pick, the kitchen was the dirtiest room in that house. We couldn't even sit and eat a meal at our kitchen table. It was piled high with papers and random stuff. The counters in the kitchen and on top of the microwave caddy were the same, piled high with bills and magazines. The counter areas near the sink were so dirty, full of scum and grease, and the sinks were always piled with dirty dishes. The stove had layers and layers of old food and grease built up. It was so filthy that we should not have been using it. Between the sink and the stove, there were always so many flies and gnats flying around. I think we even had maggots in the sink a few times. Even on the ground, against the walls, there were piles of stuff, just random stuff that shouldn't be in a kitchen. When you walked through the kitchen, your shoes would almost stick to the laminate flooring because of the amount of food, grease, dirt, and grime that had built up. The living room was pretty bad. You couldn't sit on the couches, and you tripped over piles trying to walk through it. The amount of stains and filth in the carpet were indescribable. You could smell it right when you walked in the door. My mom went shopping every single day. She would buy a bunch of stuff we didn't even need and set it in piles in the kitchen or living room. It was an everyday thing. We told her that we didn't need the stuff, that it was just more junk.

Her excuse was that we could use the stuff for something and she got a deal on it; that was what she always said. The whole house was the same, a filthy mess. My mom had a serious problem, and my dad didn't care to get her help. It was something that I tried to push out of my mind my whole childhood. There wasn't anything I could do. I knew something was seriously wrong with our house, but there was nothing I could do, so I pushed it away.

Being at Theresa's made me really be able to see just how messed up everything was at my parents' house. They needed some kind of help. Theresa helped me to realize many things, like that I was fun, outgoing, and even pretty smart. She made me truly see that I had a future, a bright future ahead of me, and that I didn't have to let anyone hold me back. Theresa made me truly realize that I was beautiful and that I didn't need to hide under a bunch of black clothes and makeup. She bought me a few little sundresses and black wedge sandals to match. I felt like a chic and beautiful young lady. Theresa gave me hair products, body lotions, and perfumes so I could pamper myself. She wanted me to feel good. She took me for a haircut. I got a long pixie cut. She also took me for a pedicure so my toenails looked nice with my new sandals. My feet looked especially good with the toe rings she got me. They were silver and looked so cute with the dresses and sandals. The toe rings matched my necklace. It was a very thin silver chain with five burgundy beads on it. I felt good when I was with Theresa. She looked at me in my eyes when she talked to me and treated me with respect. I had gotten so tired, my dad had been hitting me so much, and she came and helped me at the right time. Between not eating, drinking, using drugs, and my dad beating me, I was exhausted. For the first time in my life, I felt safe, I felt healthy, and I felt good about myself. Theresa made me understand that my life mattered and so did my happiness and my well-being. Nobody ever cared about any of those things before. I was a voiceless nobody to my mom and dad but not to Theresa. She changed her whole life around for me. She made it all work. She was dating a man, and they had just moved in together, but she still helped me. Most people would not want to be inconvenienced, especially not by an abused and damaged teenager—especially not by one who needed so much, who needed everything. Theresa was that everything. I needed her, and she was there for me in every possible way. She didn't judge me, not for the things I liked or for dating Mark, and my parents hated him. They hated him more than ever because he had just turned eighteen, and I was still fifteen and wouldn't even be sixteen for several months. I know that it must have looked bad at that time, but our mentalities were the same. Mark wasn't an old man taking advantage of a young teenage girl. We were just two teenagers in love.

Living with Theresa allowed me to date him in an appropriate manner, no sneaking out just to see each other. I talked on the phone with Carla every day, and she was happy for me that I had a safe place to live. My life finally was finally like what I thought a normal teenager's life should be like, healthy and happy. Things were going great, but somehow, I let my dad get into my head around the holidays that year. My mom had called to talk to me a few times. I had Theresa tell her that I was busy but then decided to call her back for some reason. It was a few weeks before Christmas, if I remember correctly, and my dad answered. He whispered telling me how sad my mom was. He told me that she barely decorated the house and was staying in bed a lot of days, and that actually hurt me. No matter how many times my mom allowed me dad to hit me, I still felt bad for her and cared about how she felt. She always made a big deal about Christmas, the decorations, the tree with so many ornaments and piles of presents. Even though our family life was dreadful, my mom still celebrated Christmas like we were the happiest family ever. I always looked forward to it. It was the only time of year that my dad tried even a little bit to act like we were a happy family. It was so annoying that my mom bought us tons of gifts when our family was hanging on by tiny little threads, but I still enjoyed it. My dad sounded genuine. He sounded like he actually cared about her, and I think that was what got me. I rarely ever saw my dad act caring or like he loved my mom, so when I heard compassion in his voice, it got me. He told me that she might be sleeping, and that shocked me. My mom was never sleeping in the middle of the day. Then it also hit me. My dad answered the house phone. That meant he was actually at home. My dad was at home with my mom in the middle of the day. When I realized that, my heart started to beat faster. I had to sit down. My thoughts started racing. I imagined everything changing after I left, my mom and dad in love, happiness and laughter filling the house, and my brother and sister happy. I imagined them holding hands and cooking dinner together. I could see them taking my brother and sister to the park or the movie theater. I wondered if it could be true. I wondered if we could really be a happy family. I had to take a breath and calm myself. I realized I had gone too far in my mind in the minutes. I was just waiting for my mom to come to the phone. I had to push away my hopes and fantasies of a normal home life. I didn't, though. I didn't push away my hopes of a normal and happy family. I didn't push away my fantasies of a house full of love, two parents who both not only love me but each other too. I grabbed onto the idea of it all. Like a desperate child, I grabbed onto that tiny bit of hope I had and didn't let go. When my mom did get on the phone, she sounded so sad. She sounded like me, so broken. When I heard her voice, I could also feel her sadness, and I had never felt responsible for that before. That was a feeling that I had never experienced, making my mom sad. That was my dad's job. My mom told me that she was very sad and that Christmas wasn't going to be the same if I wasn't there. She said that she just didn't feel like getting out of bed anymore and didn't care about celebrating Christmas anymore. I almost fell to my knees when I heard her say that. She actually cared about me not being there, and I was so happy. Finally, my mom was expressing herself. Finally, she was telling me that she cared about me, and it felt so good. Hearing my mom tell me these things made me want to cry. I had never cried from happiness, but I could have then. Just like that, I changed my mind about permanently living with my cousin Theresa. Even though she was about to start the legal process, even though I was happy, happier than I had ever been, I still decided to go back to my parents. Even though I felt safe, even though I felt like I finally mattered, I still decided to go back. I felt like I crushed Theresa by doing it, even though she said it was up to me and that she supported me either way. I think part of why I wanted to go back to them was that was all I knew. I loved the way I felt living with Theresa, but it scared me. It was new and scary. I was young, and I was dumb. I just didn't know any better, and I passed up an amazing opportunity. It only took a month or two before I was back in the middle of a nightmare, abuse, and hatred; my parents had deceived me. It wasn't the first time they deceived me, so it shouldn't have been a surprise, but it was. I felt so childish, so foolish, like a little kid that believed in a silly fairy tale.

After the new year came around, just when I thought I had nothing besides Mark and Carla to live for, I got a surprise. My uncle James and Mary called me to tell me that my real parents were sick. They told me that they wanted to take me there to meet them. They said that the only problem was that they didn't want to meet me. They felt horrible for years for losing me, my uncle told me. He said that they never got over it. That's why I never met them. I was told that losing me messed them up bad and they couldn't handle seeing me after all this time. He said that he told them that he wanted to bring me to meet them, and they agreed to it. I was told that they had stopped using heroin years before that but they had already caught hepatitis from it. After that, they both started drinking heavily. Maybe they did it to replace the drugs and thought it was better. Between the hepatitis and the alcohol, they both managed to severely damage and deteriorate their livers. My uncle told me that my mom's condition was a lot more serious than my dad's. Her liver damage was at a further stage. My uncle said that my mom wasn't just sick; he said that she was dying and did not have much time left. So many emotions came flooding in when he told me those things. I felt sadness, anger. I also felt some excitement. I had never met my own parents, the two people who made me, and I had never even talked to them or met them. I felt sadness that they were sick, sadness that my mom was dying, but also intense anger that even if she wanted to, she couldn't be a permanent part of my life. Past the sadness and anger, there was excitement. I was beyond excited to finally meet my real parents. It had always hurt me that they didn't want to meet me. It was confusing to hear my aunt Sarah tell me that it was complicated when I asked about it. I couldn't even believe it—I was going to finally meet my parents. My uncle planned it for two weeks from when he told me. He said that he had to make arrangements to be gone for a few days. The funny thing was that my real parents only lived five hours away; they lived in the same state as me. In my head, I repeatedly went over what I was going to say to them, what I was going to ask them and tell them. I had fifteen years of catching up to do, fifteen years of stuff to tell them. Over and over, I thought about it. I replayed so many different scenarios in my mind. I couldn't stop thinking about it. I was finally going to meet my mom and dad. I was excited. I imagined just sitting in a room with my real family. I imagined us happy and laughing together. I imagined us eating dinner or cooking with my mom and then all of us watching a movie together. I wondered what they would think about me, if they would like me, and what they would think about my life. I felt like I was moving forward in my life by meeting them. It would be the next chapter in my life, and I needed that. It was three days before we were supposed to go when my uncle told me that he spoke to them and they didn't want to meet me. Those words felt like knives stabbing me in the chest, stabbing me through my heart. I couldn't believe it. I was so confused and could understand why that would happen to me. My uncle James said that my dad thought it would be too much for my mom to meet me, she felt too stupid. I was so angry. I told my uncle—I begged him—to take me, anyway. I told him I had to meet them. He apologized so many times but said that he couldn't do it, he just couldn't help me. I must have punched so many things after that, walls, a few cars, my face. I was just so mad at the world. I was so angry that my uncle would get my hopes up and then shatter them. I was so let down by him and by my real parents. The least they could do was meet me. I replayed my uncle telling me that they didn't want to meet me over and over in my head.

I needed someone to talk to about it, so I called my aunt Sarah. I guess because she was my mom's sister, I thought she could explain why my mom wouldn't meet me. She couldn't offer much in that department. She said what she had for years. She said it was complicated but that my mom loved me. I cried and I cried while on the phone with her. I told her that I would never be okay if my mom died without me meeting her. I told her that I hated my life, I hated myself, and I wouldn't want to meet me either if I were my parents.

I was so upset when my aunt couldn't offer me any answers to why this was happening, so I hung up on her and cried so hard. I didn't sleep that night. I just lay in my bed staring at the ceiling and telling myself I hated everyone around me for letting me down. I talked out loud as if I was talking to my parents. I told them that I hated them and that they were losers who wouldn't even meet their own kid. I was completely full of anger, consumed by it, blinded by it. The next day, I was shocked when my aunt Sarah's husband called me. My uncle Will told me he would take me. Just like that, he said that he would take me even though my real parents did not want to meet me. He said we would just show up, just drive there, knock on the door, and they wouldn't have a choice. My uncle Will knew that I needed this. He was going to do it even though my parents had clearly stated that they did not want me going there. My aunt Sarah couldn't do it. She couldn't be a part of it, because she knew my mom was fragile. My aunt also knew how bad I needed to meet them, so she let her husband take me. My grandma and my parents didn't want me to meet my real parents. They were angry that I wanted to meet them so badly. I didn't care what they thought. They were probably worried that my real parents would find out that they were monsters. They probably never wanted me to meet them, because my real parents would find out what they had done to me my whole life. When we left, the further we got from my house, the better I felt. I felt free, exhilarated, and just full of life and possibility. I felt like my life had been standing still for a long time, standing still and not going anywhere. We put the windows down, and the fresh air felt like it was the best thing I had ever felt. I couldn't believe what was about to happen. The closer we got, the more relieved I felt. It was like I knew where we were going. The further we drove, the more cornfields and long roads I saw. The towns started to disappear, and we eventually got off the expressway and pulled into a small town. It almost looked like a ghost town, there were barely any people out, and it was the smallest town I had ever been in.

After a few turns, we were there. We pulled into a driveway of a small trailer, and there was a man standing outside. The man turned around, and I knew he was my father—I just knew. I had seen him before, years before, at a funeral. He shook my hand and told me how nice it was to finally meet me. I thought the way he held my hand for longer than usual was strange. Also the way he stared at me caught my attention. I quickly forgot about it, only thinking about it briefly the day after but not spending too much time on it. Years ago, I had already met him and didn't even know it. It was his eyes that I remembered the most—his eyes and the shape of his face but mostly his eyes. His eyes were light, like a greenish-brownish color. They were deep and full of pain but also they had so much mystery in them. It wasn't just his eyes that held pain. It was his face too. I can't even explain it, but he had a face that I knew went through so much. A white T-shirt and faded-blue jeans, those were what my dad was wearing when we pulled up behind him. I didn't even wait for my uncle to get out. I just got out, and my uncle Will quickly followed. My uncle said hello to him, and he realized who he was right away. My uncle Will told him that he had someone who wanted to meet him. I walked up and said hi. I said, "Hi, I am your daughter." There were so many different emotions that I could see in his eyes, in his face. What I saw was sadness that quickly turned to joy, the joy that turned to relief and happiness. He took my hand and said hello and then hugged me tightly. He held me tight, but I could feel him holding back from wanting to hold me tighter. I wanted to just burst into tears, but I held back. I pushed it down and smiled so big. This man was my father, my real father, and he was right in front of me. I must have looked like him, with so many emotions, one quickly changing to another. My dad started to explain that my mom wasn't well. He said that he didn't know what to say but just that she wasn't well. We all walked toward the house, and when I got to the door, my dad stopped and put his hand to his forehead. He said that he knew my mom wasn't going to handle it well, me just showing up there. He said it wasn't that she didn't want to meet me. She was sick, not just physically sick, he said. My parents had often said horrible things about my real parents, and that was one of them. They said my mom was crazy, just full of mental problems. It hurt to see that there was some truth to what they said. It made me mad, but it was clearly true.

I told him that it was okay. I told him that none of that mattered, and then I smiled and walked into the trailer.

As I entered, to my right, I could see a living room. There was a younger and older lady in there sitting on a couch. They didn't even look toward me at first. They continued looking at the TV that was in front of them. I could see that the older woman, my mom, did look very sick; she looked so tired. She was so skinny, such a skinny face with long brown hair falling way past her shoulders. Her hair was so straight, and it looked like she had just brushed it. It lay so perfect on her shoulders and chest. My mom had on big glasses. They were like the ones that girls wore in the '70s, big and circular. They were also kind of like the kind that much older women wore, so they looked almost strange on her. She had on light-gray jogging pants, black slippers, and a plain light-pink T-shirt. I walked all the way through the kitchen and into the doorway of the living room before they even looked up at me. All I did was smile and say hi. My mom jumped up and put her hand over her mouth and ran the other way. She had only looked at me for seconds, but she must have known who I was already. She ran down the hall and into the bathroom. I don't know why, but I ran after her. I could hear her crying through the bathroom door. She said that she didn't want me to see her the way she was and that she was so sorry. I told her I didn't care about any of that and to open the door. I told her that I just wanted to meet her. I told her I had waited so long, so many years, just to meet her. When I said that, she opened the door. She looked at the floor and kept telling me that she was sorry, but I told her that it was okay. I hugged her. I was fifteen years old and hugging my mother, my real mother, for the first time in my life. She was short. She was shorter than me, and I was only five feet tall. She wasn't just short; she was so small, so frail, and I could feel that she was sick. I felt like I was hugging her and not the other way around. I felt like I was consoling her. My mom led me back over to the couch, and we sat down. We smiled and stared at each other. We looked so similar. Our faces, our eyes, they were all the same. The only difference was that I had cut my hair short. Sitting next to me was my sister. I knew she was my sister, because she also looked just like me. She was a little bigger than us, but it was just because of her age. She had baby fat on her. She put her hand on my shoulder, so I turned around and said hi. I told her that I was her sister, Ava. She just said there smiling for a moment, and then she told me that she already knew who I was and that her name was Lisa. They said they were just watching Lifetime movies. I couldn't believe it. That is what I would have been doing too. It felt so natural. It almost felt like something I had done before, but it felt right. I could tell that it was hard for my mom to look me in the eyes. I could tell that there was so much that she was ashamed about. Like my dad, she had pain and heartache written all over her face and in her eyes. I could see it in her dark-brown eyes. I could feel it too. My mom and my sister both had brown hair and brown eyes. Finally, I was sitting with my family, and they looked like me. I wanted to just close my eyes and stay in that moment. I wanted to just hold my mother and never let go. For so many years, I existed without her. For all those years, I had been away from the person who made me. I was so content that I almost forgot that I had a brother until he walked out of the room and introduced himself. My real brother was so different from the brother I had at home. He was more of an outdoors kid. I could tell right away. My brother, Carl, had so much to show me. He brought me to his room and showed me all of his wrestling stuff. He told me that he loved wrestling and went over all his favorites with me and then took me outside to see his go-cart. Carl and Lisa took turns riding me around on the go-cart until I decided to take it for a spin myself. I would never have guessed that I could have so much fun with two people whom I had never met before. The whole time I was there, it felt like I had never left. It felt so right to be in a house with all of them. My mom had to lie down a lot. She took a lot of naps, and she looked so tired but not like she was dying. If I didn't know it, I would never have guessed that my mom was very sick, and especially not dying. She was so plain but so beautiful. She was mine. She was my mother.

My mom had a daughter from a relationship that she was in before my dad, and I had a half sister named Tanya. Tanya came to meet me and to see my mom, so that was a nice surprise. It was intriguing to meet yet another person who looked just like me. I absolutely loved it. Meeting my family was the best thing that I had ever done in my life, and I was so happy that my uncle Will brought me. Before we left, my mom gave me a charm. It was an oval with a saint on it. It said, "Saint Joseph." My mom told me that Saint Joseph was the saint of families and children and that he would protect me when we weren't together. She apologized that it wasn't fancy, that it wasn't gold, and that there wasn't any kind of chain for it. I told her I didn't even like gold and that I would get a chain for it. I told her I had one for it. I went into the room that my stuff was in, and I took a ball chain necklace that I had a guitar pick on and switched the charm with the guitar pick. That charm meant so much to me. It was something that I could hold in my hand and think about my mother. I left there a different person. I felt like a piece of my heart, a pretty big one, was healed. Driving home, I couldn't stop thinking about my real family, I had finally met them, and it wouldn't end there. We planned on having another visit the next month, and I already couldn't wait. I wanted to stay longer, but my uncle Will had to go back to work, and I had school. That next week, I felt like my life had more meaning. I felt like I was almost complete having finally met my real parents. It was a good feeling. I got a call from my aunt seven days later, and she told me that my mom died. I waited my whole life to meet her. I waited my whole life to have a relationship with her, and she was gone just like that. I was so angry. I was mad at the world for my mom dying. I wanted to blame it on anyone. I got so drunk and high that day. I drank a lot of liquor and smoked so much crack with Mark and his sister, Lynn. I felt so lost, so hurt and completely out of control. In seven days. I went from feeling complete—I finally felt okay—and then, just like that, back to feeling broken. I did as much drugs as I could that week, and even brought drugs with me when going back for the funeral. I was so mad at the world that I said horrible things to Carla and pushed her away. I wanted to apologize, because I needed Carla's friendship, but I didn't. I had been in that trailer one week before that with my mom, but she was gone when I went there again. I felt like I was in a nightmare, a horrible nightmare that I couldn't get out of no matter how hard I tried.

My real parents didn't have a lot of money, so there wasn't a funeral, just a small gathering of family and friends. It was at the town funeral home. A eulogy was given by a pastor who seemed to know everyone in that small town. My dad introduced me to everyone. When he said, "This is my daughter," those words soothed me. It was so strange meeting people who knew my mother when I didn't even know her; I knew nothing about her. I'm not even sure my mother had a headstone coming, but we went to the cemetery where my grandmother was buried. We threw her ashes into the air, each of us taking some into our hand and throwing it up into the air. I closed my eyes and talked to her when I threw them. I told her I was so sorry I didn't get to meet her sooner. I told my mother that I wished I could have gotten to know her and that I thought she was amazing even though I only spent three days with her. I wished so badly that she could hear me. I wished I could talk to her again, even if it was just one more time. I looked around after I threw her ashes at the people who were also there, and I was actually jealous of them. Those people knew her. They all knew my mother, and not even one of them probably realized how lucky they were. I had to keep telling myself that at least I could still have a relationship with my dad. At least, I could still see my real dad. I wanted to have known my mom so bad, but I had to move forward. I couldn't stay angry about it forever. When I got back home after staying with my dad for a few days, I was so depressed to have to be back there. I wished I could have just stayed with my dad. It was hard to call two people Mom and Dad who weren't really my parents, especially after my real mom just died. It was hard to even look at them. My mom and dad were horrible people, and I saw that so clearly at that point. Somehow, I managed to grow close to my brother after my mom died. He was the only person in that house who was truly sorry for my loss. My parents said they were sorry that my mom died, but it wasn't heartfelt.

I quickly went downhill with my eating issues. I went downhill with everything. The issues with my eating had gotten a lot better when I lived with my cousin Theresa but did not stay like that after my mom died. I was five feet tall and ninety pounds. I only ate a few times a week, and when I did, it was just enough to maintain my strength. Once you get past this horrible point of extreme hunger, it isn't so bad. You kind of forget about eating. I would look in the mirror and just pinch myself all over the place, just looking for anywhere that I could pinch too much. Those were the places I would obsess over, the places I would tell myself needed to be skinnier. When I would get hungry, I would go in the bathroom or in my room and yell at myself. I would tell myself how disgusting I was. I would squeeze those areas that I could pinch and tell myself I was a fat pig that didn't deserve to be alive. Sometimes, I would punch myself on my arms and legs, and sometimes, I would even punch myself in my face. If I got hungry during a time where I thought I was looking fat, I would get so angry at myself if I thought about food. There were times where I went crazy on myself, yelling, slapping my own face, and scratching my stomach till it bled. I bruised myself up so many times and would scratch my stomach so much that it would be just full of scratches and scabs. I think everyone knew I was scratching or cutting my stomach, because of the little lines of blood on my shirts. I would itch my stomach forgetting it was scabbed up, and then I would bleed through my shirts and not know until I saw people looking there. Mark was the only person whom I ever let see my stomach, and he would beg me not to hurt myself again. He never stayed on the topic, and I loved that about him. He accepted me, issues and all. He would voice his concerns, then we would move past it, and I needed that. At first, I didn't know what anorexia was, but then I saw a movie about a lady that was a singer who was anorexic. Mark always told me that I was ridiculously skinny, but I just took it as a compliment and smiled. It was shocking at first and a little scary to find out that I had an eating disorder and that it could lead to death. It made me angry, because the lady in the movie was completely out of control, and I felt like that wasn't me. I didn't want to be like the out-of-control lady with anorexia, but I was. I was exactly like her in every way. At first, I felt so proud of it, of being able to have control over something like that, but then it changed. Once I learned that it wasn't a gift or an ability to not eat, I then felt ashamed about it. I felt gross. After that, I went back to being self-conscious about my body, I felt so embarrassed to walk in front of people or when anyone looked at me. I would feel like kids or people were looking at my fat belly or my fat arms, and then I would feel so disgusted with myself. I punched myself so much and told myself I was fat and disgusting too many times.

It didn't help that I had recently met Mark's sister Lynn, who was also very skinny. Seeing her made me feel like it was okay. Lynn was in her early thirties at that time, but she was so much like me. I loved it. She had been a skinhead when she was younger, a full-blown skinhead girl. She had skinhead tattoos all over her body, and I was in love with them. I was in love with everything about Lynn, her physique, the way she talked, her tattoos, and her piercings. She did body piercings. She had all the tools and supplies at her house, and she pierced my belly button. I was only fifteen, but Lynn took me to her tattoo guy, and I got a tattoo on my upper arm of flames. It was a logo from a skateboard company. It was a flame with ombré colors in it. I was crazy about it. I loved being around Lynn. She treated me like an adult, and she felt the same way about me as I felt about her. We would smoke a lot of weed together. Mark and I took ecstasy with her a few times too. I got high on something almost every day after my mom died. It was hard to move on and get over it. After a couple of months of hanging out with her, she decided that she wanted to try smoking crack, so we went and bought some. It made me feel a lot better, so we started smoking crack every weekend. We would put our money together and get as much as we could, and Lynn would drive us all around while we smoked it. We would get so high that I thought I would lose my mind, and then we would smoke weed and take pain pills to calm ourselves down. I started getting obsessed with all of the skinhead stuff that Lynn was into, and I can now see that it was fueled by my grief. I changed the way I dressed. I wore black pants, white shirts, red suspenders, and black combat boots. The combat boots had white straight laces in them. The white laces and the red suspenders were iconic symbols for skin- heads. I put a silver-white pride cross onto my chain, right next to my Saint Joseph charm that my mom gave me. On my book bag, I put dozens of patches that Lynn gave me. Some were skinhead bands and some skinhead or Nazi symbols. I read Hitler's *Mein Kampf* and

William Luther Pierce's *The Turner Diaries*, both classic skinhead or neo-Nazi books. I was infatuated with the sick stories Lynn would tell me about what she and her skinhead friends would do to Black people. I became so obsessed with such horrific details of crimes that Lynn had committed that she started calling me Sic Pea. Sweet Pea was my nickname, so she changed it around a bit, and my skinhead name was born. On my boots in white old English letters, one said, "SIC," and the other said, "PEA." That's who I became. I was known as Sic Pea. I was no longer sweet; I was sick in the head. All I thought about was what I learned from Lynn, the books she gave me, and the stories that she told me. I even became good friends with two boys at school who were into the skinhead and neo-Nazi movement. They were exactly like me. We were all just obsessed with hatred, extreme hatred, for anyone who wasn't White. It got to the point where I was enraged when the Black or Mexican kids at school even looked at me, and I thought about stabbing them. I had a sick fantasy of curb stomping a Black person. That means to make them put their teeth on a curb, and then you kick in their skull with your boots. That's the definition of curb stomping. As sick as it may sound, I loved it and hoped I could do it one day.

My fantasies and the things I said out loud started bothering Mark, and it's not like he was a saint. I was out of control. One of the boys, Tom, who was into the skinhead movement, actually lived on the other side of my block; so we were on the same bus. Instead of catching the bus on my block, I would catch it with him, so we could talk or smoke weed together. One morning, I went to his house before we had to catch the bus, and he had made me eggs and sausage. Tom said that I was way too skinny. He said that Mark needed to start feeding me instead of getting me high. I was mad at first, but Tom's cute smile and laugh made me calm down and eat the food he made. Even though I acted mad about what he said, I was secretly so flattered by being called way too skinny. Tom knew how much Mark and I did ecstasy, mushrooms, and cocaine. He also knew we drank a lot and smoked weed up to five times a day. I couldn't be mad at him for saying that about Mark, because he didn't know that I stayed that skinny on purpose. I think that he thought it was accidental. I knew that I was out of control, but I didn't care.

I was full of hatred and sadness, and it made me feel good. That all came to a complete stop one afternoon when I found out that I was pregnant. We didn't use condoms. We had been having sex for a year without protection. I honestly thought that I couldn't get pregnant. I guess I thought that because of the drugs and being so skinny that I couldn't get pregnant, so it wasn't something that we even worried about. I had started feeling nauseous in the morning and even threw up a couple of times, but I didn't feel like I was sick. I started feeling so nauseous and sick to my stomach when I smelt cooked meat, so I knew something was wrong. I missed my period, and it was a week later, so I knew what I had to do, I had to take a pregnancy test. I bought three of them, and, of course, all three were positive. Mark really didn't know what to say when I came out of the bathroom and told him that I was pregnant. He just waited for what I was going to say. I was angry, I cried, I punched a few things, and I was so scared and mad at myself for being so stupid. I yelled at Mark and told him that it was his fault, and I told him that it made no sense that we never used condoms or anything to prevent pregnancy. I felt so dirty, and I wished so badly that I could go back and use condoms and prevent getting pregnant. I told Mark that I needed to get an abortion. I told him that we had to fix it, because we definitely couldn't have a baby. Mark told me that it was up to me. Whatever I wanted to do, he would support me. I immediately found a low-cost abortion clinic that would do the procedure for $100 due to my age, and it was scheduled for one week ago. I could afford it because I had gotten a part-time job at a miniature golf park near my house. A few kids I knew at school had applied and gotten jobs there. Apparently, they liked hiring high school kids.

It was pure relief finding a place that did low-cost abortions. A lot of the places were around $800. The abortion clinic told me that it would be $100 more to verify the pregnancy but said that I could get it done somewhere else. There were several different low-cost or free clinic-type places that did the verification, so I got it done at some kind of church facility near my school. I couldn't tell the people there that I was planning to get an abortion, and it was hard as they went through all kinds of pregnancy info with me. They went on and on about being able to help me find baby clothes, car seats, and other supplies that a person having a baby would need. They gave me so much paperwork—papers on what happens during each month of pregnancy, forms to fill out for the WIC program, and so many more. They even spent about twenty minutes role-playing with me. They wanted me to practice telling my parents. I was there almost two hours. I had to fake that I was happy about having a baby, and they even prayed with me. I walked out of there feeling frustrated and worn out, but I at least got the form that I needed to get an abortion. It was strange being pregnant, but I tried not to think about it. I just told myself that it would be over soon. My appointment was on a Monday. I found a girl at school who had a car and was willing to ditch school and take me.

That Friday, my mom came into my room crying as she held up a pile of the papers that the church facility had given me. There was no way to lie myself out of it. There was a pregnancy verification form with my name on it and tons of pregnancy literature. I told her that I was pregnant, but I was getting it taken care of in just a few days. She told me that if I got an abortion, she would kick me out, and I couldn't believe it. I was fifteen years old and pregnant, and my mom would actually rather me have a baby than get an abortion. My mom yelled at me about being so stupid, stupid enough to not be using birth control or condoms. She also said she was shocked and hurt that I was having sex, and it upset me to hear her say that. I felt so dirty. Not only was I having sex but also was pregnant and planning on getting an abortion. My mom actually called my dad, who was on a vacation by himself. He was in California, and she called him to tell him. I could hear him scream and say that I was stupid. He said *stupid* and *dumb* so many times I lost count. I was horrified that I was even going through that considering I had an appointment to fix it three days later. I felt stupid, just like my dad kept calling me. I couldn't believe my mom found the pregnancy papers just days before the appointment. My mom said that I needed to call Mark and tell him that she was coming to pick him up. She said we all needed to talk. When I told him that my mom had found out I was pregnant, there was just silence on the phone. After we picked him up, there were hours of talking, talking between us and my dad some of the time.

I really didn't have much of a choice. I was fifteen and couldn't be homeless, so I was going to have a baby. Mark said he thought it was a great idea and that we could get married and be a real family. When I heard him say that, I knew right then that I was making the right decision. A real family was all I had ever wanted, so instead of hoping for a family one day, I could make my own. In the blink of an eye, my life completely changed. I went from being an anorexic, drug-abusing, skinhead teenager to a pregnant and soon-to-be mom. It was literally like night and day. I may not have been living right, but I knew what the right thing was to do. I had to move forward as a pregnant teenager, move forward, and move past my old self and life. I did it with Mark by my side, but it was still so hard not to be able to be the kind of teenager I was before getting pregnant. No more getting high, no more drinking, no more insane concerts or drug parties. It sounds easy to stop doing all of those, but it's hard when everyone around you is still doing them. Just because I was a pregnant teenager in high school doesn't mean the whole school would change. Mark supported me, and he was there for me, but he still drank and got high, so it was hard. I was always with Mark, but it still got lonely being left out from stuff. Everyone in school stared at me like I was a monster. Even when I dressed in skinhead gear, no one looked at me like that. I know that the kids and teachers at the school thought I would be the last person having a baby.

School was weird, but things were pretty good at home between me and my parents. My dad did his yelling about me getting pregnant, and he said that he was only going to stop hitting me because I was pregnant. I think that was his way of saying that he didn't care about me but wouldn't hit an innocent little baby. Mark and I were so happy that we were going to be a family, so we went to the courthouse and got married. I wanted to do it right, get married before I had a baby. I wanted my baby to have parents who were married. I was dedicated to being a good wife, so dedicated that I stopped being friends with Carla because Mark asked me to. The month before that, I had reconnected with Carla. Finally, we had been back to being best friends. Carla had said a couple of things to Mark that he didn't like. She said he needed to stop getting high around me. She also said that he needed to start acting like someone who was about to be a father, and not a kid. Mark didn't like that at all. He thought Carla was being disrespectful to him. So just like that, I gave up our friendship. It hurt me, and I know that it hurt her, too, but I did it. A few weeks later, we drove down to visit my real dad and tell him the news of the baby and that we got married. It felt right to be with my real dad, and it felt so good that he was happy for us. I imagined my dad holding the baby and spending time with his grandchild. I was so happy being there with my dad and my real brother and sister. It was sad that my real mom had just passed months before that, but at least, I had my dad to bond with. I didn't want to leave him, but I had to get back to school but told my dad maybe we would move down there when the baby was born. My dad told me that we were all welcome to come and live with him after the baby came. He even said that Mark could get a job with him doing roofs and other work for the people he currently worked for.

When we got back, I could tell how jealous my mom was that I went to see my dad, and she almost lost it when I told her about us possibly moving in with him. She was so angry. The things she yelled and said were as if my baby was hers. She was obsessed with the baby, and I should have seen it sooner. My baby was all she talked about, from names to the outfits. She talked about it every second. When she wasn't talking about it, she was shopping in the baby isle and in thrift stores finding baby items. She was happy. I liked seeing her distracted from my dad not treating her right. I think that's why I didn't realize how obsessed she was, or I just looked the other way. My mom told me that when the baby was born, we could pretend it was hers if I wanted. She said that I could go out and do whatever I wanted if I didn't have a baby to take care of. She said I would be happier that way. She really tried convincing me to let her raise the baby, but something deep inside of me knew something was wrong with that. I realized right away all the way from when she said I had to keep the baby that my mom wanted it. She wanted a baby, she wanted more children, but she was told by the doctor that she wouldn't make it through another labor. I knew she wanted to keep my baby as her own, but I just tried pushing that out of my mind. I felt like if my mom had good intentions, then we could have been best friends. She was really there for me, but I knew deep down that it was only because I had something that she badly wanted. I think my mom had some sick fantasy of a baby fixing her and my dad's marriage. I could see it in her eyes. Everything about my mom being intensely involved in my pregnancy felt so wrong. I felt very much like I was being used. I knew my mom was obsessed with the idea of having a baby. It was the look in her eyes when she talked about it that made me know for sure. The worst was when she would talk to my dad about it, she acted as if she was talking about their baby, and not mine. It was more than just excitement with her; it was an actual full-blown obsession. About four months into my pregnancy, I got a call from my aunt Sarah, my real mom's sister, and she told me that my dad was sick and that I should take a trip to see him. I heard a sense of urgency in her voice, and then she stopped sugarcoating the situation.

My dad wasn't just sick; he was very close to dying. He had the same liver condition my mom had. It was from years of heroin and alcohol abuse. I had meant to spend more time with my real dad, visit him more, and build a strong relationship. Everything had gotten crazy after finding out I was pregnant, and now it was almost too late. I called Mark, and we drove down to where he lived that next morning. It was the longest five hours of my life. I couldn't have been prepared for what I would find when I got there. My dad was literally about to die. He was so sick, incoherent, and moaning from the pain; and it was so frightening to see him like that. I hated myself as I stood over the couch he was lying on. I was selfish and had only visited him one time after my mom died. Only three times had I ever been around my real father, and now it was too late. He was going to die. He was worse looking than my mom when I met her, so skinny, so frail that we had to help him on and off the couch. We even had to light cigarettes for him and watch him so he didn't forget he was smoking and drop it or burn himself. My dad went in and out of reality. One minute, he knew who I was, and the next minute, he thought I was my mom. I looked just like my real mom, so my dad thought I was her. He told me that I was the most beautiful wife and mother. He told me that we would be together in heaven and that he was happy to spend his life with me. After so many times of telling him that I was Ava, his daughter, I stopped and just went along with it. The day after we got there, my grandma arrived to help take care of my dad and to say her goodbyes. My grandma wasn't my grandma. She was my dad's sister, but I was told growing up that she was my grandma. My dad kept asking us for blueberry pie, so we made it for him. Actually, my grandma did, and he loved it. I was dying on the inside when I was there. I wanted so badly to have one of my real parents in my life, but it was too late. I had a baby in my stomach who would never know its real grandparents, and that hurt me so bad. I cried so much in the three days that I was there. My heart felt like it was completely dead and shattered into a million pieces. I couldn't understand why my life had to be full of pain and misery, so I would put my hand on my belly and tell my baby its life would be different. I wanted to give my baby a life full of happiness, a life nothing like I had. I felt like I had a dark cloud hovering above me, and I was going to change that once the baby was born.

I stayed for a few days, and still to this day, I don't know why I left. I had to get back to school and work, but I could have taken more time off for such a serious situation. My dad died the very next day, so we packed up and went right back. I was upset and angry that I left my dad. It hurt that he died right after I left. My grandma told me it was better that way. She said that he started bleeding out of every opening in his body. She said that he was in a lot of pain and rolled around. She said he moaned and cried right up until his last breath. I got back there the day after he died, and that night, I slept on the floor because I let my older family members take the beds. It was around midnight when I awoke to the sound of creaking floors; and right there in front of me, clear as day, was my dad. He walked over me and then stood in the doorway of the kitchen and smiled. I fell back asleep because I was so tired, and the next morning, I told my grandma before I even stood up. My grandma had slept right next to me but up on the couch, so right when she woke up, I told her. I told her that my dad woke me up, he stepped over me, and the creaking floor was what made me wake up. She told me that my dad died the day before, and I told her that I was aware of that. I feel like my dad wanted me to see him one more time so I could have closure, and I did feel a sense of peace after that. Just like when my mom died, there wasn't enough money for a funeral, so there was a small service again. My dad's ashes weren't spread like my mom's. They were given to one of his brothers to keep. If I didn't have Mark there with me, I don't know what I would have done. If I didn't have a baby in my stomach when my dad died, I probably would have taken so many drugs that I would have died. I feel like being pregnant saved me from doing bad things to try and drown out the sadness and anger that I had, because of my dad's death. I wanted to just drop out of school after that, but I decided that I would stay in school. I would take a month off when I had the baby but then go right back, because I didn't want to be a high school dropout. I definitely didn't want to be a pregnant teenage dropout. I wasn't gonna let a baby stop me. I got a postcard in the mail from Carla. She sent it to my parents' house so Mark wouldn't see it. She said that she was sorry about my parents. She said she heard it from her mom. She said she missed me. I really wanted to call her or write her back and tell her how horrible I felt about my dad dying, but I didn't. I told myself that my husband didn't want me talking to Carla, so I wasn't going to.

Things started to calm down and get better after that. It was hard, but it got better. I found out that I was having a boy. I already knew because I could feel him inside of me—a little boy whom I decided to name Kaleb, a strong and bold name. One day, I tripped over one of my mom's piles of junk, and I fell but was able to land on my butt. I didn't get hurt, but I could have if I would have fell differently. You could barely even walk through the house anymore. Piles of stuff would fall down into your path. It was insane. My mom was out of control, and no one ever did anything about it. It got worse when I got pregnant. She would go shopping sometimes three times a day and come home with huge bags. She would go to a few thrift stores so she could buy a lot of stuff with the prices being so low. My dad would say ignorant things to her about it, but he never actually tried to help her fix it. I would tell her that it was nice that she wanted to buy so much for the baby, but we didn't have any more room for it. I realized that my parents' house was just too dirty and cluttered, and I couldn't live there anymore. When school ended, Mark and I got an apartment a couple of towns over. It was just a small apartment, but it was ours. Mark had a trust fund from when his grandma died many years before that. When he wanted to use money from it, it had to be approved by a trustee. He arranged for our apartment and bills to be paid every month. He also paid for a new car out of it. The apartment wasn't spectacular, but it would be where we would take care of our son together. I hoped to share so many happy moments with Mark and the baby in that apartment. I was so excited. My mom and my grandma helped us get everything we needed for the apartment, everything from furniture to dishes. They made sure we had everything and helped me apply for food stamps so we could have food.

I started becoming good friends with a girl whom I worked with, Kat. We had gone to school together for years but just never talked even though she lived near me. She was the only person who didn't mind hanging out with a pregnant girl, but because she didn't drink or party, it worked great. We would get Chinese food after work, and she started coming over and hanging out with me. It was nice to have her there with me, especially when Mark's friends were over. We would just sit in the room and watch TV or movies and find any little thing to joke about or laugh at. Kat and her family were all so supportive of me and my pregnancy. It was nice to have that being a pregnant teenager. Around that same time, there was a fire at the gas station that I work at. It caused me to lose my job there. We wouldn't have any extra money to spend, and Mark would have to find a job fast so we could afford diapers and gas for the car. Other than diapers, my mom and grandma got me everything I would need for Kaleb for at least two to three months. We decided I would wait to get another job. We figured no one would want to hire a pregnant girl. Mark looked for jobs but couldn't seem to find any, and having no skills sure didn't help. The following month, I was out with my mom and my grandma having breakfast. We were at a restaurant where we had breakfast at least once a week. I started having cramps that I realized were contractions, so we drove and picked up Mark and then went to the hospital. It took so many hours of walking to strengthen the contractions and make the baby drop further down, but finally, it happened.

On that beautiful crisp October day in 2002, my son Kaleb was born. He was amazing, so beautiful, the most precious thing I had ever seen in my life. I looked him in his eyes, and in that moment, I knew Kaleb saved me. He saved me from myself. He saved me from being on drugs and from going further into a life as a skinhead. Kaleb was my hope, he was my newfound happiness, and I was so happy that I didn't get an abortion. Everyone was so happy when he was born. Even Kat came to the hospital to meet Kaleb. My first days with him were some of the happiest days of my life. I can't even explain what it's like to be a new mother. Being a new mother is like the biggest and brightest ray of sunshine coming down on you and filling you with a feeling that life is going to be amazing. Having a baby makes you feel like anything is possible, and it makes you feel like you can do anything. I swore to Kaleb that I would give him the best life ever and that I would always take care of him. He was a wonderful baby. Mark and I were so happy with him. We were a family. The baby brought everyone closer together. My mom, dad, brother, and sister just loved him. Kat loved playing with Kaleb. She would pick us up, and we would go to her house and play with Kaleb for hours. Jaime's parents loved having Kaleb at their house. We would take him for walks and long drives when he was fussy. My grandma and mom almost fought over who would hold him or babysit Kaleb. He was so precious. I quickly transformed from a confused and pregnant teenager to a young new mom who was eager to be a great mom.

Right away, I was in mom mode. It just came naturally to me, and I was proud to be a mom. Mark, on the other hand, didn't jump right into dad mode. He was held back by childish things. Mark would stay up all night drinking with his friends or alone and then sleep the entire next day. There were a few times where his friends would come over, and everyone took psychedelic mushrooms. Mark had found a job at a nearby department store. It was a pretty big one, so they always needed extra workers. Mark would work afternoons and have friends come over when he got off. Sometimes, they would be waiting for him to get home. His friends were still in high school, too, so they were happy to have a place where they could get high and not have to worry about anything. I would just sit there with Kaleb, rocking him and taking care of him while everyone else got high or partied. It became frustrating after a few months. I felt lonely even though I lived with Mark, because he was always sleeping. It really hurt me that I became a mom right away but Mark stayed on the same path he was on before the baby was born. One day, Kat took me to visit Mark at work and found out that he had quit about six weeks prior. Jaime drove me around to all of his friend's house to find him, and we found him at his friend Mark's house. He was in his garage, a popular hangout spot, and was getting high. Mark had been getting up and pretending to go to work every day and going and getting drunk or high with his friends instead. I had asked him a few weeks before that why we didn't have any money, and he said it was because the car needed work. It hurt to find out he had been lying to me. Instead of helping me take care of Kaleb, he was out getting drunk or high. After so many lies, lonely nights, and little drug parties, I just couldn't do it anymore. I was tired of it. I was fed up with taking care of a baby by myself. It wasn't fair, and I had gotten so unhappy. Things got very bad with my emotional state. My mom told me something was wrong. That's when I found out that I had postpartum depression. It was hard to deal with adjusting to everything and doing it on my own. I was struggling, and I wasn't getting help at home, so that is when I decided to leave. My dad came and got all of my things within an hour, and I was out of there, and just like that, my marriage was over. I had wanted us to work out so bad, but Mark wasn't even trying to be a good husband or father. Jaime's family said that I could stay with them until I figured out what I was going to do, so I did. My mom and dad talked it over and decided that I could stay with them. My dad said that he would make my mom clean the house and do something about the mess. My mom was still what I would call hoarding, so unless she did something about it, we wouldn't be able to live there. They also wanted to remodel my old room so it would be big enough for me and Kaleb, so they needed a month or two to do it. I was so happy that I had so many people who cared about me enough to do those things for me. I was lucky to have parents who would step up and help me in a bad situation, even with the bad stuff that had gone on my whole childhood. I didn't forget about everything that my dad did and everything my mom let him do. I wanted to move forward. I had a baby and wanted to leave that stuff in the past. I didn't want to move back into my parents' house, but I had to. My plan was to stay there temporarily. I would get a job and save up for an apartment. I figured I would stay there for about a year as I saved up. Plus, having my mom around to help me with Kaleb would be great. When I was pregnant, a lot of my teeth started to bother me. I knew I had tons of cavities. In middle school, my parents had gotten me braces, and at every checkup visit, they would send notes home saying that I had cavities. My mom never took me to get any of the cavities filled, even though I told her that some of my teeth were hurting. She would tell me that my dad's new insurance wasn't good, and then it would get forgotten about. When I married Mark, I was no longer on my dad's insurance. I was on government insurance. The pain got so bad in my teeth that I had to find a low-cost clinic that took my government insurance. I found one a few towns away. It was free with my insurance because of my age, and it was actually a nice place. I found out that I had thirteen teeth with large cavities, and I had four teeth that had decayed into the nerves needing root canals. My mouth was a mess, but the clinic helped me. I went to so many visits that I got to know them. One day, they offered me a job. They said they would train me to be a dental assistant, and I accepted their offer. I had planned on going back and finishing high school, but I decided to just go and get my GED. Again my life quickly changed. I went from being a jobless high school dropout to starting a promising career as a dental assistant. After a few months, I got my GED and even took some courses to help me in the dental field. Everything was great. My mom or Mark would watch Kaleb while I was at work. Mark, of course, wanted to get back together, but I said no. I made it very clear to Mark that I wanted to do what was best for Kaleb, he was everything to me, and I just wanted to be a good mother to him. I told Mark if he got a job and stopped partying, then we could talk about getting back together, but he never did. I worked and worked, and I did everything a good mother was supposed to do. Mark, on the other hand, got high and drunk every day and hung out with his friends. I couldn't do it. I had to do what was best for my son. I had to do everything I could to give him a better life than I had. Everything was going so good. I had a perfect baby, a good job, a supportive family, and a best friend. Between my family and Kat and her family, I had all the help and support I needed with Kaleb. When I moved back in with my parents, I decorated our room so cutely. I did a pale-blue-and-white color scheme, and everything matched. I used the wallpaper that was textured and painted over it. I painted the trim for the walls and the windows white and put up shelves that I also painted white. Kaleb's crib set was the exact same colors with stripes on the blankets and sheets, and two stuffed animals that matched. I had a futon bed, and I somehow found a sheet set for it that was the exact same color that Kaleb's was, but the blanket was a neutral shade of gray. Since I had to have a gray blanket, I used gray as an accent color. I bought three pillows that matched and a gray rug for in front of my bed. It was simple, but it was ours. It was our little room, and I no longer had to watch people get drunk or high. My life was actually very calm for a few months, just back and forth from work. I worked hard and got enough to buy a used car. It was used, but it really felt new, a good family-type car. I felt so independent. I had a job, my own space (even though it was with my parents'), and a new car. I was doing it. I often felt so bored, especially at night. I couldn't find anyone who wanted to hang out with someone who had a baby. I tried to hang out with an old friend from before I got pregnant, but she would pretend like she was too busy all the time. I tried to hang out with this guy whom I was best friends with before; he was one of Mark's good friends too. He did the same thing to me. He acted like he was too busy or invited me to do things that he knew you couldn't do with a baby. It hurt. It really hurt me that no one wanted to be around me after I had a baby. I got so bored, so lonely, and I even started getting depressed every time someone blew me off or lied about why we could hang out. When I would find someone that wanted to hang out, it wouldn't be for very long, and they would act like Kaleb was a parasite. The way they would look at him was like they were disgusted that I had a baby. They would act like they had no idea how to hold him and then would end up leaving when he started to cry. The only friend I had was Kat, but she worked a lot and started going to college part-time. With Kat being so busy and barely available, I was always alone when I wasn't at work. I don't know why I waited so long, but one day, I decided to go visit Carla. It had been over a year since I had talked to her, and I didn't know if she would want to see me after what I did. We had been best friends for so many years, so for me to stop being friends with her the way I did, I didn't know what to expect. One day after work, I stopped by Carla's mom's house, but neither one of them was there. A guy answered and said she wasn't home, so I gave him my number and told him to have her call me. I figured she would call me in a day or two, but she called me thirty minutes later, so I went back to her house. She definitely wasn't mad. She was happy to see me and happy to meet Kaleb. Something definitely changed in the year that we were apart; maybe she changed because we were apart. Carla brought me into the kitchen, and we sat at the table. The guy was in the living room next to us watching TV. The guy seemed to be a lot different from us. It was strange, or at least he was a lot different from me. Carla and I were always into rock music, and you would know that by the way we dressed. This guy didn't look like he listened to rock music. He looked like he was a rapper. He looked very ghetto. All through high school, we always made fun of people like him, ghetto people who listened to rap music and dressed the way he did. He had a shaved head but had a beard and mustache that were all lined up just perfect. He had on a huge red shirt. It was a lot bigger than it needed to be, and his red-and-black Nike shorts were the same. He had on a gold chain with a charm, and just like the clothes, it was big. I couldn't help but stare at the strange guy who was in front of me, and that's when I realized that Carla was dressed similarly. I had only been away from her for a year. I couldn't figure out how Carla could change so much in just one year. She introduced him as Ron, and instead of coming to shake my hand or even look at me, he just nodded and continued watching TV. Carla was different. She was more different than I could wrap my head around. She wasn't the rocker girl I had been best friends with for years. She was somebody different now. That didn't matter to me. Carla wasn't mad at me, and she loved Kaleb, so I was happy. I visited with her for an hour or so. She caught me up on everything that was new in her life and how her mom and grandma were doing. I told her that I had to get going. I had to put Kaleb to sleep. I tried to keep him on a good schedule. Carla told me that she and Ron were having a party later that night. She said that I could stop by. My mom was at work, and it was too late for my grandma to watch Kaleb, so I knew I didn't have anyone to watch him. Carla insisted that the people who were coming over were real cool people and wouldn't mind my baby being there. I went home, got ready, and came back a few hours later with Kaleb. I wasn't too nervous about it because Mark's friends were always at our old apartment, so I had been around groups of people with a baby. There were so many people there when I went back. There had to be at least other people already there. It was mostly guys there, and they were all like Ron was. They looked ghetto. They were all Mexican. Almost all of them were wearing red and black clothes. I later found out that those were their gang colors. They were all gang members in a Latin gang. Carla had brought me upstairs to explain to me that they were gang members, and it scared me at first, but I stayed. I not only stayed, but I had so much fun and didn't even want to leave. All the guys and the few girls who were there were so easygoing, not like all the people who didn't want to hang out with a girl with a baby. All night, everyone took turns holding Kaleb. No one acted like it was strange to hold or play with a baby. It was awesome. I felt so good and so accepted for what I was. I was a young mother. I was still a teenager, just turned eighteen years old. I had a baby, so there was no pretending that I was something different. I was a new mom; that's who I was. After that night, I started hanging out with a guy from the party. His name was Alejandro. He was so sweet to me and Kaleb. He wasn't in the gang yet but was affiliated. He still had to prove himself. My parents were not happy with my decision to hang out with people affiliated with gangs, and my dad had a lot of racist stuff to say about me hanging out with a Mexican guy. My dad stopped being nice to me at all. It was a combination of me hanging out with Alejandro and him using drugs.

The next months went by so fast, and before I knew it, my baby Kaleb was one year old, my precious baby. I loved Kaleb so much, and I was so happy to be his mother. I started dating Alejandro, and he took us to do all sorts of fun things like the pumpkin patch, the field museum, and the shed aquarium. I spent most nights at his house, and he even watched Kaleb when I went to work some days. Alejandro didn't have a regular job. He sold weed, so he was home all day and able to help me with Kaleb. He lived with his mom, but I didn't care. I lived with mine still, so it was okay. I quickly changed from being a rocker chick to being very ghetto. I grew out my short hair and changed my dog chain necklace to a gold chain with a cross charm. I started wearing designer sweat suits and bought several gold necklaces, rings, and bracelets. I went and got my ears pierced five times on each side and wore big gold hoops in all of them. I mostly wore red and black clothes and shoes, without even putting thought into it. I repped gang colors. I went back to calling myself Sweet Pea, and I got a window decal for my car that said, "Sweet Pea," in huge old English letters. Under the "Sweet Pea" decal, I put a big Virgin Mary decal. I didn't know anything about being Catholic, but I told people I did. I just told everyone I was Catholic even though I knew nothing about any kind of religion really. I put rims on my car and a sound system in it with speakers in the trunk. Just like that, I was ghetto, as ghetto as it gets. I started drawing so much attention to myself and didn't even realize how serious it was. Alejandro and his friends were always in my car throwing up gang signs at other people and cars and yelling out the windows. All Alejandro's friends were gang members, and almost all of them had guns on them at all times. Every other day, we either had a party or went to one, and just like that, I was back to getting high and drunk. Alejandro and his friends were big into cocaine, so I was always drunk and high on cocaine or weed. When my mom couldn't watch Kaleb, Alejandro's mom or sister did. They were so good to us. With Alejandro having a good connection for cocaine, I often bought large amounts and went driving around with Carla getting high. We would take turns driving. We would drive down the expressway to the city, then back, and then do it again. We would do it for sometimes for up to eight hours until we were so high that we started losing it. I was hung over or throwing up at work at least once a week, but I didn't care. I kept partying. It only took about six months of doing what I was doing before I got shot at one afternoon. Kaleb and I were on our way to Alejandro's house after I got off work when a car shot at me three times. Only one bullet hit the bottom of one of my doors, but we could have been killed. I was so upset. I turned around and went home questioning everything I was doing in life. I was yet again going down a bad path. I was hanging around gang members and flashing it all around town. Instead of walking away, I just moved forward and got even deeper into it all. I told Alejandro that I could no longer date him, and I couldn't be around gang members anymore. I tried to stay away from him, but things were getting bad at home, so it was hard.

My dad was always gone again. Some nights, he didn't even come home. When he was home, my dad was so mean to my mom. He would say things to hurt her feelings and make her cry. He constantly would follow me around and say mean and ignorant things to me also. One day, I was at Alejandro's house, and I had been there for four days. My mom called to tell me that my dad hadn't come home the whole time I had been at Alejandro's and she was worried. My mom said that he kept telling her that he was working on an emergency construction project. He said they were happening back to back. My dad did do jobs like that, but the longest he would ever be gone on those would be eight to ten hours. It just didn't seem plausible that he would have four or five jobs in a row and not have been home in four days. My mom gave me the address of my dad's boss. She was too embarrassed to show up at his house. I went there right away, and at first, his boss, Ronny, acted as if my dad could still be at work because they had been so busy the last few weeks. It was when I was about to leave that I turned around and told him that

I knew my dad wasn't at work, and I didn't care. I told him that I knew what kind of person my dad really was. I told him that he was garbage but my mom didn't think so. Ronny looked down at the ground and shook his head. I told him that my mom was at home worried about him. I told him that my dad had been telling her that he was on back-to-back construction projects for the last four days. He pointed south and said to go to the stop sign and then go three blocks down and look for a greenhouse with white shutters. I looked at him and waited for him to say something else. I could tell he was hesitant and thinking hard about what to say. He told me to please not tell my dad how I got that address, and he said that he was sorry in advance for what I might find there. I was annoyed and confused by that particular remark. I had no idea what that guy was talking about. I went and found the house that Ronny was talking about, and it looked like a normal house from the outside. I knocked on the door, and two young guys answered immediately looking at me like they had a problem with me being there. I told them that I was look-ing for my dad, and they told me that he wasn't there and slammed the door in my face. I was so angry. I pounded on the door and told them that my dad's truck was in the driveway and that I would call the police if I needed him to. They opened the door and pointed to a room on the right, and right away, I could see my dad. My dad was on a bed with what was clearly a prostitute, and they were smoking crack. My dad had the crack pipe in his hand with a big torch lighter to it and appeared to be shaking. I walked up to the room and told him he was so stupid. I told him that my mom was actually worried about him. When I looked directly at him, I wanted to cry. I had never seen him or anyone look the way he did. It was his eyes mostly. They were so big and frantic looking, so red and bloodshot. He was so sweaty and clammy looking, and he was steadily shaking. It was disgusting. He looked like the homeless people who come up to you and beg for money. He only had on a white tank top, the kind guys wear underneath their shirts and boxers. My dad was half naked in a room with a prostitute smoking crack. He tripped and fell trying to get around the lady that was next to him. Instead of getting up, he stayed on his knees and started apologizing to me, begging me to forgive him. The whole time he's on his knees crying, the prostitute was fumbling with the crack pipe and looking around on the floor. She asked my dad if they had any more rocks, and when I heard that, I had to get out of there. I told them both that they were absolutely disgusting and needed to get help, and I told the lady that my dad was a married man and had a wife sitting at home. All she told me was that she had nothing to do with that, and I turned around and left. I couldn't believe it. I had no idea what to even think about it. I had found my dad in a crack house with a prostitute and had no clue what I was supposed to tell my mom. My mom had done me wrong so many times in my life, but I still cared about her. I still didn't want to hurt her. I decided to call my uncle James. He knew what kind of man my dad was, so I knew he could help. I parked two blocks away from the house and had my uncle meet me there and then showed him the house where my dad was. I left at that point. On my phone, I had so many missed calls from my mom. I had not been sure what to tell her, so I didn't answer. On my way home, I called her and told her that I would be home in a few minutes and I would explain when I got there. When I got there and explained to her what had just happened, I think that she already convinced herself mentally that it wasn't true. That evening, my dad was at home sitting on the couch as if nothing happened. I didn't even hear my mom say a word to that man about the prostitute or the four-day crack binge that he had just disappeared on.

In the middle of all the chaos, Kaleb turned two years old, the terrible number two. For Kaleb's second birthday, Alejandro and his family threw a party and got him so many gifts. It was so nice. I was in love with Alejandro, and it felt so good to be able to get over my failed marriage with Mark. One day, an old friend of mine called me and told me he had something important to tell me. He said that he had to tell me in person, but I told him I would rather just discuss it over the phone. I asked him what he was talking about he told me, and that's how I found out. That's how I found out that Alejandro was cheating on me with another girl. The guy who accepted my son and that I was a teen mother, the guy who I thought loved me, he was cheating on me. My heart was completely shattered, and I felt so stupid. I spent the next three days in bed crying. At first, I tried to just avoid his calls, but he called all day and night. I tried hanging out with Carla to help with my heartache. I couldn't believe it even happened. I was devastated, so I couldn't be alone, so I had Carla come and pick me up. Carla wasn't alone. She was hanging out with a guy I hadn't really seen around much. He was almost shy, quiet, and very mysterious; but I liked it. I thought it was intriguing. His name was Ghost. Well, his gang name was Ghost. We decided to go walk around the park near our house, so we drove that way listening to loud music and joking around. It was a lot of fun. They both helped me get my mind off of what Alejandro had done to me. Even when I laughed, I still felt my heart aching and would relive finding out about Rio cheating on me in my mind. It was on the way home from the mall that I was forced to push it all out of my mind. We were just talking, and then Ghost started having a seizure. I had never seen anything like that before, so I was absolutely terrified by it. Carla had to keep driving while I tried to hold him back into the seat. I tried as hard as I could to keep his head from hitting the dashboard, but I couldn't control him. We were near Carla's grandma's house, so that's where we drove to. It felt like forever by the time we got there even though we were probably only eight minutes away from it when the seizure started. We took Ghost out of the car and brought him into the house. We laid him in Carla's old bed. Carla's grandma said that when someone has a seizure, they have to just sleep afterward. Eventually, about six hours later, he woke up. He didn't remember anything, but he appeared to be fine. The next day, there was a big party that I was supposed to go to with Alejandro, but instead, I went with Carla and Ghost. I, of course, tried as hard as I could to make it look like Ghost and I went to the party as a couple, and it worked. Alejandro was there, and he actually cried in front of everyone. He cried and begged me to take him back. Ghost, of course, wanted to know what happened, and I told him. It helped him to understand why I wanted him to go with me to the party. That night, I dreamt about him. I dreamt I was on a beach and he walked up to me, sat down, and held my hand. In my dream, I felt all these emotions, and I felt like we were talking to each other but without words.

Ghost stayed here and there in his gang's neighborhood, so I went and found him that next day. I picked him up, and he started talking before I had the chance to and pretty much said everything that I wanted to say. He just wanted someone to treat him well, to respect him, and that's all I wanted. Ghost was just like me but in male form. We both had a fire inside of us that we never allowed to get put out. We were both sweet but could be vicious the second we needed to be. When I started dating Ghost, I took myself further into the gang life. He lived in a bad gang neighborhood, so that's where I was all the time. Ghost's gang was smaller, and there was a rival gang in our area that was so much bigger. That meant occasionally getting shot at and having people shooting back out of your car. My car became a target for that rival gang. There were times I was shot at without Ghost even in the car. Before too long, I found myself right in the middle of a Latin gang with all its drugs, violence, and chaos. Ghost was living here and there, and eventually, he ran out of places to stay, so I somehow talked my parents into letting him stay with us. Ghost was younger than me, but I didn't even know it. I assumed he was my age. I was nineteen, but he was seventeen and a ward of the state who had repeatedly ran away from group homes. Ghost's dad killed himself when he was two years old, and it did something really bad to his mom's head. She gave him and his two siblings to the state. She remarried and had other children. His mom literally gave him away and just started a brand-new family without him. Off and on, DCFS placed him with his grandma who beat him and locked him in a pantry and didn't feed him. She would keep the checks that the state gave her but not use a penny of it to take care of him. I think that was where we connected the most, the abuse that we both went through at the hands of people who were supposed to take care of us. Things were really great between us for about a month or so. Ghost was so good with Kaleb, so that was a huge plus. He would feed him his bottles and rock him to sleep, and he even watched him while I was at work. The problems started when Alejandro's mom called me to say that my phone bill was still going to her house, and she opened it. Alejandro's mom said that every day at 9:00 a.m., there were calls to a certain number, and they were off and on all day to 5:00 p.m.

I worked during those exact hours every single day, so I left fifteen minutes before 9:00 a.m. and got home fifteen minutes after 5:00 p.m. So right away, those times were a red flag, and after calling the number on that bill, I found out Ghost was talking to another girl. He was sitting in my house on my cell phone and talking to a girl he met before we started dating. When I confronted him about it, he got very angry, and that's when I got very angry also. That fire that I mentioned that we both had inside of us, it wasn't a good thing when we both were angry. Ghost smacked me. It was more of a closed finger hit to the side of my head. I, of course, started hitting him back, and my mom had to scream at us and try to pull us apart. We ended up in the street in front of my house beating each other up, having a fistfight like animals. I was stupid to even stoop to his level and hit him back, but part of me was so used to being hit that it felt normal. Our relationship went up and down like that for months, full of fighting and abuse. Ghost had this manipulative thing that he did. It was similar to how Joey treated me. It kept me with him. When we weren't fighting, Ghost loved me intensely. It was like he hypnotized me but then would pull it away and have me almost begging like a dog for it. He had me wrapped around his finger. I was so desperate for his love and affection that I stayed with him. There were always rumors that he was talking to other girls, and I would confront him, but he would smack me, and it would be over. The conversations that had anything to do with him not being the kind of boyfriend I deserved ended like that. When Ghost and I weren't fighting, we were hanging out in his gang's neighborhood and dodging getting shot. Our relationship had extreme highs and lows, and it got to the point where Ghost was so abusive that I had to end it. I couldn't do it anymore. Our relationship wasn't even a relationship anymore. When I ended it, he obviously thought that I was just mad and that we would be back together in a day or two. He refused to go away. It got to the point where I was scared for my life and didn't know what to do. Ghost threatened shooting at my house so many times, and his friends said he was going to do it, so I moved out. I was a nineteen-year-old, a teen, mother who just got out of an abusive relationship who feared for her life and was homeless. I was so depressed. I started feeling like a failure, like I failed my son, Kaleb. I must have sat in my car and cried a dozen times. I was so sad and ashamed. I put my family and my son in danger. That's why I made the decision that I did after that.

I moved in with one of Ghost's friends, Jose, and his family. They had extra rooms and often rented them out. Ghost couldn't hurt me or shoot at me at least while I was in his friend's house. That's why I moved there. Jose was in the same gang as Ghost, so I was protected living in his house. I would stay there at Jose's and save up money for an apartment, and then I would get out of that dangerous neighborhood. Instead of keeping my head straight and focusing on saving up for an apartment for me and Kaleb, I got deeper into the gang life. There was another gang whose neighborhood was in the same area, on the next block from Ghost's. I started learning the ins and outs of that other gang, and they offered me protection from Ghost because both gangs were at peace with one another. I even started dressing up my son as if he was a gang member. I dressed him like a miniature one. I started getting Kaleb's hair shaved and lined up like my Mexican friends had their hair and bought him a red-and-black Bulls hat. I would dress him in plain black or red shirts, the kind that they sell at Champs or Footlocker, with blue or black jeans. Over his plain shirt, I would put red and white or black-and-white flannels, so he always had on a mixture of red and black always. I made sure that I got him the latest Jordans or Nikes that came out but only if they matched his red-and-black clothes. I pierced Kaleb's ears and bought him little diamond earrings. They made him look like a little man. He also had two gold chains with crosses, a gold nameplate bracelet, and a couple of gold rings. I dressed myself similar to my son always and would even get black-and-red weave sewed into my hair. We both definitely always looked the part of gang members. Even my car screamed out that I was gang affiliated. At that point, guns, gang banging, and constant shootings were an everyday occurrence for me in that neighborhood. One weekend, one of the guys who were in Ghost's gang was brutally killed by the bigger rival gang. The boy that was killed. Edwin was driving around in an SUV and hanging out with some other people.

Another SUV started shooting and then rammed them at a stop sign near their neighborhood. The other SUV kept ramming into them and eventually got around to the side of the vehicle where Edwin was at. Between the bullets and the impact of the collisions, Edwin was killed. He was thrown from the vehicle and ended up draped over a fence near the stop sign. Dead, brutally killed, and left to hang on a fence was the possible outcome for anyone who chose to live in the neighborhood that I did. It was painful to find out what happened, and the wake and funeral were even worse. At Edwin's wake, the rival gang started shooting at people in the parking lot, and things got bad fast. I had to get out of there, so I jumped in my car with two other people from the neighborhood and left. Right as we pulled out, we were shot at by a vehicle behind us, so the person next to me, in the front seat, started shooting at them. My vehicle was hit twice by bullets, and the guy in my backseat was shot, so I had to rush him to the emergency room. The rival gang followed us trying to run us off the road as they continued to shoot at us, and they shot at us all the way until we pulled into the ER parking lot. The guy who was shot was only shot in the arm, so he was okay. Edwin's death and then getting shot at were a lot to deal with. I found that I could really talk to Jose, and we became pretty close after that. Jose was such a caring person, had a big heart, and helped me out a lot with Kaleb. At night, we talked a lot. We confided in each other about so many things—our hopes, fears, and dreams. Jose and his family had been through a lot. A year before I moved in, Jose's stepbrother died. He actually died in the room that I rented. He was playing with a gun that one of the gangs let him keep for a while. Jose's stepbrother and two others were passing it back and forth, and someone dropped it. The gun went off, and it shot Jose's stepbrother through the bottom of his chin and out the back of his head. Edwin wasn't the only person who was killed in that neighborhood. There were several others whom I didn't really know. That neighborhood was a messed-up place, a place full of pain, anger, and sadness.

Soon after we moved there, my baby, Kaleb, turned three years old. His birthday was memorable but not in a very good way. My mom threw him a party like she normally did, inviting a few family members and some ladies whom she worked with. My mom had about five ladies from work that she had gotten close to. Some of those women not only came to Kaleb's parties but also had come to my baby shower when I was pregnant with him. I decided to bring my friend Lamont. He was someone I became good friends with and was teaching me the ins and outs of gang life. Lamont brought his brother Marshaun with him, and we were off to Kaleb's birthday party. We didn't even make it into the door when my dad came outside and told me that the Black people I was with weren't coming into his house. He said so many offensive things and then said they could stay outside but were not coming inside. I couldn't let my dad insult my friends like that. I was an adult, so if I wanted Black friends, that was up to me. I had thought that we were all adults and that my dad would act like one, but I was so wrong. I grabbed Kaleb, and we left. We took him to an arcade, and he had a blast. The whole time my mom was calling me and texting me, she told me that I should have known not to bring Black people to their home. With everything my dad said, they still made me out to be the bad guy in that situation. There was no way that I could allow my dad to disrespect my friends. I was so ashamed that they would be telling everyone what happened. I had a lot of respect for Lamont and Marshaun's mom and dad, so I was upset on what they were told about Kaleb's party. After that day. I did a lot of thinking and just watching. I just watched my surroundings. I was lost in my thoughts for weeks after Kaleb's birthday. It made me really realize the difference in people. If you sat in that neighborhood long enough and just looked around you, you could see there were levels. There was the bottom, the middle, and the top; and you could definitely tell who was on what level. Clothes, cars, rims, and jewelry were easy ways to tell what level someone was on. People who were on top were usually drug dealers. I really wanted to be on top, not in the middle anymore. I started looking up information about how to make money off of selling drugs, and one day, I had my chance to actually do it. I was standing on the block one day, just hanging out and drinking, when two kids, maybe ten to twelve, came up asking me if I was interested in buying some drugs. The kids said they took the drugs from an older family member and wanted some money for it. They pulled out two huge bags of crack rocks. They asked me how much money I would give them for it. I played it cool and said I was not really interested but I might know someone. I told them I only had $60 on me, and they said that was great. The two bags of drugs had twenty-five tiny bags in each one, and each one was worth $20. They were $20 crack rocks. Just like that, I came up on $1,000 of crack. Just like that, I started selling crack to save up money faster. I had to do better for my son. He was such a sweet little boy, and I wanted to get him out of that neighborhood. I loved my son so much, and I kept promising him that I would do better for him. I was proud to be a mother, and even though I didn't make the best decisions, I swore I would get on the right path sooner than later. I had the younger kids in the next neighborhood sell the crack for me, and I paid them daily to stand out at the liquor store and wait for customers. After two weeks, I sold all fifty bags, so I took the profit and bought more. Two weeks after that, I had enough to buy and bag up what would be a $5,000 profit for me. Things were good.

It was around that time that I fell into a serious depression. Living in the ghetto will do that to you. It was depressing where I lived. It's sad being in the middle of a neighborhood where most people will have to live their whole life. It's sad when you look around you and you just know that no one is going anywhere or doing anything with their lives. I felt so sad about having Kaleb in the middle of such a bad situation, and it got hard to keep pushing those feelings back. I felt like I was a complete failure, and I did not feel like a good mother. I felt like garbage. I felt like with what I was doing. I was a criminal. I kept moving forward, but it hurt. That's why when Ghost started calling me again, I started answering instead of ignoring them like I had been for months. I was sad, and I was lonely, and I felt like Ghost knew me, so it was so easy to confide in him about what was going on in my life. Ghost had moved to the city. He moved into a different neighborhood. His gang had several neighborhoods all over the place. Ghost always knew how to draw me in no matter what was going on, and he did. Ghost kept telling me that in the city the apartments were cheap but very nice and that I should move out there. I just brushed it off when he brought that up, and I would quickly change the subject. We started talking on the phone almost every night, and it helped bring me out of my depression. The world started to seem like it wasn't such a bad place. I was selling a lot of drugs, and I had a really good amount of money saved up. I kept the drugs and the money hidden in my room; and one day, Jose's mom, Marla, found it. She had made it very clear when I moved in that drugs were not allowed in her house, the selling or the using of drugs. Right in front of me, she took the drugs and flushed them down the toilet and told me that I was so stupid for selling drugs. I tried to offer her more money than what I was paying. I offered her a lot, but she still wanted me gone. She was so angry. I had never seen Marla angry like that, and I felt horrible. Marla had a big heart like Jose, so because of Kaleb, she gave me until the end of that month to move out. When I told Ghost what happened, he told me that he could have some of his friend's girlfriends look for an apartment out there for me. The plan started out as the apartment being for me and Kaleb but quickly changed to it being for him too. The plan changed to us getting back together, and at that time, I needed him so bad. He did sound like he had changed a bit. He had a good job installing air-conditioning units and was doing well. In just two weeks, Ghost had one of the female gang members out there find us an apartment, so all I had to do was sign papers and give our deposit.

The apartment was great. It was a tall building with only two apartments in it, and it was nice. When you went in the front door, there was a door to the right for the first apartment. Then to the left, there was a staircase with about twenty stairs that led you to the second apartment, which was ours. Through our front door was the living room. It was pretty big, wood floor and trim with fresh white walls. I did the living room in a jungle theme, mostly animal prints. We used a black futon bed as a couch, and I got two big cheetah print pillows to sit on it. On the floor was a hug rug that was also cheetah print. It matched perfectly. In the corners of the room, we had four big vases that had elephants and zebras on them, and in them, I had fake leaves. On the biggest wall, there were three staggered mirrors and a shelf with elephant statues on it next to them. The kitchen was to the right and had new grayish tiles and white countertops, and there was a big window to the far right. I did the kitchen in a fruit theme. I mostly had stuff that had lemons on it because they were my favorite. Next to the kitchen, there was a small bedroom, which was Kaleb's. It had light gray carpet and beige walls. I set his room up so neatly. I bought new stuff since he was older. I used mostly bright blue because he loved Thomas the Train, and I even found a Thomas the Train bed set for his toddler bed. I found a matching picture for the wall and a big rug that was also a playmat for the train toys. Next to the front door was the bathroom. It was small but nice, a very strange layout, though. Just inside the door was the sink, a regular pedestal sink, and then next to that a stand-up shower. Next to the shower, there were stairs, about ten stairs that led you up to a little space where there was a toilet. Next to the bathroom was Ghost and my bedroom, and it was similar to the other bedroom. I did our bedroom in black and white, black bed set with white accent pillows and a black rug. On the walls, I hung pictures. They had black frames, and each of the three had words in black on white backgrounds. The words were in cursive and said, "Live, love, and laugh." They were cute, and they matched nicely. It was just a little apartment, but it was mine; it was Ghost, Kaleb, and mine.

Everything was great for a few months. We were both working, and my mom was watching Kaleb every day. My mom worked in the evening, so it worked out good. She could babysit and drop Kaleb back off to me before she had to go to work. We ate dinner together every night and spent evenings watching movies until we fell asleep. I stopped talking to all my old friends and had even changed my phone number, so I could stay focused on being a happy family with Ghost. The only person I talked to was the lady Maria, whom I worked with at the clinic. She was the billing specialist. Maria was the only friend I had, and I liked her because she was honest with me about everything. She would tell me that I deserved better than the gang-banger guys I dated and that I was too smart for that kind of stuff. Maria had old friends who were in the same gang as Ghost, so she knew how they were and how they would be when they got older. She tried warning me about what my life would be like if I didn't smarten up and listen to what she told me. I listened to her. I always listened to every word, but I didn't use the advice. Maria was right about everything. Things between me and Ghost got bad again. After a few months, we started arguing a lot again, and the fights got worse and worse. One night, he came home drunk and very high and started saying that I didn't love or respect him anymore. He beat me up then choked me, and I must have blacked out because I woke up on the ground thirty minutes later. Kaleb was still sleeping, so I wrapped him up in blankets so we could go down the street and talk to Ghost's friends. I didn't want there to be a problem between me and the other people in the neighborhood if I called the police. I wanted to go down the street and have Ghost's friends come and get him out of the house for the night. I looked around for him, but I don't think he was in the apartment, so I left. As I walked down the alley, I noticed a dog in front of us that didn't appear to be on a leash. I tried to stand still and wait for the dog to get distracted and walk away, but it didn't. The dog stared straight at me and then started to walk toward me, so I turned and walked away quickly. The dog ran up to us growling and grabbed Kaleb out of my arms by its teeth and started shaking him. I was terrified, and all I could think about was that my son was going to die. I screamed, and I screamed for help, but no one came. I yelled at the dog, and then I noticed an empty beer bottle lying on the ground, so I picked it up. I threw the beer bottle at the dog and yelled at it like I was crazy. I can't even remember what I was saying. I didn't know much about God, but I think that was who made that dog drop my son and just walk away without it attacking me too. The dog just dropped Kaleb and walked away without even looking at me. It was the strangest thing. Lying there on the ground was my three-year-old son, in an alley in the middle of the night. Kaleb looked like he was dead, but I didn't see any blood, so all I could do was be hopeful that he was alive. I grabbed him off the ground and checked his neck and body, but there was nothing, no bites or scratches. Somehow, the dog must have held onto the blankets when it bit him. If I didn't wrap him up, then it might have been a different story.

I took my son, and I ran home. If Ghost still had a problem, then I was calling the police. I didn't care anymore. I ran up the stairs so fast and looked around for Ghost, but it looked like he wasn't there. I started looking through everything for the phone. I found it and called 911. As I stood there waiting for someone to answer on the other end, I looked up, and he was standing in the doorway of Kaleb's room. He had been there the whole time. He said he had been hiding so he could catch me on the phone with my boyfriend. I told him I was on the phone with 911 because he was crazy and had to go. I don't know why it took so long for them to answer that call. Ghost had his one hand behind his back the whole time, and I was so nervous. He finally pulled his arm out, and he had a huge knife, the biggest knife from our knife block. He started walking toward me just as the 911 dispatcher answered, and I screamed and cried to that lady to help me. I told her my name and my son's name. I told her my mother's name and number, so if something happened to me, I repeatedly told the lady that my son was with me and that he was just a little baby and that they needed to hurry. My whole life was replaying in my mind. I kept seeing Kaleb's birth and beautiful smiles. I really thought I was going to die. I told the dispatcher that there was no way that they would get there in time, that Ghost was getting closer and had a large knife. He was going to kill me. I would be dead, and Kaleb would be alone. So many thoughts flooded my mind. They were racing through one after another, and I just knew I wasn't going to make it out alive. I told him to kill me if he needed to but to just leave afterward and let them take Kaleb. Ghost kept saying that I didn't love him anymore and that if he couldn't have me, then no one could. You hear those words in movies or TV shows, but when they are actually said to you and by someone holding a large knife, it's a lot different. We take time and life for granted until the very second that we are about to lose it, then we want to appreciate it. I didn't even think anyone was on their way, but then I heard banging on the apartment door. They were there to help me. I screamed for them to help, and Ghost rushed at me as if he was going to stab me, so I closed my eyes and told my son that I loved him so much. I loved him with all my heart. I opened my eyes just in time to see Ghost cut his throat open and fall to the floor. As he hit the floor, the police and emergency medical technicians kicked open the door.

I was shaking. I fell to my knees in relief and just closed my eyes and told myself that Kaleb and I were safe. I opened my eyes and could see that Ghost was going to be okay. I could tell that he didn't cut himself too deep. At the police station, I held Kaleb so tight. I was so happy that we were safe and away from Ghost.

The officers who helped us recommended that we stay with someone for a couple of days. They said that it might not be safe to stay at the apartment. They said that Ghost would be given a call and he would almost for sure call one of his gang friends and tell them what happened. Even though I got along with his friends, that didn't matter. I was nothing to them. The officers said that in these situations, other gang members will try to finish the job. When they said finish the job, I guessed that they meant that they would shoot at my apartment. I imagined them doing more. My door was already busted, so we wouldn't be safe. I imagined someone coming in my apartment and cutting my throat like Ghost cut his throat. I had such evil thoughts as I sat there. I wished I could have finished him, did what he couldn't do to himself. I didn't want to have to be afraid, and I didn't want to start running from my problems either. I had felt relieved when the police showed up at my apartment, but then I started to feel frustrated and frantic. I didn't know whom to call. I stopped talking to everyone when I moved to the city. Plus, I felt stupid. I didn't want to have to tell anyone what Ghost did to me, what he did to us. I'm not sure why I did it. Maybe it was my emotional state, but I called Maria. At the time, it felt like the right thing to do, but later I felt stupid for involving her with my personal life. Maria let us stay with her and her family for a few days so I could figure out what I was going to do. I thought long and hard in those few days on what I should do next, because my life was in pieces. I couldn't stay with Maria for more than a few days, because it could put her family in danger, so I didn't bother to ask to stay longer. I am not exactly sure why, but I decided to call Carla and tell her what happened. I think that I called Carla because her house was one of the only places that ever made me feel safe, and safe was exactly what I needed at that time. It was embarrassing when I saw her because I still had several bruises on my face and chest. I had more than a few bruises, and they were all over my body. The most embarrassing thing was that Carla had just had a baby, and I hadn't talked to her in such a long time. Carla had started dating someone different, and got pregnant, but I hadn't talked to her in almost nine months. With Carla having just had a baby, her grandma bought her a trailer, and that's where she lived with her new baby and boyfriend. Her trailer was right down the street from her mom's house, in the same town that my parents still lived in. Carla had said that I could stay with her; but when her mom, Laura, found out I was back in town, she insisted that I stayed with her. Laura thought it would be safer that way, because Ghost was out of jail with me not having pressed charges against him. I figured that it would make the situation worse if I went to court against Ghost. In between court dates, he would be trying to ruin my life. It felt good to be back at Laura's house. It was just like when I was a kid and I was hiding from my dad. For the second time in my life, Laura came to my rescue. She was always so good to me, and now to Kaleb too. I decided that what happened to me would be the end of a chapter in my life, and I was going to put it behind me. I was beginning a new chapter in my life. I was going to move forward and not look back.

Soon after, I was back. Loneliness and depression kicked in, and I started partying again. I would have my mom keep Kaleb so I could get high. I would stay up for two to three days on cocaine and ecstasy. I met a guy, Gary, one of Carla's boyfriend's friends; and we started dating. He was a nice guy, he was calm, he was simple, and it felt safe. I didn't want wild and crazy. I wanted something that felt safe, and being with Gary felt like that. Gary would buy me flowers every few days, and even bought Kaleb a couple of teddy bears. Hanging out with Gary stopped me from partying so much. We would stay in and just order pizza and watch movies. I started feeling sick a lot, and then I realized that I had missed my period. I was pregnant. I had only been dating Gary a few weeks, and we always used protection, so I knew the baby was Ghost's. Laura told me that it would be best to get an abortion and that she would take me. I wasn't sure if that's what I wanted to do. I already had a baby, but I didn't know if that meant I should kill one. In the same week that I found out I was pregnant, in the same week that I was trying to figure out what to do, Ghost reappeared. I hadn't heard from him or anything about him in almost two months, but then he just came back out there. I only knew he was out there because Carla's boyfriend told me that he saw him in the gang's neighborhood. He said he wasn't so mad at what I did to him. Carla's boyfriend told me that he was coming for me, that he was going to make me pay for calling the police on him. When he told me that, when I heard those words, I knew that I couldn't have his baby. I had Laura take me to get an abortion. I wasn't happy about it, but I had to. Besides Ghost wanting to kill me, Kaleb needed my full love and attention. I just couldn't have another baby. Outside the abortion clinic, there were women protesting, shouting that abortion equals murder, and trying to stop women from going in. The whole process was horrible, and it made me feel like a bad, maybe even evil, person. Gary was at Laura's when I got back. He had flowers and balloons that said, "Get well." I was so surprised. Gary had looked at the situation as if it was just a medical procedure that needed to be done. He didn't judge me or even put an opinion in on the subject. After that, things were calm for a few weeks, but then for whatever reason, Gary decided that he wanted to join Ghost and Carla's boyfriend's gang. He was friends with Carla's boyfriend but hadn't been interested in joining the gang, but that changed. With Gary joining the gang, that meant that he would be around Ghost a lot of the time, which I thought was disturbing, to say the least. Within weeks, there was a huge problem between them. Gary, Ghost, and two other people were driving around; and Gary was bragging about having such a hot girlfriend. Ghost was sitting directly behind him. He pulled out a knife, held it to his throat, and threatened to kill him. Gary and I were definitely over after that. I felt like I was trapped. I felt like Ghost had me backed against a wall. Off and on over the next few months, there were tons of threats and tons of situations where I was so scared thinking that Ghost was going to come and kill me. Being trapped makes you feel alone, alone physically and mentally.

One night, I got a call. It was the middle of the night, and I was caught off guard. It was Ghost. I was so tired that I just listened to what he had to say. He went on and on about still being intensely in love with me and how sorry he was about everything. He told me that he was messed up inside of his head and that he didn't express anger properly. Ghost told me so many things that made sense. His pain was still connected to my pain, and I still loved him. I felt like other people didn't understand what it was like to have so much pain inside of them. Ghost understood. His life was all pain before he met me. We didn't need any more pain. Just like that, we were back together. After everything that happened, we were together. Over the next month, we fixed our relationship, and things were so good between us, better than ever. Laura had a boyfriend, Rick, whose house she stayed at most of the time. At least a few times a week, Ghost stayed with me at her house, even though she told me specifically not to let him. When Ghost wasn't staying with me at Laura's house, he was sleeping on someone's couch in his gang's neighborhood. Some nights, it was harder to find a place to sleep since he had been doing it for quite a while. One afternoon, Ghost was wanting to stay the night, but Laura had said that she might come home. I knew how Laura felt about Ghost being there at night, so I couldn't get caught with him there at night. He said that he would just sleep on someone's couch again, so that was that. It was around 2:00 a.m. when I awoke to my phone ringing repeatedly, and it was one of Ghost's friends. Ghost had been shot in the head. A bullet went through the window behind a chair where he was lying and hit him. I heard the words that were said, but it couldn't be real—it just couldn't be. Something like that couldn't be true. It couldn't be happening, not to me. I fumbled for my keys and wallet and struggled to get Kaleb's shoes and coat on with him half asleep. As I carried Kaleb out of the room, I looked over to Laura's room. She had never even come home. I didn't let Ghost stay the night, because Laura was thinking about coming home, but she didn't. I rushed to the ER that Ghost was taken to but was told that due to the circumstances surrounding the shooting, I couldn't see him. They said that he was in critical condition from a gunshot wound to the back of his head. They said that I should call back in the morning for an update. They told me that it wasn't good for Kaleb to be up there all night. I went back at 9:00

a.m. the next morning. I had sat rocking back and forth for hours as I watched the clock. I was told the same exact thing as the night before. They said he was in critical condition but couldn't have visitors. They said it was hospital policy when someone is shot, only parents can go into the room until they know it is safe. The nurse told me that when someone was shot and didn't die, the gang that shot them usually tried to finish the job at the hospital. I couldn't even believe what she was saying. It was hard to even imagine that ever happening. I wished I could scream at her, tell her to shut up and just let me see him. I was dying inside, my heart was shattered, and I literally felt like I would die. I felt like I was on the actual brink of insanity and didn't know what to do. I called probably twenty times a day, maybe more, and went up there several times to check and see if I could see Ghost yet. They didn't allow him to have any visitors. It was the same speech all day for the next eleven days. My boyfriend was shot in his head, but I wasn't allowed to see him, and eleven days had passed. In those eleven days, I stopped going to work. I just couldn't sit at work after Ghost was shot in the head. Maria told me that I should still go in, but I couldn't. I felt like I was dead inside. I went up to the hospital like I had been doing and asked to see him, and the nurse didn't say no. The nurse said that they just moved him to his own room in the ICU and the hospital approved me to see him.

Finally, after almost two weeks had passed, I was finally allowed to see him. It is hard to even describe the feelings that I was experiencing as I walked into his room. His head was as big as a watermelon. It looked like something from a sci-fi movie. There were bandages all over his head and what looked like a large drainage tub coming out of the bandages on the right side. His eyes were bulging out under his eyelids. They looked so frightening. The swelling pushed them forward. He had a hole in his throat with a big tube coming out of it and a few other tubes attached to it. They all went to this big machine next to him which I figured out rather quickly was a life-support machine. His head was so big that it made his body look like it was fake, and it was hard to look at. From the doorway, I could see his chest going up and down in such an unnatural way. It was horrifying. I stood in the doorway. I took it all in before I went over to the bed. It was actually a nurse coming in to check something that walked me up to the bed. She told me that her name was Karen, and then she said, "Just talk to him. He can hear you." I did just that. I talked to him and cried to him. I did it several times every single day. I poured my heart out to him every day. I begged him to wake up and told him that I loved him. I told him how sorry I was for not letting him stay with me the night he got shot. Down the hall from Ghost's room, there was a chapel. It was a Catholic hospital. I picked up some brochures one day and read them. They were about the power of prayer and how to pray the rosary. I went down to the gift shop and bought a rosary and a booklet on exactly how to pray the rosary. I learned how to do it, and I did it all day every day until I couldn't do it anymore. One day, I prayed so long and hard that I fell asleep in the chapel and woke up four hours later. The priest on call told me that he didn't want to wake me, because he could tell that I needed sleep. Day after day, I sat with Ghost. Day after day, I prayed for him and talked to him. He was in a coma for one month, and for one whole month, I sat with him. For that whole month, he had no brain activity, none at all. He also did not have any response to what they called stimuli. That's what they called it when they pinched his ankle or stuck a needle in his toe to see if he could feel it. The doctors and the nurses all started giving me this look. It was an annoyed look. They told me that I needed to get on with my life because Ghost was never going to wake up and if he did, he wouldn't be the same. They said that he would be in a coma until someone took him off life support and that he only appeared to be alive and breathing. The doctor explained that the machines were pretty much living for him. He wasn't doing any necessary functions on his own. The doctors started getting rude when they spoke to me, telling me that if Ghost woke up, he would be half brain-dead and would need to be put in a hospital so nurses could feed and bathe him daily. I am not sure why my presence there every day bothered them so much, but I did understand the picture that they were trying to paint for me. They wanted me to think that if Ghost woke up, he would be drooling on himself and making noises, maybe laughing and smacking himself for no reason. I didn't care what they said. I knew that he would wake up, that my prayers would wake him up. I had never really believed in God. I wanted to, but God always seemed like he was for people who were better than me. Up until that point, I never felt like I was good enough for God or for any of that. After learning how to pray the rosary, I felt different. I felt like my prayers actually mattered, like God really could really hear them. I felt like God was finally listening to me. Something inside me knew that my prayers were going to wake Ghost up, that God was going to wake him up. I knew that he was a gang member, and I knew that we both did bad things, but I would change that. For pretty much that whole month, my mom kept Kaleb so I could be at the hospital.

One day, I decided to get something to eat from a local Chinese food place after visiting Ghost at the hospital. I had just got back into my car, and as I sat my food down, I felt something hit my face. It all happened so fast. I barely even knew what happened until I looked over and saw two guys running away. It was then that I could feel blood dripping down my face. I had been stabbed through my cheek. I felt my face with my hand, and it was completely cut through to the inside of my mouth. I was in shock but drove myself to the nearest hospital. With everything that I had been going through, I almost forgot I was gang affiliated. It was rival gang members who stabbed me. They were probably people I had at one time shot at. At the hospital, they used some kind of medical-grade glue instead of stitches to put my cheek back together. I would find out later that I had serious nerve damage on that side of my face and would never be able to feel my lip again. I couldn't even smile properly; it was devastating. A few days later, an infection started, and my cheek had to be reopened. After a week of antibiotics, the swelling finally went down, but I was told I would need plastic surgery. A few days later, I went to visit Ghost, and there was bad news. The hospital somehow tracked down his grandma and gave her all control over whether he stayed on life support or not. I found out only one day before that they were taking him off life support, and it was just hours before it was planned that he woke up. It was his regular nurse, Karen, who called me. She told me that his grandmother was on her way to the hospital to sign the papers to take him off life support. I rushed to the hospital, and I yelled at him. I yelled at Ghost and told him how stupid he was to die like that. I told him if he wanted to live, then he better wake up, because they were going to shut off his life support soon. The doctor came in to explain to me what was going to happen when they shut off the machine and told me he would give me time to say my goodbyes. It was 2:40 p.m., and they were taking him off life support at 3:00 p.m. I cried, and I yelled at him. I grabbed his face, and I told him that he didn't have any time left, that he had to wake up now. Then to my surprise, he did just that—he woke up. He just sort of jumped up as if he was suddenly awakened from a dream and then said he was thirsty. I fell to my knees and cried so loudly. I cried and cried and thanked God for everything. The nurse yelled for the doctors to come in, and they all said it was unbelievable. No one could believe that he just woke up how he did. From the side of the bed, I could see out into the hallway Ghost's grandma and her face when they told her that he had woken up. I could see the color just drain from her face, and she almost looked as if she was going to throw up or pass out. The doctor who told her had to take her hand and walk her over to a chair to sit down. After Ghost woke up, I had to step out of the room, because at least a dozen doctors and nurses came in. They said they needed to run a lot of tests on his brain and told me that I could talk to him for a bit but then should probably go home for the day. From what we could tell, Ghost could move all of his limbs and for the most part knew exactly what was going on. I knew it was my prayers. For the first time in my life, I knew God was there. Ghost was in that hospital for maybe another month but was then moved to a different hospital in the city. The new hospital specialized in patients with brain trauma. Ghost was in that hospital for only one month, and we were only able to see him twice because of security issues. With his age and gang affiliation, that hospital was concerned for his safety and couldn't rule me out as a threat. After the evaluations, they realized he was ready to go straight to the rehabilitation phase of his recovery. He had some serious rehabilitation and intense therapy ahead of him at that point.

I started talking to my aunt Sarah a lot and found out the truth about my real parents. I knew that everything my parents told me about my real parents was a lie. Repeatedly, I was told that my real parents didn't want me and just gave me up. I found out that my parents tricked my real mother into letting them take me for a while, while she got on her feet. After they had me, they hid me and stopped answering my mother's calls and took her to court for custody of me. My aunt had tons of letters from my real mom to prove it. Thinking about what she must have gone through was enough to make me cry uncontrollably. I had so much going on, and now to find out that I was right all along about my parents and their lies, I had so much to deal with that I never even confronted them. They were already dead to me on the inside. I was unemployed for two months, but Laura found me a job at a dental office that needed an assistant. I went for an interview, and they hired me right away. It was a small office five minutes from our house. The office was only open four days a week and didn't have late hours, so I could spend enough time with Kaleb and make trips downtown to see Ghost. I thanked God that Ghost woke up and that I had a new job, and I thanked God every day for my son, Kaleb. I felt like things could somewhat go back to normal after Ghost woke up, no more sitting at the hospital all day with Kaleb at my mom's. I made my way to the city twice a week to see Ghost. Because he had so many different therapies, we could never stay too long. Ghost went into that place in a wheelchair, and was barely able to move or even get up by himself. He had to be picked up and placed into his wheelchair, and his arms and legs had to be positioned for him. The rehabilitation hospital first helped him to learn how to get up off of his bed by himself and get into his wheelchair. Then they taught him how to get up and down and eventually how to walk again. After a few months, he was able to use his hands properly and only needed a cane to walk. The only thing that he struggled with was balance and nerve damage in one of his hands. On the side that he was shot, his hand was severely affected, and he wasn't able to open it. Overall, his rehabilitation went great, and within months, you wouldn't have even known he had been shot in his head. He wasn't just affected physically; Ghost's emotions were all over the place during his recovery, and it was confusing. One day, he was happy, and the next, he was sad. Sometimes, it fluctuated hour to hour. One of the biggest emotions that was hard to deal with was his anger, but I understood why he was so angry. He was dealing with so much. When I wasn't visiting him, I was on the phone with him, so he pretty much took up all my time. Kaleb and I went back and forth from that hospital every week. It became rather exhausting constantly making that trip to the city. The two days a week that we went there were taken up by the travel to and from. Each way, it was two hours when you add in the traffic that we always sat in. We did that for six long months, and I was so relieved when he was moved to a nursing home fifteen minutes from my house. It was strange for him, being in a nursing home at such a young age and at the same time dealing with the issues surrounding a brain injury. It was so nice for Ghost to live so close to us, but it was still so hard at the same time. Every day, Kaleb and I went to the nursing home when I got off work, and sometimes, I even rushed there on my lunch breaks. On the weekends, we were there from 9:00 a.m. to 8:00 p.m., so it actually was more exhausting than when he was in the rehabilitation hospital. For several months, that was my life, coming and going from a nursing home. It was then that I started taking Vicodin on a regular basis. I had always occasionally taken it but not every day. Ghost didn't like the way it made him feel, so he would ask for it every four to six hours and just save it for me, so then I could take them every day. He never even questioned why I wanted to take Vicodin every day. He just kept them coming. I was high every day, and even several times a day, the pills had me feeling great. My mom and Laura were both against me spending all my time there and bringing Kaleb there so much.

With how busy I was all the time, I barely even noticed that I had missed my period. I took a test, and I was pregnant. With everything that God had done for me, I knew that I was meant to have the baby and considered it a blessing. I stopped taking the Vicodin but just saved them instead, because I couldn't take them while pregnant. I had saved a lot of money while living with Laura, so I was able to get us a place to live. We rented out a trailer five minutes from Laura's house. I brought Ghost home, and a few months later, I found out I was having a baby girl. I decided rather quickly that I would name her Kalli, my little baby Kalli. I was young, only twenty-one years old, and had an almost four-year-old son and was pregnant again. My mom told me I was absolutely crazy to have allowed myself to get pregnant. I didn't do it on purpose, but I wasn't mad about it. On a hot August day in 2006, Kalli came into the world. She was a beautiful baby with head full of dark-brown hair already, and I loved her so much from the moment I saw her. I had two amazing kids, Kaleb and Kalli. They were everything to me. In the hospital, I was given Vicodin, and from that moment on, I didn't go a day without it. Ghost had bottes of Vicodin sent to him monthly because of his brain injury but refused to take them, so they were all mine. Everything was going well. We were a happy family, and it felt so good.

We moved about a month after Kalli was born. We stayed in the same town but moved into an apartment. It was an old building divided into two apartments. It was cozy, a two-bedroom apartment in a nice almost-wooded area. The apartment was close to my grandma's house, so it was nice being so close to her. There were two doors to get in: one was in the kitchen and one in the dining room. The kitchen was to the far right side of the house. It reminded me of a cottage, all dark wood with bronze hardware. The whole kitchen was all dark wood, not laminate or fake wood floor. It was real hard wood. There were three windows in the kitchen, so it was nice being able to look out and see trees, birds, and butterflies in the mornings. I did the kitchen in watermelon decor. I bought most of it on sale at my grandma's job. My grandma was a waitress at a truck stop, so she got an additional 30–50 percent off of everything in the store that they had there. There had been this cute watermelon kitchen set that I just adored, so she helped me to get all of it. A lot of it, she bought me for Christmas, so I had my little watermelon kitchen. When you walked out of the kitchen, you were in the dining room, and instead of putting a dining room table, I put a pool table in there. On the east side of the room, there was the front door to the apartment. To the west, there was the kids' bedroom. It was a small bedroom; but a toddler bed, crib, and dresser fit just fine. Next to the kids' room was the bathroom. It was small but very cute. I did the bathroom in pink.

Everything was a pale and lighter shade of pink. Both the kitchen and the bathroom had a cozy cottage-type look, and I just loved it. Next to the bathroom was our bedroom. Like the kitchen, it was all dark hardwood. Large cabinets were built into the walls on both the east and west walls. They went to the ceiling and had two drawers at the bottom. The trim, the floor, and the cabinets were all the same dark hardwood as the kitchen and the same bronze hardware. I did the bedroom in a love theme, heart pictures, and "Love Is" pictures on the wall. To the right of the bedroom was the living room. It was nice. There were two huge windows on the east wall. The windows were so big, and when the sun came up, it was so nice to sit and watch it every morning. I did the living room in a dark floral theme. Both the love seat and the couch were dark blue with flowers. I put up pictures on two of the walls that were darker colors with flowers and gold retro-looking frames. I also had a big gold vase that matched the frames and had fake flowers in it that almost matched the flowers in the pictures. The apartment was small but cozy, and it was ours. For a few months, everything was great. We did what we needed to do. I worked, the kids went to day care, and Ghost was picked up for therapies and appointments.

When Ghost was in the nursing home, we thoroughly talked about it and decided that it would be best for him to not have any contact with his old gang friends. Ghost wanted a new life and understood that he was given a second chance by God, so he wanted to live right. During his recovery, almost none of his friends even checked on him, came to the hospital, or even contacted me to see how he was doing. After he got shot, his friends were all nowhere to be found. They weren't there for him. One day, I got home from work, and two of Ghost's old friends were sitting on the couch. I almost fell to my knees in disbelief. I couldn't believe it. I couldn't believe what I was seeing. We had moved from the trailer because we thought too many people knew where we lived. We moved to a new apartment in a wooded area just to be discreet, but there were two gang members sitting on my couch. Ghost asked me if we could talk in the room and, of course, started rambling about how those two people were different from the others. He said that he was getting bored sitting by himself all day. He was getting tired of watching TV all day. I was so mad, and I felt so stupid. All I could do was tell him to ask them not to tell anyone else where we lived. In just a couple of months, Ghost went downhill. Everything was going great, and he just threw it away. He stopped taking his medications consistently and started drinking beer every day. Even when his friends weren't there, he was drinking, and started staying up late at night to drink. Ghost then stopped going to his physical therapy sessions and even started doing cocaine again. I tried to keep up with him while trying not to act like I was too boring, but it got out of control. We were doing large amounts of cocaine every weekend, and Ghost wasn't doing good all around. He was off his medicine, drinking instead of eating, had to start using a wheelchair some of the again, and was just overall going backward with everything that we had tried so hard to build. I got so sick of it, and one day, we got into a big argument. The argument was over him not wanting to eat dinner. I told him that I was sick of him not wanting to get off the couch every day to do anything. I told him that choosing to keep drinking instead of eating dinner every night was ridiculous and it was really upsetting me. I told him that it was making me mad that he doesn't even come to bed at night anymore. He stayed up to keep drinking beer. I told him that he wasn't acting like a real man or a good father. I told him he was acting like a stupid little kid. I was so mad at his stupid responses that I pushed him. He then lost his balance, dropped his cane, and fell. He was near a table that had our house phone on it, so he was able to reach over and call 911.

I thought for sure that I would be taken to jail when the police arrived, but for some reason, they didn't. Since the apartment was in my name, they asked Ghost if he had a place to go. He said he just needed to make a few calls, so they took him outside to do it. In about an hour, he was gone, but I didn't see who picked him up. The police told me that he was informed to stay away for at least twenty-four hours so things could cool down between us. I was so angry about the police getting involved, but by the next morning, I calmed down. I couldn't blame him for calling the police. I did push him, and I knew it wasn't right. The next day, I waited, and I expected Ghost to call and tell me when he would be home, but I didn't get a call. Two and then three days passed, so I started calling all his old friends to see where he was at, but no one knew. I thought he was just really trying to make his point, but then the days turned to weeks, and I didn't know what to do. It was hard, and it was confusing. Kalli was just a baby, so I was confused on why he wouldn't come home. My heart broke a little more each day that I didn't see him walk through the door. I started losing hope. Halloween came around, and he hadn't come home yet, then Thanksgiving, and then Christmas. For all of those holidays, I sent the kids with my mom so I could wait at home just in case Ghost came back. I had never cried so much in my life. It was just heartbreaking to sit at home alone on Thanksgiving and Christmas. I couldn't believe that Ghost could do that to us. After everything we had been through, I just couldn't understand it. When the Vicodin ran out from Ghost, I started getting it from my grandma. She got prescriptions for her back. I would tell her that I was having problems with my back from lying around so much, but I think she knew the truth. When I couldn't get enough from her, I went to the emergency room and told them the same story, that I was having back pain. I would tell them that I was doing laundry or lifting something heavy and my back just locked up. Every time, they would give me a prescription for thirty Vicodin pills. I needed them to help ease the pain. I needed them to help me fade away.

Every week, I called all Ghost's old friends just to see if they had heard from him, but it was always the same answer: they had not. I screamed and cried to God. I asked him how he could do that to me, and I yelled at him that I hated him. I had to take my anger out on someone and Ghost just wasn't there, so I blamed it on God. I blamed God for letting months pass and my newborn daughter not have her father in her life. I blamed God for the pain and the anger that burned through my heart every single day. I was so angry. I couldn't believe that the kids or I didn't even deserve a call in his eyes; he didn't even care about us. It was hard to process it in my mind that Ghost could just walk away from his baby daughter. I had no idea other than that he was a monster. Only a monster could walk away from their baby. Kalli was a beautiful baby. She was such a good baby, and he didn't even care to be in her life apparently. I was angry, and I was hurt. I was confused, and I was so lost. I decided to wait for six full months before I moved on with my life. It would be hard, but I had to move on. I couldn't sit by the phone hoping for a call anymore; that part of my life had to be over. I started going to different emergency rooms and saying that I was in excruciating pain with a tooth and my dentist was out of town. Just like with the backstory, they would give me a prescription for Vicodin, so I stayed high. The new year started, the year 2007, and my resolution was to start a new life as a single mother. The spring came, and spring meant a new beginning. That's what it had to be for me whether I wanted it or not. I had to look at 2007 as a new beginning. I was scared and still so confused, but Ghost was gone—he was gone and not coming back—so I had to move on with my life. I mostly had to do it for the kids. I couldn't lie around crying anymore. I couldn't let life keep passing us by while I waited and hoped Ghost would come home to us. If it wasn't for running into my cousin at a store, I might have been alone forever. My cousin Andrew stepped in and helped me with the kids. I hadn't seen him in years, but it didn't feel that way. My old friend Lamont came over here and there and helped me out with them also. Life was starting to move forward again for me. My cousin was dating a girl named Katherine, and right away, we hit it off. When I wasn't hanging out with my cousin, I was with her. Each day got a little easier, and even though my heart was still broken, I learned how to live again without Ghost. Some days were a lot harder than others, but I did it. I kept moving forward for my kids.

Once my depression started to lift, I was able to really enjoy spending time with Kaleb and Kalli. It really was so nice. Katherine helped me out a lot, and together, we took the kids to do so much fun stuff. Katherine and my cousin Andrew had just had a baby, so she was always more than happy to do fun kid stuff. We were always at the park, the zoo, and at Chuck E Cheese even when it wasn't someone's birthday. It couldn't have come at a worse time, but my aunt Sarah called and told me that my sister Tanya had died. I sat on my front porch, and I cried. I looked at the sky, and I told my sister that I wish I could have gotten to know her. She died of a heroin overdose. She took several types of painkillers, too, so it could have been a suicide. I had planned on having a relationship with my sister Tanya at some point in my life, but it just never happened. Now I would never have a relationship with her. She was gone forever. I was angry at her, but at the same time, I understood her even without knowing her well. If her pain was anything like mine, then I totally understood what she must have been feeling and why she did so much drugs. Taking Vicodin every day helped me ease the pain that I felt from not even knowing her. Ghost leaving us and then my sister Tanya dying were a lot to deal with all at once, but I decided that I was going to live. I was going to enjoy life and not only love the kids but love myself also. I couldn't let my life get to the point that my sister had. I had to take charge and be happy. I made sure that the kids and I were always dressed very cute, and I started dressing up a lot. I bought a bunch of skirts, wedge heels, summer dresses and so many accessories to match everything. I started tanning every day, dyed my hair platinum blonde, and even wore blue contacts. I guess I wanted to be somebody new. The girl whom Ghost walked out on was gone. I became brand-new, a new sexy and flirty girl who always had a smile on her face. I started selling ecstasy so that I could have extra money. My job barely paid the rent and bills. With the extra money, I was able to buy us nice clothes and shoes and pay for us to do fun stuff. I was also able to buy all the extra Vicodin that I needed to stay high every day and didn't need to visit the ER so much. Since I had the extra money, I started going out on the weekends when my mom would watch Kaleb and Kalli. Sometimes, Katherine and I went to bars, and sometimes, we hung out with her friends. We were both young and beautiful, so it wasn't hard to find people who wanted to have a good time with us. One day, we were with a girl who was looking for her boyfriend. They had gotten into a huge fight earlier in the day, so she was frantic to find him. Her boyfriend was a drug dealer and supposedly was drunk even though it was early in the day. She said that her boyfriend took the drugs that he kept in their house and had them on him wherever he was at, so she was worried. She was worried that he would get pulled over being drunk and get caught with the large amounts of drugs that he took from the house.

We checked a bar that she said he normally would hang out at, but he wasn't there. When we were about to pull off, a car next to us signaled to roll our windows down. The car had four people in it, two younger Mexican guys in the front and one older guy in the back. The two guys in the front had big smiles on their faces for me and Katherine, and they were pretty cute. I have no clue why, but I gave one of the guys my number. His name was Marco. I had never talked to a guy like him. He was a very big guy but had such a mysterious and genuine smile. Marco told me to call him, and after Katherine and I left a bar that night, I called him. Right away, he made me feel good, and when I told him what happened with Ghost and my sister, he reassured me that everything happens for a reason. Marco made me feel good about myself, and he said all the right stuff to make me feel completely comfortable with him. That night, we talked on the phone until we both fell asleep, and we definitely connected that night. I was lonely, and my heart was still hurting from my sister's death, so Marco couldn't have come into my life at a more perfect time.

We started dating pretty fast, and it didn't take more than a couple of weeks to realize that Marco was a drug dealer. After going out one night, Marco dropped me off and gave me $200 and said to buy myself something nice. I thought Marco was seeing someone else because he was so busy on the weekends, but I came to find out it was because he sold cocaine. Most people wouldn't be comfortable with the fact that someone sold drugs full-time as if it was a legitimate job, but I was. I was already selling ecstasy, and the profit was hard to turn away from, so I understood why Marco sold drugs. Plus, I was so lonely. I needed my heart to feel something other than pain. I was worried that my heart would permanently die if it stayed in its current state of sadness and darkness. I wanted to feel something. Just the thought of love and happiness sounded so good. That's why I think I fell for Marco so quickly. I had felt too much pain. I just wanted to feel love, to love and to be loved. I knew Marco loved me for me, because we waited several months to even engage in any sexual activity. For months, Marco made me feel like I was a princess, and at just six months in, we decided to move in together. We had so much fun when we were out together, and I was crazy about him. I realized how crazy I was for him one night when an old girlfriend approached him in a bar. We had all been drinking for several hours, and his ex mumbled something under her breath as she passed me. Immediately, I felt enraged and started punching the girl in the face. I just kept swinging and swinging. I was so angry and out of control that I just kept going. I must have hit that girl until every one of my fake nails was broken off and bleeding. If I hadn't taken so much Vicodin, I am sure I would have been in a lot of pain. It lasted several minutes until the bar's security dragged me out and threw me out of the bar. I wasn't satisfied with the fight. I felt she deserved more, so I asked the people outside if they knew her. I found someone who knew of her, and I asked them which car was hers, and they told me. At the time, I had a big old Chevy Caprice, the kind of car that the police used to drive. On the front of the car, I had what you would call a rammer bar, so I rammed the girl's car repeatedly. I was embarrassed and ashamed that night, but it showed Marco that I loved him.

I was out of control, and it wasn't just because of the fight. I had taken a second job at another dental clinic, just for a few hours every afternoon. I only took the job because I wanted a chance to be able to write myself prescriptions for Vicodin. I got the chance to do it right away, and I did. The first time I did it, it went smoothly. The second time I did it, the pharmacy told me that there was a problem with the prescription. They called my job about it, but no one said anything to me, and about five days had passed. The following week, I got called to the HR department, and there was a room of people waiting for me. There were four ladies in a small room all staring up at me, and it was terrifying. I knew why I was there; that was even their first question. I told them that I did, and they asked me to have a seat. They told me that what I did was serious, and they knew I had already done it once before. One of the ladies went on and on for probably about ten minutes on what could legally happen to me because of what I did. They told me that unless I admitted that I had a drug problem that they would press charges. At first, I didn't say anything. I just sat and started at the table. Then out of nowhere, I started crying, not just a little bit but a lot. I cried and cried as I told them that I was addicted to the pills and took them every day. I cried and poured my heart out to them that they couldn't even look mad anymore. After that, the four ladies asked if they could have the room to talk amongst themselves, so I stepped out into the hallway. I was only out there for five minutes, and then they called me back in and told me that they had come to a conclusion on what to do. They told me that they, of course, had to let me go but that they decided not to press charges. I had already known that they weren't going to press charges. I just knew. They told me that I needed to act fast and get help for my addiction. They explained that an addiction to Vicodin can lead to serious problems and can ruin your entire life. I paid no attention to anything they said and only felt embarrassed that it even happened. I told myself that I was stupid and that I couldn't do something so careless again.

I don't know why I even tried the whole prescription thing, because Marco had a connection at a local pharmacy near where we lived. He was good friends with a girl who worked there's brother, Roberto. The girl would steal large bottles of Vicodin and sell them to Marco for only $100. He would then sell them for $10 a pill and make $1,000 on each bottle. I would get a bottle for myself. I told him that I liked taking them here and there but sold most of them to friends. I would hide most of them away and tell him that I sold them and made a big profit. I didn't tell Marco that I took Vicodin every day. I told him I just casually took it. I didn't even tell him what happened with me getting caught up with the prescriptions. We had just moved in together, and I didn't want him to think I was some kind of addict. Everything was going so great for us, but not too long after we moved in together, I found out I was pregnant. Even though we had always used protection, I was pregnant. I didn't even know what to think. Marco and I had only been dating for 6 months. We had been going out so much, so I was worried about drinking and taking pills so much. Marco was also shocked to find out that I was pregnant but considered it a blessing. At first, I wasn't sure what to do. I already had two small children and didn't know if it would be right to have a third child. Kaleb was five years old, and Kalli was only one, so I just wasn't sure what to do about a pregnancy. I was sitting back and thinking about it and then thought that Marco's mom, Gloria, had ten kids, so I thought three would be okay. I loved my kids to death, so a third child would be great, and I decided to keep the baby.

I, of course, stopped drinking, taking pills, and going out at all. Marco's family didn't seem thrilled to hear the good news, but we didn't care. There was always constant drama in Marco's family, sometimes just because he had so many siblings. The drama between him and his two older brothers was always because of the drug dealing, usually when the correct amount of money wasn't acquired the night before. I tried to stay out of it for the most part, but it was hard, because his brothers were always trying to take advantage of him. Marco was different from the other members in his family. They all lacked something that he had. It was passion. Marco had a certain passion for life, and he had a certain love in his heart that they didn't have. The moment I got pregnant was when I could tell that Marco's family really didn't like me, maybe because I was White but maybe just because. It was hard dating a drug dealer already because of the long nights and constant coming and going, but his family made it worse. His mom, Gloria, and his oldest sister Angela always told me that I should worry about him being out all night at the bar. We decided to move in with Marco's family for six months so we could save up a lot of money before the baby came. When we lived at Marco's mom's house, I really saw all of his family's true colors. They weren't good people. His mom and sister constantly tried putting things into my head about Marco being out all night. He spent his nights at a small local bar. It's what you would call a coke bar. Most towns have them. He would bag up around fifty $40 bags of cocaine and then sit at the bar and try to sell them all, so he was always gone all night. I was never worried because the money was always there to show for his long nights out. It seemed like the further I got in my pregnancy, the more money he made and the more gifts he gave us. Marco had bought Kaleb and Kalli both several gold bracelets, gold rings, and several pairs of Jordans. I had everything to show for being the girlfriend of a drug dealer. I had so much gold jewelry, gold chains, earrings, and large rings. I had leather coats and boots that people traded Marco for drugs. We had huge TVs, DVD players, PlayStations, WII consoles, and every household item that held any value. People would knock on our door with their arms full of things to sell or trade us. Marco was like the bank. People knew to see him if they had anything to sell or needed to trade for drugs. We were well taken care of. Marco really stepped up and handled his responsibilities as a man, stepdad and soon-to-be father.

His family grew increasingly jealous of us and by the amount of money that he was making, so we moved out and to the other side of town. Our apartment was actually pretty big for an apartment, and because Marco knew the guy, our rent was on $650 per month. I decorated the rooms so nicely, and we had so many nice things in our apartment. It was such a warm home. Marco made sure that he traded for any items that we could use for the apartment, and he even had a group of people that went out to find anything we needed. If I said I needed a KitchenAid blender, then he sent out his crew of people, and they would come back with one. We found out right after we got our apartment that we were having a little boy. I was having another little boy. It was right after that, that I got a surprising phone call. I was on my way home from work one day when Ghost called. Almost two years later and Kalli's dad called to say he wanted to come home. I couldn't even believe the words that I was hearing. He asked to come home as if it had been a few days. Not only had I moved, but I had moved on. I had found a new boyfriend, and I was pregnant. Ghost told me that I was wrong and that he couldn't believe that I would do something like that to him. How dare him for saying that to me—he left us and never came back. I took a few weeks, but I eventually forgot about the phone call. Ghost said he wanted his daughter, and I told him that he could see his daughter, and then he hung up on me. I never heard from him again after that. Marco and I were doing great. We were in love, and then on a cold January day in 2008, Kris was born. Kris had a full head of hair just like his sister when she was born, and he had big beautiful brown eyes. We would set Kaleb on the couch and put Kris in his arms. He looked so cute holding him. I had a perfect family. I had three of the most beautiful kids and a loving boyfriend. For the first time in a long time, I could look around and say that things were good. Right after Kris was born, I was back to taking Vicodin, but instead of every day, I only took it several times a week. It was around then that I started regularly seeing a psychiatrist to get Xanax and other medications. At first, I was prescribed Xanax twice a day. Within months, it was increased to five times daily. Here and there, in addition to the Xanax, I was also prescribed Klonopin and Valium for what I called anxiety. I'm not sure if at that point I really ever had anxiety. I think I just wanted to feel good and be in a great mood all the time. I wanted to be a supermom, a mom who did everything she was supposed to do while looking and feeling fabulous. Between working full-time, taking care of three small children, and trying to be a good girlfriend, I was stretched thin. A combination of Vicodin and Xanax always kept me going. People always asked me how I did it all. No one, not even Marco, understood the severity of all the pills or that I had been taking Vicodin for years. I had gained a lot of weight while pregnant with Kris, so I went to a weight loss clinic and was given phentermine to help lose the weight. The weight came right off, and I not only looked great but felt great too. Phentermine makes you feel like you are on cocaine, so I balanced myself out by taking extra Xanax.

We moved into a big house on the other side of town shortly after Kris was born, and Marco's dad and cousin moved into the basement. With having built-in babysitters, we went out a lot and threw a lot of parties. I threw a lot of nice dinner parties also, inviting every adult we knew, including my parents. I really tried to have a good relationship with both my mom and dad, but it was hard because they were always causing drama. I think that it was around that time that I realized my parents were never going to want a good life for me. They were always going to try and bring me down. My parents made me so depressed—the constant back and forth, constantly having to try and win their love and approval. I started getting tattooed every four weeks. My goal was to tattoo my entire left side of my body. My tattoo guy, Mike, was a family friend, so I got very good deals on tattoo sessions. I found out that I loved tattoos and that I could express myself better being tattooed. Getting tattoos was painful, but afterward, you felt so relieved, and you felt a sense of accomplishment. Mike, my tattoo guy, started asking Marco if he could get something besides cocaine. He asked for something stronger, something like heroin. He said it was because he knew several people that were doing it and you could make so much money off it. Marco found a connection to heroin and started supplying Mike with it every week or two. We would have parties where everyone got completely wasted, and Mike normally came to them, but he stopped coming. I threw a huge birthday party for myself, and Mike came, but he only came to see if Marco had any more heroin to sell him. Mike looked different, and his girlfriend who was a model stopped looking like a model. She looked off. There was something about Mike and his girlfriend that was different, and at that time, I just wasn't sure what it was. I later put two and two together and realized that Mike was using the heroin, not selling it. Marco often had me bring Mike heroin to the tattoo shop that he worked out of, and one day, I decided to take some out of the bag. I took my ID and scooped some out, and then I put it onto a piece of paper and then folded it up and hid it in my wallet. I wasn't sure what I was going to do with it. I just wanted it, and I would decide later.

The drinking and the parties got out of control at that point. Tequila was my drink of choice, and it made me angry the more I drank. One night, I was out with a friend at the local bar that Marco sold cocaine out of, and someone said something rude to me. The whole bar started fighting, and people held me back from the girl I was fighting with, so I ran to the door. The girl I was with, Angel, and I went back to my house; and I ran in and got a gun. On the way back to the bar, Angel was panicking because I had a gun, so I kicked her out right on the side of the road. I went back to the bar and told the girl to come outside, and when she did, I held the gun to her face and told her I would kill her. I told her that if she ever said anything to me again, then I would shoot her and her boyfriend in the head. After that night, I knew I was out of control, and I don't know if it had something to do with it, but our house got raided. The police were there looking for guns and drugs, and they found both. I had just sat down to eat dinner when the door was kicked in and police swarmed in. They all yelled at everyone to get on the ground, even the kids. They kept yelling at them to get down. I quickly went to where Kaleb and Kalli were playing and held them tight as I pulled Kris close to us. Kris had been in his little walker, so I pulled it over toward us and then pulled him out of it even though I had a gun in my face and was told to stop. It was worth the risk for me to be able to hold my children during a traumatic time like that. There were so many cops, so many guns pointed at us, and just so much yelling. The cops said they would destroy our house if Marco didn't show them where the drugs were kept, so he did. They not only took the drugs but also the bags full of money that we kept in our closet. It was scary to see Marco get cuffed and taken away like that. It all happened so fast. That night, it was hard to sleep. I kept replaying the cops busting down the door and yelling at us to get down. The biggest thing I couldn't push out of my mind was the kids' scared faces and them crying for me. Marco only spent one night in jail, and Mike bailed him out the next morning. It was a frustrating day, to say the least. Mike was looking worse and worse every time I saw him, and I thought it was strange him bailing Marco out without even talking to me. When Marco and Mike got home from the police station, that's when I saw it and when I really understood what was going on. Mike was sweaty and pale. He was shaky and almost looked frantic. Right away, he and Marco went into the bedroom, and I could hear them talking. Mike was begging Marco to call and get him heroin, and when I heard that, my heart just broke. I couldn't believe it. Mike said he was selling it. He did not say he was using it too. I was so upset. Mike was one of my best friends. I couldn't believe Marco would let this happen. Marco let one of my best friends get strung out on heroin. I was so hurt and didn't know what to do.

It was at that point that I decided to live separate from Marco, so he went to live with his mom, and I got an apartment a few towns over. We were still together. We just were going to live separately until things settled down. Marco had a long road ahead of him when it came to court dates, and within a year, he would have to go to prison. I needed my own place so the kids and I wouldn't be affected when that happened. It was a lot to stress about, and I was tired of pretending that it was okay to deal drugs for a living. I had convinced myself over and over that as long as everything was paid and taken care of, then it didn't matter where the money came from. I was angry at Marco, but I think I was even angrier at myself for being so stupid. It was my second week there when I decided to open that little folded-up piece of paper in my wallet and try what was inside. That was when I first tried heroin. It was 2009, and I decided to see for myself what the big deal was. The first time I did it, I made a line out of the powder, and I sniffed it. Within minutes, everything felt so funny, but it felt so good. It felt like when I took a few Vicodin pills but a lot stronger. I definitely liked it. I do not remember much about that night, but I do remember how good it felt to drift off to sleep. The next morning, I was so sick that I threw up for hours. I felt absolutely horrible. I don't know why, but that night, I did it again, and it felt even more amazing than the night before. I had to reconnect with my old high school friend Melissa to find out where to find heroin, because I couldn't tell Marco. Melissa was raised by her grandma because her mom was a crack addict, so I knew she could ask her mom where I could buy it. Sure enough, Melissa's mom found me a connection to heroin. Her name was Eshe, and I became a regular customer. She wasn't a dealer; she was a middleman, but a middleman was better than nothing. At least, I found heroin. I asked Eshe about shooting up the heroin. She told me how to do it and what kind of needles I needed to buy. For my first purchase, I spent $200 and got ten $20 bags, and then I went to Walgreens right after and bought a box of syringes. Marco spent a lot of time at my new apartment, so I had to keep what I was doing hidden. The kids went to bed hours before Marco even left for work, so I didn't have to worry about them seeing me. When he went to work, I took out my secret supply of paraphernalia and a belt for my arm. In just minutes, I went from being a regular girl to an IV heroin user, just like that. The first time I did it, it was nothing less than euphoric, a warm, happy, and safe feeling. A warm rush into your vein and then through your entire body, and then you feel like you're in paradise. You feel like you are floating, you feel invincible, maybe even magical. Hands down, it was the best feeling in the whole world, and I couldn't even believe it. I couldn't believe that I hadn't tried heroin sooner. I lay back and thought about my real parents, and for the first time, I understood how they ended up the way they did. I swear I felt them that first time I shot up. I felt them as if they were right next to me.

Within months, I was a full-blown addict, and it didn't happen gradually—it happened right away. At first, I just stopped shopping at fancy stores so much, just that alone was almost enough to support my habit at first. Then I stopped getting my nails and hair done, and then I had to stop buying myself pretty much anything. At first, I had things under control, at least financially. I paid the rent, the bills, and for groceries, and bought the kids new clothes and shoes often. With all the extra money that we had when Marco was selling drugs, I had a lot of extra stuff that built up like nice clothes, out-fits, shoes, purses, makeup, and even jewelry. I just started wearing those clothes that were in the back of the closet. A lot of them still had tags, so for one whole year, I really didn't need anything new. I used all those shoes and purses, too, so you really couldn't tell at first that I wasn't buying myself stuff anymore. Even Marco never noticed. Everything went on the way it always did, except that I was doing something every night that no one knew about. Every night the kids went to bed, Marco went to work, and I shot up heroin. I loved it. I was so happy that I had finally found something that made me happy. I couldn't wait for the night to come every day. I really didn't have any bad side effects until about five months in. That's when I started not feeling so good in the late afternoon, and at first, I just thought I wasn't feeling good. I quickly found out that I was feeling sick because my body needed heroin. I had been shooting up at night, but then my body started to need it earlier, so I had to do it after work. On days where Marco would come over before work, I would just say my stomach hurt and do it in the bathroom. The first times I did it when Marco was home, I said that I wasn't feeling well and needed to lie down. After several times of doing it around him, I was able to not lie down. I just said I was really tired. I knew when I did it, I looked tired, and my eyes would get low, so I would say I couldn't sleep the night before. Marco never said anything to me about it. He never said that I looked funny or anything.

The following month, I started to get emotional by the fact that no one even noticed I was on heroin. It started to make me feel so far away from Marco. I started to feel ashamed that I could do that to my kids and family. I felt so bad about it. The more I thought about it, the more I felt stupid about the decision I made to use heroin, so I decided I was going to stop. I also decided that I was going to tell Marco and my family about it before I did. I picked Saturday night because Marco didn't have to go to work, and I started out by telling him that I felt like we were getting too far apart. I told him that I felt like we didn't know each other anymore and that I had something I had been keeping from him. I told him I had been shooting up heroin for six months and he never even noticed. His first instinct was to say that I was joking or messing with his head. He didn't believe me, and even made me show him the heroin and needles, so I did. He was very confused and upset to see that I wasn't joking about it, and he just sat there with his hand over his mouth. He looked me in the eyes and just shook his head. He then started to tear up. I told him that I was going to stop using, and he made me promise. We then went, and just like I told Marco, I told my parents. Their response was the same, but they also told me that I didn't want to end up like my parents. I felt sick for one day. It was nothing too bad. I only felt sweaty off and on, and my stomach hurt. I even went to work. The very next day, I felt like I was back to normal. I was shocked that it was that easy. I am not sure why, but I kept a few bags of heroin and a few needles in the back of my closet. After six days, I told Marco that heroin wasn't as serious as everyone said it was. I told him that he saw for himself that I didn't even get really sick when I stopped using it. It wasn't a big deal. I felt like I deserved to be able to use something that made me feel better, and that's what I told him. We came to an agreement that I should only do it in the evening and at night and keep it under control. Marco's biggest concern was the financial aspect of it. He didn't want me to start spending all my money on heroin. I lied and told him that I would only spend $50 a week on it, but really I spent $200 a week on it. Just months after that, I realized it was hard to keep up with the rent and bills if I was going to use heroin. I contacted Carla and asked her if I could come and live with her at her grandma's. She said yes, so I told Marco that I hated living in my apartment. I made up several excuses. I told him I wanted to move in with Carla so I wouldn't be alone when he went to prison. I also made a good point to say that when he was in jail, I would have to pay all the rent and bills by myself for a long time. So I said it made sense to live with Carla so I could save up my money and get a big apartment or house before he got out of jail. I said all the right stuff to make everyone think I had things under control when the truth was I was very close to losing control of everything.

When I moved in with Carla and her kids, it was good at first. It was like a permanent sleepover for the kids. They got to play with her three kids all day, and then they got to sleep together in the same rooms, so it was fun. While we were there, I would say that my addiction spun out of control. It was at the one-year mark of using. Kaleb was eight years old at that point, Kalli was only four, and Kris was only two. So I think Kaleb was starting to notice that something was off with us living with Carla, and with me in general. Sometimes, I would come out of the bathroom, and Kaleb would be there, just sitting on the ground. It hurt me to know that he felt that there was something wrong. I think it hurt even worse that he never even knew how. He couldn't understand what was happening to me. Maybe he just didn't want to ask me if there was something wrong with me because he was scared. After one year of using in the evening and then at night, I started feeling sick in the morning. I started needing more heroin every day, so I had to start shooting up three times a day. That was when I started to get worried; shooting up three times a day was expensive. That put me at $350 a week that I would need to get high, and even though I had a good job, that was still a lot. It started to get impossible to buy anything that I needed. I had to spend all my money on drugs. If I didn't shoot up three times, a day then I started to get sick, and it was such a nasty feeling. It is hard to even describe what it feels like to be sick and needing to shoot up. It's called being dope sick, and it's something that no one should ever have to feel. The hairs on your arms start to raise, your stomach starts to turn and ache, and you feel like you might throw up. Your head starts to hurt as your mind races and repeats the need to shoot up over and over. You become frantic, you become scared, and the thought that you won't be able to get drugs is terrifying. The longer your body goes without drugs the worse you start to feel, and you start sweating worse and throwing up, and the pain in your stomach becomes unbearable. Your skin starts crawling and itching, and your veins and bones ache for the heroin. Even the hair on top of your head hurts, you grind your teeth, and you pretty much lose your mind. The need to get heroin becomes all you can think about, and that's the only thing you can do—you have to find heroin. You become an animal, you are stripped down to your basic instincts, and it's almost like you are an animal hunting prey. You will do anything—you will do anything and everything you have to. It feels amazing, and that is why you continue to get high, because you have to. There were days that I threw up on myself on the way to get drugs because I had to wait till work was over, and I started feeling sick early. There were days where I cried because I couldn't find a vein fast enough and had already been sick for an hour. There were also days where I was so sick that I shot up on the bathroom floor with the door wide open because I was too sick to even close the door.

In 2010, after a year and a half of doing drugs, I decided to go to rehab. I was scared, broke, and tired of being sick. I was ashamed at the kind of person and mother that I had become. I hadn't done anything fun with my kids in several months when I decided to go to rehab. I had to do it for them. They were my everything, and I let heroin get in front of that. I was a disgrace. I had to change my life around fast for them. I told my parents that I never stopped using drugs when I told them I did the year before. I rarely saw my parents, and I told them it was because I was busy with work and the kids. When I did see them, it was just like when I had first started using heroin; no one noticed. I only saw Marco a couple of times a week, so I would really pull myself together for him, so he didn't know how bad things really were. When I told my parents, they cried. When I told Marco, he was almost embarrassed of me. He told me that he was worried about what people would say. He was worried his family would find out. I moved back in with my parents, and they were to take care of Kaleb and Kalli while I was away, and Marco would take care of Kris. I planned on at least doing a full thirty-day program, no exceptions. I needed to get better. I quit my job three days before I planned on going to the rehab center, because I wanted to just focus on getting clean. I didn't want to have to worry about getting back to work or people wondering where I was at. My boss had been on my case so much around that time. He was working at two different offices and was always stressed. There were several occasions where he got in my face and yelled at me over stupid stuff. My parents were very helpful in the process of helping me move in with them and get ready for rehab. I found a women's rehabilitation center down-town, and it was first come first serve to get a bed. My dad took off a morning of work to have me down there and in line by 4:00 a.m. I really appreciated him for that. It's true when they say the city never sleeps, and you really see that standing in line of a rehab center at 4:00 a.m. The rehab center didn't open and start taking patients until 7:00 a.m., so there was a lot to make it through before you even got in. There was so much going on, so many homeless people, so many alcoholics and addicts trying to get into that building. On one side, there were people lying on the ground sleeping, and on the other side, there was a group of what looked like homeless people drinking cups of liquor. All around me, there were random people hollering at each other, and everyone was asking each other if they had any cigarettes or change to spare. People were walking up from all directions and asking people if they had any extra drugs on them that they could buy before going into the rehab center. Most of the people in line were high and could barely stand up. Some were sick, sweaty, and shaking. I waited in my dad's truck for a while, but at about 4:15 a.m., people started lining up, so I had to get out and get in line. There were two people already in line but lying on the ground. They must have gotten there the night before so they would for sure get a bed and not have to worry. I had called the week before, and they told me that most days they have three to five beds open up, so I made sure I was the third person in line.

When my dad pulled off, it was a bit scary. I had never really been around so many people like that. I had never been around any other heroin users except for Eshe, the lady who got heroin for me.

Every time someone would ask me for a cigarette, change, or drugs, I would get nervous and just keep my head down as I said no. I started to mimic what other people were doing and acted like I was too messed up on drugs to respond. I shot up one bag before I left and was told that they administer medicine as soon as you are admitted to help with withdrawal symptoms. The lady whom I spoke to when I called explained the whole process to me. She said that they give you methadone, which tricks your body into thinking it has heroin, so then you don't get sick. I was ready to get better. I wanted and needed to be clean for my kids. All I thought about was doing right for my kids when I stood in that line. I started to get nervous and worried that I would get sick before I got admitted because I heard the girl in front of me talking about it. I asked her what time she thought we would be admitted, and she said that this was her third time there and you don't get admitted until the late afternoon. I had thought I would be in by 9:00 a.m. or 10:00 a.m., so the words "late afternoon" sent chills down my spine. I asked a girl who was next to me in a group of people who were drinking and asked if she knew someone who sold drugs. I told her I would pay her $50 to go and get me $50 of heroin. I didn't have any needles, but I knew if I sniffed it, then it would keep me from getting sick. I felt horrible to be doing something like that as I was trying to get into a rehabilitation center to get clean. The girl said she knew someone and would be back in thirty minutes. I knew there was a good chance that she might not come back and just keep the money, but it was a risk I was willing to take. The girl didn't come back until almost 7:00 a.m., and the doors had just opened, so I had to just put the bag in my pocket and hope to find a bathroom inside. Once I got in, there was, what I was told, a lengthy intake process, and I was told to "just be patient." I was able to find a bathroom after putting my name down at the first desk I went to. I sniffed the bag and was so high that I almost hit my head on the metal toilet paper dispenser. After the initial sign in, there was an hour wait, and then a nurse checked your vitals and asked what drug you were needing to get off. After that, they send you to the next room where you wait to speak to a counselor, and that was about an hour and a half wait. After meeting with the counselor, which was an hour of intense questions about my heroin use, I waited to see if they had a bed available. I was told that it would be about an hour until they found out, because 9:00 a.m. was when people were discharged. Finally, at 11:00 a.m., I found out that they had a bed for me and would be taking me to the detox floor soon. They explained that for the first seven days, you are on the detox floor. Then once you are detoxed, you go to the rehab floor for the twenty-three remaining days. It wasn't until around 1:00 p.m. that I actually made it to the nurses' station on the detox floor. A nurse came and talked to me to make sure I was serious about wanting to be there. She said she hated when people wasted her time. I was then taken into a room where I undressed, and they checked my body to make sure I didn't have any drugs or items that were not allowed in there. I had brought a bag of clothes with me, but they said that they weren't allowed and put them in a locker along with my phone and wallet. I was given a set of very big and very worn-down scrubs that said the name of the rehab center on them. After that, I was taken to another room where a lady came in and explained to me how everything works. At 2:00 p.m., I was shown where my bed was, and at 3:00 p.m., they took me to medicate. They gave me a little cup with orange liquid in it. They said it was methadone and would help with withdrawal symptoms. They said that they give you forty milligrams on the first day; then thirty milligrams on the second day; then twenty milligrams on the third day, and then on the fourth, and last, day, ten milligrams. The nurse did tell me that the methadone might not take away the withdrawal symptoms completely, and that made me nervous.

By the time I got back to my room, I was exhausted, and the medicine made me tired, so I just went to sleep. I slept until the middle of the night and was awakened by a sick feeling in my stomach. I got up and realized I was soaked in sweat, freezing, and needed to throw up. I rushed to the bathroom but didn't make it. I threw up all over myself and the floor. At first I thought I was alone until I looked around, and there were four other beds with women in them. Two of the women woke up and started cussing at me for throwing up and then went to tell a nurse. They gave me a clean set of scrubs and sheets and then told me to get back in bed and try to get through the night. After that, I couldn't go back to sleep. I was sick. I was anxious. I was hot, and then I was cold. My stomach was in knots and hurt so bad. I was sweating and felt like I had bugs going up and down my legs. My legs not only felt like there were bugs on them, but they were hurting and aching so bad that I had to keep moving them. It felt like when you have restless legs but so much worse. I couldn't stop moving around. I was in pain, and it made me clench my teeth so hard that my head was pounding. My whole body was aching. It felt like my bones were rotting inside me, and my chest felt like I had a brick on it. I cried that night. I moaned, and I wanted to die. I can't even explain what it was really like—words aren't enough. I must have fallen asleep for an hour, because a nurse came in and woke me up at 7:00 a.m. for my medication. They allowed me to stay on just one of my medications while I was there, but they only allowed me to take it twice a day. So I stayed on Xanax, and it helped; it helped a lot to get that first thing in the morning. They asked how my night was, and I told them. They gave me two Benadryl and said that it would help. I went back to my room after that and slept through breakfast. A girl who was my roommate came and woke me up. She said that at 9:00 a.m., you line up for methadone. I was so happy that she woke me up, or I would have missed it. I was still feeling so sick. As soon as they gave me the methadone, it made me feel so much better. It took most of my horrible symptoms away. On the way back up to our floor was the first time I even looked around me at the other women. I had been too sick to even look before. There were all types of women there, but most looked like they were there for heroin. I later found out in a therapy session that there were mostly heroin addicts, some crack addicts, one meth addict, and one alcoholic. The four women in my room were all trying to get off heroin. Two were in their fifties and two in their forties. On the whole floor, out of twenty women, there were only four other women my age; the rest were all older. The four women in my room were all prostitutes. I was the only one who actually had a legitimate job prior to going there. It was scary to see that being on heroin will make you get so desperate that you will have sex for money. At night, the women in my room told stories about getting raped, robbed, and even beaten while trying to make money as prostitutes. The stories that they told were hard to listen to. The details of some of them almost made me sick. I was happy that I was getting help. I could never imagine ending up like those women.

The first week wasn't so bad. By the third day, I no longer felt sick, just restless. By the second week, all I could think about was getting high, but I pushed it out of my mind. By the third week, I was about to lose my mind. I needed to get high so bad; it was all I thought about. When they told me that I could leave to go to a medical checkup, I was so happy. They trust you when you tell them that you are serious about getting clean, and within the first thirty days, you have to visit a nearby clinic for a checkup. I asked the women in my room how to get drugs, and they explained it to me. You have to be picked up by a family member for your doctor's appointment, so I told my dad to pick me up at a later time. The nurses never asked me what time my appointment was, so I told them it was at 12:00 p.m., when it was really at 3:30 p.m. I had three hours to go to an ATM, find someone who sold drugs, go buy needles and a lighter, and then make it back for my dad to pick me up at 3:00 p.m. I got the money from the ATM at a liquor store right down the street from the center, and then I bought needles and a lighter. After that, I went to an area where one of the women told me to go. Sure enough, there were three people standing out asking me what I was looking for. Within fifteen minutes, I had $200 worth of drugs, so I went and bought water and a can of pop so I could use them to shoot up. I dumped the pop out, and then I used a piece of glass off the side of the road to cut the pop can in half. I went and found a bathroom at a bus station right by the center, and then I went in and shot up. Since I hadn't gotten high in three weeks, it felt amazing. It almost felt as good as the first time. I felt so good but so ashamed at the same time. I told myself that the $200 of drugs I just bought was it, no more after that. I wanted to get clean. I needed to leave that rehab center as a clean and sober person. It was too hard in the center to shoot up. Needles, a lighter, and a spoon or can were too hard to hide. So I kept the bags in my underwear and snorted them in the bathroom over the next two days. The bags were gone, and I had to be done with heroin, no more getting high. I spent the next few days after that writing my kids letters. I wrote all three of them. I wrote them long and heartfelt letters. I wrote notes to my parents on the side telling them to please read the letters to them before they went to bed. I wrote Marco a few letters too telling him how I was going to be better than ever after going through rehab and that I would never touch drugs again.

I made it through my thirty days, and I got out. I felt like I was on top of the world. I was positive and ready to live right for my kids. I was ready to be the best mom possible for them. I decided to take it easy for a while. I had plenty of money in my savings still and just wanted to go slow. I didn't want the pressure of a job, taking care of the kids, and dealing with my parents. Things were good the first week. I felt great and was motivated to stay sober for the kids. The kids were so happy to see me, and their faces gave me hope that I could stay clean. That first week, I took the kids to the park every day and to get ice cream. I played with them in the sprinkler and bought them a small pool. It was summer, and everything felt so fresh and new. That week, we found out that we had five months left until he had to go to jail for eight years. I knew it was coming. We knew he was going to get jail time for the large amount of drugs found during the raid. Marco said that ten years meant he would only do seven years, and he said that wasn't so bad. I was scared but kept pushing it out of my mind, because I wasn't ready to deal with it. I just wanted to enjoy the summer with my family. I just wanted to live and enjoy our time together as a family. It was my second week out of rehab when I was cleaning my room upstairs. My parents let us turn their computer room into our bedroom while we were there. I still had a lot of my clothes and toiletries in suitcases from when I moved out of Carla's grandma's house. I was taking clothes out of a suitcase and putting them away when I found two syringes with heroin in them. My heart dropped when I found them. I fell backward because I was so shocked that they were still in there. On the way to rehab, I told my dad that I had two syringes left with heroin in them and asked him to get rid of them. I couldn't believe they were still there. I couldn't believe that he didn't throw them away. I hurried up and got out of the room. I went downstairs and paced back and forth. My mom and dad were both at work, and the kids were in day care in the mornings still. I was all alone with the heroin that my dad didn't get rid of. I felt like I needed to run away, like I needed to get out of there fast. I went upstairs and grabbed the needles. I was going to squirt them out and throw them in the garbage cans outside. I got to the sink, but I couldn't do it. I couldn't squirt out the heroin. Right there in my hand, I had a syringe full of something that would make me feel so good. I didn't throw them away. I did them both. Again. I told myself that was the very last time. I couldn't be a heroin addict. I had three beautiful kids who needed me, and I just couldn't be an addict. It felt so good to be high, but I felt so guilty that I cried until I fell asleep. After that, I didn't stop. I kept going, and I let myself and my kids down. I started getting high again every few days. I told myself I couldn't do it every day, or I would get sick. I couldn't do it so much that my parents could tell. Also I had to stay sober when I was around Marco, because I didn't want him knowing that I was using again. Marco wasn't worried about me, anyway. He was worried about going to jail. I applied for unemployment even though I quit my job. I found out that because of how my boss was treating me, I was eligible for benefits even though I quit. I started getting $1,042 every week, and that made my drug addiction so much worse. I got high all day and still got paid as if I was still working. It was the worst thing that could have happened; getting unemployment fueled my addiction.

A few months later, the time came for Marco to turn himself in for his jail time. It was so hard to leave him. It was hard knowing that I would be away from him for years—not days or weeks but years. It scared me. I was addicted to heroin, and now my boyfriend had to go to jail for eight years. Everyone knew that Marco went to jail. Word got out fast. Jose, my old friend, called me up to say he was sorry about Marco going to jail. I hadn't talked to Jose for years, pretty much not since I lived with him and his family. It felt good to connect with an old friend. I knew being around people would help. I started hanging out with him every day, and it did help to take my mind off Marco and drugs. Being around an old friend made me want to be my old self again, but I ended up letting him know that I was using heroin. Jose convinced me that I needed to get help. He told me that I was too good to be using heroin. He was right. I was too good for that. I needed to keep trying to be sober. It had been about six months since I got out of rehab, and I decided to tell my parents that I needed to go back. My parents were not happy. They were baffled on how I ended back up in the same place. I told them to tell the kids that I was away at a hospital, but Kaleb was old enough to know something was wrong. I hated myself for not being a better mother. I loved my kids so much but had let myself become an addict. I had to go to rehab, and I had to get clean but for good, no more games. It was hard to admit to my parents that I was using drugs again. It felt so dirty. My grandma's face was upsetting when I told her. It was the face of some who is losing all trust in you. Her face was the face of someone who is just about disgusted with you and doesn't even want to look at you. After I told her, I wished I could take it back. I wished I could take back telling my parents too. When I went to the rehab center the second time, I got there at the same time to make sure I got in again. The whole process was exactly the same as the first time, and so were the first couple of weeks. I didn't get as sick the second time I was there. It was actually a lot easier. I thought I really had it that time, but just like the first time, I started thinking about it. Once I started, I couldn't stop. I was three weeks in and losing my mind because I wanted to get high. I stopped sleeping, and I couldn't do anything because I was so anxious and frantic. In the mornings, I was so tired and stressed from not sleeping, and my veins would be crawling and itching. I started staring at the other girl's arms. Their veins were so perfect looking. It made me want to get high even more.

One morning, my legs were so restless that I was moving all around for hours. It was about 4:00 a.m., and I didn't realize that the girl across the room was awake. I looked over, and she was staring at me. I told her I was sorry if I woke her and that I was going crazy. Her name was Rosalina, and she said she was going crazy too. She said she hadn't slept since she got there. Rosalina was thirty-eight years old, but she looked like she was twenty-five. She was very beautiful. She was Puerto Rican but looked like she was some kind of Indian.

She reminded me of Pocahontas with her long straight dark-brown hair. Her eyes reminded me of her too. Rosalina was married. Her husband was in the marines and was killed two years prior. She said she started taking OxyContins and ended up trying heroin the year before. We exchanged stories and talked about how we would love to be getting high and how we talked about exactly how we would do it if we were out of rehab. I told her I would transfer a few thousand from my savings and go get a hotel room and get high for days. She said that is exactly what she would do, and that's when my fantasy seemed like a possibility. Within ten minutes, we had a plan to check ourselves out of the rehab center, transfer money, go to ATMs to get a few thousand dollars, and find a place to get high. Rosalina made a call to a lady whom she knew and set it up for us to stay with her. She wasn't a heroin user but a crack addict. The lady, Lawanda, inherited a nice condo from her husband, who passed, so Rosalina set it up for us to stay there. The lady just wanted $100 a day for us to stay there, and we could have our own room and bathroom. With me spending $2,000 on heroin, Lawanda was able to arrange for us to be picked up by the guy selling the drugs. Rosalina and I decided on staying for five days. we would stay at Lawanda's condo for five days and get high. I just wanted to be able to get really high for five straight days. that was $400 of heroin a day for us to get high on. I figured if I got high enough, then maybe I would get it out of my system. Maybe I could get the need to get high out of my system. I had to get it out of my system. In that five days, I got higher than I ever had before. I came so close to death. I think I was trying to kill myself. I think I was so ashamed that I was a heroin addict. I couldn't do it anymore. I should have been at home with my kids or still in rehab, but instead, I was out shooting up drugs. I was a bad mother, and I knew it. I just kept telling myself I would get better. After five days of getting high, I set it up for my mom to pick me up outside of the rehab. We chose five days at Lawanda's because then we ended up back at the rehab on our thirtieth day. I went into the entrance of the rehab center at 2:20 p.m. asking to use the bathroom, because my mom was scheduled to pick me up at 2:30 p.m. My mom thought I was walking out thirty days clean and sober, but I was walking back out as the same heroin addict. I didn't feel bad about it because all she did was complain the whole ride home. For one hour, she told me how bad the kids had been for the last thirty days. She complained about every possible thing she could; it was so stressful. My mom told me that I should be ashamed of needing to go to a rehab center twice. I don't know why, but then she started talking about how I needed to break up with Marco. She went on and on about how I made a bad decision by having a third child with him. She told me that my life was messed up enough and that having my son Kris was a mistake. I couldn't believe that she was saying such things to me and on the ride home for rehab. It was during that ride home from the city that I remembered just how much my mom didn't care about me. I don't know why she was doing that to me, but it hurt to hear her say that. When we got home, my dad wasn't home, and she continued complaining to me. I just sat and listened. I let her go on for another hour before she stopped talking. I was stressed, and I was getting sick. I needed more drugs. It was a hard decision, but I decided to be sick and not go and get drugs. I decided to really stay clean for my kids, no more doing heroin.

I actually made it through being dope sick for five days. For five full days, I rolled around wanting to die. It took five days of sickness to pay for those five days that I spent getting so high. After being dope sick, I made it for fourteen full days, but I just couldn't do it. I relapsed again. There was something wrong inside of me, something that just wouldn't let me stay sober. There was like there was some kind of evil inside of me that always won. I wanted so bad to be a good mom, but I just felt like I needed heroin. It's something I will never be able to fully explain. It's like you are a starving animal looking for prey. Nothing else matters. The only thing your brain and body both want is to get high. Things went downhill pretty fast with me continuing to live at my parents' house because they knew I was getting high. I was at Eshe's house picking up $200 of heroin when I was telling her how bad it was when I was dope sick two weeks earlier. She told me that she always has methadone for when she can't afford to get high. I was shocked to find out that you could buy methadone on the streets just like drugs. I bought ten tablets of methadone for $100, so then I could get high without getting sick. If I got high for five days and then ran out of money, instead of being dope sick, I could take one tablet a day for two days and avoid being sick. After two months of going back and forth from heroin to methadone, my parents knew I was using drugs. I was up one day and down the next. They could see a huge difference in me, and they just knew something wrong. My parents started accusing me of using, and both started being very mean to me. They started fighting a lot, and I could hear through the walls that they were fighting about me. I could hear my dad's anger toward my mom for letting me continue to stay there even though they both knew I was getting high. Their argument started getting worse and worse, and a few times, they even fought before my dad went to work at 4:00 a.m. Just as their fighting got worse, so did my addiction. I started taking my old jewelry and the kids' jewelry and selling it. I tried to just focus on waiting for Marco's calls from prison and writing him letters, but it wasn't enough. I told myself that I would get clean for Marco and the kids, but it wasn't as easy as it sounded. I had started talking to Jose again, and I spent most days at his house until I had to pick them up from school. Jose made me feel good about myself and kept telling me that I should stop using drugs and methadone. Marco's dad Raymundo and uncle had their own apartment, and Marco said that I should ask them to stay there. I did, and they were okay with it as long as I paid a third of the rent, so we moved in with them. It was a lot more relaxed there without having to deal with my parents' constant judgment. It was great not having to answer to anyone or hear them fight anymore.

I tried so hard to stay sober for the kids, and a few times, I stayed sober for weeks. I started going to a methadone clinic instead of buying methadone off the streets. At the methadone clinic, I had a counselor, Wanda, who was really great and made me want to stay clean. Every morning, you go to the clinic before 9:00 a.m., and they give you the methadone to take in front of them. The kids motivated me, and I was able to stay clean for thirty full days. I don't know what happened after that, but I started using heroin again. After that, I started buying methadone off the streets again and went back and forth from heroin to methadone. I wanted to stay clean for my kids, but it was like something was seriously wrong inside of me. I tried to just take my medication to stay calm and relaxed, but it wasn't enough. Every time I got sober for a few days, I would start to feel very stressed out and anxious, and that caused me to use heroin. I stayed talking to Jose, who was a big help. Our conversations always made me feel good about myself. Talking to Jose and hanging out with him caused a lot of drama with Marco's family. They would tell Marco that I was cheating on him with Jose, which put our relationship under a lot of stress. His family constantly harassed me about it, and that made it even harder to stay clean. That summer, I started selling my food stamps for drug money and stealing from grocery stores to feed the kids. I did it so much that one day I got caught and arrested. I was with the kids at the Mexican grocery store down the street from our apartment. The kids saw me shoving food in my large person, so Kalli grabbed a pack of snack cakes and put it in my purse. Someone must have seen it, because I was stopped at the door. I was so embarrassed and ashamed. Seeing the kids' scared faces killed me inside. I had to call Marco's dad, Raymundo, and have him come and get the kids so I could be taken to jail. Fortunately, the Mexican store didn't press charges, so I was released and went home. Just a few months later, I was arrested at a department store for doing the same thing. The worst part was that Raymundo's suspicions of me being on drugs were confirmed. After being arrested for stealing food, he knew that I was on drugs. When I got home, he told me that I was stupid and that he knew I was using heroin. He said that everyone told him I was a heroin addict, but he didn't believe it. He said that I was too good for that and didn't understand how I could do that to my family. It was so embarrassing to tell Marco what I did, but I had to because I knew his dad would tell him if I didn't. Marco was so angry. I had been lying to him the past few years and had been telling him that I was clean. Marco thought I was clean since rehab and had no idea that I had been using the whole time he had been in jail. I was letting my family down. I had to get clean for Marco and the kids. My kids were still little. I couldn't let them grow up and have a drug addict as a mother.

It was soon after I had gotten arrested that I started getting a bad feeling about Marco's dad, Raymundo. He was constantly trying to get Kalli to come into his room or to sit on his lap, and I just felt something from it. I think it was my gut telling me something was off about him. I asked Kaleb what he thought, and Kaleb said that he was always making Kalli kiss him on his cheek before he gave her candy or ice cream. I started keeping Kalli close by me all the time, but I didn't feel like that was enough, so we moved out. I told Jose everything and that I felt like we had to get out of there. Jose talked to his mom, Marla, and she said that I could move in there if I paid $150 for rent. I know it was confusing for Marco, and I know how upset he was about it, but I had to move in with Jose's family. It wasn't like I was moving in with just Jose. It wasn't even his house. It was his mom and her boyfriend's house. Jose also somehow convinced me to get clean off heroin—off everything. I knew that I wouldn't be able to get off drugs and methadone living with Marco's dad. Jose agreed to take care of Kaleb, Kalli, and Kris while I got better. He helped me out so much, and he was so good to the kids. He picked them up from school, took them to the park, fed them dinner, and bathed them every night. The plan was that I would stay there for three to six months and detox from heroin and methadone. If I knew how hard it was to get off methadone, I probably wouldn't have tried. It was a hundred times worse than being sick and getting off heroin. I couldn't eat, I couldn't sleep, and the pain that I felt in my stomach was unbearable. I could barely do anything, except roll around crying. I threw up on myself every day for months. I couldn't even make it to the bathroom most of the time. I lost so much weight that Jose brought me to the emergency room three times to see if there was anything they could do for me. I got so weak that I could barely walk, and if I even tried drinking water, I threw it up. I hated that the kids had to see me like that, and I hated that I couldn't take care of them. I went through that for five months, and then I decided that I couldn't do it anymore. It was Kris's fourth birthday in 2011 when I went back on drugs so I could celebrate his birthday with him. I didn't want to miss another birthday, because I was too sick. I hadn't been able to celebrate Kaleb or Kalli's birthdays earlier in the year, because I was so sick. Just months later in 2012, my unemployment benefits ended unexpectedly, and I couldn't pay rent to live at Jose's house. Jose's mother, Marla, was already fed up with me going back on drugs. Even though I denied it when she asked if I was on drugs, she knew, everyone knew, I was back on heroin. Marla said that I had to move out and gave me one week to find someplace else to go.

I reached out to my aunt Sharon, my dad's sister, and asked her if I could stay there for a while. She let us move in, but my addiction messed it up. I tried to stay sober most days, but I couldn't. With only having a little bit of money saved, I couldn't get high every day, which left me sick a lot. It was hard explaining to her and my uncle why I was sick off and on, and they quickly realized something was wrong with me. My cousins, her grandkids, told her that I was a heroin addict; but I repeatedly denied it. I know that she realized that it was true—everything that her grandkids told her was true. I needed a job badly and found one right down the street, so I was able to start using regularly again. I went back to using methadone and heroin to avoid being sick, so that helped but wasn't enough. My aunt kept asking me if I had enough money saved for an apartment, but I didn't. I had been spending check after check on heroin, so I didn't have any money saved at all. My aunt also kept asking me to buy groceries, but I didn't. I kept just eating hers. Finally, my aunt and uncle said that I needed to find someplace else to live. I hated moving the kids from place to place, because I couldn't pull myself together. I hated letting them down. I was a horrible mother and a horrible drug addict but just couldn't pull myself together. I called Marco's sister Angelica, whom I hadn't talked to in years, to see if we could stay with her for a while. She was very happy to hear from me and said that we could stay with her for as long as we needed to. A couple of weeks later, we moved in with Marco's sister Angelica, her girlfriend Lakesha, and her four kids. The kids had their cousins to play with every day, and I had Angelica and Lakesha to confide in. It took only one month for Angelica and Lakesha to figure out that I was on drugs. Angelica, surprisingly, was okay with it as long as I gave them money for rent and bought groceries. It worked out, because soon after moving in there, I found a better job that paid a lot more money. I applied for food stamps and actually got $500 a month, so that paid for our groceries. Things were going good there. It felt good to be accepted for who I was. The kids got to go to the same school as Angelica's kids, and they liked it. Angelica's daughters did Kalli's hair every day and got her ready for me. She slept in the same room as Angelica's youngest daughter. Kaleb and Kris slept in the same room as Angelica's youngest son, and he helped them get ready in the mornings too. We finally were in a good situation. Angelica and her family were good to us. Angelica treated me with respect and didn't look at me just as a heroin addict but as a regular person. Angelica and her girlfriend, Lakesha, were so good to me and the kids. They helped us so much. After about a year of living there, Marco was moved to a center where he was able to visit us twice a month.

In 2013, I started getting worse and got a serious infection in the middle of my arm from shooting up with a dirty needle. I was in the hospital for five days, and they had to do a minor surgery on my arm. I stopped regularly paying Angelica and Lakesha rent, and that made things not so good between us. I was a disgrace to my children, and it was sad that a serious infection couldn't even make me stop getting high. I was out of control, and I knew it at that point. I was getting sick every week because I was needing more and more heroin. I couldn't afford to do as much drugs as my body needed and as often as my body needed it, so I would get sick. It was disgraceful for me to be sick like that around Angelica and her kids. It just wasn't right. Even with all the things I was doing, Angelica still treated me with respect and was kind to me. There were so many days where I got so sick that I would be driving to get drugs while throwing up on myself. I left Angelica's house at all hours of the night. I came and went like a crazy person when I needed drugs. I was a mess, and I know I disrupted Angelica and Lakesha's house a great deal. Angelica's kids were always watching me, and I know I had to look crazy to a child. Most days, my attitude and appearance were bad, and I know it had to be crazy to live with me. So many days I rolled around dope sick with Angelica's kids staring at me. I was so disrespectful to everyone; it was bad. Everything finally came to an end one day when I came home and the kids said that Angelica and Lakesha were fighting about me.

They had been fighting about watching the kids for free and me not paying rent anymore. They were fighting about me getting high and not paying for pretty much anything. They had a right to be mad about it. I had turned into a complete loser and wasn't contributing to anything. I was so bad on drugs that I just couldn't make stuff work anymore; everything was falling apart. I called my mom and asked her to come get us. I asked her to let Kaleb and Kalli stay with her for a little bit. I called Marco's mom and asked her if she could start taking care of Kris more for me because I was going through some stuff. She agreed and told me that I could drop him off over there right away. I decided to move back in with Marco's dad so I could get clean and save for an apartment of my own. I was determined to fix my life. I couldn't let my kids down anymore. I told my mom that I had a weird and bad feeling about Marco's dad so she needed to keep them for a few months. At first, my mom was shocked that I would ask her to do something like that, but she said that it might help my dad stay with her. I told her I would keep them on the weekends if she could take care of them during the week. I had to get better. I had to be a good mother again. I couldn't be a heroin addict anymore. I was going to do it. I was going to get clean for my kids. I decided to slowly get clean so I wouldn't fail like my previous attempts. I would stay clean from Monday through Thursday and only get high on the weekends, and I would do that until I felt like I could stay sober all week. I had tried several times to get clean by completely stopping, and it never worked. I started keeping up with my appearance more, dyeing my hair again and even getting pedicures. I bought the kids and myself some new clothes, and when I had them on the weekends, I took them to the waterpark. It was nice having money again, with only getting high on the weekend. I could afford stuff again. I was doing well. I was actually slowly getting myself together.

One day, I was sitting outside, and there were two gang members walking up the street near me. Right after they passed me, a car sped up and started shooting at them, and they started shooting back. Before I could even react, I felt a painful burning sensation on my right wrist. I had been shot and was bleeding everywhere, and I was so scared. I called 911, ran and got a towel for the blood, and then waited for them to arrive. I closed my eyes, rocked back and forth, and hoped that the ambulance would get there fast. I found out that I was only grazed by the bullet, but just that gave me pretty bad damage. Several nerves were hit, and I couldn't feel or move my hand. The recovery took months, but after eight months, I was able to move my hand in somewhat normal motions. At work, I would tuck my hand into the pocket of my scrubs. I couldn't let people at work see it. I definitely couldn't let people know that I couldn't use it. I just kept it in my pocket, just acted like I was always getting something out of my pocket. I never even told my parents that I had been shot, because I knew they wouldn't let the kids come over anymore. I already knew that my mom would tell me that it was too dangerous and that I needed to move. I didn't have enough money to move, so I just kept it to myself and kept on a long-sleeved shirt when I saw my mom. Right after my hand healed, I started shooting up right near where the bullet grazed me because a big vein was popping out. Soon after that a large bubble formed, it was a huge infected abscess. The abscess got so big that it pushed my hand toward the opposite direction. I was hospitalized for six days after they had to do an emergency surgery to remove infected tissue. The doctor said that I almost lost my hand, that a couple of more days and there would have been no saving it. It took me months to recover from yet another trauma to my hand.

Not too long after recovering from the infection, something much more serious happened. I was at work one day when I got a call. My coworker told me that I had to take it right away. She said that it was a detective, so I took the call right away. The detective said that I had to go to the police station right away and that it was about one of my children. I felt like my heart was ripped out of my chest, and my thoughts started racing. One horrible thought after another, I imagined every possible scenario about my kids getting hurt and even dying. I had already thought of the worst possible things, before the detective told me that my kids were all okay. My heart was beating so fast that I had to go to the bathroom and sit on the floor for a moment. I just needed to catch my breath. I had to just breathe. I had to focus for a moment on just breathing, because I felt like I was going to pass out. I had no idea what a detective would need to tell me. All I could think of was that it was because I was a drug addict. I was dying inside. If I lost my kids because of my addiction, then I would never forgive myself. I drove home before going to the police station so I could take out all my drugs and paraphernalia. I was going to hide them out in an alley and just get them after going to the police station. When I went to go into the apartment, I noticed that the door looked like it had been kicked in. There were wood and pieces of the doorframe all over the ground in the doorway. The door was open. I just pushed it, and right away, I could see that something happened there. Stuff was knocked all over the ground, and Marco's dad was gone. I started to think that maybe this was about Marco's family selling drugs and my kids being around it. Marco's dad, Raymundo, sold drugs just like Marco and his brothers did, so that's what I started to think that the police wanted to talk to me about. They probably wanted to talk about me letting my kids be around drugs. When I checked my room, all my drugs and paraphernalia were all still where I left them. That made me realize that whatever was going on wasn't about me. No matter what it was about, I couldn't stop thinking about losing my kids. When I got to the police station, there were detectives waiting in the lobby for me, and they brought me back into what looked like an interrogation room. I was so scared that I had to try so hard not to cry and just act normal. I was surprised when the police started off by asking me if I knew Marco's sister Angelica and her kids. They said that they called me there because one of Angelica's daughters came forward and said that Marco's dad had molested her. I felt my heart start to beat so fast, and all I could think about was that feeling I had in my stomach about him months before. In my head was Kaleb's voice saying that Marco's dad always made Kalli kiss him on the cheek. I felt the blood rush to my face, and I felt like my ears were on fire. I felt like I was going to have a panic attack. That's when I realized that they wouldn't have called me there if this was just about Angelica's daughter. I told them that I needed to take my medicine. I told them that I needed my Xanax in my purse. I had to take a Xanax pill and wait fifteen minutes before I could continue with them. They left

333

the room and told me to take a little bit to calm down before they continued. When they came back in, they said that they were going to ask me some serious questions about my daughter. When they said that, I knew what was happening. They asked all kinds of questions about Marco's dad Raymundo's behavior. They asked if I thought he was molesting Kalli, and I just wanted to die. I told them that I had started having bad feelings about him. I told them what Kaleb said about Raymundo always wanting Kalli to kiss him on his cheek. I told them that my three kids had been staying with my mom because I had to move back in with Marco's dad, Raymundo, to save money. The officer who was with me, Officer Tomez, said that he already knew the kids were living with my parents. He said that they had already been in contact with my mom and that Kalli said that she had been molested. I jumped up from my seat and gasped for air. I couldn't breathe. How could this be happening to me? I didn't know what to do. I started panicking. I started replaying everything that made me have a funny feeling about him in my mind. All I could think about were the times I heard him telling Kalli to sit on his lap. I wanted to die. I couldn't stop thinking about that sick man touching her, my innocent little daughter. I wanted to die, and I wanted to kill Marco's dad. They told me that they already had him in custody, and he admitted to everything. They said it wasn't just Angelica's daughter and Kalli that he molested; it was a lot of kids. Officer Tomez said he admitted to it right away as if it was a completely normal thing and that it sickened him. He said that he has seen a lot of bad things and a lot of bad people as a police officer. He said that Raymundo was one of the worst people he had ever seen and that the way he talked about molesting kids with a smirk on his face was disturbing even to him. Officer Tomez and two detectives told me that they would need to talk to Kris at some point to make sure that Marco's dad didn't molest him too. They said that they were confident that he had only been molesting girls and had said that he never touched my other two children. Then it hit me that Kris was with Marco's family and that I would have to face them to get him. I just knew that everything was going to get really crazy and that there were going to be problems between me and Marco's family. My thoughts started racing. I felt like my head was going to explode. I felt so frantic and scared. I cried and couldn't stop.

Officer Tomez and the two detectives who had been coming in and out had to give me a few minutes to calm down again. They both explained to me that there were a lot of steps that had to happen right away—that after a child is molested, there are procedures. They said we had to take Kalli to this center to be interviewed by special child psychologists. Officer Tomez said that they would have to video record the interview with Kalli just to make sure she was telling the truth. They said that they believed her, of course, but that there were procedures that had to be followed. My mom came and got me with Kalli. All I could do was cry and ask her why she never told me. I sat in the back of my mom's van and held her tight. I told her I would never let anyone hurt her again. We were met by two officers and a team of psychologists at some kind of center near my house. They informed us that it would take a few hours to get all the information they needed from Kalli. Here and there, one or two of the doctors came out and let us know what exactly was being done or talked about. It was about twenty minutes in when a doctor came out to say that Marco's dad told Kalli that if she said anything, then he would kill me. He brainwashed her, and that's why she didn't tell me or anyone. That monster tricked her into keeping such a horrible secret for months. It killed me to hear that. The doctor said she wanted me to know that because she could only imagine what I was going through. After about two and a half more hours of waiting, they called me back for my portion of the reports and interviews. Once I gave my report and signed a lot of papers, we were done for the night, and I had to go back home. My mom took Kalli like she normally did during the week since it was a Wednesday. We decided that we would keep her on the same schedule she had. We wouldn't let what happened throw her off. The psychologists said that Kalli seemed to have processed what happened to her very well, because they did not see psychological damage yet. When I got home, I thought everything was going to be okay until five members of Marco's family showed up and were angry because Raymundo was in jail. Right away, they said that I must have made Kalli lie and say those things about him. Marco's sister, his uncle, and three of his cousins all said that I set Raymundo up, that he would never do something like that. They told me that it was messed up to do that to him after everything he had done for me. I tried to tell them that I had nothing to do with it, that it was Angelica who went to the police. I tried explaining to them that I knew nothing about this and that Raymundo admitted to molesting several kids. They didn't care. I think they wanted or expected me to look the other way. They started yelling at me, telling me they hated me and wished I would have never met Marco. Marco's uncle, who was Raymundo's brother, pushed me into the wall and screamed in my face. He said that I "better hope that Raymundo gets out of jail" and that I "better watch my back." They pushed over things in my apartment and broke several things before they left.

The guy who lived upstairs, Curtis, came down to see what was going on. I had met Curtis the week before when I was sitting outside. He had just got out of prison, had been in there eight years, and was staying with his parents upstairs. He was a nice guy and was concerned when he heard yelling from my apartment. Even though, Curtis and I barely knew each other, I told him what happened to Kalli. He was very sympathetic and told me that he was there if I needed him and would help me with anything. From that day on, Curtis was there for me. We were great friends, and even started dating. I didn't know what I was doing. I had never cheated on Marco before. I had planned on waiting for him to get out of jail and then us being a happy family again. I just wanted to feel alive again, being with Marco, and while he was in prison, it was killing me. I was alone. I was sad and going through something so serious. I needed someone to be there for me. Curtis put a smile on my face every time I saw him, and I liked the way it made me feel. Curtis made me feel alive again, and I had felt dead inside for so long; it was killing me. He understood me. I just knew he did, and we barely even knew each other. He was intriguing. You could tell when you looked into his eyes that he had been through a world of pain, just like me. Curtis's parents let him come and stay with them when he got out of prison, so he didn't have a plan yet. He was fresh out of prison and really didn't know what he wanted to do with his life after eight years of being locked up.

The next day, Marco called, and I had to explain to him everything that happened, and his response just wasn't what I thought it would be. I expected yelling, cussing, and maybe even something getting broken; but there wasn't any of that. Maybe it was because he was in a work release center and didn't want to get in trouble, or maybe it's because he knew his dad was a monster. His voice stayed the same even after I told him details of his dad molesting Kalli. He didn't even sound mad. The only thing he kept saying was how messed up the whole situation was. When I told him that his family came and harassed me the night before, he still didn't seem surprised by any of it. He actually told me that I needed to see it from their point of view to understand why they were so mad. I told him that the only point of view I could see it from was from the mother of a child who just got molested. I told him that I needed to pick up Kris and that I wanted him to have his mom call me so we could set up a time. He told me that his mom wasn't going to want to talk to me after everything that happened. I couldn't help but to start yelling at him. I told him his family was messed up in the head and I couldn't do it anymore. I was so hurt and upset that he wasn't angry like I was. I was so angry that he never even asked me how Kalli was doing. I waited all day for Marco's family to call me about me picking up Kris, but they never did. That afternoon, I was going to just go to Marco's family's house to get him, but my car wouldn't start. I was actually surprised that my car lasted as long as it did with me not taking care of it. I hadn't done an oil change or anything to that car in years because of being a drug addict and spending all my money on drugs. I had a mechanic shop that was a few blocks away look at it, and they said it was the transmission. The mechanic said it would be thousands to fix it, and there were a lot of other problems that they could see. They actually offered to buy it from me, so I sold it for $800, so I could get really high. I didn't care about the car, because I worked near a train station. I already took the bus and then a train to get to my office, so it didn't matter. The next day, Marco called, and we got into a big fight over the phone. I told him that he needed to tell his family to drop off Kris right away. He said that they didn't want to give Kris back to me because I got his dad put in jail. Curtis was there with me, and I thought I had hung up on Marco, but I didn't, and he heard me talking to Curtis. When I saw that the phone was still on and that Marco was still there, I picked up the phone. Marco had heard me kissing Curtis and me telling him that I was happy that I found him. Just like that, my relationship with Marco was over. I thought I would feel horrible, but I didn't. I felt like I had the chance to live again.

Kaleb and Kalli loved Curtis, but my parents were mad to find out that I was dating a Black man who was over ten years older than me. Kaleb cried when he found out that my parents were racist against Black people. He cried and told Curtis how sorry he was. Weekends were nice with Kaleb and Kalli visiting us, and Curtis fit great with us. After that, Curtis moved in with me, and he helped me out so much. We would talk for hours about everything. Curtis really got me, and it felt good. I was so happy to finally have someone that liked me for me, someone who accepted me even as a heroin addict. After that, I thought that I would be able to keep doing well, keep only getting high on the weekends. That didn't happen. The longer I went without Kris, the worse I got. The more I thought about what happened to Kalli, the worse I got. I started getting high during the week again, and then after a month, I was getting high every day again. Curtis gave it his all when it came to trying to get me back on track with my life, but he couldn't. He tried to get me to start only using on the weekends again, but the pain in my heart had grown too much. I was too sad, and I had too much pain and regret over Kalli being molested. I let myself drown in pain and sorrow. I went from almost being clean to being the worse I had ever been. Curtis really tried to help me in every way that he could, but at that point, I was too far gone. My pain for what happened to Kalli was too much to bear, and I was missing Kris too much. I called Marco's mom's phone every day, but she either didn't answer, or she hung up on me. I also called Marco's sister's phone, but she changed her number, probably because I called it so much. There were two times where I was so sad that I did triple the amount of drugs that I usually did, just to try to drown out my misery. Things were bad with my mom and dad. They started telling Kaleb and Kalli that I was a drug addict. They told the kids that I didn't love them and that I only loved sticking needles in my arms. My mom and dad told Kaleb and Kalli horrible things about me, and even told them that I would die soon. After a few months, Kaleb chose to stop coming to see me, but Kalli still came every single weekend. Kalli was so happy to see me every Friday. Her little smile was all that I had left. Almost every time she got dropped off, she would be crying because of all the horrible things my mom would tell her on the ride there. My mom hated that she still wanted to see me, and even started making her do tons of chores just to come see me. Kalli never gave up on me, and she was the only reason I didn't just kill myself. I couldn't be mad at Kaleb for not wanting to see me. I had let him down too many times. Even when I wasn't a drug addict, I was making bad decisions, and he suffered because of it. After Kaleb stopped coming over on the weekends, a part of me died inside. I let my life get so out of control, but I just couldn't pull myself together to fix it. I barely ever ate. I only ate snack cakes every few days when I was high. Curtis always saved enough money to buy Kalli food when she was there, because we never had food in the house. When Curtis was hungry, he ate lunch at work and went and bought food from a local food place. I don't know how Curtis did it. I don't know why he stayed with me. I was a mess. I didn't buy groceries. I didn't buy stuff for my apartment. I didn't cook, and I definitely didn't clean anymore. After Kalli got molested, I stopped doing everything, and barely even bathed anymore.

One day, I did so much drugs that I almost didn't wake up. The day after, I had a horrible pain near my stomach. I had to go to the emergency room because the pain got so bad. I found out that I had a kidney infection. The doctors and nurses were horrified and I think even disgusted by me. The doctor told me that my left kidney wasn't doing well and that I was going to fail my kidneys if I didn't stop using heroin. They kept me there for six days, but I had Curtis sneak me in heroin and methadone every day so I wouldn't get sick. I didn't care about my kidneys. I didn't care about anything except for getting high to drown out my pain. Before I left the hospital, a nurse told me to hold on a little longer because God had something special coming for me. Every few days, my mom would call just to tell me that I was garbage and turned out to be a drug addict just like my parents. I hated how nasty my parents were. I hated that I let myself get to the point where I ever needed them to take care of Kaleb and Kalli. The longer I went away from Kris, the worse I got. I went to work and got high the minute I got home. That's all I did, nothing else. I just went to work and then got high and then did it over again. I cried every morning on the bus and the train. I was always so high that I fell asleep while crying. I was miserable and wanted to die, but I refused to leave my kids alone in such a horrible world. After three months of not seeing Kris, Marco started coming home on the weekends, so he brought Kris to me. I had been scared to death that I wouldn't be able to see Kris. I was scared Marco's family would hide him or keep him forever. Marco and I promised that we would never keep Kris from each other, that even though we weren't together, we would still get along for him. Marco said he was sorry for what happened to Kalli and that he was sorry that we ended the way we did. I was sorry, too, but it was the way it was. I was just happy that Curtis was there for me. I don't know why, but he was. I was shocked that Curtis could watch me get high day after day and not even be tempted to try it. The kids were all getting older. Kaleb was twelve, Kalli was eight, and Kris was six at that time, and I was twenty-nine years old and a complete mess. I got so bad that I stopped consistently paying my rent and all the bills. I just paid a little bit here and there. I got so bad on drugs that I needed more to keep me from going crazy every day, and Curtis started giving me most of his money. He worked as a laborer but didn't make much money. He only made about $300 to $350 per week. He saved enough out of it to buy himself beer and himself and Kalli food, and then the rest was for my drug habit. I don't know why he did it. I don't know why he cared so much about me getting sick, but he did.

Just months after losing my car, I got a paper in the mail about tickets that had to be paid. I had $300 in tickets that were never paid. If they weren't paid by a certain date, my license would be suspended. The date was two months away, so I planned to pay it, and it was tax time, so I had extra money. During tax time, I was the most out of control. With having so much extra money, it was hard not to be. I would get so high that I would wake up on the bathroom floor. Sometimes, I would get so high that I didn't wake up for hours. Curtis did the best he could trying to get me to stay sober, and I constantly told him I would try harder. Every other week, I told him and myself that I was going to get sober but failed miserably. For years, I had told myself that I would get better, but I just kept using heroin. Every paycheck, I told myself that I would pay my rent and the bills, but I didn't always do that. I paid pills only to avoid them being shut off, and I only paid rent every other month and strung the landlord along. I got so high every day that I almost couldn't go to work the next day but always somehow managed to. I would get high just to be able to get up in the morning. My addiction was as bad as it had ever been. I had found a ride the day I needed to go and pay the tickets to keep my license from being suspended but didn't go. I chose to spend that $300 on heroin and get so high that I tripped and fell outside. My legs and knees got pretty scraped up on the pavement. It was embarrassing that I even got that impaired. It didn't matter to me, because my arms, hands, wrists, and ankles were always swollen from shooting up. My arm and the marks that the drug use left were disgusting and disturbing, to say the least, but I didn't care. The bruises and scrapes were only the beginning of the problem. Not paying the tickets caused me my license. I started not even caring how high I looked at work and would let them see me so high that I would let them see my head nod down. When you get so high, you nod. Your head nods down. When you nod, people know you're on heroin. Everyone at my office and my previous two offices had to know that I was on heroin. They just didn't care enough to say something. In 2014, I was so strung out that people at work were starting to talk, but I just told them I was prescribed Xanax. I told them that I have a panic disorder that had been acting up, so my doctor increased my Xanax. Either my coworkers and boss believed it, or they didn't care.

I was so high all the time that even Curtis became curious and wanted to try it. I was so high that I didn't care whether or not he tried it, so I let him shoot up a very little bit. As soon as it hit him, he just slumped over, and I knew something was wrong. I pushed him back to try to wake him up, but he just fell onto the bed. Seeing him like that scared me, so I smacked his face, but he still didn't wake up. I didn't know what to do, so I called Keisha, one of the other ladies I got my heroin from. I asked her what to do in a situation where someone wasn't waking up from heroin. She rushed over, living only one block away, to see if she could help me wake him up. She told me to dump water on his face, so I did, and she said to punch him in his private area, and I did. Nothing. Curtis wasn't waking up, so we decided to call 911. When the emergency medical team got there, I told them that I came home from work and found Curtis like that. They immediately gave him a shot of Narcan in his leg, and he instantly woke up. Just like that, he jumped up. The only problem was that Curtis said he couldn't see; he said everything was black. The EMTs took him to a hospital that was about five blocks from where we lived, to find out what was wrong with him and why he couldn't see. At the hospital, the doctors couldn't figure out what was happening to Curtis's vision, and it was frightening. Curtis was in the hospital for seven days to monitor his high blood pressure and his eyesight. In those seven days, the doctors still could not find the cause of his loss of vision, and he was discharged. They said that it could have been something in the heroin or his blood pressure got so high after he shot up that his eyes were affected. It was hard to go to work every day knowing that he was sitting at home and couldn't see anything. Curtis was depressed and wanted to die, so it put even more stress on me, because I felt responsible. With Curtis unable to see, he was unable to work. That meant that we would have a lot less money, and that made it harder for both of us to get high. About a week later, just as quick as it had left, his vision came back. I thought the whole ordeal would make Curtis not want to use heroin again, but it didn't. He still wanted to get high. I couldn't tell him not to use something that he bought me almost daily. It just wouldn't have made sense.

Curtis spent almost all his money on me, on buying me heroin, so I couldn't tell him not to use it too. After that, I gave him the smallest amount possible, just enough for him to feel it but not enough for him to almost die again. When he started using, things got even worse. That meant two habits that had to be taken care of. Two people with heroin addictions, two people who had to get high. The worst part about it was that there were now two people who would do anything to get high. My tolerance had grown, so I needed more heroin just to keep me from getting sick and a lot of heroin if I wanted to actually get high. In our town, I often saw women prostituting themselves for money, so I decided to give it a try. Curtis wasn't very happy with my decision to prostitute myself, but he knew that once I set my mind on something, there was no changing it. The next afternoon, I put on a little skirt and walked up and down the street in a part of town that was known for prostitution. I walked up and down the same three streets for about an hour and a half, but no one stopped or even looked interested in me. I just started walking back toward the apartment when a man stopped and rolled down his window. He told me that a pretty girl like me would get hurt walking around in a bad neighborhood like that. He told me that girls like me who were trying to have sex for money used websites, and he gave me the information for them. He said that it was a safe way to go about it, and then I could screen who I wanted to have sex with or not. The man said that walking up and down the street made me look desperate and that would make men not want to pay me much. I was happy that the man actually gave me some good advice, so I went home and made an ad on the website he told me about. On the site, there were a lot of women doing what I was doing, but it looked like there weren't too many doing it near where I lived. I put an ad up for twenty minutes of sex for $150, and after putting it up, I got a response the next day. I e-mailed the person back, and they said they were interested but only wanted to pay $100, so I agreed to it. The person came the next night. He was a college kid from Afghanistan named Amir and was actually very polite. Curtis didn't want to, but he sat in the kitchen just in case something went wrong. Amir said he was in medical school to be a doctor and didn't have time for girls or dating. I told him I just needed the extra money for bills because I only worked part-time. I figured it sounded better than telling him

I was a heroin addict who needed extra money to get high and that my paychecks weren't enough. The whole thing actually went very easy. He paid me $100, and the sex only lasted about fifteen minutes. Amir said that he would be interested in coming over every week or two, and I told him that worked for me. Just like that, I was officially having sex for money, something I told myself that I would never do. After a few days, I got a second response to my ad, and he was an older man named Muhammed who owned an auto parts store in the city. Just like Amir, he said that he didn't have a lot of time to try and meet or date women. Muhammed paid me the same as $100. I guess that was a common price to pay for sex, and then it was over. He, too, said that he would be interested in coming to see me every week or two, so then I had two regular clients. I decided not to respond to any of the people who were contacting me about the ad. I just didn't want to risk it. I didn't want to risk getting set up by the police or something. I couldn't go to jail for prostitution. I was also worried about someone being violent. I had heard women in rehab say that they were beat up several times by men when they were prostituting. I couldn't risk being beat up or being set up by the police, so two clients had to be enough. I made sure that I only had them come over Monday through Thursday because Kalli and Kris came over on Fridays.

After I started having sex for money, something inside of me died, and my depression got worse. I didn't even want to be alive anymore. I was only living to get high, and I just couldn't do it anymore. I stopped eating most days, and barely even slept. I only went to work then got high and saw Kalli and Kris on the weekends. That was my life; my entire existence was pretty much getting high. I was so depressed that I would get high and hope that I would overdose and not wake up. In just a few months, I was in the hospital twice for a kidney infection from using so much heroin. The doctors said that my kidneys couldn't filter that much heroin at one time and that if I didn't slow down, they would shut down. I didn't care. I didn't care if my kidneys shut down, and I didn't care if I died. I would have done it, just killed myself, but I just couldn't do that to my kids. I knew how bad I was, and I think that's why I was so depressed. I wanted to die. I was a complete disaster and a horrible mother. I almost wasn't even a mother at all. My oldest son hated me and my younger children would end up hating me if I didn't get better. I started going to work so high that I lost my job, and everything got so much worse. I struggled with having enough money to get high but then quickly found a new job. I would have ended up a full-time prostitute if I wouldn't have found another job. My new job was so short-staffed that no one seemed to care how high I looked every day, so it worked out. Around that time, Marco got out of the work release center and was talking about us getting back together. I didn't know what I wanted to do. I thought it might be good for us to get back together because of the kids. I wasn't sure what to do because I lived with and was sort of dating Curtis still.

One day, I got a Facebook invitation for a party for my biological sister Lisa's two-year-old son, and Kalli saw it. She begged me to take her, and with me not having a license or a car, I asked Marco to take us. Marco said he would take us and thought it was a good opportunity for us to talk about getting an apartment together. Marco was set on us getting back together and picking up where we left off with our relationship. The day of the party, Marco said he would have to drop me and Kalli off and then Kris and he would come back later. He said that he forgot about his sister's daughter's birthday party that he and Kris were supposed to attend at the exact same time. My sister's party would end up turning into more of an adult get-together, so Marco said he would drop us off at 1:00 p.m. and be back by 6:00 p.m. to spend time with us. I got myself ready and had to get high three times just to prepare myself to be around people. I hadn't been around people socially or went to any parties for so many years, so it was hard for me. Everybody pretty much knew I was a heroin addict, so I hadn't gone to any get-togethers or parties in so long. When Kalli and I went in we were greeted by my sister Lisa and her boyfriend, Jim, it was nice to see them. I had once been close to them. I had partied with them a lot before I started using heroin. They were into drinking and doing cocaine, so they had parties almost every weekend, and I was often there until I discovered heroin. I hadn't seen or talked to Lisa or Jim in at least five years, so I figured it would feel strange, but it didn't. We made our way through the living room and the kitchen and ended up outside where most of the guests were. I saw and spoke to my aunt Sarah, my real mom's sister, and her husband, my uncle Will. They were kind and happy to see me and Kalli, but I could see disappointment in their eyes. I don't know why, but I told them I was sober and had been sober for almost a year. They both told me that they were happy to hear that, but I could tell that they didn't believe me. As I talked to them, a man across the room caught my eye. He was cute, he was so intriguing, and I couldn't stop looking at him. I had never seen him before, but I found myself drawn to him, so I went over and stood near him. I was eating a plate of food and trying to figure out what I would say to him. I just said hi, and I walked away and then went into the house to talk to my sister. Right away, my sister told me that Jim had a friend whom they wanted me to meet; they thought we would be a great match. I told her that Marco was going to be coming back later that evening and that we were talking about getting back together. Jim came up to me, and he repeated the same thing Lisa had just said. He said he had an old friend who was there and that I should talk to him. I told them both that Marco and I were probably getting back together, and I didn't want it to be weird when Marco got there. They talked me into going outside to meet this guy, Robert, and when I did, I immediately fell in love with him.

Up until that point, I had never believed in love at first sight, but I was experiencing it. We introduced ourselves, and I could tell that he was into me. I could tell that he was intrigued by me. The way this guy, Robert, looked at me. It made me feel like I was the only girl in the world. He was so handsome, muscular, and dressed so neatly. He had beautiful brown hair and eyes and looked like he was Italian. From head to toe, he looked perfect to me. He was beautiful. Right away, I knew we would be together, and he was all I could see. We talked all afternoon, and Kalli ended up liking him just as much as I did. Afternoon turned into the evening, and Marco said that he was sorry that he couldn't make it to the party. He asked me if I could find a ride home, and I did. I knew it was fate. We were supposed to be talking about getting back together, and he didn't show up.

Instead of us talking, I met Robert and I knew we were going to end up together. We talked for hours, and we sat cuddled up on a couch and talked about everything. I liked him so much, so I couldn't tell him I was still using heroin. He, of course, had heard from Lisa and Jim that I was either using or used to use heroin, so he knew about the issue. I told him that I had been clean and sober for one whole year. Robert told me that he just inherited a house and asked me if I would come in live with him, but I told him I lived with someone. I told him about Curtis and how we were sort of together but mostly just good friends. I also told him all about King and how he went to prison but was out and wanted to get back together. The only thing that I wasn't honest about was that I was still a heroin addict. I was still an out-of-control addict. Kalli and I stayed there until 10:00 p.m., and I would have stayed later, but I started not feeling good because I needed to get high. Robert drove us home that night, and Curtis could see that I had a smile on my face, so he knew that I met someone. I told Robert I would call him that week but got the stomach flu, so I never did. The week after that, I responded to his Facebook messages, and we talked about our jobs. Robert told me that he had to see me and that he wanted to come pick me up from work, so I let him. The day he came to get me, I watched him from my building. I already loved the way he moved. I watched him walk to the passenger side of his truck and then clean the mirrors and windows so neatly. When I walked down to his truck, I could see that he was nervous as he stood and waited to open my door, Robert was just so cute and sweet. Our conversations were endless, and I found that I was so comfortable around him and that I already liked him so much. The first time he picked me up from work, he took me to a cute little nail shop. We both got manicures and just talked the whole time. It only took that one day for me to know that he was the one. I just had to figure out how to get clean before he found out. It only took four times of seeing Robert after work before I decided to take him up on his offer and move in with him. I just moved out and left almost everything behind so I didn't have to face Curtis. I made sure to buy enough methadone so I could take that instead of using heroin and not get sick. I made it a few days before I couldn't do it anymore and needed to get high very badly. I told Robert that I was going to pick up my stuff from the apartment slowly so he would take me there every day or every couple of days. I would have Curtis get me a few bags of heroin, and then I would get it when Robert took me there to get my stuff that I never took when I moved out. Even after leaving him, Curtis was still willing to help me get drugs. He still cared about me that much.

After only living with Robert for two weeks, he caught me shooting up heroin. I was in the bathroom, and he was outside doing yard work when he caught me. He came up to the bathroom window and was going to try and scare me but saw what I was doing. He was so mad but said that part of him knew that I was still a heroin addict. Robert told me that I needed to get clean and that he would help me in any way he could. He said that he knew about addiction and the behavior of an addict, because his mom was a recovering heroin addict. After a few weeks, Kalli came to live with us, but it got stressful with me still being on drugs and working so much. My cousin Theresa offered to let Kalli stay with her, so I took her up on that offer, and Kalli went to live with her for a while. I just needed to get myself together and get sober before I could take care of my kids again. With me still using things got stressful between me and Robert. I don't think he knew what to do to help me at first. We decided to start drinking to take the edge off, but that quickly turned into a problem. After drinking didn't work at helping me to not want to get high, I decided to try pills. I got Robert to get me one hundred Xanax pills in hopes that I could take the Xanax instead of using heroin. That also didn't work. I started using both and got so high that I didn't even know what was going on. For the two weeks that I took the Xanax, I still don't remember it. It was stupid to think that taking pills would help me. Robert did everything he could on his end to help me to get back on my feet. He paid thousands to get my license back and get me a car so I could be more independent. For six months, there were so many ups and downs, and it finally came to an end one September afternoon. I went to get my usual three bags of heroin for $50. Curtis had it already, so I just had to pick it up. I was feeling sick and needed it fast, so I left the car running and had him meet me at the front door of the apartment building. I put the bags in my bra, got in the car, and pulled off; but right away, there were lights behind me. I got pulled over by the police. They had been watching that block for drug sales, and I was arrested. When they asked me for the drugs that I just purchased, I only gave them two, because I knew I would get sick without any drugs in my system. In the back of the police car, I had to wiggle around to get the bag out of my bra. I was able to get it to drop into the seat. I then got it in my hand and was able to push it into my underwear so I could use it later. I thought it was the bag of heroin that I managed to keep hidden when I got arrested that got me through the night, but if I went to jail, I would be so sick. I got down on my knees in that jail cell, and I prayed. I told God that if I didn't go to prison, I would never use heroin again. The next day, the judge was going to give me twelve months in jail, but Robert told her he would help me get clean. The judge then changed her mind and let me go with just drug classes. I walked out of that courthouse a different person, a person who was going to be sober.

September 25, 2015, was the first day of my new life, my new sober life. I went to a methadone clinic the very next morning and started taking methadone the proper way and with counseling. God must have really listened to my prayer, because I didn't even crave heroin after that. It wasn't even hard to stay sober. After five months, Kalli came back to live with me and Robert, and Kris came to visit every weekend. I tried to get Kaleb to want to spend weekends with us, but he didn't believe that I was clean. Kaleb thought I was still using, or he thought I was going to let him down again. Kaleb was already thirteen years old, and I had been such a bad mother to him, so I couldn't blame him for not wanting to see me. Kalli was nine, and Kris was seven, so they were a lot younger and less affected by my drug addiction. Being clean made me want to fix any broken relationships in my life, so I reached out to my parents. Robert helped me to try and have normal relationships with them, but it didn't work. I had never told Robert about my childhood and the abuse, but after meeting my dad, he knew something wasn't right. Robert felt the evil that was inside of my dad and the awkward tension between us. Soon after I got sober, my mom and dad both repeatedly tried to start problems between me and Robert, and I couldn't allow that. It didn't take long for me to realize that they were the same bad people that they were when I was younger. They didn't want me to be sober and have a good life. They wanted me to have a miserable life like they did. My dad was still cheating on my mom and not even trying to hide it, and I couldn't deal with it. I couldn't let my parents suck me in, no matter how bad they wanted to. I tried to mend the relationship between me and my younger sister, but it was the same thing. She was too damaged from our childhood and wanted to cause problems just like my parents. My dad and my sister both didn't like Robert, so they tried getting in between us, but I didn't let them. That's when I had to make the decision to cut my family off. I broke all ties to them and moved forward. After I stopped talking to them, I really realized how bad of people they really were.

One day after being sober for six months, I started having flashbacks of being molested as a child, and it really messed me up. I wanted to get high so bad every time those horrible thoughts went through my mind, but I didn't. It was hard with Kaleb still living with my parents. I missed him so much and so badly wanted him in my life. I cried so many nights over Kaleb not wanting to see me or to come and stay the night. I cried so many nights because it hurt me that I messed up so bad that my son had so much hate toward me. I got the chance for Kaleb to live with me around that time. My mom and dad were finally separating, so they were going to sell their house. My mom was going to find an apartment, and my dad was going to move in with one of his girlfriends. Kaleb came to our house one weekend, and he was so mean and angry at all of us. He told me that if he had to live with me, he would make my life miserable, because he hated me. Kaleb said that he didn't even know me, and he was right. I was on drugs for so many years that I no longer had a relationship with him. I tried to tell him that I couldn't go back and change his past with me, but I could promise him a good future with me. Too much damage was already done, and there was nothing that I could say to him that would fix it. The whole weekend, Kaleb sat in our garage and talked on his phone, and when he did come in the house, it was unpleasant. Kaleb made it clear that he didn't want to live with us, and I was only six months sober, so I couldn't argue his decision. Kaleb said he wanted to live with my mom or dad, so we set it up for him to live with my dad. I went to court and signed over temporary guardianship of Kaleb to my dad. We would see if he was ready to live with us again in one year, so I was okay with the decision. I needed to get further in my sobriety before I could take on an angry teenager, and he needed to forgive me.

I thought getting sober would be the hard part, but getting back to my normal self was the hard part. I was on drugs for so many years that I didn't even know who I really was anymore, so I didn't know what to do with myself. The first thing I did once I got sober was eat. I ate everything. Robert and I went out to eat almost every day for the first six months, and before I knew it, I gained a hundred pounds. I hadn't even noticed the steady weight gain until it was too late. The second thing I decided to do after getting sober was stretch my ears. I had always liked the way it looked, so I decided to buy an ear stretching kit and go for it. I started at one millimeter and told myself that I would stretch my ears to twenty-five millimeter—that's one inch. After getting sober, I decided to quit my job in the city and find a job close to home. I didn't want to work at the same place as when I was getting high, so I figured I needed a change. Just two days after quitting my job, I already had an interview at a local office and got the job immediately. Working so close to home gave me the chance to do things before and after work. I actually had time for myself. With having gained so much weight, I joined a gym and went most mornings in an attempt to lose the weight I gained. I did lose some weight with exercise and meal prepping every week. My biggest problem after getting clean was my emotional state. It was hard to know how to live again. After being an addict for so many years, it was hard to know who I was, and even harder trying to figure it out. My confused emotional state and my continuous ups and downs made it hard on Robert. I know being with me when I was high was completely different from being with me sober, so it was hard for him too. Our relationship suffered in my first year of being sober, and it was both of our faults. My mood swings were confusing for the both of us, and his angry outbursts were just as bad. The love that we had for each other overcame all of that, and as time went on, our relationship grew stronger. I tried to find as many things as I could to keep me busy and to help with my anxiety. After so many months of suffering from anxiety and depression, I made an appointment to see a doctor for it and to try medication. I was diagnosed with depression and prescribed a mild antidepressant for it. I was excited to get help for my depression because I knew it was affecting my life, but I had horrible side effects with the medication. I became very agitated and frightened. I was so scared out that I waited in the corner of the bedroom for Robert to come home. By the time he got home, I was shaking and sweating so bad that I didn't know what to do. I was scared to try another medication, but I did it, anyway, and it was just as bad. Almost the whole year of 2016, I tried to get my mental state more balanced out. After several failed attempts at medication, I decided to try a more natural approach and started taking herbs and meditating. I constantly felt like there was something I was missing in my life that was causing me to have emotional problems. I thought maybe it was because I didn't have a good relationship with my family, so I tried to get closer to my mom. Every time I tried to talk to her or visit her, she almost always turned it into something negative. She would constantly give her opinion on Robert and say that Kaleb probably didn't want to live with me because he didn't like him. Instead of trying to get close to my mom, I decided to talk to my cousin Theresa more. Theresa had always been there for me whenever I needed her, so I thought maybe more time around her would help me. I went to the gym almost every day. I walked a few miles almost every day, but nothing I did ever felt like it was enough. Nothing I did ever felt like it was enough. Nothing helped my anxiety and depression. Some days I got so bad, so depressed that I wanted to die. Some days, I thought that I wasn't good enough for my kids and shouldn't be alive. I hated myself for being on drugs for so many years and ruining my relationship with my son Kaleb. I realized that the feeling of inadequacy was because I didn't have him. For almost a whole year, I suffered from debilitating depression, and it was so hard because I couldn't do anything about it. I started getting harassing messages on Facebook from my dad's girlfriend, and that made my emotional state a lot worse. Her messages were horrible. She called me the worst names you could possibly call someone. She said that she didn't want Kaleb there and that she hated me for allowing him to live there. She wrote that Kaleb was ruining her life and that she wanted him gone. I reached out to Kaleb a few times just to tell him that I was there if he ever needed me. I called and texted my dad about it, but he brushed it off and said that it's not true what she said. It was confusing and upsetting that my dad's girlfriend felt that way about Kaleb. It also hurt knowing he was fifteen years old and growing up without me. It hurt knowing that he probably would always hate me and would never want anything to do with me.

One day, unexpectedly, Kaleb texted me asking how we were doing, and he said he was ready to come and live with us. He said he just needed to get away from my dad, and that worried me a little. I asked him if he was okay, and he said that he was but just wanted to live with me. It was around the holidays in 2016, and we planned on him coming to live with us after he finished school. I asked if he wanted to come immediately, but he said it could be after he finished school. I asked him several times if he needed to tell me anything and if he and my dad were having problems. Every time, he said he was fine and didn't feel like talking about it. I was worried about him but told myself that he would tell me if something was wrong. My heart was full of joy and a newfound hope that one day I could have a relationship with my son. I was hopeful that Kaleb could forgive me for everything I had done and that we could all be a happy family together. Over the next few months, we planned on adding on to our house to accommodate Kaleb and give him his own room. We made so many plans with Kaleb, and even bought him a four-wheeler so he could have something fun to do when he came. I talked to him here and there. Things were good. We were going to have so much fun when he came to live with us. There was a court date in the summer, and that's when full custody would get transferred from my dad back to me. My dad had no objections, and Kaleb said it was definitely what he wanted. The lady whom I spoke to at the courthouse said that as long as there's no objections to Kaleb coming back to live with me, then it's a quick process. At first, I was worried that I needed a lawyer to end my dad's temporary guardianship, but the lady assured me I didn't, so I was happy to hear that. When it got closer to the court date, I started to hear from Kaleb less and less. When I called or texted him, he didn't answer or respond back. I didn't get nervous or anything because I figured Kaleb was a teenager, and that's what I figured kids his age did. Even though I didn't talk to her much, I called my mom a few times and let her know what was going on in my life. I confided in her about not having heard from Kaleb, and she said he hadn't been calling or texting her much either. I asked if he had a new number, and she said that she thought he did change his number but wasn't sure what it was. I had no one else to talk to about it besides Robert, so I continued to confide in her all the way up to the day before the court date. I cried to her so much. I was so confused at why I hadn't heard from Kaleb. Even though I hadn't heard from him in two months, I still planned on going to the courthouse and getting full custody of him back. Kalli and Kris were both so excited to be able to see and talk to their brother again. It was going to be great. We were all getting ready for bed the night before court when there was a knock at the door, and it was Kaleb. We were so happy but so surprised to see him, and I was relieved to be seeing him before court. We showed him how we were going to build him his own room in the back of the house and the jeep that we bought for him. I was rambling on and on because I was so happy to see him, but he wasn't saying much. Robert did the same. He went on and on about the four-wheeler he had bought for Kaleb and how he could customize the jeep to his liking. Kalli told him how she was so happy to see him and couldn't wait to see him every day. Kaleb was acting strange, and then he finally said something as we walked back into the kitchen. He said that he didn't want to come and live with us. He said it would be weird because he didn't even know us. I wanted to die when those words came out of his mouth; it hurt. I held back tears as I told him that we could all get to know each other and that shouldn't be an issue. I frantically stated good reasons for him to come and live with us, but none of them were good enough for him. Kaleb told me to stop acting like I was dying and that he could still come to visit us. He said that he didn't want me to go to court that next day. He said he wanted everything to stay how it was. Kaleb said he thought I knew because he had told my mom he didn't want to live with me. I asked him if he regularly spoke to my mom. He said he spoke to her almost every week. That meant, the whole time, my mom had been lying to me about not talking to him. I told him that it was time for him to come back home and that I was still going to court. He got very mad and started crying, and that made my tears that I was holding back just pour out. Kaleb told me that if I went to court, he would hate me and not forgive me for it. It hurt so bad to hear him say that, but I told him I was his mother and was going to fight for him. Seeing Kaleb cry hurt me, and it tore me up inside to hear him tell me that he didn't want to live with me. I tried to hug Kaleb, but he didn't want to hug me, and I tried to tell him I loved him, but he didn't want to hear it. After he left, it came to me about him acting strange, and I almost had a panic attack. My dad was probably hurting him. He was probably hitting him like he used to hit me.

That night, I decided that I was done with my mom. I couldn't take her lies and manipulation anymore. My mom had been lying to me the whole time. She pretended like she was on my side. I called her and told her how I felt and she told me that she didn't think that Kaleb should live with me. She was rude and negative as she told me that I missed too much of his life and that he didn't want anything to do with me. She said that Kaleb was better off with my dad and that I had Robert now. She made it seem like I chose Robert over my own son, and it made me so mad. I couldn't believe it. I couldn't understand why everything was suddenly going downhill. The next day in court, it was even worse. Kaleb didn't even pick his head up. He kept it low. He looked like a dog that had been beaten too much, and it was horrible. The way he moved reminded me of how I had looked at that age and what my dad had been doing to me. Kaleb's shirt was dirty, and his pants were so short and clearly didn't fit him. His shoes were the worst. They were so dirty and stained up with frayed laces. I was horrified and didn't know what to do. All I could do was go to the bathroom and cry before it was time for court to start. I couldn't have prepared myself for court and how the judge would treat me. It didn't go well. My dad was asked if he thought Kaleb should live with me, and he said no. The judge said I needed a lawyer if we didn't all agree on whom Kaleb should live with, and I told him I would get one. The judge was very mean to me and said that I should have never signed over temporary custody of my son. He wouldn't even look me in my face and, apparently, only liked to speak to lawyers. I found out the hard way that temporary custody actually isn't temporary. We were given another court date a couple of months out and sent to talk to a lady down the hall in the courthouse. The lady was some kind of mediator for the court and would talk to both sides involved. I explained to the lady that, up until the night before, my son wanted to come and live with me and all parties had been in agreement. We waited while she spoke to my dad and Kaleb. I was so upset that it was hard to just wait. When she came back in, she said that Kaleb didn't want to live with me, but I said that he needed to. The lady asked about my relationship with my dad, and I told her everything. I told her how I was worried that my dad was hitting or abusing Kaleb because of how he was acting. I told her how he reminded me of me at that age by the way he kept his head down and looked scared around my dad. She said that there was nothing she could do but give us the information to some lawyers that the judge would take seriously. I was so mad that I screamed and cried on the way home. I was devastated, and I was angry that my dad told the judge that he didn't want Kaleb to live with me. I told myself to calm down and to start calling lawyers if I wanted to get my son back. When I called the lawyers, I found out that it would be around $20,000 start to finish for my case. I also found out that because of Kaleb being almost sixteen, by the time the case was over, he would probably be eighteen years old. I talked to several lawyers hoping that they would say something different, but it was similar with all of them. They all said that the judge would probably listen to Kaleb if he said that he didn't want to live with me. Even though I really wanted to hire a lawyer, it wasn't looking good. Two of the lawyers even told me that they wouldn't feel comfortable taking so much money for a case they didn't think they could win. It took me two weeks of driving myself crazy to finally come to the decision to not hire a lawyer. I decided to let Kaleb have what he wanted. I couldn't force him to live with me. It hurt me so bad. I cried so many nights because of it, and it took so long to feel okay about it.

After seeing Kaleb at court, there was no communication with him after that, no calls or texts. It took a lot to get the kids to forget about what happened, because it hurt them so much too. After that, I lost myself for a while. I fell into a deep depression that it took several months to get out of. I put Robert and the kids through a lot during those months, and I didn't mean to. It got to the point that I had to see a doctor again, so I started seeing a psychiatrist for my depression. Unfortunately, I had another bad experience after trying a medication, so I stopped going. When I finally started feeling better, I started going to the gym every day to help with my stress and anxiety. I made it an obsession out of it. I focused on losing weight all day every day. I had to focus on something to get my mind off of everything that happened with Kaleb. I walked three to seven miles a day and went to the gym too. I did it just to help release my anxiety over it all. Still with everything that I was doing, I still felt like I was missing something in my life. In 2017, I finally started letting go of the past and focusing on moving forward with my life, moving forward with Robert, Kalli, and Kris. I was thirty-two years old and trying to enjoy my new sober life. I was a year and a half sober, and it was great. That year, we did all sorts of things as a family, trips to the beach and to state parks. It was great being sober. Being sober gave me back my life, and I was loving every minute of it. In September of that year, Robert and I got married. I married the love of my life, and it was amazing. We didn't have a ceremony, just the two of us, together at the courthouse. I would have married Robert anywhere. He was everything to me, and I loved him with all my heart. Soon after that, I discovered other ways to help my anxiety; healing stones and yoga became my new hobby. I felt like I needed to be more connected to the universe, so I used crystals and started following the cycles of the moon. I felt like we were all lacking some kind of spiritual element in our lives, so that is what I started looking for. Following moon phases and using crystals just wasn't enough, so again I started looking into other things. I started looking into Wicca and spells and chanting and using the earth to achieve certain things. I bought colored candles, all sorts of herbs, more crystals, and several things with pentagrams on it. I started praying to the moon goddess for everything and wanted so badly to be connected to her. I wanted so badly to be connected to anything. I still felt a large void in my life. In October of that year, we were on our way home from a restaurant when Kris told us something horrible. Kris brought up what his grandpa did to Kalli and asked us if it was bad. We assured him that it was very bad and that's why his grandpa was in jail. We told him that molesting a child is more than just bad; it was a sickness that his grandpa had. Kris then told us that his dad was molesting him, just like that he told us. He said that it had been happening for years, and that's why he hated going back to his dad's house during the week. I was so shocked. I couldn't believe that his dad would do that to him. I was horrified by it. We went to the police station that night, and Marco was arrested the next day. My heart was shattered by the details that we heard Kris tell the police. It was hard to listen to it. Kris was only nine years old, and his dad had been molesting him as long as he could remember. We also found out that Marco's family knew about it and would walk in on him doing it. Kris said that they would just tell him he was sick and to stop it, but not do anything else. It took some time, but we eventually moved forward from it. Both kids went to therapy every week to make sure that they were coping properly.

For months after that, there were no issues until my depression came back. The holidays that year were the worst. My depression was debilitating, to say the least. Most days were so bad that I didn't want to get out of bed, and I would cry before my day even started. Going to work was such a struggle, and it was hard to even want to talk to patients or my coworkers. My depression took a toll on my relationship with Robert because I pushed him away. I let everything that was bothering me build up until I exploded with pain and frustration, and most times, I directed it at him. I had completely stopped taking the kids to do anything fun. I was hurting so bad inside that I wanted to die. For Thanksgiving and Christmas, Robert cooked. I was too depressed and bothered by everything to even get out of bed. I was mad at myself. I was disgusted with myself and took my anger out on Robert like I had been doing for months. I started taking my anger and frustration out on myself in an attempt to not take everything out on my husband. Every time the razor or knife cut my skin, it was an intense relief, and I felt a lot better afterward. It helped at first, but then we started fighting about me doing it. I was a mess, and we were suffering as a family because of it. We went into 2018 being seriously affected by my mental state and depression. In the spring, Robert finally put his foot down and told me that I needed to get help, because he couldn't take it anymore. I decided to go back to the psychiatrist whom I had seen before with hope that they could help me. The doctor tried me on another antidepressant, and yet again I had very bad side effects to the point where I missed several days of work. I wanted to give up on taking medication, but Robert convinced me to try one more time. When I went back, the doctor thoroughly went over my history, my symptoms, and all the medications that didn't work for me. Robert was with us in the room, so the doctor said he wanted to hear from Robert on what was going on with me. The doctor said that in a lot of cases, a spouse can tell him more details of a patient's behavior. After twenty minutes of going over what it was like to live with me and deal with me, the doctor said he didn't think I had regular depression. He said that I had bipolar disorder and that I was experiencing extreme depression because of it. He tried me on a medication for bipolar, and it helped. I was finally able to move forward from the horrible mental state that I had been in for at least six months. Once I was back to feeling better, I started doing yoga again, and I started working with my healing stones and crystals. After months of trying to become more spiritual, I was still lacking something, but I didn't know what it was. I got further into trying to do Wicca spells, connecting to the earth, and praying to the moon goddess. I started having the kids pray to the moon goddess, too, and live according to moon phases. I was constantly outside doing spells and chanting as I tried to deepen my connection to the universe. I went on like that for months until I became frustrated that I didn't feel connected to anything or anyone.

Toward the end of 2018, Kalli and Kris both started hanging out with the wrong crowd. Kalli had friends who were into fighting and gang banging and were proud to be bad kids. The girls whom she called her friends were always starting problems with other kids, and even had her fight girls in the bathroom at school. She started talking to boys who were affiliated with gangs, and we found inappropriate messages in her social media messages. When we finally took her phone away, the stuff we found in it was so bad that we swore we would never allow her to have a phone. Kris was doing similar things and following boys who were always out getting into trouble. When we looked in Kris's phone, we found long search histories full of pornographic images and videos. His phone had to be taken away as well, and we couldn't get him to understand why. I didn't know what to do. Both kids were out of control and didn't seem to care. Finally, I felt better. Finally, my depression was gone, and then I had to deal with both of my kids being out of control. Kalli was suspended from school a few times for fighting and for talking back to teachers. Just weeks later, Kris was suspended from school for talking back to teachers and then for stealing. For months, the kids' bad behavior got worse, and it started affecting me and Robert's relationship. We both had different views on how we should deal with the kids and punish them, so it caused conflict between us. We started fighting a lot as it got worse, and there were days that we didn't even talk to each other. We had a few fights early in 2019 where we talked about separating out of anger and frustration. Kalli was twelve, Kris was ten, and they were both headed down a bad path, but I didn't know what to do. I took them both to a children's behavioral health facility, and they started counseling for their behavior. The counselors were great, but the kids still didn't fully understand that the things they were doing were wrong. I tried as hard as I could with doing Wiccan spells and rituals to make the kids behavior change, but it didn't work. I spent hours praying to the moon and to the moon goddess, but that didn't help either.

In April of 2019, I was sitting in bed one night when this strange but relaxing feeling came over me. It was like a thought was placed right into my mind, and I knew what I had to do. I looked over, Robert was sleeping, but I woke him up and told him that we needed to go to church. Robert looked at me like I was crazy. He took a deep breath and just said that I could go, but he wasn't going to go to church. I know I must have sounded completely crazy, because I had been into Wicca for years. I was confused by it, but it was right there in my mind—something told me that I had to go to church. I didn't know anything about church. I had only gone there a few times when I was a kid and didn't like it. I figured the kids and I would go at first, and then maybe Robert would follow at some point. I didn't know much about the different kinds of churches, so I looked up the church that I went to as a child. I found out that they closed down a few years prior, so I picked six churches in the area and e-mailed them all about joining or becoming members. The next morning, I checked my e-mail and had no responses, so I almost wanted to forget about it. The next day, I decided that if there were no responses from any churches, then I would forget about the whole thing. I checked my e-mails, and there was an e-mail from a Christian church. It was from the pastor of the church himself. He invited us to come to church that Sunday. He even said he would meet us at the door. When I read the e-mail, I had that strange feeling again. I felt like we were meant to go there that Sunday. The kids were completely shocked when I told them that we were going to church. They said that they thought we believed in other stuff. I told them I wasn't sure about anything, but I wanted to check it out. I was nervous, but we went there that Sunday, and the pastor was waiting by the door just like he said. When we sat down and the church service started, I just closed my eyes. I felt relief. I felt all my stress fade away. For the first time in my life, I felt something spiritual. I felt like that was exactly where I was supposed to be. The church service was so amazing, and I learned that Jesus forgives you of your sins if you accept him as your Savior. I felt this feeling that I wasn't alone. I finally felt connected to everything, and it felt good.

We continued going to church, and Robert even started going to. It was great. I developed this newfound sense of peace, and I felt like it made all my worries disappear. As a family, we all accepted Jesus Christ as our Savior, and the kids' bad behavior quickly changed.

Everything changed. Our relationships with each other became stronger, and there was no more fighting. Every day, the Bible spoke to me. It felt like it was just for me. I felt peace in my heart. I finally felt okay about Kaleb's decision not to live with us. I was finally able to forgive my mom and dad for my childhood, and I was finally free of that pain. I had hope for the future. I knew that God was going to lead us to great things in all of our lives. Just like that, I became a child of God. Just like that, I was born again. Jesus cleansed me of all the horrible things I had done, and I no longer had to feel guilt in my heart. Instead, I felt peace. I was no longer lost. Jesus found me and brought me to a place where I could live a new life through him. Jesus accepted me. He took all my sins with him to the cross, and his blood saved me. By the blood of Jesus, I am now healed. I am reborn, and I am finally able to accept my past and all my mistakes. I am able to wake up every day knowing that I am not alone and the Lord is with me and always will be now. I am no longer angry at anyone. I am moving forward and leaving the past behind me. I have faith that the Lord will heal my heart and my children's hearts. I have faith that he will help me to forgive myself and also for my son Kaleb to forgive me for everything I have done. The world tried to break me, but God lifted me up into his arms, and now I can live. I now know that throughout everything, my life was always *in the hands of the Lord*.

> For I can do everything through Christ who gives
> me strength.

> —Philippians 4:13 (NIV)